Macroeconomic Policies in Indonesia

T0330817

This book gives insight on the dynamics and route of economic policies that have been taken and implemented since the point of institutional reforms in 1998, which were triggered from the context of the financial crisis in 1997/1998. The condition brought a different paradigm to the landscape of economic and development policies, especially in the case of the monetary and financial structure, the international trade sector, the manufacturing sector, the taxes administration policy and the evolved context of decentralization and development of public sector policies in general.

Given the state of current economic development, this book offers suggestions to address economic issues that require improvements. This book is unique as: (1) it is about Indonesia, a country mostly affected by the 1997/1998 financial crisis, which also led to a change in regime; (2) it covers a broad range of thematic topics on sectors of development and institutional changes from major policies that have been taken; and (3) it posits both existing and future challenges on monetary and financial sectors, trade, manufacturing and competitiveness, as well as on development of decentralization policies.

Anwar Nasution graduated from the Faculty of Economics, University of Indonesia, in 1968. He obtained a Master's degree in Public Administration from the Kennedy School of Government, Harvard University, in 1973, and a PhD in Economics from Tufts University in 1982. Anwar was a member of the International Policy Advisory Group (Shadow G-20) in 2013, under the Chairmanship of Professor Jeffrey Sachs of Columbia University, the Dean of the Faculty of Economics at the University of Indonesia (1988–2001) and the Sasakawa Distinguished Professor for the Chair in Development Economics at UNU/WIDER Institute in Helsinki, Finland. He was consultant to UN-ESCAP, UN-ECLAC, US-AID, ADB, the World Bank, IMF and MITI of Japan. He was a visiting research fellow at NBER in Cambridge, MA, USA, IDE in Tokyo, the Research School of Pacific Studies at the Australian National University in Canberra and Kyoto University.

Macroeconomic Policies in Indonesia

Indonesia economy since the Asian financial crisis of 1997

Edited by Anwar Nasution

Routledge
Taylor & Francis Group

LONDON AND NEW YORK

First published in paperback 2016

First published 2015
by Routledge
2 Park Square, Milton Park, Abingdon, Oxon OX14 4RN

and by Routledge
711 Third Avenue, New York, NY 10017

Routledge is an imprint of the Taylor & Francis Group, an informa business

British Library Cataloguing in Publication Data
A catalogue record for this book is available from the British Library

Library of Congress Cataloging-in-Publication Data
Macroeconomic policies in Indonesia : Indonesia economy since the Asian financial crisis of 1997 / edited by Anwar Nasution.
    pages cm
  Includes bibliographical references and index.
  1. Finance—Indonesia.   2. Banks and banking—Indonesia.
3. Monetary policy—Indonesia.   4. Financial crises—Indonesia.
5. Indonesia—Economic policy.   I. Nasution, Anwar.
  HG187.I7M33 2015
  339.509598—dc23
  2014022471

ISBN: 978-1-138-79763-5 (hbk)
ISBN: 978-1-138-19510-3 (pbk)
ISBN: 978-1-315-75698-1 (ebk)

Typeset in Galliard
by Apex CoVantage, LLC

Contents

Contributors

Frank Bosch works for the International Monetary Fund and has conducted IMF missions in Indonesia, Egypt and Moldova.

John Brondolo has been involved in various IMF missions. He has extensive knowledge on tax administration and tax reform. He has been involved in several tax reform country strategy plans.

Lili Yan Ing, Economist for Economics Research Institute for ASEAN and East Asia (ERIA), and Lecturer at the Faculty of Economics, University of Indonesia.

Lloyd R. Kenward was a staff member at the World Bank office in Indonesia for several years at the time the crisis began and has also worked in the IMF's representative office in Jakarta. Dr Kenward holds a PhD from Queen's University in 1974.

Ari Kuncoro is Professor and Dean of the Department of Economics at the University of Indonesia. He received his PhD in Economics from Brown University.

Eric Le Borgne is a World Bank Lead Economist. He has been the IMF's Senior Economist since June 2001 and during his post for 20 years with the IMF, he has worked on numerous countries such as Indonesia, Thailand, Lebanon, Azrbaijan, Libya, Tanzania and Cameroon.

Raksaka Mahi is a Senior Lecturer and Researcher in the Department of Economics at the University of Indonesia. He received his PhD from the Department of Economics, University of Illinois at Urbana Champaign, in 1996.

Dionisius Narjoko is a Trade Economist at the Economic Research Institute for ASEAN and East Asia (ERIA), and was previously a researcher at the Department of Economics, Centre for Strategic and International Studies (CSIS) in Jakarta, Indonesia. He received his PhD from the Australian National University.

Anwar Nasution was a member of the International Policy Advisory Group (Shadow G-20) in 2013, under the Chairmanship of Professor Jeffrey Sachs of Columbia University, the Dean of the Faculty of Economics at the University of Indonesia (1988–2001) and the Sasakawa Distinguished Professor for the

Chair in Development Economics at UNU/WIDER Institute in Helsinki, Finland. He was consultant to UN-ESCAP, UN-ECLAC, US-AID, ADB, the World Bank, IMF and MITI of Japan.

Mari Elka Pangestu was the Minister of Trade for Indonesia for seven years (2004–2011) prior to her current position as Minister of Tourism and Creative Economy. Mari Pangestu obtained her PhD in Economics from the University of California Davis, specializing in macroeconomics and international trade and finance.

Riatu Mariatul Qibthiyyah is Associate Director in Research at LPEM-FEUI. She is a public finance expert who has been involved in various research projects on policy evaluation and monitoring, design of fiscal related schemes, intergovernmental transfer and regulatory impact assessment.

Sjamsu Rahardja is a Senior Economist for the World Bank office in Indonesia and leads the World Bank country program on competitiveness. Dr Rahardja has a PhD in Economics from Georgetown University.

Marta Ruiz-Arranz is Deputy Division Chief in the Fiscal Affairs Department of the IMF, and coordinates the work of the Fiscal Monitor team. She holds a PhD in Economics from Harvard University.

Carlos Silvani is an independent consultant working in projects supported by the World Bank, the IMF, the Inter-American Developing Bank (IDB) and the Gulf Cooperation Council (GCC).

Maria Monica Wihardja received her PhD (2009) and Master of Science degree (2008) in Regional Science from Cornell University, Ithaca, New York. She also received a Master of Philosophy in Economics from the University of Cambridge in 2002, and Master of Arts in Economics from Brown University in 2002.

Milan Zavadjil is the Director of MTM Advisors Ltd. Pte, based in Singapore. He teaches at ESSEC business school and other institutions and has had numerous consulting assignments with both private and public sector institutions.

Acknowledgements

The editor expresses his appreciation and gratitude to the authors of the articles in this book: Lloyd R. Kenward, Marta Ruiz Arranz and Milan Zavadjil, John Brondolo, Carlos Silvani, Eric Le Borgne and Frank Bosch, Raksaka Mahi and Riatu Mariatul Qibthiyyah, Lili Yan Ing, Mari Elka Pangestu and Sjamsu Rahardja, Dionisius Narjoko, Ari Kuncoro and Maria Monica Wihardja. Special thanks go to: Riatu Mariatul Qibtiyyah who served as Secretary to this book project; Anton Gunawan, who was involved during early stage of the process; and Ashintya Damayanti and Veny Nanin Puruitasari, the Secretaries from the Department of Economics who offered their great assistance to processing the manuscript. Also the Department of Economics of the Faculty of Economics, University of Indonesia, and KANOPI FEUI, the economic student organization, jointly organized two public seminars in Jakarta to get valuable inputs for improvements to the articles. Last but not least, special thanks go to Denise File from Apex CoVantage Limited, the Project Manager and editor of this book, Elisabet Ainsworth, the Production Editorial Manager at Routledge, and Yong Ling Lam of the Routledge office in Singapore who edited and published the book.

Introduction

This book identifies progress in some aspects of institutional reforms introduced in Indonesia after the end of President Suharto's 32-year period of administration in February 1998, particularly in the economics field. It offers suggestions to address economic issues that require improvements. In general, the reforms replaced a military-led authoritarian political system with a democratic multi-party system and a centralized government with broad-based decentralization and state-led economic policies with a market-based and more globalized open system. In contrast to most of the countries that give autonomy to provincial and state levels of the government, the autonomy in Indonesia is transferred to the regency or district at the sub-provincial level.

Indonesia was one of the main victims of the Asian Financial Crisis in 1997. The economy that had respectable growth at an average of 7 per cent per annum before the crisis between 1990 and 1996 sharply shrank to minus 13.1 per cent in 1998. During the same period, the inflation rate rose from 6 per cent to 60 per cent while the interest rate rose from 14 per cent to 63 per cent. The external value of the Rupiah devalued from Rp2,300 per US dollar before the crisis to Rp10,261 in 2001. These combinations had caused solvency problems for banks and the corporate sector particularly those that had great exposures to foreign debt.

As phrased in Chapter 3 the banking industry is the core of the financial system of Indonesia and a large portion of investment is financed through bank credit. The non-bank financial institutions, such as insurance and pension funds, had been growing fast since 2000, but their share in the financial industry remained limited. The Post Office has not been developed to become a narrow bank, mobilizing small savings and selling insurance policies to the masses. The mobilized funds can be used to absorb the Rupiah-denominated SUN (*Surat Utang Negara*) or sovereign bonds, SBI (*Sertifikat Bank Indonesia*) or Bank Indonesia's Certificates and equities traded in the Jakarta Stock Exchange.

The financial crisis in 1997 had impaired banks' balance sheets and their ability to lend. Such a crisis was costly to clean up due to the fiscal cost of recapitalization and purchases of non-performing assets of domestic banks. This reduction in fiscal space and deleveraging by the banking sector reduced both private and public investment which lead to slower economic growth, rising unemployment and further deterioration of asset quality. These deteriorated tax bases caused forgone tax revenue and ultimately a larger fiscal burden.

The Indonesian economy quickly recovered due to deep devaluation and rising prices of energy, food and primary products. Since 2000, the economy had been growing between 6 to 7 per cent per annum, benefiting from three booms. The first boom had been the boom in international prices of primary products. The rapid growth in China and India, between 9 to 10 per cent per annum, as well as the mechanization, motorization and urbanization in these rapidly growing economies, demanded energy and raw materials exported from Indonesia. The more affluent consumers in these rapidly growing economies also demanded better quality of foods, among others, marine and agriculture products from Indonesia. Second, there were remittances from low-skilled and uneducated labor working overseas particularly in the Middle East, Malaysia and Hong Kong. The third boom was the massive capital inflows to take benefit of high domestic interest rates in Indonesia, particularly after the quantitative easing or massive liquidity injections in the US between 2007 and 2011.

In the past two or three decades, East and South East Asian countries have been a large manufacturing hub where industrial spare parts and components are produced, making the region an important player of the global supply chain. Indonesia, however, fails to participate in the process. This is mainly due to a combination of bottlenecks, high cost of logistics and the appreciation of the Rupiah. The bottlenecks include the shortage of infrastructure and complicated investment regulations and business climate. A poor legal system and weak economic institutions have made it difficult to protect property rights, correct market failures and government failures. The strong external value of the Rupiah since the year 2000 occurred due to the boom in the primary products, labor remittances and inflow of short-term capital inflows. The stronger external value of the Rupiah erodes financial incentives for producers of traded goods and export. As a result, the structure of the Indonesian economy at present is not significantly changed from those during the colonial past. Indonesia remains to be a supplier of raw materials and a cheap unskilled and uneducated workforce.

The move to a market-based economic system was encouraged by the IMF and World Bank programs to rebuild the economy from the deep crisis in 1997. The programs consist of the short-run economic stabilization program and medium- to long-term structural program. The IMF short-term program consists of monetary and fiscal policies. It replaced the government-led or repressed macroeconomic policy that had been applied during the 32-period of President Suharto's administration between 1966 and 1998. The main elements of the economic policy before the crisis include: (1) the 'balanced budget rule', (2) fixed exchange rate, (3) repressed financial system and (4) distorted trade policy because of wide practices of corruption, collusion and nepotism. The winners in business competition are not necessarily the most efficient but rather the most politically connected. In the repressed financial system, Bank Indonesia, the central bank, set detailed credit ceilings, credit allocations by economic sector and class of customers, provided refinancing and credit guarantees and heavily subsidized interest rates.

In spite of various reforms, tax ratio or the ratio of government tax revenue to GDP remains very low around 13 per cent. This is mainly because of the weaknesses in tax administration that implements the reforms. Tax audit for example is only done internally by the Directorate General of Taxation. Audit by external auditors such as the State Audit Board requires permission from the Minister of Finance. As expected, self-assessment without auditing gives a license for tax evasion. Much of the evasion in Indonesia occurs on types of income that are difficult to monitor such as self-employment income, bad administration and transfer pricing by large companies that have branches and subsidiaries in neighboring countries such as Singapore with lower tax rates. Tax reform of December 1983 unifies and simplifies the personal and corporate income tax systems, simplifies reductions and exemptions, reduces tax brackets into three groups (15, 25 and 35 per cent), modernizes tax administration and shifts it to self-assessment. The value-added tax with a single rate of 10 per cent was introduced in April 1985 to replace the complicated indirect and sales taxes. In 2002 the Directorate General of Taxation established large taxpayer offices in cities such as Jakarta, Medan, Bandung, Surabaya and Makassar (Brondolo). To improve customs clearance, the government, between 1985–70, brought in a privately owned Swiss firm, SGS (*Societe General de Surveillance*) to provide custom clearance for shipments valued above $5,000.

For 32 years of President Suharto's administration, the entire budget deficit was financed by official development aid (ODA) from Indonesia's consortium of international donors (IGGI, the Inter-Governmental Group on Indonesia). Such budget debt rules were called 'balanced budget policy' and government revenue from foreign aid and loans was called development revenue that was earmarked for development expenditures. In 1998, the government started to issue sovereign bonds both to recapitalize the financially ailing banks and to finance the budget deficit. To prevent 'the original sins' the bonds are mainly denominated in domestic currency and sold in the domestic market. The securities are shielded from currency crisis but not from interest rate risks. In 2004 the government started to float sovereign bonds denominated in the US dollar sold in international markets. In 2009 the authorities issued the Samurai bonds partly guaranteed by the Japanese government.

The new short-run macroeconomic policy under the IMF Program of 1997–2003 replaces the fixed exchange rate system with a floating one and set inflation targeting as its new target and uses interest rates as its operating target. Modeled after the Bundesbank of Germany, Bank Indonesia is given an independent status, banned from buying government bonds in the primary market and the only objective of its monetary policy is to achieve an inflation target at a low rate. During the Suharto era, Bank Indonesia was supervised by the Monetary Board chaired by the Minister of Finance. The monetary policy adopted since 1997 is supported by fiscal policy that uses strict fiscal rules of the Maastricht Stability Rule of the European Union. The fiscal rule set a ceiling of both central and local governments' budget deficit to 3 per cent of annual GDP and Regional Domestic Product. The debt rule sets the ratio of public debt to GDP at a sustainable level of 60 per cent. The new budget and debt rules replace the previous 'balanced budget' rule and the debt rule of maximizing the ODA.

The central bank sets the reference or policy real interest rate lower than the neutral rate to stimulate the economy to full employment level. On the other hand, it sets the policy real interest rate above the neutral rate to dampen economic growth and avoid overheating. The difference between the actual policy rate and the neutral interest rate is called the interest rate gap. Aside from the interest rate gap, the monetary stance is also determined by the output gap, namely the difference between actual output and potential output. Interest rates should be reduced when real GDP fall below its potential.

In theory, Bank Indonesia needs a smaller amount of foreign exchange reserve as it has shifted its monetary policy to floating exchange rates and inflation targeting. The need for market intervention is reduced under a floating system as an exchange rate target is no longer used as a nominal anchor for monetary policy. The need for self-insurance is also reduced with the availability of loan backup after the revision of the IMF conditionality, multilateralization of the Chiang Mai Initiative and bilateral currency swap agreements between central banks in this region. Indonesia and other Asian countries accumulated large international reserves following the Asian financial crisis in 1997–98 (Ruiz-Arranz and Zavadjil, 2008) for a number of reasons. First, to avoid extreme fluctuations of the exchange rate and thus prevent adverse impacts on the economy. Second, to hedge against speculations and foreign exchange instability due to shortfalls in exports and capital flow reversals. Third, to maintain adequate fiscal space when facing economic crisis. Asian countries, including Indonesia, are reluctant to turn to the IMF for help, because they were treated improperly when they sought help during the crisis in 1997–98.

The progress of the economic reforms has been relatively slow to take benefit of political democratization, local autonomy and economic globalization. This is because of the slow progress in rebuilding the required institutions and degradation of quality of human resources that are needed to design policies and implement them. The current weaknesses in public institutions are particularly evident in three areas. First, poor legal and accounting systems that raise transaction costs as they cannot properly protect property rights and enforce contracts to make the economy more productive. This is also evident from the spread of corruptive practices in three branches of the government: executive, legislative and judiciary and in all layers from the top to the lowest level. The cost of market transactions is high because the legal system cannot protect property rights. As the system is perceived to be slow, conflicted people resort to debt collectors, thugs and take the law to themselves. Second and third are, respectively, the existence of market and government failures.

The Bank Bali scandal in 1999 and the Bank Century scandal in 2008 indicate the failures of Bank Indonesia (BI) as the bank's regulator and supervisor to implement prudential rules and regulations as well as its independency status. Pressed by the ruling government, Bank Indonesia gave its blessing to illegitimate claims of payments to Bank Bali from the Bank Restructuring Agency (IBRA) in 1999. Without having adequate capital and properly checking the integrity of the owners and management, BI gave permission to three small banks to merge and form Bank Century in December 2009. The bank is a small-sized bank and collapsed because of violation of prudential rules and regulations including legal lending limits and other criminal acts such as outright theft of its customers' deposits by the controlling owners of the bank. BI assigned an onsite supervisor at the bank, but did nothing to the various violations of prudential rules and regulations until the bailout in 2008. Without a proper license, the bank acted as a custodian to PT Antaboga, an unlicensed Trust Fund Company owned by one of the controlling owners who had a bad reputation. Like any other Indonesian bank, Bank Century was not a player in the US prime mortgages. The contagious effect of the bank's failings should have been contained because of its small size. The facilities to help address the liquidity and solvency problems of the bank were designed in a rush by BI. At the end, Bank Century was taken over by the state-sponsored LPS (*Lembaga Penjamin Simpanan*), the Deposit Insurance Company.

The decentralization or local autonomy program gives freedom to local governments at regency or sub-province level to set the size and structure of their budgets to deliver a variety of public services such as primary education, health care, local infrastructure. Taxing power, however, remains at the central government while local governments are only given rights to collect minor taxes. Collecting land and property taxes, for example, is still in the hands of the central authorities even though the country is rapidly urbanizing where over 49.4 per cent of its population in 2011 was living in big cities. This means that wealth is increasingly vested and locked up in land and property. The low municipal revenue-to-GDP ratio, at less than 1 per cent, indicates that urban tax and property are still untapped.

At present, the central government transfers two kinds of revenue to the local government, namely, general allocation (DAU-*Dana Alokasi Umum*) and revenue sharing (DBH-*Dana Bagi Hasil*) from general tax revenues and revenues from exploitation of natural resources. Some areas receive revenue sharing for reforestation. Special allocation funds or *Dana Alokasi Khusus* (DAK) are given to finance central government initiatives implemented by the region, particularly in remote and less developed areas. In 2012, over 39 per cent of central government expenditure was transferred to regions, mainly regencies and cities. The large vertical imbalance inherent in the massive mismatch between functions and finances of local governments, particularly urban local bodies, violates the principle of 'subsidiary' that is the cornerstone of fiscal autonomy.

As shown by Ing et. al in Chapter 7, the dilution of power because of democracy and decentralization of the government make the decision-making process more difficult. In contrast to the centralized system under the previous authoritarian regime, the decision makers under the present messy democracy have to accommodate interests of conflicting political parties and districts. Technical capabilities of the Parliament and political parties are insufficient to meet the rising law making and oversight responsibilities. Most of the districts do not have technical staff to implement the newly obtained power. Because of the high transportation costs and the lack of infrastructure, Indonesia has no integrated national market that takes benefits from its large population (2011: 242.3 million). Markets for goods and services and factors of production such as labor and financial markets are segmented across regional markets. The eastern parts of Sumatra and provinces in Kalimantan remain the hinterlands to supply both unprocessed raw materials and cheap labor to their neighboring countries, particularly Malaysia and Singapore.

The reforms gradually replaced the quota and non-tariff barriers with tariffs and at the same time reduced the level of tariff rates. Business licenses and investment climates have been slightly improved to attract private sector investment. Nevertheless, logistic costs remain high in Indonesia, partly because of infrastructure bottlenecks including electricity, roads and seaports.

The government failures are reflected in the inefficiency of state-owned enterprises, including the state-owned and regional development banks (RDB). This group of public sector banks enjoys monopoly rights to deposit financial wealth of the public sector at large, including state-owned enterprises. This unfair competition has caused segmentation in the financial market. Among the ASEAN5 countries (Thailand, Malaysia, Singapore, Brunei Darussalam and the Philippines), the net interest margin (NIM) or the gap between lending and deposit rates is the highest in Indonesia. NIM at state and RDB banks is the highest among the domestic banks.

The lack of well-developed economic institutions and high dependency of foreign financing have added to fragility in the economy. Over one third of the Rupiah-denominated SUN, SBI and equities traded in the Jakarta Stock Exchange is owned by foreign investors. This makes their prices and yields sensitive to movement of capital flows. At the same time the flows also affect the exchange rate and interest rate. Capital inflows increase prices of domestic equities and subsequently increase capital as well as assets of their holders including recapitalized banks that received capital injection in the form of government bonds in 1998. The rise in banks' capital reduces the ratio of their dud loans or the non-performing loans (NPL). Capital outflows reduce prices of equities that erode values of capital and assets of the recapitalized banks and increase their NPL. Kenward (Chapter 3) shows that the crises in the mutual fund industry in 2003 and 2005 were because of the sudden massive capital outflows.

This book is a collaborative effort by faculty members and researchers from the Faculty of Economics, University of Indonesia, and foreign researchers that had been working on Indonesia. The writers have benefited from two public seminars held in Jakarta in September 2011 and February 2012. The purpose of the book is to enrich a public discussion of macroeconomic formulation, implementation and evaluation in this country. We look forward to continuing our joint efforts to improve future economic management in a more democratic and decentralized Indonesia.

Jakarta, 5 August 2014
Anwar Nasution
The Editor

1 Towards a market-based monetary policy

Anwar Nasution

I. Introduction

This chapter discusses the formulation of monetary policy since the financial crisis in 1997–98. Special attention is given to how monetary policy instruments developed following the shift of economic management in 1997 from direct government control to a market-based system. The tools of monetary policy give the central bank a commanding position in respect of money supply. In the present market-based system, Bank Indonesia uses interest rate as the operating target of monetary policy. The central bank sets the real interest rate level neutral if the monetary policy is neither expansionary nor contractionary. The neutral or equilibrium interest rate depicts stable inflation with a closed output gap over the medium term. The central bank sets the real interest rate lower than the neutral rate to stimulate the economy to full employment level. On the other hand, the central bank sets the real interest rate above the neutral rate to dampen economic growth. The difference between actual policy rate and the neutral real interest rate is called interest rate gap that can be used to evaluate the monetary stance to close the output gap.

The use of interest rates as the operating target of monetary policy requires a set of pre-conditions. First, the existence of a financially healthy banking system and deep well-developed money and capital markets which are not sensitive to the vagaries of short-term capital flows. The underdevelopment of the money and capital markets in Indonesia is partly because of the long period of financial repression prior to banking sector reform that began in October 1988 and continued up to the crisis in 1997. During that era, there was no need to issue short-term Treasury bills or SPN (*Surat Perbendaharaan Negara*) or long-term government bonds (SUN or *Surat Utang Negara*) as the government budget deficit was entirely financed by official development aid (ODA) from a consortium of foreign creditors. Domestic business sector is either owned by the state or tightly close family-owned that are reluctant to either issue bonds or equity shares for raising capital. During the past financial repression, the financing of long-term business sector investment was provided by the credit programs of the state-owned bank with both low interest rates and credit risks.

Second, the existence of a competitive, effective and efficient financial market characterized by low transaction costs. Such a market will only exist in the absence of discrimination as regards bank ownership, and based on good legal and accounting systems that protect private property rights, enforce contracts and ensure symmetric transmission of information. At present, the banking system is segmented because the government deposited its financial wealth only at state-owned banks. Meanwhile, the private banks are more interested in financing their business affiliates. The system also requires good supervision of the financial system with prompt and strict implementation that is equally applied to all financial institutions, including state-owned banks and non-bank financial institutions (NBFIs). The third requirement is the existence of sound non-inflationary monetary policy, exchange rate policy, fiscal discipline and sustainable public debt management policies to promote both short-run macro-economic stability and long-term economic growth so as to allow the financial system and business sector to flourish and avoid crisis. Lastly, the availability of up-to-date and reliable information on the banking system's liquidity position – the supply and demand for reserve balances.

As noted in the previous chapter, three major policy instruments are now being used to preserve financial stability. First, upgrading prudential supervision and regulation of the banking and financial systems so as to bring them into line with the Basel Accords. For this, Indonesia has increased the risk-weighted capital ratio to above the 8 per cent required by Basel I and has implemented the Core Principles for Effective Banking Supervision. To comply with Basel II, Indonesia has moved from a practice of supervision based on compliance-checking towards the implementation of risk-oriented procedures. Second, building up external reserves at times of high commodity prices and short-term capital inflows. Third, establishing deposit insurance and a financial system stability forum to facilitate better coordination between the central bank, Treasury, Deposit Insurance Company and the Financial Sector Supervisory Authority including for resolution of bank failures.

In an open economy the central bank can use macroeconomic prudential policies as complementary tools to conventional monetary policy or substitute to conventional interest rate policy. Surges in capital inflow, for example, have expansionary effects on money supply and credit. On the other hand, during the period of positive terms of trade shock and surges of capital inflows, the central bank can use the macro prudential policies to tighten its credit or monetary stance without altering policy rate.

The rest of this chapter is divided into eight sections. Section 2 discusses the new monetary and fiscal rules first introduced under the IMF program in 1997 and which are still being used today. Section 3 analyzes the accumulation of external reserve policy introduced following the crisis in 1997. Section 4 describes the new role of Bank Indonesia, the central bank, following the crisis in 1997–98. Section 5 analyzes the shift in monetary rule from quantity rule to interest rate rule. Section 6 evaluates the operational implementation of Inflation Targeting and the Taylor Rule in Indonesia. Section 7 analyzes the monetary transmission mechanism. Section 8discusses the monetary policy instruments available to Bank Indonesia to control money supply. Finally, a number of conclusions are set out in Section 9.

II. New monetary and fiscal rules

The IMF Programs of 1997–2003 force Indonesia to adopt stringent macro-economic policies to control inflation and stabilize the exchange rate and restore economic growth. In addition to monetary and fiscal policy, structural reform is equally important to achieve these objectives. The short-run macro policies included replacing the exchange rate management from managed floating or pegging to independent floating. This, supported by (soft) inflation targeting and strict fiscal discipline, has been the monetary operating strategy in this country ever since, which means that an exchange rate target is no longer used as a nominal anchor for monetary policy. The maintenance of inflation target-ing as an operating strategy of monetary policy indicates the firm commitment of Indonesia to price stability, disclosure transparency, central bank independence and the avoidance of printing money to finance budget deficits. An explicit inflation target, along with a more flexible exchange rate regime and explicit fiscal discipline that ensure a stable government debt-to-GDP ratio, are now the three main pillars of the macroeconomic stabilization framework in Indo-nesia (Table 1.1). In addition to these monetary and fiscal rules, the authority also reforms the real sector of the economy and ended the practices of collu-sion, nepotism and corruption to improve economic efficiency and competitiveness.

Law No. 17 of 2003 on the Public Finances imposes fiscal rule by setting the budget balance rule or ceilings of the central government budget deficit at 3 per cent of annual GDP, and of each local government at 3 per cent of its Regional Domestic Product (RDP). The law calls for the adoption of the internationally recognized classification system and unification or consolidation of the fragmented fiscal reporting of the public sector. Implementation of the law is, however, very slow because until now, fiscal reporting in Indonesia was only confined to the budget of the central government and covered only cash transactions and debt of central government entities. Fiscal statistics exclude self-funded fiscal plans of central government entities, local governments out-side the Ministry of Finance including state-owned enterprises. All govern-ment departments, agencies and local governments and state-owned enterprises maintain registers of their fixed assets and produce partial operating statements and balance sheets. Actuarial estimates of public sector pension liabilities are periodically undertaken.

The new debt rule sets the ratio of public debt to GDP at a sustainable level of 60 per cent. During an economic slowdown, the government budget is deficit that is financed by public borrowing. In an upswing, the government runs a budget surplus which allows it to pay back its debt. To avoid transfer problems, a country has to have a surplus in its balance of payments to repay its external

Table 1.1 Elements of monetary policy in ASEAN+3 countries following the Asian financial crisis of 1997

Country	Exchange Rate Arrangement	Year of Adopting Inflation Targeting	Goal Autonomy	Target Autonomy		Instrument Autonomy		Bank Restructuring[2]
			Legislated Goal	Target Specification[1]	Government Override	Credit to Gov't	Gov't Participation in Policymaking	
Brunei Darussalam	Currency board arrangement	–	–	–	–	–	–	–
Cambodia	Managed floating	–	–	–	–	–	–	Yes
China	Pegged to USD	–	–	–	–	–	–	Yes
Hong Kong	Currency board arrangement	–	–	–	–	–	–	–
Indonesia	Independent floating	January 2000	Currency stability	G + CB	No	No	No	Yes
Japan	Independent floating	–	–	–	–	–	–	Yes
Korea	Independent floating	Apr–98	Price stability	G + CB	No	Yes	Non–voting	Yes
Laos	Managed floating	–	–	–	–	–	–	Yes
Malaysia	Pegged	–	–	–	–	–	–	Yes
Myanmar	Pegged	–	–	–	–	–	–	Yes
Philippines	Independent floating	December 1989	Price stability	G + CB	No	Yes, limited	Voting member	–

Singapore	Managed floating	–	–	–	–	–	–	–
Thailand	Independent floating	May 2000	Price stability	CB	No	Yes	No	Yes
Vietnam	Pegged	–	–	–	–	–	–	Yes

Sources: IMF. 2009. 'Annual Report on Exchange Arrangements and Exchange Restrictions 2008'. Washington, DC: IMF. Ito, T. and T. Hayashi 2004. 'Inflation Targeting in Asia'. Hong Kong: Hong Kong Institute for Monetary Research. HKIMR. March. Roger, S. 2009. 'Inflation Targeting at 20: Achievements and Challenges'. IMF Working Paper No. WP/09/236. Washington, DC: IMF. October. Filardo, A. and Genberg, H. 2009. 'Targeting Inflation in Asia and the Pacific: Lessons from the Recent Past'. BIS Representative Officer Asia and the Pacific. August.

Notes: [1]G = Government; CB = Central Bank; [2]Finance Minister may delay implementation of decision for two weeks.

debt. The explicit new budget and debt rules replace the 'balanced budget' rule that had been applied for 32 years under the administration of President Suharto, which ended in 1998. Back then, the budget deficit was financed by low-cost official development aid (ODA) from Indonesia's consortium of international donors (IGGI-the Intergovernmental Group on Indonesia). Law No. 23 of 1999 on Bank Indonesia bans the central bank from buying government bonds in the primary market to finance the budget deficit. Additional revenue is generated from privatization of SOEs and selling off state assets. These strict macroeconomic policies have protected the country from deep devaluations and steep increases in the interest rate that devastate the balance sheets of banks and non-bank financial firms, particularly those with large foreign currency debt, as happened in 1997. Fiscal consolidation is also necessary for facilitating sustained long-run growth by minimizing the crowding out of investment and by creating fiscal space for countercyclical fiscal policy and crisis-related spending. Central bank accountability under the inflation targeting framework imposes costs on an incompetent and opportunistic central bank.[1]

The budget and debt rules limit automatic stabilizers and discretionary policy actions of the government. Tax collections and non-tax revenues decline when the economy slows down. At the same time, social spending and other subsidies rise. In other words, when the budget worsens fiscal policy is automatically expansionary. Discretionary fiscal policy needs explicit decisions by the government and the Parliament to change both taxes and government spending. In reality the ratios of fiscal deficit and public debt to annual GDP were maintained by the government much below the upper limits as set by the Public Finance Law of 2003. The budget deficitrose from 1.5 of GDP in 2010 to 2.4 per cent of in 2013 and the public debt to GDP was around 27 per cent. These conservative ratios are good for building images in international markets to upgrade Indonesia's rating and reduce yields of Indonesia's sovereign bonds. The policy, however, is bad for economic growth because of the lack of financial resources available for building the badly needed infrastructure. On the other hand, because of inefficiency of tax administration, tax ratio remains very low at 13 per cent of GDP. Most of the budget expenditures go to Personnel, Material and Subsidies and capital expenditure is only about half of outlays for subsidies for fuel and electricity.

The procedural rules issued under the Public Finance Law of 2003 require the application of the principles of transparency and accountability in designing, implementing and assessing fiscal policy. They require the government to commit in advance to a monitor-able fiscal policy strategy over a multiyear period and to report and publish fiscal outcomes and strategy changes on a routine basis. The Law prescribes the submission to Parliament of yearly statements on medium-term fiscal policy, fiscal policy strategy and the macroeconomic framework that outlines rolling targets for prescribed fiscal indicators. These statements should include the underlying macroeconomic assumptions, and the policies of the government, particularly on taxation, expenditure, borrowing and other key fiscal measures, including privatization of SOEs and selling off state assets. The Minister of Finance is obliged to prepare quarterly reports highlighting trends in revenue and expenditure to Parliament,

Table 1.2 Foreign reserves and currency in circulation, 1998–2011

Year	Foreign Reserves as % of				Currency in Circulation as % of			Inflation	Short-Run Interest Rate	Rate of GDP Growth	Budget Deficit as % of GDP	Ratio of Public Debt to GDP	Nominal Exchange Rate IDR/USD
	MB	PSD	SBI	GDP	MB	PSD	GDP						
1995	115.7	—	252.5	8.3	80.5	—	4.6	9.4	13.6	8.4	1.72	30.1	2248.6
1996	121.3	—	225.0	10.4	65.4	—	4.2	8.0	14.0	7.6	1.98	23.9	2342.3
1997	101.6	—	665.4	9.0	61.7	—	4.5	6.2	27.8	4.7	1.32	38.0	2909.4
1998	316.8	—	556.4	24.9	64.6	—	5.1	59.6	62.8	-13.1	-1.84	58.0	10013.6
1999	208.8	—	337.1	19.3	71.3	—	6.6	2.1	23.6	0.8	-3.68	85.0	7855.2
2000	197.1	—	414.1	17.8	71.4	—	6.5	9.0	10.3	4.9	-1.2	89.0	8421.8
2001	225.0	—	518.3	17.5	71.4	—	5.5	11.9	15.0	3.6	-2.4	77.0	10260.9
2002	215.8	—	386.9	16.4	71.2	—	5.4	9.6	13.5	4.5	-1.3	67.0	9311.2
2003	187.0	38.6	295.4	15.5	67.7	14.0	5.6	4.4	7.8	4.8	-1.7	61.0	8577.1
2004	162.8	80.7	316.0	14.1	63.6	31.6	5.5	6.2	5.4	5.0	-1.1	57.0	8938.9
2005	140.5	84.3	466.5	12.2	60.4	36.2	5.2	16.2	6.8	5.7	-0.5	47.0	9704.7
2006	131.3	93.2	188.1	11.7	60.1	42.6	5.4	6.4	9.2	5.5	-0.9	39.0	9159.3
2007	137.1	108.0	212.1	13.2	58.2	45.8	5.6	6.4	6.0	6.3	-1.3	35.0	9141.0
2008	145.3	94.3	282.5	10.1	76.7	49.8	5.3	11.2	8.5	6.0	-0.1	33.0	9699.0
2009	170.8	112.8	277.2	12.2	69.4	45.8	5.0	2.8	7.2	4.6	-1.6	28.3	10389.9
2010	168.7	142.1	437.0	13.6	50.2	42.3	4.1	7.0	6.0	6.1	-0.7	26.0	9090.4
2011	138.2	98.9	658.4	12.2	56.7	40.6	5.0	4.8	5.6	6.5	-2.1	25.0	8770.4

Sources: Bank Indonesia, *Indonesia Financial Statistics*, various issues; IMF, *International Financial Statistics*, May 2011. Ministry of Finance, *Buku Saku Perkembangan Utang Negara* (Pocket book on Government Debt), various editions.

Notes: MB = Monetary Base; PSD = Public Sector Debt, which is the total of government bonds plus Treasury Bills (data for 1995–2003 are not available) and *sharia*-based government bonds issued in international markets; SBI = Bank Indonesia Certificates of Deposits; GDP = Gross Domestic Product; Short-Run Interest Rate = JIBOR 1 Month.

and provide explanations in cases where there are substantial deviations from fiscal targets, as well as remedial measures to address them.

Law No. 22/1999 and Law No. 32/2004 transfer significant responsibility to local governments. Unlike in other countries, autonomy in Indonesia is given to sub-province levels, namely municipalities, or *Kota*, and regencies, or *Kabupaten* governments. The obligatory sectors for local government include health, education, public works, environment, communication, transport, agriculture, industry and trade, capital investment, land, cooperatives, manpower and infrastructure services. During the *Orde Baru* administration, everything was centrally decided by the central government. At present, the central government is only responsible for six areas, namely (1) foreign policy; (2) defense; (3) security; (4) administration of justice; (5) monetary and fiscal policy and (6) religious affairs and the rest is transferred to local governments.

At present, approximately 40 per cent of the budget expenditure of the central government is transferred to finance budgets of local governments (*Anggaran Pendapatandan Belanja Daerah*, APBD). Revenues of local governments are heavily dependent on this transfer as local governments are only given power to tax minor sources such as restaurants and entertainment to generate their own-source revenues. Taxing power on major revenues remains at the hands of the central government which is given back to local governments in the form of the balancing funds or fiscal equalization funds. Borrowings of local governments require permission from the Ministry of Finance at central government. The balancing funds consist of three components, namely: (1) general allocation funds (*Dana Alokasi Umum*, DAU) which cover about 70–80 per cent of local governments' budgets, (2) *Dana Bagi Hasil* or DBH or tax sharing from general tax revenues and revenues from exploitation of natural resources and (3) general allocation funds (*Dana Alokasi Khusus*) to finance central government initiatives implemented in the region.

Long before this, Indonesia had liberalized the balance of payments capital account in April 1970, while the current account remained heavily regulated. At that time, Indonesia moved to a fully convertible foreign exchange system with a unified fixed exchange rate and practically no limitation on capital flows. The liberal exchange rate system did not cause problems at that time because of the limited access of economic agents to the international financial markets.

The first attempt to develop the financial markets began in February 1984 with the issuance of Bank Indonesia's own short-term debt certificate, SBI – *Sertifikat Bank Indonesia* (Bank Indonesia Certificates). In the absence of short-term government securities, at that time SBI was the principal instrument for controlling money supply through open market operations (OMO). To absorb excess liquidity, Bank Indonesia introduced the FASBI facility (*Fasilitas BI*) in 1997, paying interest on overnight placements with Bank Indonesia. In addition, the central bank opened a discount window to allow depository institutions to borrow during temporary shortfalls in reserves. In addition to ending financial repression, further improvements in the legal and accounting systems were introduced to make the markets work more effectively and efficiently, particularly for the development of corporate debt instruments.

The issuance of government bonds to recapitalize financially distressed banks in 1997 and diversify the funding of the government budget deficit has also contributed to the development and deepening of a liquid domestic debt market. On a trial basis, the government began to issue short-term SPN in 1990. But, the amounts were very small and, therefore, were incapable of replacing SBI as the primary instrument for OMOs. The broadening range of financial assets available to local institutions and investors provided alternative channels for financial intermediaries aside from the banks, and paved the way for market-based monetary policy. In spite of the shift to a flexible exchange rate system, Indonesia continues to accumulate a large foreign reserve buffer to avoid exchange rate volatility.

In addition to exchange rate policy, there are now seven other broad policy measures typically used by the central bank to implement monetary policy. These are as follows: loan to deposit ratio, loan-to-value ratio, legal lending limits, net open position, reserve requirement system, open market operations and standing credit facilities made available to commercial banks as depository institutions. The first four policy instruments are part of the prudential rules of the banking system. These instruments are generally called macro prudential instruments that are typically used in mitigating systemic risks, either over time or across institutions and markets. Loan-to-value ratio limits credit to certain economic sectors. The reserve requirement affects the demand for liquidity in the banking system. Open market operations and credit facilities are market-based instruments designed to adjust the supply of liquidity so as to influence the target interest rate in the interbank money market and maintain the discount rate the central bank charges on the loans it makes to commercial banks. Banks make overnight loans to each other in the interbank money market. As it affects the money multiplier, the reserve requirement ratio is a powerful tool for controlling the quantity of money, which is equal to the money multiplier times the monetary base. Computing the required reserve, however, is complex and involves time lags.

III. Accumulating external reserves

Indonesia is primarily a commodities exporter and, hence, is exposed to terms of trade shocks and the adverse effects of volatility in commodity prices. Located on the ring of fire, Indonesia is also vulnerable to frequent natural disasters, such as the devastating tsunami in the Province of Aceh and the Nias Island in December 2004 and frequent volcanic eruptions. These calamities not only destroy infrastructure, but also productive capacity that adversely impacts on loans in the financial system.

At present, Indonesia has no Sovereign Wealth Fund (SWF) to mitigate the impacts of external shocks on domestic economy. A SWF plays five roles (Truman, 2011), namely, first, as a stabilization fund to insulate the government budget or the economy against global price swings; second, as a savings fund for future generations; third, as a reserve investment fund; fourth, as a development fund; and, fifth, as a contingent pension reserve fund. To some extent, the increase in foreign exchange revenues due to positive external shocks has only been used for traditional purposes, namely, the early retirement of external debt, appreciation of the Rupiah, strengthening the capital of state-owned enterprises, including banks, and removing their non-performing loans (NPL), modernizing infrastructure and productive capacity in the economy, and accumulation of foreign exchange reserves by the central bank.

In theory, a flexible exchange rate requires a smaller amount of foreign reserves as the system reduces the need for market intervention. The central bank is free to respond to shocks, but cannot commit ex ante to the monetary policy that it will follow. On the other hand, under the fixed exchange rate system, the central bank subordinates monetary policy or domestic credit expansion to maintaining the constant nominal exchange rate. The flexible exchange rate system provides a greater degree of monetary policy autonomy and protects output better from real external shocks because the exchange rate can adjust and stabilize demand for domestic goods through switching expenditures. The flexible exchange rate system is expected to reduce one-way bets against the Rupiah, thereby discouraging short-term capital inflows that can be easily reversed. The need for self-insurance is also reduced as it discourages a buildup of large un-hedged foreign currency positions by reducing the implicit exchange rate guarantees resulting from the pegged system. The flexible exchange rate system also stimulates the development of the foreign exchange market as market participants are encouraged to apply prudent risk management and hedge against potential exchange rate risks.

The need to build up external reserves has been further reduced thanks to the availability of back-up loans under the Chiang Mai Initiative (CMI) and bilateral currency swap facilities between Asian central banks. The CMI was established by the meeting of ASEAN+3 countries in Chiang Mai in May 2000. Eight years later, the meeting of 13 ASEAN+3 Finance Ministers (AFMM+3) in Madrid 2008 resulted in an agreement to multilateralize the CMI to become CMIM (Chiang Mai Initiative Multeralisation). At the same time, the ministers agreed to enlarge the size of the facility and increase the portion that is non-linked to IMF Programs. In March 2012, the size of the CMIM was doubled to $240 billion, but the money remains in the individual central banks. Each member country has access to the amount it has committed times a multiple (5 for poor countries and 2.5 for better-off ASEAN members, 1 for Korea and 0.5 for China and Japan). The CMIM facility is, however, very small in comparison to the 1997 bailouts of Thailand ($17.2 billion) and Indonesia ($42.3 billion). In addition, the IMF and other international and regional financial institutions have relaxed their loan conditionality and now offer flexible credit lines to meet the liquidity needs of those countries with good track records and sound macroeconomic policies.

In reality, for a number of reasons Indonesia has continued to accumulate large international reserves since the Asian financial crisis of 1997 (Calvo and

Reinhart, 2002, and Ruiz-Arranz and Zavadjil, 2008). Table 1.1 shows that between 2000 and 2010, the nominal value of Indonesian external reserves rose more than 100 per cent, although as a percentage of GDP they declined from 15 per cent in 2003 to 12 per cent in 2010. Indonesia has benefited from high international raw materials prices since the early 1990s, mainly due to rapid economic growth both in China and India, as well as rapid industrialization, mechanization and urbanization in those countries. As will be discussed further, massive short-term capital inflows to Indonesia to buy Bank Indonesia papers (SBIs) and sovereign bonds since 2005 have been encouraged by high interest differentials. Foreign investors mainly book their investments through Singapore to benefit from the tax agreement that provides an exemption to the 20 per cent withholding tax charged on investment returns in Indonesia. Another incentive has been the appreciation of the Rupiah, which has allowed investors to acquire more foreign currency for the same amount of the Rupiah.

The first reason for the accumulation of reserves is to enable the government to avoid extreme fluctuations of the Rupiah exchange rate or excessive exchange rate volatility in a relatively shallow foreign exchange market, and thus prevent adverse impacts on the economy. Less volatile exchange rates minimize currency risks and provide incentives for overseas borrowing, particularly when international interest rates are lower than domestic rates. Strong financial sector policies with strict implementation of prudential rules and regulations, such as the net open position (NOP) of the banking system, encourage banks to hedge risks and avoid currency mismatches. Second, less volatile exchange rates avoid the harmful balance-sheet effects on economic units, including the banking system. The third reason is the fear of inflation from exchange rate pass-through under greater exchange rate flexibility, particularly given the limited technical and institutional capacity of the central bank to implement transparent inflation targeting. By lowering the prices of imports, an appreciating exchange rate suppresses inflation.

The fourth reason is because exchange rate policy is one of the principal policy instruments to pursue export-led growth as it affects both the international competitiveness of the economy and its efficiency. The exchange rate strategy is also a very powerful tool for attaining the inflation target of the central bank. There are two ways to measure exchange rates, namely, nominal exchange rate with trading partners (NEER) and real effective exchange rate (REER). NEER refers to the nominal price of foreign currency, while REER is the relative price, measured in the same currency, of a bundle of goods in the foreign country compared with the same bundle of goods on the domestic market.[2] On the external front, a rising REER provides financial incentives to help improve the external competitiveness of the domestic economy in international markets and, hence, promote exports. This, along with fiscal discipline and structural reforms that increase productivity, helps to improve external competitiveness.

On the domestic front, a rising REER gives incentives for economic resources to migrate from the less productive non-traded sector of the economy to the more efficient traded sector.[3] Productivity can also be raised through transfers of technology and economy-wide deregulation and structural reforms. Prior to the Asian financial crisis of 1997, a strong Rupiah triggered an asset bubble in the non-traded sector of the economy, such as the land-based sector, including the property market. As noted earlier, with the availability of official development aid from Western creditors and inflows of foreign investment, Indonesia ended its strict foreign exchange controls in April 1970. The country liberalized its capital account while the current account continued to be heavily regulated. With liberalization, Indonesia moved to a fully convertible foreign exchange rate system, with a unified fixed exchange rate and practically no limitation on capital flows. Figure 1.1 shows the development of the Rupiah nominal (NEER) and real exchange rate (REER) indices against a basket of foreign currencies with which Indonesia trades. Both NEER and REER declined between April 2007 and April 2009, and have been gradually increasing again since then. Again, REER indicates a country's competitive position over time. As it is defined as the ratio of international prices over domestic prices, a rising REER indicates an increase in the competitiveness of the economy in international markets and provides incentives for economic resources to be reallocated from the non-traded sector to the traded sector of the economy. On the other hand, a declining REER indicates a loss of international competitiveness and provides financial incentive for the allocation of domestic resources to the inefficient non-traded sector of the economy.

The fourth reason for the accumulation of reserves is to hedge against speculation and foreign exchange instability resulting from shortfalls in exports and capital flow reversals. Indonesia's exports mainly consist of raw materials, such as energy and agriculture products, whose prices are inherently volatile and cyclical. Figure 1.2 shows that a large portion of both Rupiah-denominated SBI and SUN is owned by foreign investors. Both SBI and government bonds have been attractive to foreign investors because of the high differential between domestic interest rates and those in foreign markets, and expectations of Rupiah appreciation. The significant presence of foreign investors helps boost both the

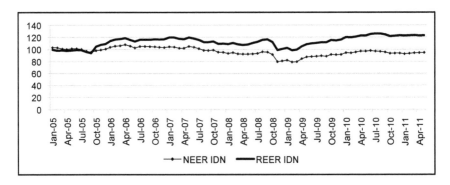

Figure 1.1 Nominal and real effective exchange rates, 2005–11

Source: Bank for International Settlements, Annual Report, (2010).

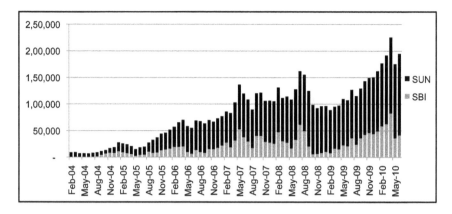

Figure 1.2 Foreign ownership of government bonds (SUN) and SBI, 2004–10 (in billions Rupiah)

Sources: *Indonesia Financial Statistics*, various issues.

liquidity and growth of these two commercial papers. Domestic institutional investors (such as insurance companies, pension funds and mutual funds) are still at the early stages of development in Indonesia and mainly invest in short-term securities. Unlike Japan, Indonesia has no Postal Savings Bank that can mobilize low-cost domestic savings to absorb SBI and Indonesian sovereign bonds. Other large holders of these securities are domestic banks and local governments, which recycle unused transfer funds from the central government back to Jakarta. Foreign investors have played a crucial role in boosting the liquidity and the growth of the newly established bond market. In the future, it is expected that both local investors and non-residents will borrow in local currency to fund investments in a more mature bond market.[4]

The fifth reason for accumulating foreign exchange reserves is to maintain adequate fiscal space when facing a crisis. Indonesia and other Asian countries were quite reluctant to turn to the IMF for help during the global financial crisis in 2007–08 as they were treated improperly when they sought help during the Asian financial crisis of 1997–98. As noted in the earlier chapter, a combination of significant Rupiah depreciation and the injection of large-scale liquidity support by Bank Indonesia to contain and manage the crisis had fueled inflation.

IV. New role of independent Bank Indonesia

Modeling after the Bundesbank of Germany, Law No. 23 of 1999, as amended (Law No. 23 of 2004) accords independent status to Bank Indonesia, and assigns Bank Indonesia an overriding task, namely, stabilizing both the internal and external value of the Rupiah. To achieve this goal, Bank Indonesia is assigned three roles, namely: (1) to set and implement monetary policy; (2) to regulate and preserve the health of the payments system; and (3) to regulate and supervise the banking system. The legislation bans the central bank from financing the government budget deficit by buying government bonds in the primary market. Bank Indonesia issues and revokes banking licenses and prudential rules and regulations governing the banking system, which constitutes the core of the Indonesian financial system. Bank Indonesia also supervises the BPR (*Bank Perkreditan Rakyat*), which are small, non-depository rural banks. As of February 2011 there were 1,617 BPR in existence, with 3,928 branches spread across Indonesia. During the colonial period, the BPR were supervised by BRI (Bank Rakyat Indonesia, then known as Algemene Volkscrediet Bank), which at that time specialized in serving cooperatives, and small-scale agricultural and fisheries enterprises.

Law No. 23 of 1999 directs Bank Indonesia to focus on systemic stability so as to preserve the stability of the payment system and monetary policy by stabilizing both the internal and external values of the Rupiah. The internal value of the Rupiah can be maintained by keeping inflation low, while its external value can be maintained by stabilizing the Rupiah exchange rate. Drawing on the Financial Services Authority of the UK, the Central Bank Law requires Bank Indonesia to transfer its role as bank supervisor to the newly established OJK (*Otoritas Jasa Keuangan*), an independent super institution that will supervise the entire financial sector, including both banks and NBFIs. The OJK is fully functional at the beginning of 2014.

Law No. 23 of 1999 elaborates the capital structure of Bank Indonesia. The minimum or basic capital of the central bank is set at Rp2 trillion. Thirty per cent of Bank Indonesia's financial surplus is to be used to build up specified reserves, while the rest of the surplus is to be used for accumulating general reserves until their value, plus the basic capital of Bank Indonesia, amount to 10 per cent of the monetary liabilities of Bank Indonesia. An additional surplus above the specified and general reserves is to be transferred to the Treasury. With the consent of Parliament, the Treasury can inject extra financing to provide Bank Indonesia with a minimum capital of Rp2 trillion in a case where it falls below that level.

The financial cost or the quasi-fiscal cost of holding large reserves is high for Bank Indonesia's balance sheet. For example, in order to sterilize short-term capital inflows, Bank Indonesia issued SBI with a coupon rate of 6.75 per cent per annum in early 2011. By contrast, the return on its foreign assets (mainly in the form of US government bonds) was only 3 per cent. In addition, Bank Indonesia also holds non-traded, low-interest government bonds that were issued as repayment for the liquidity injected into financially distressed banks during the crisis in 1997. Part of the collateral pledged to secure these liquidity credits is of low quality. Bank Indonesia also currently pays interest on deposits owned by the government and commercial banks. On the other hand, its revenue from seigniorage, or the printing of currency, is not that great, while its interest income has eroded with the elimination of the credit programs of the past. As a result, Bank Indonesia has suffered losses over the past few years up to 2012 that could erode its minimum capital. Moreover, the current crises at the periphery of the euro zone indicate that securities denominated in domestic currencies are shielded from currency risks but not from interest rate risks that raise the debt burden of the government. Capital flow reversal puts pressure on the balance of payments and results in the devaluation of domestic currencies, thus depressing the value of the capital and assets of domestic banks and companies.

Like any other central bank, Bank Indonesia administers the foreign exchange reserves of the state. Buying and selling foreign exchange is one of the powerful policy instruments available to Bank Indonesia, particularly so given the limited amount of SBI and short-term Treasury papers (SPN – *Surat Perbendaharaan Negara*) for use in open market operations. The purchase of foreign exchange from the general public by Bank Indonesia raises both the stock of its foreign exchange reserves and its monetary liabilities. On the other hand, its stock of external reserves and monetary liabilities decline with the selling of its foreign exchange reserves.

A sterilization operation is a combination of the expansion of the monetary base, for example the purchase of foreign exchange from exporters or borrowing from foreign lenders, and a contraction in the same amount through the sale of SBI or government papers. The supply of base money remains the same as a result of such an operation. As shown in Table 1.3, from the source or supply side, the stock of base money is equal to the summation of foreign exchange reserves of the central bank plus its domestic credit to both government, commercial banks and others, and its net other assets. As banker to the government, Bank Indonesia holds government deposits and provides credit to the government backed by its securities as collateral. From the use or demand side, monetary base is a summation of fiat money circulated by Bank Indonesia, its securities (SBI), deposits (of the government, commercial banks and others) and its equity capital. As net other assets and the equity capital of the central bank are relatively constant, the monetary base is mainly affected by its foreign

Table 1.3 Bank Indonesia's balance sheet

Assets	Liabilities and Capital
1. Foreign Exchange Reserves (R)	4. Currency in Circulation
2. Domestic Credit (D)	5. Central Bank Securities (SBI)
2a. Government Securities	6. Deposits
2b. Loans and Discounts to Banks	6a. Government
3. Net Other Assets	6b. Commercial Banks
	6c. Others
	7. Equity Capital
Monetary Base (Sources) = H^S= 1 + 2 + 3	**Monetary Base (Uses) = H^d= 4 + 5 + 6 + 7**

reserves and domestic credit on the asset side. The law gives a monopoly to Bank Indonesia to issue fiat money that is accepted as a medium of exchange simply because of government decree. The summation of currency in circulation plus central bank securities and deposits of both government and the commercial banks is the monetary liability of Bank Indonesia.

There was a debate in the 1990s about the appropriateness and effectiveness of sterilization operations. On the one hand, Calvo, Leiderman and Reinhart (1992) criticized sterilization operations for leading to excessively high domestic interest rates, thereby perpetuating capital inflows and quasi-fiscal costs. The fiscal cost, according to Calvo, Leiderman and Reinhart, is equal to the interest differential between the domestic and international markets, multiplied by the size of the sterilization operation. By contrast, Reisen (1993) defended sterilization operations by highlighting the experiences of many Asian countries that successfully used sterilization policies in the early 1990s to defend their monetary independence. Frankel (1994) bridges the gap between these two extreme views by pointing out that the appropriateness of the response is dependent on the source or nature of the shock. If the shock is caused by a fall in foreign interest rates that subsequently increases the attractiveness of domestic assets, a sterilization operation will push domestic interest rates down by supplying the excess demand of investors for securities issued by both the government and the central bank. On the other hand, if the inflows are attracted by, for example, a stabilization program that subsequently increases demand for money by domestic residents, sterilization will lead to higher domestic interest rates that will increase its fiscal cost. In such a situation, Frankel recommends that sterilization be avoided, and that the domestic money that residents want be supplied.

Bank Indonesia was for long a fiscal or quasi-fiscal agent of the government. During the last period of the President Sukarno administration (1960–65), known as the 'Old Order', Bank Indonesia was predominantly a payment agency for the government. Modeled on the banking systems of the socialist countries, Bank Indonesia was part of one consolidated state-bank. This allowed it to directly control all of the activities of the state-owned banking system, which formed the backbone of the financial services industry. Quasi-fiscal activity was carried out through credit programs with credit guarantee and subsidized interest rates. Bank Indonesia had no autonomy as the governor of the central bank held a ministerial position in the government. The government budget deficit was mainly financed by printing money, which led to hyperinflation of more than 650 per cent per annum in 1965 (Aghevli and Khan, 1977).

The 1968 Central Bank Law introduced by President Suharto's 'New Order' administration provided some autonomy to Bank Indonesia, and assigned it the primarily responsibility for bank regulation and supervision and for setting an appropriate legal structure for banks. As in the previous era, prior to 1966, monetary policy continued to be determined by the government through the Monetary Board, whose members were mainly Cabinet ministers, with the governor of Bank Indonesia being only one of them. The Monetary Board approved selective credit policies based on subsidized interest rates. Through this credit policy, the previous quasi-fiscal operation of monetary policy was continued under the New Order administration.

In contrast to the earlier practice, the balanced budget fiscal and debt rules under the New Orderbetween1966–98 relieved Bank Indonesia from financing the government budget deficit. This allowed Bank Indonesia to focus on other aspects of monetary policy and management. Credit ceilings cum selective credit policies with subsidized interest rates were made more detailed during the oil boom period between 1973 and 1983. The credit policy was ineffective in constraining growth in both money supply and inflation due to the increasing foreign exchange reserves of Bank Indonesia. The increase in foreign exchange was also due to a continuing increase in the international oil price and massive capital inflows, including the reckless foreign borrowings of Pertamina, the state-oil company, in 1973–75 (Cole and Slade, 1996: 39). The windfall from the high price of oil in the 1970s was directly spent by the government.

As the bankers' bank, BI holds the deposits of the commercial banks and provides various types of credit to them. The commercial banks' deposits include the required reserve, excess reserve and overnight deposits. The size of the reserve requirement is calculated as a certain ratio or percentage of third-party deposits with commercial banks. As will be discussed further in a later section, the reserve requirement ratio is varied by the central bank as a monetary tool to affect the capacity of commercial banks to create inside money though extending credit and making investments. As they cannot be used for lending and investment, the reserve requirement acts as a tax on the commercial banks. To reduce the effective tax on deposits Bank Indonesia pays the interest rate on deposits. The rate is set below the interbank interest rate or interest rate on overnight loans of reserve from one bank to another. In extraordinary circumstances, the central bank can extend credit to non-bank business entities, thereby bypassing the commercial banks. To soak up liquidity, the government and the central bank can encourage the shifting of deposits of public entities and state-owned enterprises, as well as the private sector, from the commercial banks to the central bank.

The Bank Indonesia Laws of 1999 and 2003 preserve the role of the central bank as a lender of last resort in preventing the bankruptcy of a solvent bank unable to meet its payment obligations by, for example, helping it to cope with deposit runs during a crisis. The lender of last resort facility provides ailing banks with funds when market sources of liquidity dry up. To restore the normal functioning of the money market and payment system during the crisis of 1997–98, Bank Indonesia injected massive liquidity assistance into the banks, even those suffering solvency problems. In exchange for the financial assistance, the recipients were required to submit collateral in the form of eligible private-sector papers and real estate. Some of these assets turned out to be of low quality. The non-performing assets of the financially distressed banks were shifted to IBRA and financial assistance to support insolvent banks was injected by IBRA and the Ministry of Finance.

The Bank Indonesia Laws of 1999 and 2003 ban the central bank from buying government bonds in the primary market so as to prevent inflationary financing or the printing of money to finance the government budget deficit. At the same time, financial repression was ended with the shifting of credit allocation from non-market and non-economic considerations to a market-based system. This resulted in the discontinuation of Bank Indonesia's role as a provider of liquidity credit to finance selective lending at subsidized interest rates as part of the financial repression system. It also brought to an end Bank Indonesia's quasi-fiscal operations through selective lending programs with subsidized interest rates.

The stock of money supply (M) is equal to the multiplication of the monetary multiplier (m) by the monetary base (H), or $M = m \cdot H$. The size of the monetary multiplier is a function of the reserve requirement ratio, the ratios of money and demand deposits to total money held by the public, and the ratio of excess reserves as a percentage of total reserves held by the commercial banks. The ratios of money and demand deposits held by the public are determined by the payment system, as well as the behavior of the money holders. Meanwhile, the holding of excess reserves by the commercial banks is also determined by the payment system and their own behavior.

V.   Changing monetary policy rules

The IMF Program in 1997 shifted the monetary policy rule of Bank Indonesia from a money supply/credit policy instrument to an interest rate instrument. One of the issues in monetary economics is how the monetary authority or central bank should formulate its policy decisions so as to achieve its policy objectives, namely internal and external stability and full employment in the economy. It is widely believed that monetary policy can be used to counteract macroeconomic disturbances so as to promote economic stability and economic growth. When economic growth falls below its potential, accommodative monetary policy can stimulate aggregate demand to restore full employment. On the other hand, monetary restriction can be used to dampen inflationary pressures and restore price stability.

Quantity Theory of Money

Monetary policy using money as the policy instrument was introduced at the beginning of the New Order to suppress the hyperinflation of the mid-1960s. This was in line with the traditional IMF-conditionality criteria that imply a commitment to achieving quantitative targets for key macroeconomic aggregates. A stabilization agreement with the IMF usually imposes a ceiling on the level of net domestic assets of the central bank (Ghosh, Zalduendo, Thomas, Kim, Ramakrishnan and Joshi 2008). The key monetary policy instrument during the past long period of financial repression was setting detailed credit ceilings by economic sector and class of customer, accompanied by heavily subsidized interest rates. This policy was in accordance with the classical Quantity Theory of Money of Irving Fisher, and the modern version postulated by Milton Friedman (1960), as part of which Bank Indonesia maintained a constant rate of growth of money supply based on consideration of price stability, or an optimal rate of inflation or deflation:

$$\frac{\Delta M}{M} + \frac{\Delta V}{V} = \frac{\Delta P}{P} + \frac{\Delta y}{y} \tag{1}$$

where:

$\dfrac{\Delta M}{M}$ is the rate of growth of money supply;

$\dfrac{\Delta V}{V}$ is the rate of growth of income velocity of money;

$\dfrac{\Delta P}{P}$ is the rate growth of inflation;

$\dfrac{\Delta y}{y}$ is the rate of growth of real output.

The classical long-run quantity theory postulates that the economy is in full employment ($\Delta y = 0$) and the velocity of money ($\Delta V = 0$) is fairly stable due to stability in the payment system. This stabilizes the demand for money. The rate of growth of money supply, therefore, raises the inflation rate proportionally. The classical and neo-classical quantity theories are basically a model for a closed economy and there is no reference to interest rate parity and the pass-through effect that describes the effect of changes in exchange rates on import prices and hence the general price index.

Milton Friedman agrees that monetary policy has a strong impact on the economy. However, this impact has a long and variable lag because the course of the economy cannot be foreseen long in advance. This monetarist believes that changes in money supply cannot affect the 'real variable' in the long run. For this reason, he recommends that discretionary policy should be avoided and that money supply should grow at a given constant percentage.

McCallum monetary rule

In contrast to the passive Friedman rule, the McCallum monetary rule is driven by the belief that central banks should respond actively to evolving economic conditions. Equation (1) can be interpreted in nominal terms (McCallum, 1988). Let Δa be the sum of the natural rate of growth of nominal income plus the central bank's inflation target, or $\Delta a^* = \pi^* + \frac{\Delta y^*}{y^*}$. The rule for constant money growth can, therefore, be seen as targeting this nominal natural rate of growth.

The raft of banking and lending reforms (Pakto) of 1988 produced significant changes in the regulatory system and affected stability in the demand for money.

Disturbances were also caused by the Asian financial crisis in 1997, as well as rapid financial innovation resulting from technological progress in the payment system. To capture the change in velocity of money due to the regulatory and technological changes in the payment system, the McCallum (McCallum, 2000) specifies the growth of the monetary base (instrument) in a non-discretionary feedback rule for nominal GDP (target) as:

$$\Delta H/H = \Delta Y^*/Y^* - \Delta V/V + 0.5 \ (\Delta Y^*/Y^* - \Delta Y_{t-1}/Y_{t-1}) \qquad (2)$$

where:

$\Delta H/H$ is the rate of growth of the monetary base;
$\Delta V/V$ is the rate of growth of base velocity;
$\Delta Y/Y$ is the rate of growth of nominal GDP, assumed to be 5 per cent by McCallum for the US, which is equal to the sum of the target inflation rate (2 per cent) and the long-run average rate of growth of real GDP (3 per cent per year).

Partly because of the instability in demand for money due to regulatory reform, financial innovation and rapid technological changes in the payment system, the IMF stability program of 1997–2003 called for a change in monetary policy from the rule with money as the policy instrument to an interest rate instrument. An earlier classical interest rate policy rule was proposed by Wicksell, (1936) under which interest rates would move in proportion to the inflation rate. The Wicksellian reactive monetary rule focuses exclusively on price stability and does not refer to real economic activity (Orphanides, 2007):

$$\Delta i = \theta \pi \qquad (3)$$

where θ is an adjustment coefficient.

As noted earlier, appreciation of the Rupiah reduces the international competitiveness and efficiency of the economy. On the other hand, a stronger Rupiah reduces the price of imported foreign goods and suppresses inflationary pressures. Liberalization of foreign trade that has replaced non-tariff barriers with tariffs and reduced the level of tariffs has increased the portion of imported foreign goods in the consumer price index. This, in turn, has heightened the elasticity of the exchange rate pass-through effect, which makes changes in exchange rates more sensitive to import prices and hence domestic prices. The undervaluation of the Renminbi further lowers the prices of imported goods from China. This can be seen from the following simple inflation equation. The consumer price inflation in the domestic economy (π) is made up of a weighted average of domestic goods price inflation (π_d) imported foreign goods price inflation measured in the domestic currency (π_f). λ is the weight or share of domestically produced goods price inflation in the general domestic price inflation rate and $(1 - \lambda)$ is the share of imported foreign goods and $0<\lambda<1$. This gives us:

$$\pi = \lambda\pi_d + (1 - \lambda).\pi_f \qquad (4)$$

Purchasing Power Parity relates the price of imported goods in foreign currency (P^*) to their price in the domestic market in domestic currency P_f or

$$P_f = e.P^* \qquad (5)$$

where e is the exchange rate, or the price of one unit of foreign currency in domestic currency.

The price inflation of imported goods (or the rate of change in the prices of imported goods) or π_i is therefore equal to the rate of change in domestic currency ($\Delta e/e$) and the rate of change in international prices, or π^*.

$$\pi_i = \frac{\Delta e}{e} + \pi^* \qquad (6)$$

Taylor rule

The modern interest rate policy instrument of monetary policy was first prescribed by Professor John B. Taylor in 1993. The Taylor rule is based on the idea that a central bank actively influences economic activities through the interest rate. It is a simple monetary policy rule on how a central bank should set the short-term interest rate in response to developments in inflation and economic activity. In a simple form, the reaction function of a central bank is an additive function based on inflation, the real equilibrium interest rate and capacity utilization, as follows:

Short-term interest rate = inflation rate
+ real equilibrium interest rate + a(inflation rate
– the desired long-run inflation target) +b(output gap) (7)

where:
a and b are the response coefficients for, respectively, inflation and output and $a + b = 1$; the inflation gap is equal to the difference in the actual inflation rate and the inflation target, and the output gap is equal to the percentage deviation of real or actual GDP from its potential level or full-employment output.

The Taylor rule says that monetary policy rate responds to deviation of (a) inflation rate from the central bank's target and (b) real output from its potential level. Excessive inflation and capacity utilization are to be countered by higher short-term interest rates. When inflation rises beyond the target level, monetary policy needs to raise the real interest rate in order to slowdown the economy and reduce inflationary pressures. The real interest rate should also be raised when real output rises above its potential and be reduced when real

GPD falls below its potential. When the economy is in a steady state with the inflation rate equal to the target and the output gap close to zero, then the real interest rate (the nominal rate minus the expected rate of inflation) equals the equilibrium real interest rate or the neutral real interest rate. Taylor (1993) focuses on quarterly observation and suggests measuring inflation as a moving average of inflation over four quarters. For the US economy, he sets the equilibrium interest rate at equal to 2 per cent, and the target long-term inflation rate equal to 2 per cent, while simulations suggest that the response coefficients on inflation and the output gap are close to 0.5.

The equilibrium or the neutral interest rate that depicts a stable inflation rate within a closed output gap is not an observable variable. According to Blinder (1998), the equilibrium interest rate is 'difficult to estimate and impossible to know with precision'. It is more difficult to estimate because of the structural change in the capital market, low global interest rate and changes in macroeconomic fundamentals (Magud and Tsounta, 2012).

Like in other IT (Inflation Targeting) countries,[5] Bank Indonesia, by law, formally announces a numerical target for inflation and is required to twice a year present detailed inflation reports to Parliament. Credible inflation targeting dampens the inflationary expectations of the public. The minutes of Bank Indonesia board meetings, however, are not made public, and the remuneration of the central bank governors is not linked to their success in achieving the inflation target.

Operational implementation of it and Taylor rule in Indonesia

The execution of market-based monetary policy through open-market operations using the overnight interest rate as an instrument requires well-developed interbank and money markets. As pointed out earlier, Bank Indonesia established its overnight FASBI facility in 1997 to influence the shallow and segmented interbank money market. To absorb liquidity, BI also pays interest on the placement of excess reserves with the central bank, and pays term deposit rates. A domestic money market started to develop with the trading of SBIs and recapitalization bonds. The repo market, however, is still underdeveloped due to a combination of legal uncertainty and double taxation of the relevant instruments. Nevertheless, Indonesia is gradually developing institutions that understand the monetary transmission process and inflation forecasting, as well as better coordination between IT policies with fiscal and debt management policies. However, it is difficult to predict optimal monetary policy instruments in an emerging country, such as Indonesia, for two reasons. First, it has an economic structure that relies greatly on the production of raw materials, such as agricultural and mining products, that are subject to external shocks and the vagaries of the international business cycle. Second, very few studies have been carried out on the transmission mechanism by which policy instruments relate to inflation and other economic variables.

Orphanides (2007) points out that the design and operational implementation of a Taylor rule is dependent on the reliability of data, particularly, the measures of inflation and economic activity that the policy rule is intended to respond to. The appropriate concept and sources of information to be used in the analysis in the Indonesian case are very crucial as some of the variables are unobservable, such as the real equilibrium interest rate, inflation target and output gap. Conclusions about the performance of a particular Taylor rule are sensitive to assumptions regarding the availability and reliability of data.

One of the problems is how to measure inflation (Lebow and Rudd, 2006). Indonesia's Central Bureau of Statistics (BPS) measures inflation based on the cost of living index (CPI or consumer price index). Since October 1999, the CPI calculation has been based on a survey of 249 to 353 goods and services consumed by households in 126 large and small cities all over Indonesia. The CPI measures the expenditure needed for the optimizing consumers living in those urban areas to maintain a specified level of utility as prices change. The CPI is therefore urban biased and is not a price index for overall GDP, which is defined as including the prices of all domestically produced final output, bought by consumers, producers, the government sector and the rest of the world. The CPI does not capture implicit flows of services that are not generated by market transactions or directly purchased by consumers. An example of the former is owner-occupied housing, while the latter includes free banking services. Asset prices are also excluded from the CPI.

It is assumed that core inflation is directly affected by the monetary policy of the central bank. Core inflation in Indonesia is the CPI minus administered prices, or the prices of the state-vended products, minus the prices of volatile foodstuffs. The main components in administered prices are the prices of refined petroleum products and electricity, which are heavily subsidized by the government and adjusted based on political considerations. Food prices are subject to external shocks, such as weather conditions. The measure of core inflation is therefore aggregate household inflation excluding the contribution of price changes from food and energy.[6] The removal of volatile and transient components from headline inflation is expected to predict the monetary phenomenon of inflation. But Walsh (2011) found that shocks to food inflation in developing countries can be directly transmitted to non-food inflation. Because of this, he argues that the use of core inflation as a measure of inflation is subject to severe bias. Bank Indonesia ascertains public inflationary expectations from its regular business survey based on a sample of 2,000 companies.

Core inflation is not easily controlled by the monetary authority. The reason is because of the long time lag in the effect of monetary policy on inflation outcome and revealed only after a substantial time lag. The rigid rule imposed by the inflation target limits the ability of the central bank to adjust to unforeseen circumstances particularly in emerging economies like Indonesia that is subject to many kinds of external shocks. The rigid rule of the inflation target can have substantial effects on real economic activities. It potentially fluctuates output and lower economic growth.

Indonesia began to adopt (soft) inflation targeting in 2000, and the Taylor-type reference interest rate has been fully implemented since 2005. Starting on

9 July 2008, the operational target was changed from the interest rate on one month SBI to the interest rate in the overnight interbank market. In consultation with the government and the Central Bureau of Statistics, Bank Indonesia announces its annual inflation target for the coming budget/calendar year in the middle of the preceding year when the government presents its macroeconomic assumptions to Parliament at the beginning of the budget cycle. The extent to which the target is realized is announced in Bank Indonesia's quarterly monetary policy report, on its website and in public hearings with Parliament. Between 2000 and 2010, Bank Indonesia set its inflation targets at between 4 per cent (2010) and 8 per cent, over periods of 3 and 5 years, respectively, within a band of ±1 per cent. The period of 2004–06 was of particular interest as international oil prices started to increase in 2004 and continued upward until early 2006. To reduce budget subsidy spending, the government adjusted the domestic price of petroleum products upward in October 2005, which in turn increased the level of core inflation. Headline or CPI inflation has hovered between 6 and 13 per cent per annum between 2000 and 2010, and for the period between 2010 and 2012, the government has set yearly inflation targets (5.0 per cent, 5 per cent and 4.5 per cent, respectively). Each target had a band of ±1 per cent.

Following the adoption of an inflation target, Bank Indonesia sets the BI rate as the Taylor-type reference interest rate based on the following equation:[7]

$$i_t = 0.75i_{t-1} + 0.25\left[\bar{r}_t + \pi_{t+1}^T + 1.9\left(\pi_{t+3} - \pi_{t+3}^T\right) + 0.25\left(\Upsilon_t - \Upsilon_t^*\right)\right] \tag{8}$$

Where:

> i_t is the BI policy rate;
> $\bar{r}_t$ is the long-run natural real interest rate;
> π_t is the actual rate of inflation;
> π_t^T is the inflation target;
> Υ_t is the logarithm of real GDP;
> Υ_t^* is the logarithm of potential GDP.

Bank Indonesia estimates that the equilibrium natural real interest rate over the long run is 2 per cent, exactly the same as stated in the formulation of the Taylor rule for the US economy. The coefficient for the inflation gap is nearly 2 and for the output gap 0.25. This indicates that Bank Indonesia's policy of raising its reference interest rate is a powerful tool for controlling the inflation rate. Potential output is estimated based on the DSGE (Dynamic Stochastic General Equilibrium) model, which links real growth and changes in employment according to Okun's law (Okun, 1981). Aside from the unemployment rate, the model also contains CPI inflation and capacity utilization in the manufacturing sector. Equation (7) is also basically a model for a relatively closed economy of developed country and not for a small open economy of emerging economies such as Indonesia. In addition, Okun's law is handicapped in estimating potential output in Indonesia because of limited data on the labor market, financial market, and capital stock and utilization. In contrast to developed economies, inflation and inflationary expectation in emerging economies, such as Indonesia, are not only driven by excess demand, but also by a number of shortcoming in the supply bottlenecks, such as transport system, storage and distribution. Some distorted government policies create segmentation in markets for goods and services, finance and labor. It may be also useful to include the real effective exchange rate as a variable in estimating the Philips curve for a small open economy.

Equation (7) does not refer to interest rate parity[8] and the pass-through effect that describes the results of changes in the exchange rate on both the CPI and core inflation through changes in import prices. Such an equation may be true for a large economy, such as the US, which has a low level of interaction with the rest of the world. The model has no reference to positive export-market shocks, such as the oil boom between 1973 and 1982 and the boom in the prices of energy and raw materials since the early 1990s. The increases in prices of raw materials have been mainly ignited by the rapid economic growth, industrialization and urbanization in China and India. Activity in infrastructure, construction, real estate, mechanization and automobile manufacturing have all contributed to the strong demand for broad-based primary products, including energy, minerals and other raw materials.

Too dominant a role of foreign investors in the ownership of the SBI and sovereign bonds creates distortion in the policy or benchmark interest rates. Rising capital inflows that provide liquidity to the narrow markets lower yields and interest rates that contribute to booms. On the other hand, uncertainty encourages capital outflows and drives up interest rates that could result in a credit crunch. As shown by the events during the global financial crisis in 2008, the jump in the yield of sovereign bonds drove up government debt repayment. The capital inflow reversals that lower down prices of SBI and sovereign bonds had ignited the collapse of the mutual funds industry in 2003 and 2009.

Another positive external shock to the Indonesian economy has been low international interest rates resulting from relaxed monetary policy in the industrialized countries prior to the global financial crisis of 2007–08, and quantitative easing policies subsequent to the crisis. Lower interest rates in the international market eased the constraints on international borrowing. The appreciation of the Rupiah, mainly due to external shocks in the goods and capital markets, has caused the Dutch disease to emerge in the Indonesian economy. There is also no reference to the undervaluation of the RMB that has caused a negative external shock for the Indonesian economy. The combination of Rupiah appreciation and the undervaluation of the RMB has reduced prices of imports that help to lower both the inflation rate and debt-to-GDP ratio. On the other hand, the stronger Rupiah has reduced the competitiveness of Indonesia's manufactured products vis-a-vis the PRC, which has resulted in deindustrialization in Indonesia and promoted growth in the less productive non-traded sector of the economy.

The advanced economies, such as the US, have a labor shortage while Indonesia is a dualistic economy with labor-surplus mostly engaged in agriculture sector (36 percent) and non-formal sector with low productivity. The non-formal sector includes small scale industry, transport, wholesale and retail trade. The surplus labor is mainly occurred on the small island of Java the resident of about two-third of Indonesia's population (2011: 242.3 million). The average farm land on Java is less than 0.5 hectare per farmer. About seventy percent of labor force in manufacturing industry is absorbed by small and medium scale firms that produce only about 20 percent of industrial output. Inter-island labor mobility is limited due to inefficient transportation system. Government sponsored transmigration program to move people out of Java stopped after the financial crisis in 1997 due to the budget constraint.

It is true that Indonesia has enjoyed a potential demographic premium since the 1970s as the dependency ratio has declined due to a fast growing population working age. This potential, however, can only be tapped if enough jobs are created to absorb the large labor force, and better education is provided so as to produce highly skilled labor. This will require a number of policy changes to address the present bottlenecks constraining growth in the Indonesian economy. First, relaxation of the current tight fiscal policy to provide fiscal space for building badly needed infrastructure. Second, the provision of exchange rate incentives to producers of traded goods and exporters of non-raw materials. Third, the introduction of radical supply-side reforms to reverse a decade of lost competitiveness and boost long-term growth. Structural reforms are particularly needed in the input markets, including electricity, seaports, airports, labor and land, as well as the streamlining of the regulatory system to relieve the bottlenecks that are adding to production costs. The high severance pay and minimum wage in the formal sector of the economy deters employers from hiring more workers under formal contracts and instead encourages informality.

The fourth policy that is needed to address the bottlenecks constraining economic growth is to build strong and solid public institutions. As pointed out earlier, there are four objectives of such institution-building: first, to facilitate the development of an effective and efficient market with low transaction costs. Second, to correct market failures. Third, to ensure stable markets, including macroeconomic stability so as to allow business and investment to flourish. Fourth, to address market failures by the state-owned sector so as to allow state capitalism to work.

VI.   Monetary transmission mechanism

Very few studies have been conducted on the monetary transmission mechanism in Indonesia. The textbook studies on the subject investigate how monetary policy affects real economic activity and inflation in advanced industrial countries. Information about this mechanism is needed to evaluate monetary policy and how to set policy instruments to achieve the macroeconomic objectives in those advanced countries. Interest rate plays a crucial role in stimulating activity in the manufacturing, trade and modern services sectors of their economies. On the other hand, a large portion of economic activity in a country such as Indonesia is in the primary sector, including mining and agriculture, and the prices for products depend more on the vagaries of the international business cycle than on interest rates.

Boivin, Kiley and Mishkin (2010) reviewed how the monetary transmission mechanism has evolved over time in the United States and other industrialized countries. They observe that during the past 30 years there have been dramatic changes in both the conduct of monetary policy and in the way financial markets operate. The focus of monetary policy has gradually been placed more on price stability. They divide monetary transmission into broad categories, namely (1) neoclassical channels in which financial markets are assumed to be perfect; and (2) non-neoclassical channels that involve financial market imperfections, which is usually referred to as the credit view.

During the long period of financial repression in Indonesia, the government directly intervened in the credit markets by setting the detailed ceilings for credit programs channeled by state-owned banks, capping both deposit and lending rates and identifying the recipients of credit. Central bank decisions on the availability of credit-program refinancing, interest rates and credit guarantees gave rise to an important channel of monetary transmission rooted in credit policy. To avoid disintermediation, or the loss of deposits from the banking system due to low deposit rates, banks supplemented them with other types of compensation, such as draws offering attractive prizes in the form of durable goods.

Monetary policy is transmitted to the real sector of the economy also through investment, consumption and the exchange rate. In a simple neoclassical model of investment decisions, the demand for capital for investment goods, residential housing and consumer durables (and inventory investment) represent a negative function of the user cost of capital. The interest rate is part of the user cost of capital because it is the cost of borrowing funds or interest income forgone in the case of using own funds. In a more sophisticated version of the neoclassical investment model, the user cost of capital not only consists of the interest rate, but is also influenced by other variables, such as the expected real appreciation of capital assets, the depreciation rate and the marginal tax rate. Because capital assets are long-lived and the adjustment of capital stock involves costs, the user cost of capital is a function of the long-term real interest rate. Expectations of further tightening of monetary policy, for example, could lower interest rates and the expected rate of appreciation of capital goods, and raise the current user cost of capital. In the present value criterion for investment, the investor will invest in a project that produces the highest present value. The present value of an investment project is a negative function of interest rate. Thus, an increase in the market interest rate reduces the present value of an investment project.

Keynes suggested a different type of investment decision, namely, the marginal efficiency of investment criterion. The marginal efficiency of investment is defined as the rate of interest that will discount the present value of the project to zero. Investors will invest in projects that produce the highest marginal efficiency of investment.

Investment decisions may also be considered in the Tobin's q framework as proposed by James Tobin. The q is defined as the market value of a firm divided by the replacement cost of capital. High q encourages investment spending as the market price of firms is high relative to the replacement cost of capital and new capital goods are relatively cheap as compared to the market value of the firms. Lower interest rates due to monetary expansion will raise demand for stock and push stock prices upward and thereby increase investment expenditure and aggregate demand.

The wealth effect operating through asset prices is an important element in the monetary policy transmission mechanism in the life-cycle consumption hypotheses, as developed by both Friedman (1957) and Ando and Modigliani (1963). Both camps postulate that individual consumption at one time is an increasing function of the present value of his income at that time. Their analyses differ in their treatment of the present value of income. Friedman assumes that the typical individual consumer wants to smooth his actual income stream into more or less flat consumption expenditure. This means that the level of permanent consumption is proportional to permanent income. The ratio of permanent consumption to permanent income is dependent on the interest rate as the return on saving, taste as reflected by indifference curves and the variability of expected income. Total consumption in a period of time is the sum of permanent consumption and random transitory consumption. Similarly, total income in a given period, in Friedman formulation, consists of permanent income and random transitory income. Friedman makes three strong assumptions that there are no correlations between: (1) transitory and permanent incomes and (2) permanent and transitory consumption. A transitory change in income, therefore, will not immediately change consumption. As a result, the marginal propensity of consumption (MPC) in the Friedman formulation is lower than the average propensity to consume (APC) or MPC < APC.

Like Friedman, Ando and Modigliani hypothesize that the typical individual has a relatively low income stream at the beginning and end of his life when his productivity is low during youth and old age, and high during the middle of his life. On the other hand, the individual maintains a more or less constant, or gradually increasing, level of consumption throughout his life. The constraint on this consumption stream is that the present value of his consumption does not exceed the present value of his total income.

In the Ando-Modigliani model, income consists of labor income and income from wealth, whether from financial assets, other assets or property. There are many assumptions on how to link average expected future labor income to current variables. One of them is to estimate average future expected labor income as a multiple of present labor income. Assuming that the capital markets are reasonably efficient, the present value of the income from an asset is equal to the value of the net asset itself, measured at the beginning of the current period. As the consumption to income ratio is constant in the long run and inversely related to income in the short run, then MPC < APC in this model.

Lower interest rates, because of the expansion of monetary policy, stimulate the demand for financial and physical assets, such as common stock and housing. The increase in their prices raises total wealth and then drives up consumption and aggregate demand. Changes in short-term interest rates in inter-temporal substitution effects alter the slope of consumption expenditure and raise current consumption.

The exchange rate channel is probably the most powerful channel in a less-developed economy with underdeveloped financial markets. Monetary expansion lowers interest rates and, in an open economy, reduces the return on domestic assets relative to foreign assets. This encourages depreciation of the domestic currency that makes traded goods produced in the domestic market cheaper than similar goods produced in other countries. As noted earlier, currency depreciation leads to expenditure switching from imports to domestic products and to a rise in exports and hence aggregate demand. As has also been discussed earlier, exchange rate depreciation provides an incentive for greater production of more efficient traded goods relative to inefficient non-traded goods, and thereby increases the productivity and efficiency of the whole economy. But, exchange rate depreciation also raises the ratio of external debt to GDP. The importance of the exchange rate channel is dependent on, first, the sensitivity of the exchange rate to interest rate movements or the validity of uncovered interest rate parity; and, second, on the cost of the movement of factors of production from the non-traded sector of the economy to the traded sector.

Studies by Bank Indonesia (e.g. Goeltom, 2008) confirm that the exchange rate mechanism is the leading monetary policy transmission mechanism in Indonesia. By means of the pass-through effect, the exchange rate affects the inflation rate and balance sheets of economic units. At a certain level, Bank Indonesia has found that exchange rate appreciation will support the export of manufactured products with high import content. Conversely, a number of studies indicate that the current combination of Rupiah appreciation and Renminbi undervaluation has resulted in rapid deindustrialization in Indonesia (e.g. Giap, Abeysinghe and Yam, 2011). This is because the appreciation of the Rupiah has eroded the financial incentive for the production of traded goods and has not been accompanied by improvements in productivity.

VII.   Monetary policy instruments

The instruments available to Bank Indonesia to conduct monetary policy can be divided into three groups, namely, reserve requirements, open market operation (OMO) and discount rate and loans to commercial banks. Through OMO the central bank affects the monetary base by buying and selling securities and foreign exchange. Pumping liquidity through discount and loans and OMO is called monetary easing.

Figure 1.3 shows the policy instruments in a more detail, namely: (1) the loan-to-deposit ratio (LDR); (2) legal lending limit regulations; (3) the reserve requirement system; (4) open market operations; (5) the loan-to-value ratio, which restricts sending to certain economic sectors, such as real estate, credit cards and motor vehicles; (6) standing facilities/fine tuning operations; and (7) net open position (NOP). NOP is intended to serve two purposes: first, to tame speculation in the foreign exchange market and, second, to prevent exchange rate risks on the balance sheets of deposit-taking institutions. At present, NOP is

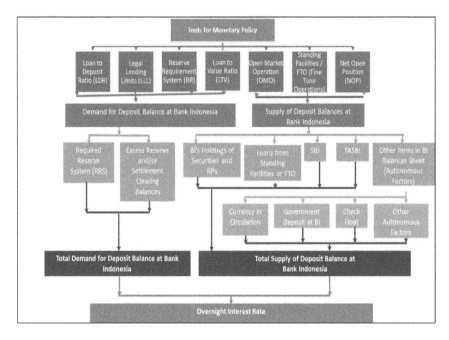

Figure 1.3 Monetary policy tools

set at 20 per cent of a bank's capital. [9] Because of the time lag for recognition, the design and implementation of monetary policy in emerging economies takes much longer than in the advanced economies, where the use of macroeconomic prudential policies is more popular. In addition, macro prudential policy instruments can be tailored to the risks in specific economic sectors or loan portfolios at minimal cost of policy intervention.

If the banking sector hits foreign currency funding problems, the central bank can respond by providing support using its foreign exchange reserves and availing of intra-central bank foreign exchange swap arrangements between the ASEAN and the ASEAN+3 countries. At present in Indonesia, the policy instruments used in open market operations are limited to Bank Indonesia's SBI (*Surat Berharga Bank Indonesia*) or Bank Indonesia Certificates, including *sharia*-based SBI. Conventional SBI come in three maturities: 1 month, 3 months and 6 months. Bank Indonesia provides a range of *sharia*-compliant facilities and instruments that allow Islamic banks to manage their liquidity. A *sharia* Certificate (SBIS) has a maturity of 1 month. The value of *sharia*-instruments, however, is relatively small. In addition, Bank Indonesia offers *Wadiah Certificates* (SWBI). As regards standing facilities, since the 1997 crisis Bank Indonesia has absorbed excess liquidity of depository institutions through its Overnight Deposit Facility (FASBI – *Fasilitas Simpanan Bank Indonesia*) with interest rate remuneration. In addition, Bank Indonesia conducts Fine Tune Operations both for expansion and contraction purposes.

As noted earlier, because of the underdevelopment of the money market and the limited number of money market instruments available to affect the supply of deposit balances at Bank Indonesia, the central bank mainly uses those policy instruments that affect the demand for liquidity. In addition, Bank Indonesia buys and sells foreign exchange swaps to influence the stock of base money. As noted earlier, by buying foreign exchange, the stock of its external reserves and monetary liabilities rises by the same amount, and increases stock of base money and money supply. On the other hand, the stock of money reduces with the selling of foreign exchange by the central bank. In June–July 1987, the supply of base money was sharply reduced with the transfer of deposits of large state-owned enterprises, mainly at state-owned banks, to Bank Indonesia. At the cost of the liquidity position of the state-owned banks, the Minister of Finance ordered the transfers to suppress speculation against the Rupiah. At that time, state-owned banks were using their excess reserves to directly accumulate foreign reserves or lend to their own customers who could then lengthen their foreign exchange positions (Cole and Slade, 1996: 52–53). This transfer of deposits to Bank Indonesia reduced the monetary liabilities of the central bank but, at the same time, raised its non-monetary liabilities by the same amount.

To summarize, Bank Indonesia mainly uses four policy instruments for open market operations. First, its own certificates of deposit – the conventional SBIs and *sharia* instruments. To affect both the volume and composition of liquidity, in 2010 Bank Indonesia introduced a 1-month holding period for SBI and phased out shorter maturity papers. Then in May 2011, Bank Indonesia lengthened the SBI holding period to 6 months during which the SBI cannot be traded or repoed. The SBI, however, can be used as collateral to access Band Indonesia's lending facilities. Second, daily auctions of term deposits with varying maturities up to 6 months. There are typically 3 maturities, namely, short-tenors of 14 days, 3 months and 6 months. The third instrument is the outright sale and purchase of government securities, short-term SPN and long-term SUN. Finally, the fourth instrument is the sale and purchase of foreign exchange and swap facilities.

Reserve requirement

Like any other central bank, Bank Indonesia has a monopoly over the issuance of 'central bank money', which consists of currency and deposit balances held by depository institutions at Bank Indonesia. Bank Indonesia has the power to set reserve requirements, that is, the minimum percentage of a bank's liabilities that must be held either as vault cash or deposits at the central bank. As noted earlier, the reserve requirement affects the demand for liquidity in the banking system. The traditional money multiplier theory assumes that banks can always expand loans, and hence deposits, subject only to the constraint of adequate reserves. Because it is a strong monetary policy instrument, the reserve requirement ratio (RRR) is rarely changed. A small change in the size of reserves will have a large impact on the level of deposits and liquidity in the banking system.

Raising the reserve requirement can immediately cause liquidity problems for banks with low excess reserves.

The reserve requirement has been used in Indonesia as a principal monetary tool for many purposes. The portfolio theory sees the reserve requirement as one element of a bank's portfolio. Because the reserve requirement affects the asset mix of the banking system, during the past period of financial repression the reserve requirement was used as a tool to allocate bank credits as a supplement to a selective credit policy. It was also used in the past to influence the availability of credit and credit interest rates in various sectors of the economy so as to stimulate targeted activities and particular geographical locations, underserved communities and classes of customers and to tax unwanted sectors. The reserve requirement can also be used to influence the maturity structure of bank credit. For example, to encourage a bank to provide long-term credit, the reserve requirement ratio could be lowered for longer maturity deposits. Particularly before the establishment of the LPS (*Lembaga Penjamin Simpanan*– Deposit Insurance Corporation) in 2004, another purpose of the reserve requirement was to avoid liquidity risk by ensuring banks were sound and thereby reassure depositors that they could withdraw funds on demand. As noted earlier, the government provided a blanket guarantee for bank deposits following the crisis in 1997. Traditionally, deposits at state-owned banks and BPDs were implicitly guaranteed by their owners, that is, the central and local governments.

For a number of reasons, the use of the reserve requirement as a monetary policy tool in emerging economies has gained popularity with the rise in volatile short-term capital inflows. The first reason is that the reserve requirement system can be effectively used to reduce the volume of short-term capital inflows and to alter their composition towards longer maturities. To control capital inflows, in 1990 Chile, for example, imposed a 20 per cent non-remunerated reserve requirement to be deposited at the central bank for a period of one year on liabilities in foreign currency for direct borrowing firms. By contrast, since 2010 Bank Indonesia has only applied the reserve requirement to foreign borrowings of the banking system with a shorter holding period of one month. The second reason is that it can be used as a tool to slow down the growth of bank lending. Bank Indonesia raised the reserve requirement ratio for Rupiah deposits from 5 per cent to 7.5 per cent in 2008, and to 8 per cent in 2010. The third reason is that the reserve requirement can complement monetary policy as raising the reserve requirement can act as a substitute for raising interest rates to dampen bubbles in the non-traded sector of the economy, such as the real estate sector. Lastly, the reserve requirement can be used to contain liquidity risks, particularly during downswings.

The definitions of reserve and current liabilities have changed over time, reflecting changes in monetary policy. At present, reservable liabilities include all types of deposits and their currency denominations: demand, savings and time deposits and other liabilities in Rupiah and foreign currencies. The same reserve ratio is applied to all maturity deposits. During the past period of financial repression, the reserve requirement ratio was differentiated based on the geographical location of the head office of the bank (urban versus rural) and on classes of customers – small scale, medium and large depositors. Since

2010, a no-interest bearing, or unremunerated, reserve requirement (URR) has been applied in Indonesia to discourage short-term capital inflows by making them more costly. Since the opening of the capital account in the early 1980s, residents can open foreign currency–denominated accounts with domestic banks, but only foreign licensed banks are allowed to borrow abroad. Commencing with the banking reforms of 1988, the authorities have imposed open position limits on the commercial banks.

A reserve requirement imposes three kinds of cost on depository institutions that can encourage market disintermediation. The first cost is the opportunity cost of the interest-bearing assets that are locked up in the reserve account. As pointed out by Friedman (1969), interest-free commercial bank and government deposits at the central bank are actually interest-free loans from the depositors to the central bank.[10] By reducing the reserve requirement ratio and by paying interest on commercial bank excess reserves and on government deposits, the monetary authorities have corrected some of these externalities. Bank costs have been reduced somewhat and their profits from demand deposits have increased. A reduction in their costs should enable the commercial banks to lower their lending rates. On the other hand, the monetary authorities lose some of their monopoly profits in the form of seignorage and inflationary taxes.

The second cost imposed by a reserve requirement on the commercial banks is the loss of liquidity of the reserve balances, while the third cost is associated with managing the required reserves. To reduce the burden on the depository institutions, Bank Indonesia has gradually reduced the reserve ratio and since 2004 has remunerated the depository institutions for the required reserve balances. Bank Indonesia now pays interest on all bank reserves at a rate below the interbank overnight market rate and policy rate. At present, the remuneration rate on reserve balances at Bank Indonesia is 3 per cent per annum. On the other hand, Bank Indonesia also imposes penalties in respect of any failure to comply with reserve requirements. Such penalties are charged at a rate that is well above the interbank overnight money market rate.

The modernization of the payment system, including the introduction of Real Time Gross Settlement, has reduced the need for banks to hold excess reserves. To further reduce the burden imposed by the reserve requirement on depository institutions, Bank Indonesia accepts reserve balances at the central bank, vault cash and holdings of its SBI as eligible assets to meet the reserve requirement. The central bank requires depository institutions to hold reserve balances in domestic currency. However, foreign currency–denominated liabilities must be held in euro or US dollars. As vault cash is normally held to meet customer needs, its application for meeting the reserve requirement can cause two problems. First, it makes monitoring of reserve requirement compliance by the central bank more complicated. Second, it may decrease the effectiveness of the reserve requirement in functioning as a buffer to absorb autonomous fluctuations in the markets in the case of reserves that subsequently increase volatility of the overnight interest rate in a maintenance period.

When it was first introduced in May 1957, the reserve requirement ratio was 30 per cent of the current Rupiah liabilities of commercial banks. The rate was reduced to 15 per cent on 30 December 1977. The reserve requirement for foreign exchange liabilities was first introduced in August 1971. A minimum of one third of the reserves must be kept on deposit with the central bank. Since 9 April 1974, part of a bank's excess reserves at the central bank – up to 10 per cent of a bank's current liabilities – carries an interest rate of 10 per cent per annum. The need for banks to maintain excess reserves has been reduced with improvements in telecommunications technology and the introduction of Real Time Gross Settlement by Bank Indonesia in 2000.

In July 2011, Bank Indonesia increased the primary reserve requirements on both foreign and Rupiah deposits to 8 per cent, from previously 1 per cent and 5 per cent, respectively, while in June 2011 Bank Indonesia imposed additional reserve requirements (RR) on banks that have a loan-to-deposit ratio (LDR) of below 78 per cent or above 100 per cent. Banks with LDRs outside the range of 78–100 per cent and CAR (Capital Adequacy Ratio) below and above 14 per cent are required to build their reserve requirements based on the following formula:

1) For LDR below 78 per cent, the additional RR = 0.1 × (78%-LDR%) × Rupiah third-party funds (TPF);
2) For LDR above 100 per cent and CAR below 14 per cent, additional RR = 0.2 × (LDR%-100%) × Rupiah TPF;
3) No additional RR required for banks with LFR above 100 per cent and CAR above 14 per cent.

This regulation encourages banks to expand credit to the relatively inefficient non-traded sector of the economy and for consumption expenditure, mainly on the purchase of goods that can be insured and used as collateral for the credit. The non-traded sector of the economy includes real estate, shopping malls and golf courses that produce goods and services solely for the local market. The consumption sector includes automotive, telecommunications equipment and household appliances. To slow down lending to the real estate and automotive sectors, on 15 June 2012 Bank Indonesia introduced a loan-to-value regulation that links the amount of the loan to the size of the collateral or down payment required in the case of housing and automotive loans. The ratio for the purchase of houses of over 70 square meters, motorcycles, vehicles for business purposes and vehicles for personal use are, respectively, 70 per cent, 25 per cent, 30 per cent and 20 per cent.

Unlike in other countries, such as Chile and Brazil, Indonesia has not applied the reserve requirement and net-open-position regulations to the non-bank sector as a policy tool to discourage capital inflows through non-bank chan-nels. The bank deposits of this sector are, however, subject to the normal reserve requirement and prudential rules and regulations that are applied to the banking system. As part of the protective features, every mutual fund, for example, is required to appoint a licensed custodian bank to act as a trustee whose primary responsibility is to safeguard the fund's assets and calculate their value daily.

High and volatile short-term interbank money market rates

As shown in Figure 1.4, high and volatile short-term interest rates in Indonesia are also caused by inefficient reserve money management and segmentation in the banking industry. The inefficiency in reserve money management is partly because the money market instruments that are available to mop up liquidity are mainly limited to SBI issued by Bank Indonesia based on various maturities, and BI's overnight deposit facility (FASBI). As seen from Table 1.4, these two instruments accounted for, respectively, 61.62 and 8.21 per cent of the monetary base in 2009. Those with high levels of excess reserve balances at Bank Indonesia are mainly state-owned banks and Regional Development Banks. Since the crisis of 1997, many banks have been content to park their cash with the central bank, rather than lending it out to other institutions. Only a small amount of bank liquidity is traded on the interbank money market. As noted in other chapters, market segmentation has results from government regulations that accord an exclusive right to public banks to hold deposits of public sector funds. Meanwhile, domestic private banks mainly serve their business affiliates.

As banks hold high levels of excess reserve balances at the central bank in both SBI and FASBI, at attractive rates, there is no need to generate liquidity in the interbank money market. Placements by commercial banks in FASBI have been continuously rising, and amounted to over 10 per cent of the monetary base in September 2011. Central bank action to purchase short-term debt that would expand the stock of money would subsequently have both a portfolio balance effect and an expectationary effect on the long-term interest rate. The use of different SBI maturities to drain excess liquidity affects both the level as well as slope of the long-term yield curve, and drives it away from its longer market equilibrium, thus impeding market development. This is because less predictable and more volatile short-term interest rates raise the risk premium that investors will demand for providing longer-term funds.

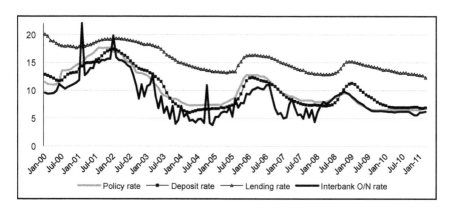

Figure 1.4 Bank Indonesia's policy rate, and interbank interest, deposit and lending rates, 2000–11 (per cent per annum)

Sources: IMF, *International Financial Statistics,* December 2002, December 2004, December 2006, December 2008, December 2010 and December 2012.

Table 1.4 Actual inflation, expected inflation and inflation targets and monetary policy credibility

Year	Actual CPI	Inflation Expectation*	CPI Target	Difference between Expectation and Target	Surprise	Anchoring	Credibility**
	(1)	(2)	(3)	(1) − (3)	(2) − (1)	(2) − (3)	
2000	9.35	10.61	6	3.35	1.26	4.61	24
2001	12.55	14.29	7.25	5.30	1.74	7.04	21
2002	10.03	12.12	9.50	0.53	2.09	2.62	26
2003	5.06	8.04	9.00	−3.94	2.98	−0.96	46
2004	6.40	7.38	5.50	0.90	0.98	1.88	42
2005	17.10	9.75	6.00	11.10	−7.35	3.75	32
2006	6.60	9.20	8.00	−1.40	2.60	1.20	23
2007	6.60	7.47	6.00	0.60	0.87	1.47	47
2008	11.06	7.75	5.00	6.06	−3.31	2.75	37
2009	2.78	4.90	4.50	−1.72	2.12	0.40	51
2010	6.96	5.70	5.00	1.96	−1.26	0.70	53

Source: Harmanta, M. et al. 2011. 'Inflation Targeting under Imperfect Credibility Based on ARIMBI (Aggregate Rational Inflation Targeting Model for Bank Indonesia); Lessons from Indonesia', *Bulletin of Monetary Economics and Banking*, Vol. 13 Nr 3, January: pp. 271–306.

Notes: *Estimated through Bank Indonesia's Business Survey, based on 2,000 companies as respondents; **Credibility is the percentage of respondents whose inflationary expectations coincide with the Bank Indonesia inflation target.

Government bond market

The emergence of both long-term and short-term government bonds was a direct policy outcome of the Asian financial crisis of 1997–98. To develop the bond markets, the government has taken some measures to expand the investor base, the issuer base and financial intermediation. The reforms include measures to reduce barriers to entry, narrowing information gaps and disclosure standards, administrative controls, capital rules and other statutory and prudential provisions, as well as monopolistic behavior. Accounting and regulatory standards have been upgraded, including full balance sheet disclosure. A modern central securities depository was established to improve market efficiency, reduce the number of securities accounts and connections required by investors and traders, and economize on the cash settlement leg. The procedures associated with the offering of securities have been streamlined to reduce regulatory costs. The authorities have also strengthened oversight of key information providers, such as credit ratings agencies and auditing firms. As pointed out earlier, the significant presence of foreign investors in the nascent bond market has boosted its liquidity and growth.

Adherence to fiscal discipline and inflation targeting has helped resolve the 'original sin' dilemma, as highlighted by Eichengreen and Hausman (1999) after the Tequila crisis in Mexico in 1994–95. The 'original sin' dilemma describes the choice faced by emerging economies with past experience of high and unstable inflation of whether to issue sovereign bonds denominated in foreign currency with long-term maturities or in domestic currency but with very short-term maturities. A sustainable budget deficit and low inflation help reduce risk premia and facilitate a lengthening of the maturity of domestic currency debt. The issuance of domestic currency sovereign bonds reduces reliance on foreign currency debt and variable rates.

In the early phase of the global financial crisis of 2007–08, Indonesia also faced financial stress and a sharp rise in the interest risks of her sovereign bonds as a consequence of a significant outflow of capital, changes in investor demand and the effective drying up of international liquidity and capital markets after the closure of Lehman Brothers in October 2008. The impact of that stress was controlled thanks to the availability of large foreign exchange reserves, rapid financial assistance from Indonesia's developing partners, including a currency swap facility from China, and guaranteed by the Japanese government for Indonesia's Samurai bonds.

Indonesia, however, withholds 20 per cent tax on both interest income and capital gains from investment in debt securities and *sukuk*. However, the country has a tax treaty with Singapore, the neighboring regional center, which does not apply withholding tax. To benefit from this tax treaty and thus avoid Indonesian withholding tax, non-resident investors hold Indonesian bonds via Singapore.

Between May 1999 and October 2000, the government issued Rp666. 9 trillion in Rupiah bonds with 5–10-year maturities, which was the equivalent of over 50 per cent of GDP in 1999. Of this, Rp438. 9 trillion (65.8 per cent) was used to recapitalize financially distressed domestic banks, Rp218 trillion (32.7 per cent)to finance the government budget deficit and the rest (Rp10 trillion) to refinance the credit program. On 4 March 2004, the government floated 10-year maturity US dollar bonds amounting to US$1 billion on the international markets, and in 2008 issued Samurai bonds on the Tokyo market. As noted earlier, during the administration of President Suharto from 1966–98, the government debt strategy was to maximize the availability of long-term concessionary official development aid to finance the government budget deficit. Because of the availability of cheap foreign financing, there was no need to float short-term Treasury bills or long-term government bonds. Because of the availability of cheap and low-risk credit programs from the state-owned banks during the financial repression period, only a handful of banks and non-bank enterprises issued short- and long-term bonds.

Table 1.5 shows the distribution of recapitalization bonds, their coupon rates and their trading positions in June 2001, nearly two thirds (63.6 per cent) of the recapitalization bonds were received by the seven state-owned banks, 25.4 per cent went to banks that were taken over by IBRA, 4 per cent were received by private commercial banks, 3.7 per cent went to non-recapitalized banks and 0.3 per

Table 1.5 Financing of bank restructuring (as of June 2001) (in Trillion Rupiah)

	Total Bonds	%	Fixed Rate	Variable Rate	Hedged	Traded on Secondary Market
Recap. Banks	438.9	100	183.2	219.5	36.2	48.2
State-owned Banks	279	63.6	128.7	114.1	36.2	15.8
Private com. Banks	17.5	4.0	3.2	14.3	–	2.0
Nationalized Banks	117.7	25.4	37.1	74.6	–	7.7
Regional Dev. Banks	1.2	0.3	0.4	0.8	–	0.1
Non-Recap. Banks	16.5	3.7	1.8	14.6	–	14.1
Sub Registry	13	3.0	11.9	1.1	–	8.4

Source: Bank Indonesia.

cent were received by the Regional Development Banks. The other 3 per cent were placed in the sub-registry at Bank Indonesia. About half (50 per cent) of the recapitalization bonds carry variable rate coupons, 41.7 per cent carry fixed rates and the other 8.3 per cent are hedged or indexed. The interest payable on the variable and hedged bonds is sensitive to interest rate, inflation rate and exchange rate developments. The state-bank group received over 70 per cent of the fixed rate bonds, nearly 52 per cent of the variable rate bonds and all of the hedged bonds. Other banks (private commercial banks, nationalized banks, non-recapitalized banks and regional development banks) mainly received variable rate bonds, fewer fixed rate bonds and none of the hedged bonds.

The fixed rate bonds have two maturities, namely, 5 years and 10 years. The interest rate on the 5 year fixed rate bonds is 12 per cent and 14 per cent for the 10-year maturity bonds. Interest payments are made every 6 months. The interest rate on the variable rate bonds is linked to the SBI rate. They have maturities of up to 15 years and interest is payable every 3 months. The interest rate on the indexed or hedge bonds is 3 per cent. They have maturities of up to 20 years and interest is payable every 6 months. To smooth out their maturity structure, in November 2002 the government restructured or reprofiled the sovereign bonds and extended their maturities to 20 years. Reprofiling is a fancy word for saying that the money will not be paid back in full or on time. The present values of the reprofiled bonds are equal to those of the old exchanged bonds. Investors prefer to hold short-to medium-term bonds due to Indonesia's long history of high inflation and social instability, lack of information on the government's ability to service its debts, and the weak legal and judicial infrastructure.

Taking advantage of low international interest rates, Indonesia changed its debt strategy in 2004. As noted earlier, beginning in 1998 the government issued a large amount of Rupiah-denominated sovereign bonds to recapitalize the collapsed domestic banking system and finance its budget deficit. In 2004, the country started to issue US dollar-denominated sovereign bonds on international markets, followed in 2008 by Samurai bonds guaranteed by the Japanese government. Low international interest rates represent a positive external shock as they reduce the cost of borrowing. The interest rate risk on Rupiah-denominated government bonds is relatively high because of the shallowness and narrowness of the domestic money market. An increase in interest payments can cause a punitive fiscal crisis as it reduces non-interest outlay, which is the summation of the primary deficit and total revenues of the government. At the same time, the increase in interest payments increases the total deficit, which is the summation of the primary deficit and interest payments. The recent crises on the periphery of Europe indicate that a dominant role played by foreign investors in domestic debt can also cause a balance of payment crisis as the debtor countries need foreign exchange to service their debts.

Sovereign bonds are regarded as riskless bonds as the government has the power to collect taxes from its citizens. The emergence of riskless sovereign bonds improves risk analysis and the bonds can serve as benchmark assets for pricing private sector bonds. The existence of a term structure for riskless lending also affects monetary policy in setting interest rates. At present, yield curves in Indonesia are comparatively steep due to the relatively high inflation rate and relatively weak banking system. The real inflation rate is always well above Bank Indonesia's target, while the relatively weak banking system is evident in part from the high spread between deposit and lending rates.

The existence of riskless sovereign bonds and the end of credit programs have increased the need for the corporate sector to raise funds on the bond market. The government yield curves can serve as benchmarks for pricing and hedging of corporate bonds. The maturity structure of corporate bonds has also been largely concentrated on short-to medium-term maturities due to uncertainties about the viability and lifespan of firms and the inadequacy of the legal, informational and accounting systems, as well as an unreliable judicial infrastructure. At present, institutional investors, such as insurance companies and pension funds, are still in the early stages of development in Indonesia. Moreover, these underdeveloped insurance companies and pension funds prefer to hold bank deposits. Meanwhile, unlike Japan, Indonesia has no cash-rich Postal Savings Bank that can mobilize low-cost funds from small savers. As a result, the commercial banks are the major investors in the bond market. As their liabilities comprise mainly short-term deposits, to mitigate maturity mismatches the commercial banks tend to hold short-term bonds.

Transactions involving both sovereign and corporate bonds have gradually increased, thereby increasing the liquidity of the bond market. A portion of the recapitalization bonds held by the state-owned banks is non-traded and must be held to maturity. The supply of traded bonds is gradually increasing in tandem with an increase in the portion of the recapitalization bonds that are tradable. The portion of recapitalization bonds that are tradable has gradually increased from 10 per cent in February 2000 to 15 per cent in September 2000, then to 25 per cent in December 2000 and finally to 35 per cent in February 2001. The turnover ratio of the recapitalized banks has also increased with improvements in the registration and settlement systems, market makers and the repo market.

Short-term papers: Treasury bills and SBI

Articles 23 and 71 of the Law No. 1 of 2004 on the State Treasury requires Bank Indonesia to pay interest on government deposits at the central bank at a rate agreed between the Governor of Bank Indonesia and the Minister of Finance. In return, the Ministry of Finance is required to start issuing short-term Treasury Notes (SPN – *Surat Perbendaharaan Negara*) commencing in 2005 to replace Bank Indonesia Certificates (SBIs) as a monetary instrument for open market operations. To meet its short-term liquidity needs, the Ministry of Finance has issued small amounts of SPN with tenors ranging from 3 months to 1 year. Replacing SBI with SPN transfers the cost of running open market operations from the central bank to the Treasury. As the market for SPN is likely to be deeper than for SBI, this will broaden the base of investor assets and encourage the development of the secondary market for government paper. During the transition period, both the existing SBI and the small amount of SPN (Treasury bills) will be used by the central bank as monetary instruments for open market operations. As they are both regarded as riskless assets, the commercial banks are likely to regard the two of them as being equally attractive. From the perspective of general investors, SBI are more appealing as they have short-term maturities and Bank Indonesia has never repudiated its debts. By contrast, the government has repudiated its long-term debts either through inflation, restructuring or reprofiling, or has simply not paid them.

As noted earlier, a sterilization operation involving a combination of the purchase of foreign exchange and the selling of SBI will raise the interest rate differential. This, and the appreciation of the Rupiah, will simply serve to attract even more capital inflows. As the focus of Bank Indonesia has been the management of short-term capital inflows through the banking system, the prudential rules and regulations governing the banking system do not apply to either non-bank financial institutions or the corporate sector.

VIII.   Conclusion

The use of interest rate as the operating target of market-based monetary policy requires strengthening of the banking system and improvements in the money and capital markets. After it financially collapsed during the Asian crisis, the banking system has gradually recovered. The system, however, is segmented as the government only deposited its financial wealth in state-owned banks. The Regional Development Banks exclusively deposit financial wealth of their owners, the local governments. Meanwhile, the private banks mainly finance their business affiliates. Financial and labor markets, as well as markets for goods and services, are segmented because of a combination of high inter-island transport cost and distorted government regulations. The financial instruments that can be used to control the monetary base are limited to short-term SBI, Bank Indonesia Certificates of Deposit, and long-term government bonds. The Treasury only issued a small amount of short-term Treasury bills. As a result, Bank Indonesia relies on non-market instruments such as the reserve requirement, legal lending limits, loan-to-deposit ratio, net open position and direct allocation to favored economic sectors such as small-scale enterprises.

For a number of reasons, the use of the reserve requirement and other non-market instruments are popular in Indonesia. First, the reserve requirement and net open position, for example, raise the cost of foreign borrowing so as to reduce inflows of volatile short-term capital. Second, loan-to-deposit ratio, legal lending limits and loan-to-value ratio are used to slowdown the growth of bank lending to specific economic sectors and classes of customers. Third, they can be used to deflate bubbles in non-traded sectors of the economy, particularly in the land-based or real estate sector. Fourth, the non-market instruments can be used to help reduce liquidity risks, particularly during downswings.

An explicit (soft) inflation target, along with a more flexible exchange rate regime and explicit fiscal discipline that ensures sustainable government debt are now the three main pillars of the macroeconomic stabilization framework in Indonesia. The flexible exchange rate system provides a greater degree of monetary policy autonomy and protects output better from external shocks as the exchange rate can adjust and stabilize demand for domestic goods through switching expenditures. The flexible exchange rate system is expected to reduce one-way bets against the Rupiah, thereby discouraging short-term capital inflows that can easily reverse. For a number of reasons, the central bank continues to accumulate external reserves and intervene in the foreign exchange market: first, to avoid excessive exchange rate volatility in a relatively shallow foreign exchange market; second, to guard against inflation from exchange rate pass-through resulting from the greater exchange rate flexibility, particularly given the limited technical and institutional capacity of the Indonesian central bank to implement inflation targeting; third, to use exchange rate policy as a tool to help improve external competitiveness and encourage the shifting of resources to the more efficient traded sector of the economy; and fourth, to hedge against speculation and foreign exchange instability due to shortfalls in exports and capital flow reversals.

Positive external shocks, particularly since the early 1990s, have allowed Indonesia to accumulate external reserves and strengthen the external value of the Rupiah. Since the early 1990s, Indonesia has enjoyed two positive external shocks. The first shock was the continuous increase in the international prices of her exports of broad-based primary commodities (energy, raw materials and food) mainly due to rapid economic growth, industrialization, mechanization and urbanization in both China and India. This generated a current account surplus in Indonesia's balance of payments. The second positive shock has been low international interest rates, except during the global financial crisis of 1998–99. This low interest rate environment lowered the cost of Indonesia's borrowings on the international financial markets. Significant amounts of SBI and Rupiah-denominated sovereign bonds are owned by foreign investors. Most of the investments are booked in Singapore to take benefit of the tax treaty between Indonesia and Singapore that exempts investors from Indonesian withholding tax.

To achieve its inflation target, Bank Indonesia has allowed the external value of the Rupiah to appreciate so as to lower the prices of imports on the domestic market. The overvalued Rupiah helps reduce the inflation rate but deter exports of manufactured products and provides incentive for allocation of resources to the non-traded sector of the economy. The undervaluation of the RMB has further lowered the prices of imports from China. In addition, the appreciation of the Rupiah has helped reduce the debt-to-GDP ratio. On the other hand, however, the appreciation of the Rupiah has eroded the international competitiveness of the Indonesian economy and precipitated a relocation of resources to the inefficient non-traded sector of the economy.

For at least three reasons, a Taylor-rule type of interest rate policy should be carefully used as a guide of monetary policy in Indonesia. First, because of the difficulty in estimating the fundamental concepts such as the natural rate or potential output, employment and interest rates. Second, an economy that relies on primary industry is subject to the vagaries of the international markets. Third, the sensitivity of policy or benchmark interest rates on volatile capital inflow due to the dominant role of foreign investors in the SBI and sovereign markets. In addition, there is no information on how monetary policy is transmitted to the real sector of the economy.

In general, the trends for bank deposit and lending rates follow developments in the policy rate. The interest rate in the interbank money market, however, is highly volatile because of inefficiencies in reserve money management and the segmentation of the banking industry. Only a small amount of bank liquidity is traded on the interbank money market. Those with high excess reserve balances at Bank Indonesia are mainly state-owned banks and the Regional Development Banks. These groups of banks have more extensive branch networks and monopoly rights over public sector deposits. The use of SBI with various maturities to mop up excess liquidity affects both the level and slope of the long-term yield curve, drives it away from its longer equilibrium and impedes market development. Meanwhile, the domestic private banks are mainly interested in serving their own business affiliates.

Notes

1 The main elements of macroeconomic policy during the New Order administration, 1966–98, include: (1) the 'balanced budget rule'; (2) fixed exchange rates; and (3) repressed financial system where Bank Indonesia set detailed credit ceilings, credit allocations by economic sector and classes of customer; provided refinancing and credit guarantees; and heavily subsidized interest rates. The availability of foreign aid allowed Indonesia to end the policy of inflationary budget deficit financing that was adopted in the previous regime of President Sukarno's administration that ended in 1966.

2 REER can be expressed as REER=e. P^*/P
3 Balassa (1964) and Samuelson (1964) argue that because technological advancement and automation are more advanced in the traded sector of the economy, labor productivity in this sector is higher than in the non-traded sector. Also, due to differences in the use of modern technology and technological advancement, labor productivity in the tradable sector in developed countries is higher than in developing economies.
4 Administered by the Bank for International Settlements (BIS) Representative Office in Hong Kong, the 11 members of EMEAP (the Executives Meeting of East Asia-Pacific Central Banks) established ABF 2 (the Asian Bond Fund 2) in 2005. This is a \$4 billion plus fund invested in Asian local currency government bonds.
5 New Zealand was the first country to adopt inflation targeting in 1990.
6 For alternative measurement of core inflation see, among others, Robert Rich and Charles Steindel. 2007. 'A Comparison of Measures of Core Inflation', Federal Reserve Bank of New York, *Economic Policy Review*, Vol. 13 Nr 3: pp. 19–38.
7 BI's Taylor-type equation is provided courtesy of Dr Hartadi Sarwono, Deputy Governor of Bank Indonesia in charge of Research and Monetary Policy, and Dr Yuda Agung of the Directorate of Monetary Policy Studies.
8 Using the uncovered interest rate parity condition, the nominal domestic interest rate (i_t) is equal to the international interest rate (i_t^*) plus the expected nominal rate of depreciation of the domestic currency (e^e) plus the country risk premium ($\dot{\rho}$) or $i_t = i_t^* + e^e + \dot{\rho}$. In turn, the expected nominal rate of depreciation (e^e) is equal to the rate of depreciation of the real exchange rate (ΔRER) and the difference between domestic inflation rate (π) and international inflation rate (μ^*) or $e^e = \Delta$RER $+ (\pi - \pi^*)$.
9 Bank Indonesia Regulation No. 12/10/PBI/2010 of 1 July 2010.
10 Milton Friedman (1960) argued that the central bank should pay interest on all kinds of bank reserves. On the other hand, James Tobin (1960) recommended that interest be paid on excess reserves only, with mandated reserves continuing to be non-interest bearing.

2 Rebuilding the banking system in Indonesia since 1997

Anwar Nasution

I. Introduction

The twin banking and currency crisis in Indonesia in 1997–2001 was one of the costliest crises ever (Laeven and Valencia, 2012). It was caused by a combination of indebtedness of both banks and the corporate sector. The crisis was preceded by a prolonged period of high credit growth for financing long-term projects, mainly in the non-traded sector of the economy, that were significantly funded by short-term foreign borrowing that caused maturity and currency mismatches. Under a system of financial repression prior to the crisis in 1997, credits from state-owned banks were channeled to specific economic activities and classes of customers at subsidized interest rates. Meanwhile, in violation of net-open-position (NOP) and legal-lending-limit regulations, most of the loans of privately owned banks were extended to their business affiliates. Lax regulatory oversight by Bank Indonesia, the central bank, was another key contributor to the crisis.

The crisis led to a deep recession with the rate of growth of GDP contracting by 13.1 per cent in 1998 as compared to positive growth of 4.7 per cent in 1997 and 7.8 per cent in 1996. The inflation rate rose from 6.2 per cent in 1997 to 60 per cent in 1998, and the Rupiah devalued sharply from Rp2,300 per US dollar in 1996 to Rp10,014 in 1998 and Rp10,261 in 2001. The short-run interest rate climbed from 14 per cent in 1996 to nearly 63 per cent in 1998. All this devastated the balance sheets of banks and non-bank financial firms, particularly those with large foreign debt. The output loss amounted to 67.9 per cent of annual GDP of 1998, while the fiscal cost was 56.8 per cent of GDP. Peak liquidity, measured as a ratio of central bank claims on commercial banks and liquidity support from the Treasury to total deposits and liabilities to non-residents, stood at 23.1 per cent. As a percentage of total loans, liquidity support amounted to 17.2, while peak NPL (non-performing loans) soared to 32.5. As a percentage of GDP, the public debt increased by 67.6 per cent and monetary expansion rose by 4.5 per cent.

The authorities adopted a number of policies to cope with bank failures. As the lender of last resort, Bank Indonesia temporarily relaxed prudential rules and regulations and injected massive liquidity credit into the devastated banking system. Capital adequacy ratio (CAR) was temporarily reduced from 8 per cent to 4 per cent in 1988 and raised back to 8 per cent in 2001. The central bank upgraded regulatory oversight by introducing the Basel core principles and standards, and adopting risk-oriented banking supervision. At the same time, Bank Indonesia ended financial repression and shifted monetary and credit policies to a market-based system. The Ministry of Finance established a deposit insurance mechanism to strengthen the financial safety net and recapitalized ailing banks to meet the minimum required capital ratio of 8 per cent. On 27 January 1998, IBRA (the Indonesia Bank Restructuring Agency) was created to take over impaired loans from the banks and to temporarily nationalize, or take a majority stake in, 13 of a total 237 banks. Prior to that, in November 1997, Bank Indonesia liquidated 16 private banks. IBRA later sold the nationalized banks and assets to private investors.

The rest of this chapter is divided into nine parts. In part 2, we discuss the bank-centered financial system, while part 3 elaborates on strategies to restructure the commercial banking system. In part 4, we discuss the bank recapitalization program, while part 5presents an analysis of the present structure of the banking industry. In part 6, we look at the market concentration of banks, while part 7 discusses the high interest margins, followed by the financial performance of banks in part 8. Then in part 9, we set out a summary of the financial architecture based on the Basel core principles and standards in connection with insider trading, accounting standards, financial sector supervision, deposit insurance and financial stability forums. Concluding remarks are presented in the last section.

II.   Bank-centered financial system

Table 2.1 shows that the financial intermediation system in Indonesia is one of the least developed in Asia. In terms of assets and branch networks, the commercial banking industry is the core of the financial system in this country. As a percentage of GDP, the assets of deposit-taking financial institutions, market capitalization and total bonds outstanding in Indonesia in 2010amounted to, respectively, only 14.9 per cent as compared to 75.5 per cent in Singapore. Bank loan penetration, defined as the ratio of bank loan to annual GDP, at 30 per cent in 2010 was also the lowest as compared to neighboring countries at over 140 per cent in Thailand, around 112 per cent in both Singapore and Malaysia and at 111 per cent in Vietnam.

Despite the rapid growth of their assets, the role of non-bank financial institutions (NBFIs) is still relatively small and only beginning to pose a competitive challenge to the banks. The leading NBFIs are insurance companies, pension funds and mutual funds. Like the pension funds for the civil service and military, most pension funds provide defined benefit plans. Under such plans, the employer provides determinable benefits, usually related to the employee's length of service and/or pay. Their portfolios are also mainly invested in time deposits and short-term securities. The Postal Saving Bank (PSB) that was inherited from the colonial past was destroyed during the Second World War, and there was a series

Table 2.1 Size and composition of financial system (per cent of GDP)

	Financial Sector Assets[1]						Market Capitalization[3]			Total Bonds Outstanding[4]								
Economy	Deposit-taking Financial Institution[1]			Non-Bank Financial Institutions[2]						Government			Corporate			Total		
	2000	2005	2010	2000	2005	2010	2000	2005	2010	2000	2005	2010	2000	2005	2010	2000	2005	2010
Bangladesh	46.8	52.0	57.3	0.8	3.8	5.0	2.5	5.9	29.0	...	10.0	8.5	...	0.0	0.0	...	10.0	8.5
PRD	168.8	202.8	229.8	8.8	15.5	21.5	27.1	12.5	45.0	16.6	36.4	39.9	0.3	2.8	10.7	16.9	39.2	50.5
Hong Kong, China	505.5	524.2	703.1	196.4	415.4	509.4	363.9	586.8	1,198.0	8.2	9.2	38.8	27.6	38.8	34.2	35.8	48.0	73.0
India	60.0	78.0	98.0	15.0	25.6	35.2	32.0	69.7	97.9	23.2	33.1	43.3	0.4	1.4	11.1	23.7	34.5	54.4
Indonesia	70.8	38.9	34.4	7.5	10.9	14.1	18.7	28.9	50.6	35.4	17.1	13.1	1.4	2.1	1.8	36.8	19.2	14.9
Kazakhstan	13.9	50.9	70.2	4.6	11.0	17.7	7.3	18.4	65.6	...	...	...	...	...	...	4.2	6.1	11.1
Korea, Rep. of	147.9	150.1	169.9	44.1	48.3	71.6	31.2	75.7	98.1	25.7	45.9	47.3	48.8	42.1	63.1	74.4	88.0	110.3
Lao PDR	...	23.4	33.0	...	0.8	1.1	...	...	...	...	...	2.1	...	...	...	...	...	2.1
Malaysia	154.2	178.3	202.3	16.5	19.9	22.5	124.7	133.1	166.5	38.0	44.4	58.2	35.2	33.0	40.4	73.3	77.4	98.6
Nepal	57.0	69.8	84.1	...	10.7	18.3	14.4	16.5	38.9	13.3	14.9	12.2	0.0	0.0	0.0	13.3	14.9	12.2
Pakistan	73.7	86.1	84.6	2.4	12.7	13.2	10.0	42.4	21.0	36.1	31.0	32.4	0.0	0.0	0.0	36.1	31.0	32.4
Philippines	99.2	82.0	84.9	22.4	21.2	21.3	76.8	109.3	104.1	31.1	40.1	31.3	0.2	1.0	4.1	31.3	41.1	35.4
Singapore	243.4	234.7	287.0	36.0	49.4	48.7	239.6	249.3	270.9	26.6	37.4	43.6	20.9	28.8	31.9	47.5	66.2	75.5
Sri Lanka	...	68.1	64.0	...	28.8	22.7	6.8	23.8	22.2	...	...	...	...	...	...	...	...	...
Taipei, China	256.0	309.4	287.2	29.4	67.1	94.8	80.4	133.2	174.9	14.1	26.7	36.5	25.9	32.8	15.9	40.0	59.5	52.4

| Economy | Financial Sector Assets[1] | | | | | | | | | Total Bonds Outstanding[4] | | | | | | | | |
| | Deposit-taking Financial Institution[1] | | | Non-Bank Financial Institutions[2] | | | Market Capitalization[3] | | | Government | | | Corporate | | | Total | | |
	2000	2005	2010	2000	2005	2010	2000	2005	2010	2000	2005	2010	2000	2005	2010	2000	2005	2010
Thailand	132.3	143.5	150.5	10.7	28.1	40.1	26.0	72.0	82.5	22.8	37.6	54.4	4.5	8.1	12.4	27.4	45.7	66.8
Uzbekistan	39.7	35.4	35.5	. . .	. . .	. . .	. . .	. . .	. . .	. . .	. . .	. . .	. . .	. . .	. . .	. . .	. . .	. . .
Average	138.1	136.9	157.4	30.4	48.1	59.8	70.8	105.2	164.4	24.3	29.5	33.0	13.8	14.7	18.1	35.4	41.5	46.5
Median	115.7	82.0	84.9	15.0	20.5	22.0	27.1	69.7	82.5	24.5	33.1	37.6	3.0	2.8	11.1	35.8	40.2	50.5
Euroxone	230.0	275.9	315.9	142.0	190.5	234.7	. . .	. . .	. . .	48.8	45.9	58.7	38.1	35.4	48.3	86.9	81.3	107.0
Japan	311.3	303.4	323.6	272.0	275.1	232.2	64.1	77.9	37.0	77.5	145.1	213.1	44.6	38.8	38.5	103.6	165.3	198.4
United States	79.6	92.0	106.3	279.3	305.4	304.8	115.9	107.9	91.4	41.3	46.8	76.1	96.8	109.5	95.9	138.0	156.3	172.0

Source: Park (2011).

Note:

. . . = data not available.

PRC = People's Republic of China, GDP = Gross Domestic Product, Lao PDR = Lao People's Democratic Republic.

[1] Data for 2000 refer to 2001 for Bangladesh and Nepal, and 2002 for the PRC. Data for 2010 refer to 2009 for the PRC, India, Kazakhstan, the Lao PDR, Nepal, Pakistan, Sri Lanka and Uzbekistan, and to 2008 for Bangladesh.

[2] Data for 2000 refer to 2001 for Bangladesh and Nepal, and 2002 for the PRC. Data for 2010 refer to 2009 for the PRC; Hong Kong, China; India; Kazakhstan; the Lao PDR; Nepal; Pakistan; Sri Lanka and Uzbekistan; and to 2008 for Bangladesh.

[3] Market capitalization as per cent of GDP in local currency units. Data for US refer to NYSE Euronext (US); 2010 data refers to 2009 for Bangladesh, Kazakhstan, Nepal, Pakistan and Sri Lanka.

[4] Total bonds outstanding data for 2010 refer to 2009 for Bangladesh and Kazakhstan, and 2008 for the Lao PDR.

of civil wars and mismanaged economy with a high inflation rate during a period after independence until 1966. PSB operates as a narrow bank to cheaply mobilize savings from the general public to be invested in government bonds. In Japan, PSB also sells insurance policies.

Financial intermediation primarily takes the form of bank lending rather than the issuing of bonds and equity on the capital markets. Bank operations are mainly concentrated on traditional deposit taking and lending, and less focused on the capital and bond markets. The small fixed income market is dominated by recapitalization bonds issued in 1998–99. Domestic financial institutions employ few financial innovations such as structured products, derivatives and securitization. There was no exposure to toxic assets that sparked the global financial crisis in 2007–08. In addition, their lending to the consumer and housing sectors are still relatively small. The relative backwardness of institutional investment makes competition among financial intermediaries relatively non-existent, with implications as regards financial innovation and the development of the new financial products that are needed by investors.

In 2010, the total assets of the various components of the financial services industry were, respectively, 34.4 per cent of annual GDP for deposit-taking institutions and 14.1 per cent for NBFIs. In the same year, the ratio of market capitalization to GDP stood at 50.6 per cent, while the ratio of market capitalization to total outstanding bonds amounted to 11.8 per cent. The rapid growth of the mutual fund industry in recent years is the outcome of the recapitalization of collapsed banks following the financial crisis in 1997. A mutual fund is a retail investment vehicle designed to allow relatively small investors to hold a diversified portfolio of financial assets. The types of assets held by such funds are mainly recapitalized bonds, together with small amounts of short-term Treasury bills, SBIs (Sertifikat Bank Indonesia), equity shares and corporate bonds.

The domination of commercial banks in the financial industry indicates that financial assets are mainly held in the form of bank deposits, with a heavy reliance of businesses on debt financing. In 2009, outstanding loans from commercial banks stood at 24 per cent of GDP, while outstanding deposits with commercial banks amounted to 33 per cent of GDP (IMF, 2010). A number of factors have deterred the development of capital and corporate bond markets in Indonesia. First, there is bank dominance and the availability of cheap and low-risk credit from the state-owned banks during the period of financial repression under the long-running administration of President Suharto (1966–98), when state-owned enterprises (SOEs) relied on capital injections from the government. Indonesia's state banks were given in 1997 an exclusive monopoly over public sector deposits and funding, including as regards state-owned enterprises. Jointly owned by provincial and regency (county) governments, Regional Development Banks (RDB) act as cashiers for their owners, local governments. Second, close family-owned companies do not like to share ownership with outsiders. Third, the small size of companies makes raising funds through the capital and bond markets more expensive than bank financing. To save on the regulatory cost of public listing, those companies that resort to bond financing prefer private placements to a small number of investors. Fourth, there is the weakness of the country's legal institutions, particularly as regards insolvency processes to protect creditor and investor rights. Indonesia's corporate bond scene has only gradually developed since 2003.

Other sources of financing are internal financing or borrowing from family members, use of retained earnings and revenue from tax evasion, tax avoidance and transfer pricing. Reputable companies can borrow on the international financial markets, mainly through nearby Singapore. Foreign-owned firms rely on retained earnings and internal funding from their parent corporations. During the era of financial repression prior to the Asian financial crisis of 1997, state-owned banks were the providers of long-term investment credit to the business sector. The cheap and low-risk loans extended as part of credit programs were refinanced by the central bank and guaranteed by PT Askrindo, the state-owned credit insurance company. Such highly leveraged financing had adverse effects at the microeconomic level as it led to an unbalanced funding structure among firms in the real sector of the economy. In an economy that depends on the export of raw materials, highly leveraged financing renders enterprises and their banks vulnerable to internal and external shocks, such as changes in interest rates, exchange rates and international prices.

Dubbed 'agents of development' during the period of financial repression, the public-sector banks were mandated to direct lending so as to support government industrial policy, frequency exercised through state firms or politically well-connected business groups. Bank Indonesia also set interest rates, mostly below the inflation rate, and restricted the activities of banks. The main source of funds for financing specific priority areas were liquidity credits provided by the central bank either through an expansion of its balance sheet or from government foreign borrowing. The state-owned banks provided long-term investment credit financed by long-term official development aid (ODA) from the group of Indonesia's international creditors. The financial repression allocated credit to specific economic activities and classes of customers (Nasution, 1983). In addition, the government provided credit guarantees. Under the authoritarian political system and centralized government, the authorities directly intervened in the day-to-day operations of the state-owned companies, including banks. A combination of financial repression and direct control by the government made the state-owned banks arm's-length extensions of the government bureaucracy.

Following the international trend at that time, Indonesia established a group of development banks in the 1960s, one at the national level, Bapindo (*Bank Pembangunan Indonesia*) the Indonesian Development Bank, and a BPD (*Bank Pembangunan Daerah*) or Regional Development Bank (RDB) in every province. The original objective of these institutions is to mobilize long-term funds, such as bonds, for financing long-term development projects. None of these materialized because of political turmoil, civil wars and economic mismanagement and high inflation rates. In reality Bapindo only channeled long-term project aid from the World Bank and Indonesia's international creditors and later operated as a commercial bank. The bank is now part of the newly established Bank

Mandiri. The BPDs operate as cashier to their owners, the provincial and sub-province governments. In 2013, 16 out of the 26 RDBs had not achieved the minimum core capital of Rp1 trillion.

Because of the long period of financial repression, banks in Indonesia suffered from weak commercial orientation and limited risk management discipline for self-protection. There was no incentive for bank managers to monitor and manage risks, upgrade transparency in corporate reporting or provide relevant business information. As credits were allocated based on non-economic considerations, the supervisors classified loans based on repayment of the credit rather than on the creditworthiness of borrowers or the market value of the collateral they pledged. Such inefficient allocation of financial resources resulted in poor asset quality and a high level of non-performing loans (NPL). In addition, without reliable, up-to-date and comprehensive information, the markets were unable to work effectively and efficiently.

As a part of economy-wide reforms, Indonesia introduced a wide range of banking sector reforms in October 1988 (Nasution 1995, 1998 and 2001, and Cole and Slade, 1996). The banking reform package was known as Pakto88 (*Paket Kebijaksanaan 27 Oktober 1988*). In the banking sector, the reforms improved market competition by allowing new entrants to the banking industry and relaxing the requirements for opening branches. Prudential rules and regulations were strengthened by adoption of the CAMEL (capital adequacy, asset quality, management, earnings and liquidity) system, under which capital adequacy, asset quality and liquidity are the key variables. The reforms eliminated the traditional functional specialization of banks and the major areas of specialization for state-owned banks[1] and served designated economic sectors and classes of customers.

The government started to corporatize the state-owned financial institutions to enable them compete in a more competitive market. Nevertheless, the rights of minority shareholders are not protected as the government still holds the *golden share* of these institutions that retains its exclusive rights to appoint management of state-owned banks. Penetration of foreign banks into the domestic market was enlarged by relaxation of market entry requirements and the takeover of financially distressed domestic private banks from IBRA (the Indonesian Bank Restructuring Agency), or small banks that could not meet the standards of API (*Arsitektur Perbankan Indonesia*), the Indonesia Bank Architecture program. Launched on 9 January 2004, the API program erected barriers to entry and exit that make it impossible to establish a new bank without buying the license of an existing bank. The new rules issued by Bank Indonesia in July 2012 to limit shareholding in banks allows for greater ownership by foreign investors of Indonesian banks.

There are only two types of bank recognized by Pakto 88, namely, commercial banks and banks specializing in providing services to small customers (BPR or *Badan Perkreditan Rakyat*). BPR do not receive demand deposits, deal with foreign-exchange transactions, make investments or involve themselves in the insurance business. There are also two types of bank operations: conventional banking operations and Islamic *syariah*-based banks whose operations are based on risk-sharing. After the crisis, the number of banks and BPR institutions, as well as the assets of Islamic *syariah* banks, have been growing rapidly. New *syariah*-based institutions have either been established as independent banks or as separate parts or units of conventional banks. Meanwhile, the postal savings bank system, which efficiently mobilized savings from small savers, was devastated by past armed conflicts and high inflation rates, devaluations and monetary purges prior to 1966.

Through separate subsidiaries, Pakto 88 allows banks to establish financial conglomeration by setting up non-bank financial institutions, such as those operating in the field of securities, leasing, venture capital, insurance, pension funds or mutual funds, subject to requirements for additional safeguards. The increasing integration of the banking and securities and insurance markets has led to a blurring of distinctions between the financial sector and national financial markets. Indonesia, for example, does not have regulations governing one-bank holding companies that ban owners of banks from owning non-financial subsidiaries and, as a result, nearly all banks and BPR are owned by business conglomerates. Such a separation would eliminate the temptation for banks to evaluate a commercial affiliate's loan application less objectively than that of an unaffiliated firm.

III. Restructuring of commercial banking

There were seven components involved in the restructuring of the commercial banking industry in Indonesia following the financial crisis(Nasution, 2001, Pangestu and Habir, 2002, Enoch, et al., 2004, and Suta and Musa, 2004). The first component was to restore public confidence and stop destabilizing bank runs by introducing a blanket guarantee on both the domestic and foreign liabilities of banks. The banking crisis had the potential to cause the payment system to collapse and drain foreign reserves. Prior to the introduction of the blanket guarantee in Indonesia on 1 January 1998, severe market turbulence was also caused by political uncertainty due to increasing pressure for President Suharto to step down, as well as the reopening of a previously closed bank owned by one of the sons of the president. The blanket guarantee was expensive and significantly increased the fiscal cost of resolving the banking crisis. After stability had been restored, the blanket guarantee was replaced in 2004 by a regular deposit insurance scheme that covers bank deposits of up to Rp100 million and was raised to Rp2 billion in October 2008. The revised limit covers about 90 per cent of the depositors. After the creation of the Deposit Insurance Corporation or LPS (*Lembaga Penjamin Simpanan*) in 2004, the fund was created and filled with premiums paid by banks on covered deposits. The availability of the insurance fund allows the government to rapidly close a financially collapsed bank and bail out depositors, thus preventing bank runs.

The second strategy was to address the solvency and illiquidity problems of financially distressed banks by recapitalizing, liquidating, consolidating and temporarily nationalizing weak financial institutions. The solvency problem was resolved by injecting a large amount of sovereign, Rupiah-denominated recapitalization bonds into these banks. Meanwhile, the illiquidity issue was resolved by injecting liquidity support from the central bank and cleaning up bank balance sheets through the taking over of their non-performing loans. A number of specialized restructuring agencies, such as IBRA and INDRA (Indonesian Debt Restructuring Agency), were established to manage and dispose of the sour assets. The second component of the strategy was to modernize the payment system. Real Time Gross Settlements (RTGS) was established in 2000 to ensure that interbank transactions are completed safely and on time and to minimize overdrafts. Deregulation and the rapid development of telecommunications technology encouraged the rapid expansion of ATM, credit and debit card use, as well as e-banking, which has also benefited low-income groups. Under the administration of President Suharto, the commercial use of a telecommunications satellite was only available to BCA, which was jointly owned by his family and cronies.

The third component of the strategy was to bring financial repression, or government-directed lending, to an end for the most part. This transferred the responsibility for taking risks from the central bank and government to bank managers. The Basel II Capital Accord requires banks to internally evaluate and test their own risk management systems to measure the safety and soundness of their institutions. The models require up-to-date and accurate data provided by banking organizations and the auditing profession that validate accounts and records, valuing risk assets and verifying the accuracy of financial statements. In reality, however, Indonesian banks do not have the capacity to assess the overall capital adequacy in relation to their risk profile. This is partly because of the interlocking of ownership, management and business in the family-owned company. Prior to the financial crisis in 1997, all business conglomerations had banks and each of them used its bank to control the entire group and allocate funds to companies in the group.

The government uses a combination of moral suasion and the provision of refinancing facilities to encourage commercial banks to provide credits to special classes of customers, particularly small and medium enterprises. The moral suasion includes a Bank Indonesia regulation, introduced in March 2011, that encourages banks to increase their loan-to-deposit ratio (LDR) to between 78 per cent and 100 per cent by imposing a higher reserve requirement ratio on banks whose LDR falls outside this rage. In April 2011, Bank Indonesia issued a maximum loan-to-value regulation for property and car loans to reduce credit growth to these economic sectors. All banks are required to submit to BI a plan for lending to SMEs by economic sector, province and credit scheme. In December 2012, Bank Indonesia issued a regulation that obliged commercial banks to allocate at least 20 per cent of their credit to micro, small and medium enterprises.[2]

Funded by the national budget, the Ministry of Finance provides subsidized funding to banks to channel loans under the KUR (*Kredit Usaha Rakyat*) program to small and medium enterprises. Meanwhile, all SOEs are required by the Ministry of State-Owned Enterprises (SOEs) to allocate 4 per cent of their after-tax profits to SME credit and environmental protection programs as part of their corporate social responsibility requirements. The Ministry of Cooperatives and Small and Medium Enterprises operate its own savings and loans program while the National Family Planning Program offers loans to participants in the birth control program. All of these non-market-based schemes are competing with the normal commercial lending of the banks and BPRs, and have the potential to weaken monetary policy based on market mechanisms and the use of the interest rate as operating target.

The fourth component of the restructuring program was to overhaul the financial infrastructure by strengthening institutional and prudential rules, and standards and regulatory structures so as to comply with the risk-based Basel standards. The reforms included modernization of the legal, judicial and accounting systems. Nevertheless, enforcement of business contracts as well as protection of property and creditor rights are still very weak, which makes it impossible to define, pledge and execute collateral and poor recovery rates particularly in unsecured lending. The low recovery rate also indicates the low capacity of and professionalism of the implementing institutions and inefficiency in the administration to deal with rehabilitation and insolvency. These and the lengthy legal process and unpredictability of legal decisions in the courts have made banks turn to debt collectors.

The prudential framework for the banking system was revised to bring it into line with the recommendations of the Basel committee, with the three pillars consisting of regulations on capital requirements (Pillar I), supervision (Pillar II) and market discipline(Pillar III) to measure particularly bank equity and debt based on market value. In 2002, Indonesia adopted the 40 recommendations of the Financial Sector Assessment Program (FSAP), introduced legislation on money laundering and became a member of the Financial Action Task Force (FATF). As the objective of the credit program prior to the crisis in 1997 was to deliver credit to the targeted economic sectors and classes of customers, the focus of bank supervision was mainly on the delivery of the credit program and not on asset quality. The adoption of Basel II changed the practice of bank supervision from compliance-checking towards risk-oriented procedures.

The IMF provided technical assistance from 2000 to 2008 to upgrade prudential rules and regulations and the banking supervision unit of Bank Indonesia[3] to comply with Basel I. In addition to regular periodic supervision, on-site supervision has been instituted so as to ensure tighter oversight of problem banks. Bank supervisors have been retrained in the field of credit analysis and risk management in banking organizations so as to understand recent financial innovations, such as derivatives, and the sophisticated risk management models that evolved because of advances in information technology. The risks specific to the banking industry are divided into eight categories: capital or gearing risks, credit risks, counterparty risks, liquidity or funding risks, market or price risks (which include currency and interest rate risks), operational risks, and sovereign and political risks. Bank supervisors are also expected to detect arm's-length transactions between banks and their affiliates. Reform of the accounting system has upgraded transparency through the provision of reliable and on-time information. This, and the creation of the Credit Bureau at Bank Indonesia in 2005, has promoted market development and market discipline, and prudential lending and investment.

However, the poor handling of the Bank Century (BC) case in 2004–08 revealed the inadequate implementation of the banking rules and regulations, and a lack of discipline on the part of the central bank in taking prompt corrective action. The poor implementation of the prudential rules and regulations causes market failures. Established in December 2004, BC was produced by the merger of three small banks with histories of inadequate capitalization, poor management and fraudulent practices. The new bank was given the opportunity to correct the deficiencies it had inherited subject to the proviso that the owners open an escrow account at a reputable bank in Jakarta in mid-2004. The size of the escrow funds was to be equal to the capital deficiency and should be used only for strengthening the capital base of BC with the consent of the central bank. However, it turned out that BC had to be placed under intensive supervision in February 2005, barely three months after its establishment. Despite repeated warnings from the supervisors, no firm corrective measures were taken. Meanwhile, in early 2005 Bank Indonesia allowed the owners of Bank Century to transfer its funds from the escrow account at Citibank in Jakarta to their own personal accounts in Switzerland.

The Bank Indonesia Law (No. 23 of 1999), as revised by Law No. 23 of 2004, makes the central bank an autonomous and independent institution. The role of Bank Indonesia, according to the legislation, should be focused on preserving the systemic stability of the payment system and monetary policy management so as to ensure the stability of both the internal and external value of the Rupiah. As noted earlier, the legislation requires Bank Indonesia to transfer its role as bank supervisor to the newly established *Otoritas Jasa Keuangan* (OJK), the Financial Supervisory Agency, an independent, fully integrated supervisory agency that is in charge of micro-prudential supervision of the entire financial system (both bank and non-bank financial institutions). After a long delay, the OJK finally commenced operations in late 2012.

The fifth component of the strategy was to change the culture and image of Indonesia's banks through improvements in their governance, the hiring of highly qualified managers and professionals and the introduction of new banking products. For the first time, private bankers were hired to manage state-owned banks and foreign owners of private banks hired foreign professionals to manage their newly acquired banks. Market segmentation in the banking industry has been relaxed through the stricter enforcement of legal lending limit regulations, rapid growth of NBFIs and greater penetration of foreign banks. However, the government has retained the monopoly of state-owned banks and regional development banks over public deposits. The private banks are mainly interested to finance their business affiliates. Foreign banks serve foreign businesses, those who need extensive international networks, and those who perceive that these banks have better services and reputations, are sounder and better managed, and are closely supervised by their head offices. The foreign-owned banks, such as PT Bank Danamon, also serve small and medium businesses and operate mobile banking services to reach out to customers. Through injections of recapitalization bonds and the taking over of their non-performing loans, all domestic private banks were practically nationalized in 1998.

In line with WTO rulings, Pakto 88 (the Deregulation Package of 1988) allows foreign investors to own up to 99 per cent of an Indonesian bank. Greater penetration by foreign strategic investors into the domestic banking industry came about via two channels. First, through the acquisition of financially distressed banks that had been taken over by IBRA, and second, through the acquisition of existing small banks. The takeover of existing small banks is encouraged as part of the API program. The transfer of ownership to foreign investors has ended the concentration of bank ownership primarily in affiliated companies. Foreign owners brought professional managers in to create new cultures and images for their banks. Management of the newly recapitalized state-owned banks also began to mobilize professionals with appropriate expertise. Increased market competition has encouraged banks to offer more extensive financial services to small and medium enterprises. The issuance of large quantities of sovereign bonds to recapitalize the financially distressed banks in 1998–99 encouraged the development of deeper financial intermediation.

The sixth component of the strategy has been to develop the secondary bond market. This is crucial to implementing both Pillar I (risk-based capital adequacy requirement) and Pillar II (market discipline) of Basel II as most bank capital consists of recapitalization bonds. The seventh element of the bank restructuring strategy was to create a banking sector safety net and the financial stability forum. A state-owned deposit insurance company was established in 2004, while a credit bureau was set up at Bank Indonesia in 2006 to promote consumer credit. Chaired by the Minister of Finance, the Financial Stability Forum (FSF) was created in 2007 to serve as a forum for cooperation, coordination and exchange of information between the central bank, the Ministry of Finance and the LPS to maintain the stability of the financial system.

The eight component of the strategy to restructure the Indonesian banking system involved bank closure, intervention and nationalization, and merger and acquisition. Four large state-owned banks (Bank Bumi Daya, Bank Exim, Bapindo (Bank Pembangunan Indonesia) and BDN (Bank Dagang Negara)) that were collapsed during the crisis were merged into the newly established Bank Mandiri in September 2008. The number of banks was reduced from 237 in June 1997 to 149 in June 2001 due to liquidation and suspension (69 banks), merger (21 banks) and new establishments (2 banks). As mentioned earlier, the API program encouraged the merger and consolidation of small banks to strengthen their capital base, upgrade technology and improve human resources so as to allow them to operate as sounder and safer full-service commercial banks. On the negative side, however, consolidation of the banking industry has created what the World Bank and International Finance Corporation (2009) describe as a medium-concentration oligopoly. The Bank Century scandal in

2008 shows that a merger combined with a failure by Bank Indonesia to take strict and prompt measures on violations of rules and regulations can create an inefficient, rent-seeking oligopoly and concentrated credit risks (Nasution, 2010).

IV. Bank recapitalization

The solvency and liquidity problems of Indonesia's devastated banking system began to stabilize in 2001. The negative shock that hit the balance sheets of both banks and credit clients during the crisis had a direct adverse impact on bank capital. The low effective capital levels of financially distressed banks provided a small cushion for shocks. Bank runs started in September 1997 followed by flight to quality or shifting of deposits from domestic banks to better-capitalized and better-managed foreign banks. At the same time, the financial problems cut access of domestic banks to international markets as foreign lenders raised concerns about low capitalization levels. The annual interest rates jumped to over 70 per cent in 1998 as banks competed to attract deposits.

To recapitalize the financially distressed banks, the government issued Rp439 trillion (34 per cent of GDP in 1999) in long-term bonds between May 1996 and October 2000, and injected these into the banks through IBRA, which was a government institution established on 27 January 1998 to manage the bank restructuring program and take over non-performing loans (NPLs) so as to address the liquidity issues faced by the banks. IBRA merged the 13 banks that were taken over into 7 new banks. Prior to the establishment of IBRA, 16 poorly managed domestic private banks closed in September 1997. The capital injections allowed the banks to meet the mandated risk-weighted capital adequacy ratio (CAR) of 8 per cent by the end of 2001 and thereby solved their solvency problem.

The group of state-owned banks received 63.6 per cent of the recap bonds, 25.4 per cent were injected into IBRA banks, other private commercial banks received 4 per cent, non-recap banks received 3.7 per cent and the BPD group received 0.3 per cent. The other 3 per cent was placed in the sub-registry. Half of the recap bonds carry variable rates that are linked to the SBI rate, with maturities of up to 15 years and interest payments made every 3 months. Nearly 42 per cent of the recap bonds carry fixed interest rates. Those that carry an interest rate of 14 per cent have 10-year maturities, while those with a 12 per cent interest rate have a shorter maturity of 5 years. The indexed rate bonds carry 3 per cent interest rates with maturities of up to 20 years and interest payments every 3 months. The variable – and indexed – rate bonds are sensitive to interest, inflation and exchange rate movements.

There are three reasons why the state banks received the lion's share of the recap bonds. The first is because this group of banks controlled the biggest portion of the bank credit market at 48.2 per cent in June 2001, while the group of taken-over banks, or IBRA banks, controlled 17.5 per cent and the BPD group 3.4 per cent. The second reason is because traditionally the state-banks had low capital bases and, therefore, used the crisis to strengthen their capital bases as they had smaller buffers to absorb losses, thus leaving them open to high capital or gearing or leverage risks. Third, being the main channels of the credit program of the past, this group of banks had the highest average ratio of NPLs at 17.1 per cent (BNI 25.7 per cent; BTN 21.9 per cent and Mandiri 16.9 per cent). Under the previous financial repression policy, the state-owned banks were used to achieve the industrial policy goals of the government, and to reach underserved regions and targeted classes of customers and communities. The state-owned banks were also used by the government to maintain a countercyclical stance during periods of credit contraction during the crisis. The average NPL ratio of the taken-over banks was 16.3 per cent (Bali 33.2 per cent, Niaga 25 per cent and BII 22.2 per cent). The high level of NPLs in the state bank group was due to the fact that the financial repression policy created more of an incentive for bank staff to extend program loans than to collect loan repayments as repayment was guaranteed by the state-owned credit insurance company. This shows that the state-owned banks represented a fiscal contingency as they were prone to engaging in risky activities to exploit implicit guarantees.

The capital injections and takeover of banks' NPLs by IBRA restored the financial health on Indonesia's banks in 2001, four years after the outbreak of the crisis. By the end of March 2001, the average CAR of the state-owned and IBRA banks amounted to 20 per cent. The average CAR of the state bank group (Mandiri, BNI, BRI and BTN) was 18.2 per cent while that of the IBRA banks (BCA, Bali, BII, Danamon, LIPPO, Niaga and Universal) was 23 per cent. Banks with high CAR were BCA (58.8 per cent), Lippo (44.1 per cent), Mandiri (32.2 per cent), BII (22.2 per cent) and Danamon (21.2 per cent). At that time, IBRA also took over subordinated loans and emergency liquidity credit (BLBI – *Bantuan Likuiditas Bank Indonesia*) that had been extended by the central bank to financially weak banks since November 1997. The NPL takeover by IBRA helped solve the liquidity problem of these banks as their NPLs shrunk from 48.6 per cent in 1998 to 16.6 per cent in June 2001. At the same time, revenue from the coupons on the sovereign recapitalization bonds generated income for the recipients so as to allow them to rebuild their capital. The state-owned banks are doing well as they earn double digit rates on the government bonds while paying single digits on government deposits. As of March 2001, on average 55.8 per cent of the total assets of state-owned and IBRA banks consisted of recapitalization bonds. The share for state-owned banks was 59.4 per cent and 49.1 per cent for IBRA banks. Those banks that had recap bonds worth more than 50 per cent of assets were Mandiri (66.8 per cent), Danamon (65.2 per cent), BCA (60.5 per cent), BTN (58.1 per cent) and BNI (58.1 per cent).

The high percentage of banks' capital and portfolio in sovereign bonds makes the recapitalized banks vulnerable to the country credit rating as well as to the movement of short-term capital. This is because about 33 to 35 per cent of government bonds, SBI and other equities traded in the Jakarta Stock Exchange is owned by foreign investors. The short-term capital inflow provides liquidity to the bonds and equity markets. It raises prices of equities and reduces interest rates and push pressures for appreciation of the Rupiah. Sterilization operation of Bank Indonesia raises its external reserves. The increase in the prices of securities subsequently raises capital ratio (CAR) of the banks and reduces the ratio of their non-performing loans. On the other hand, sudden stop or capital flow reversal reduces prices of equities that subsequently reduce both CAR and NPL ratios of the banks. Bank Indonesia depletes its external reserves to prevent sharp depreciation of the Rupiah because of the capital outflow. The mutual fund industry that traded the equities was in crisis in 2003 and 2005 due to a massive redemption of funds because of the sharp decline in the prices of equities ignited by the capital outflows (Kenward, 2011).

V.   The present structure of banking industry

Thirteen years after the Asian financial crisis, as of May 2010 there were 121 commercial banks in Indonesia and 1,706 BPRs. Four of the commercial banks are state-owned, while there are 26 BPD and 92 private banks (Table 2.2). As

Table 2.2 Number of banks and branches, 2005 and 2010

	December 2005	August 2010
A. Commercial Banks		
1. State-owned banks	5	4
1a. Number of branches	2,171	4,047
2. Domestic private banks licensed to conduct forex transactions	34	36
2a. Number of branches	4,113	6,358
3. Domestic private banks without forex licenses	37	31
3a. Number of branches	709	1,029
4. Regional development banks	26	26
4a. Number of branches	1,107	1,398
5. Joint venture banks	18	15
5a. Number of branches	64	260
6. Foreign banks	11	10
6a. Number of branches	72	229
Total Number of Commercial Banks	*131*	*122*
B. Sharia Commercial Banks and Sharia Business Operations		
1. Number of banks	22	34
2. Number of offices	436	1,632
C. Rural Banks		
1. Number of banks	2,009	1,706
2. Number of offices	3,110	3,910

Source: Bank Indonesia, *Indonesia Banking Statistics*, August 2010.

pointed out earlier, PT Bank Mandiri, the biggest state-owned bank, resulted from the merger of four other large state-owned-banks: Bank BumiDaya, Bank Exim, BDN (*Bank Dagang Negara*) and Bapindo (*Bank Pembangunan Indonesia*), which had collapsed during the crisis. The secession of East Timor from Indonesia to form the independent Republic of Timor-Leste in 2000 reduced the number of BPD (Regional Development Banks) from 27 to 26. Of the private banks, there were 16 joint venture banks and 10 foreign-owned banks. Ten of the private banks are licensed to conduct foreign-exchange transactions. As noted earlier, the BPRs (1,706 banks) do not accept demand depositor engage in foreign-exchange transactions. With rapid improvements in the payment infrastructure, the number of bank branch offices had also expanded to 12,958 as of end of May 2010. Of this figure, 3,892 branches are operated by state banks, 7,229 by private banks, 1,369 by BPDs, 239 by joint venture banks and 229 by foreign banks.

Bank Indonesia encourages BPDs and commercial banks to become apex or central banks for BPRs. An apex bank functions similar to the central bank to manage funds of BPRs, provide credit lines to solve their liquidity problems and give access to a modern payment system. As a patron and creditor, the apex supervises its clients. The success of the plan is determined by the capacity of the BPDs to execute their central banking task for BPR as well as the willingness of these rural financial institutions to become clients of the BPDs.

Islamic financial products have been growing rapidly since the crisis of 1997 as around 89 per cent of the 213 million population of Indonesia is Moslem. The products consist of financial instruments that are structured so as to comply with Islamic *Sharia* law, especially concerning the payment of interest. Indonesia has a dual banking system in the sense that conventional banks are allowed to open *Sharia* units. Established in 1992, Bank Muamalat Indonesia was the first and the only pure *Sharia* bank to exist before the Asian financial crisis of 1997. As of December 2010, there were 11 pure *Sharia* banks with 1,253 offices, 23 *Sharia* units with 264 offices and 151 BPR *Sharia* with 291 offices. The other *Sharia* banks and units were established after the crisis. Two of the state-owned banks, 14 of the BPD and 10 of the private commercial banks have opened *Sharia* units. As of December 2010, the assets of *Sharia* banks and units remained relatively small at 2.73 per cent of total bank assets.

Greater penetration by foreign strategic investors in domestic private banks following the crisis in 1997 strengthened their capital bases and governance structure, created healthier market competition, reduced financial costs and brought about transfers of technology, technical expertise and better management practices. Staff trained by foreign bankers often move to local institutions. Foreign investors entered the domestic market through a combination of mergers and acquisitions, and the privatization of nationalized collapsed banks by IBRA following the Asian financial crisis of 1997–98. Foreign investors have also acquired small private banks. The Indonesian Bank Architecture Plan (API) of 2004 calls for the consolidation of national banks through mergers and acquisitions for the purpose of strengthening capital and governance. Bank Indonesia envisages that banks will be categorized into three strata, namely, international-class banks, national banks and non-depository rural banks (BPR).

Sixteen out of 26 BPD have not achieved the minimum target of core capital of Rp1trillion. Starting from December 2013, minimum capital for a newly established commercial bank has been raised to Rp3 trillion and Rp1 trillion for *syariah*-based banks. Minimum capital of a branch office of a foreign bank is Rp3 trillion. To diversify ownership of banks, Bank Indonesia only allows one controlling shareholder in one commercial bank. In addition, Bank Indonesia set the following maximum limits of bank ownership for each shareholding category as follows: (1) bank and non-bank financial institutions at 40 per cent; (2) non-financial institutions at 30 per cent and (3) individual shareholders at 25 per cent for commercial banks and at 25 per cent for *syariah* banks. Individuals and/or legal entities may hold 99 per cent of equity share of commercial banks by purchasing their shares either directly or through the stock exchange.

Beginning from December 2012,[4] Bank Indonesia differentiates the size of the requirement for core capital of banks by business activities, type of bank office and geographic location. Banking operation of the banks (Buku) is divided into four classes, namely, Buku 1, Buku 2, Buku 3 and Buku 4. Business activities in Buku 1 are limited to basic banking services with core capital amounted to between Rp100 billion to Rp1trillion. Banks in Buku 4 have more complex business activities and are subject to a minimum core capital of Rp30trillion. The type of bank office is differentiated to five, namely, branch office, operational regional office, sub-branch, functional office conducting operational activities, cash office and other offices of an operational nature overseas or Representative Office if conducting operational activities. Branch Offices of Buku 1 and Buku 2 are subject to a minimum core capital of Rp8 trillion and Rp10 trillion for Buku3 and Buku 4. The minimum capital requirement for Representative Office for Buku 1 and Buku 2 is Rp1 trillion and Rp2 trillion for Buku 3 and Buku 4. Indonesia is divided into six zones and the highest core capital is required in Jakarta, which has the most densely concentrated bank offices; opening banks in some provinces in the eastern part of Indonesia requires a smaller core capital.

As noted earlier, penetration by foreign institutions of the domestic banking market has been much easier after the Banking Reforms of 1988 that allowed foreigners to own 99 per cent equity shares in joint venture banks and gradually liberalized the rules governing the opening of new branch offices. At the same time, the reforms also relaxed geographical restrictions on foreign banks. As also mentioned earlier, IBRA sold the taken-over banks to foreigners and foreign investors also bought small banks that were unable to meet API Standards. The privatization of state-owned banks began more rapidly after the economic crisis of 1997, partly for the purpose of financing the government budget deficit. The government, however, retains the golden share in such banks and exclusive rights over the appointment of management. Top managerial positions in state-owned banks are reserved for locals and foreigners can only work as advisors. The tighter market competition that has resulted from this process has influenced

Table 2.3 Foreign ownership of domestic private banks (as of August 2010)

Name of the bank	Foreign investor	Equity share (%)
1. CIMB Niaga	CIMB Group SdnBhd, Malaysia	77.0
2. Danamon	Temasek Holdings, Singapore	67.9
3. Panin	ANZ, Australia	35.0
4. Permata	Standard Charter, U.K.	44.5
5. BII	Maybank, Malaysia	54.3
6. Buana	UOB, Singapore	91.0
7. EkonomiRaharja	HSBC, Hong Kong	99.0
8. BTPN	Texas, Pacific, USA	71.6
9. ANK	Commonwealth Bank, Australia	83.0
10. Bumiputra	Che Abdul Daim, Malaysia	58.3
11. Mestilka Dharma	RHB Capital Berhad, Malaysia	80.0
12. Nusantara	Tokyo Mitsubishi, Japan	75.4
13. HalimInternasional	ICBC, China	90.0
14. Swadesi	Bank of India	76.0
15. Indomonex	Bank of India	76.0
16. BCA	Farindo Investments Ltd	47.2

Source: Bank Indonesia, *Indonesian Banking Statistics*, August 2010.

the conduct of banks and helped contribute to an improvement in market discipline.

Table 2.3 shows the dominant foreign ownership in leading private domestic banks. Through Farindo, Faralon of the United States partly owns BCA, the leading domestic private bank. The greater presence of foreign banks in the domestic market requires closer collaboration between financial authorities, particularly with respect to consistency in the calculation of risk-weighted assets, and the treatment of sovereign exposure and liquidity standards (Caruana, 2012). Foreign banks may transmit foreign shocks to the domestic economy when their funds consist mainly of borrowings from their parent companies. These risks can be mitigated if foreign banks are mostly financed through domestic deposits.

VI. Market concentration

The banking system in Indonesia is dubbed by the World Bank and International Finance Corporation (2009) as a 'medium concentration oligopoly' because third-party funds, assets and credit outstanding are highly concentrated in a few state-owned and private banks. Six leading banks (Mandiri, BRI, BCA, BNI, BRI, CIMB Niaga and Danamon) held 57 per cent of total third-party funds and provided 52.23 per cent of total bank lending at the end of December 2010. Four state-owned banks (Mandiri, BRI, BNI and BTN) have a dominant market share mainly due to a combination of their wider branch networks and government regulations giving them a monopoly over public sector financial transactions. In December 2010, this group of banks controlled 37.2 per cent of the total outstanding deposits of commercial banks. Meanwhile, the private bank group's share of bank deposits stood at 44.8 per cent, joint venture and foreign banks at 8.9 per cent, regional development banks at 7.7 per cent and the BPR at 1.4 per cent. As they are neither allowed to receive demand deposits nor conduct foreign-exchange transactions, the BPR only offer savings and time deposits. As regards lending, the domestic private banks are more aggressive in extending loans, accounting for 43.5 per cent of total bank lending, while the state bank group supplied 35.3 per cent of bank loans, the joint venture and foreign banks 11.3 per cent, the regional development banks 8.0 per cent and the BPR 1.9 per cent. The state-owned banks and BPR are the main providers of funds on the interbank money market and private and the joint venture and foreign banks are the main users or buyers. The BPR also receive funding from commercial banks.

The banking market is also highly segmented and characterized by a high degree of government ownership. The Coordinating Minister for Economic Affairs issued a regulation in 1967 to require the entire public sector, including state-owned enterprises, to deposit their financial assets with state-owned banks and only conduct financial transactions through these public banks. The public banks are also implicitly guaranteed by the government, their owner. In return, these banks are required to meet the credit needs of non-bank state-owned companies. The public banks are also the main public service payment agents, such as in the case of taxes. The banking reforms of 1988 retained this monopoly over public sector deposits and financial transactions. Each of the 27 provinces that existed prior to 2000 also has a BPD. In reality, the BPDs act as cashiers for their owners, namely, the provincial and sub-provincial local governments.[5] In addition, as the government stands by its own banks, depositors tend to prefer them over private-owned banks. The weak performances of state-owned banks and the BPD indicate government failures.

The central role of the public banks, owned by the central and local governments, in the economy is another source of potential vulnerability. This is not only due to the large market share enjoyed by this group of banks but also their interconnection with other financial institutions through the interbank markets. Because of these factors, the failure of a public bank would inevitably lead to government or the central bank bailing out depositors, thereby creating moral hazard and a high fiscal contingency. Large-scale injection of liquidity from the central bank to bail out such large public banks would fuel inflation and currency depreciation that in turn would trigger macroeconomic instability.

The second reason for market segmentation is the fact that all domestic private banks (and BPRs) are owned by business conglomerates and their main objectives are to mobilize funds to finance their business affiliates. Until recently, there were no regulations in place governing one-bank holding companies that separate the ownership of banks from non-financial subsidiaries that ensure arm's-length transactions between banks and their commercial affiliates. Banks and non-bank business enterprises in one group of companies are interlocked though ownership, business and management. Prior to the crisis in 1997, a number of business conglomerates owned several banks. This, together with a lack of reliable information and a weak legal system, makes it difficult to implement the legal lending limit regulations so as to limit credit to bank owners, management and business associates.

Under a weak and unreliable institutional framework, privately owned banks lent only to people they could trust: themselves, family members and business associates, or the banks were looted by transferring funds overseas. Against a background of weak market infrastructure and a lack of creditworthy entrepreneurs, related lending to affiliates helps improve credit efficiency as bankers have more information on borrowers compared with non-affiliates. Banks can also use internal information to assess the ex-ante risks of investment projects or persuade borrowers to abandon risky projects. Related lending, however, is prone to insider trading and the principal-agent problem. A regulation was issued by Bank Indonesia in October 2006 to limit the ownership of one ultimate owner to only one bank. This regulation is, however, scarcely being implemented due to a lack of information and a weak legal system.

VII.   High interest rate margin

The net interest margin (NIM – the margin between lending and deposit rates) in the Indonesian banking system is the highest among six ASEAN member countries. Banks make most of their income from the spread. In 2009, NIM in Indonesia was 5.9 per cent per annum as compared to 3.9 per cent in the Philippines, 3.4 per cent each in Vietnam and Thailand, 3 per cent in Malaysia and 1.8 per cent in Singapore. The high spread is partly because of bank consolidation and concentration, as well as subsequent regulatory tightening following the Asian financial crisis of 1997. The consolidation has resulted in a marked reduction in the number of banks. It has not, however, resulted in a decline in the intensity of competition, partly because it was accompanied by easier entry for foreign banks through the acquisition of small banks.

The high banking spread in Indonesia is also because of the high cost of intermediation and lower efficiency of the banking system in this country. The high cost of intermediation indicates that banks do not effectively function as intermediaries and optimally channel financial resources from savers to investors. The high NIM is partly due to poor market infrastructure, including the legal and accounting systems and weak creditor rights. This makes for lower recovery rates and a longer time to repossess loan collateral. Availability of information about borrowers is also limited in Indonesia, whether as regards the non-affiliated corporate sector or SMEs. Increasing reserve requirements, partly intended to slowdown short-term capital inflows, have also contributed to the wide gap between deposit and lending rates, particularly as the reserve requirements are remunerated at below-market rates. The banks in Indonesia use the maximum interest rate guaranteed by the Deposit Insurance Company as a benchmark for setting deposit rates. In addition to interest rates, they also compete by running drawings offering expensive prizes to attract deposits. The prizes including luxury cars such as Mercedes Benz S-500 series, Lexus, BMW and Range Rover models, motorcycles and Blackberry telephone handsets. The prizes add another 0.5 per cent to 1 per cent to the interest costs of the leading banks.

A number of studies have identified other possible causes of high interest margins,[6] including the application of oligopoly power to extract rents in a non-competitive banking system structure. Bank operating costs increased with the adjustment from a repressive system to a market-oriented environment that required the retraining of staff and modernization of operations. The modernization process included mechanization, such as the introduction of automatic teller machines and e-banking, as well as the expansion of branch networks for retail-oriented operations. Some of the overhead costs and (implicit and explicit) taxes have been passed on to bank customers in the form of higher lending rates.

Other possible explanations are, first, because of the high proportion of debt instruments of Indonesia (SBI and SUN) that are in the hands of foreign investors. This restricts the degree of freedom for monetary policy as the high interest rate differential is required to attract foreign capital. As pointed out earlier, the capital flows also affect prices of the equities traded in the Jakarta money and capital markets, interest rate as well as exchange rate. In addition, market segmentation of the banking industry and low domestic savings are also pushing up market-determined interest rates. The market segmentation is also caused by monopsony position of the state-owned bank group on deposits and financial transactions of the public sector including state-owned enterprises. This policy causes segmentation of the money market.

Table 2.4 shows that the highest NIM in August 2010 was at non-foreign-exchange banks (9.47 per cent), followed by RDB (8.86 per cent), state-owned banks (6.26 per cent), foreign-exchange private banks (5.30 per cent), joint venture banks (3.79 per cent) and foreign banks (3.53 per cent). The high NIM of non-foreign-exchange banks reflects restrictions on their operations as they are not permitted to facilitate import-export trades that require transactions in foreign exchange. The banks in this group have limited branch networks, are less automated and offer limited financial products. At the other extreme, joint venture and foreign banks are managed by professionals, are equipped with more advanced technology and offer a wide variety of financial products, including products that produce fee-based income, credit cards, debit cards and e-banking. Supported by better reputations, more extensive financial products and international networks, foreign banks can apply strategies to rely more on fee income than other banks. This group of banks also caters to the financial needs of large companies from their home countries. Overstaffing and overextended branch networks are more prevalent among state-owned banks and

Table 2.4 NIM of bank by ownership, 2005–10 (per cent per annum)

Bank Grouping	December 2005	December 2009	December 2010
State-owned banks	5.78	5.81	6.11
Foreign-exchange banks	5.24	5.64	5.35
Non-forex banks	5.35	7.97	9.10
Regional dev. banks	9.56	7.88	8.74
Joint venture banks	3.81	3.77	3.83
Foreign banks	4.78	3.78	3.54
All banks	*5.63*	*5.56*	*5.73*

Source: Bank Indonesia, *Indonesian Banking Statistics*, 3 February 2011.

regional development banks. This is partly because during the long period of past financial repression, public financial institutions were used as political patronage and operated as arm's-length extensions to the government bureaucracy.

Without much success, the central bank has adopted a variety of measures to encourage banks to lower their lending rates. In turn, lower lending rates are expected to reduce the level of undisbursed loans and raise LDR (loan-to-deposit ratio). In December 2010, the LDR of domestic banks ranged between 71.54 per cent (state-owned-bank group) and 79.11 per cent at non-foreign-exchange domestic private banks. The first measure to encourage banks to lower their lending rates was to set the upper limit for deposit rates at 50 basis points above BI's policy rate. The banks, however, were reluctant to lower their deposit rates as they had committed to paying higher than the capped rates. The second attempt by the central bank was to encourage the banks to set prime lending rates as a reference for interest rates on their loans. This also failed as the basic problem of distorted market infrastructure had not been addressed.

There is no information available on the sources of income and profit of the banks. Some of the revenues probably come from interest income on SBI, FASBI, term deposit rates and government bonds and excess liquidity held at the central bank. Another major source of income for the recapitalized banks has been revenue from the repayment of sour loans that have been fully written off from their books.

VIII. Financial performance of banks

Key financial indicators in the Indonesian banking sector have improved markedly since the crisis in 1997. This is due to a combination of a massive injection of sovereign bonds in 1998–99, strong macroeconomic policy and improvements in banking supervision, as well as prudential rules and regulations. Macroeconomic stability allows business and investment to flourish, while improved banking regulation and supervision prevents socially costly bank runs and crisis. As the same time, Indonesia has also benefited from favorable terms of trade due to soaring commodity prices and surging capital inflows. The combination of favorable terms of trade and surging capital inflows has allowed Indonesia to lower its debt-to-GDP ratio and accumulate higher international reserves. The average CAR in the Indonesian banking sector was 17.18 per cent in 2010 (Table 2.5), more than double the required ratio of 8 per cent. Financial institutions in Indonesia were not exposed to toxic assets during the global financial crisis of 2008–09. Because of this, the adverse effects produced by the liquidity crunch brought about by the collapse of Lehman Brothers and the downturn in the advanced economies only slightly affected the financial soundness of Indonesia's financial industry.

With relatively high CAR, it is expected that Indonesian banks will have no difficulty in meeting the capital requirements under Basel III between 2013 and 1 January 2019. As of December 2010, NPL (non-performing loans) was 2.71 per cent, classified loans were 2.36 per cent, ROA (return on assets) was 2.96 per cent and loan-to deposit ratio (LDR) was 75.21 per cent. A combination of increasing reserve requirements and attractive yields from SBI and SUN has encouraged commercial banks to increase placements in these papers. This reduces loanable funds in the banking system, particularly to the risky small and medium enterprises. Rosengard and Prasetyantoko (2011) point out that one fifth of the total assets of Bank Central Asia in 2009 was placed in SBI and another 16.6 per cent in government bonds. In the same year, 26 per cent of Bank Mandiri's assets were invested in government bonds and 8.4 per cent in SBI. This is much higher than the average bank portfolio placements in government bonds in 2011 in Europe, which stood at around 6 per cent. As happened in March 2005, the rise in interest rates depressed bond prices and drove down net asset value (NAV), thus creating losses on bondholders including domestic financial institutions. At the same time, a mutual fund managed by BNI abruptly collapsed and some investment managers failed to use mark-to-market valuations, especially for corporate bonds. The resulting confusion led to a massive redemption of funds from the newly established mutual fund industry (Kenward, 2011).

The relatively small and less sophisticated banks in Indonesia do not have the expertise needed to develop their own technical models to evaluate risks. In addition, as has been discussed earlier, during the past long period of financial repression Indonesia banks did not pay attention to risks. For these reasons, the banks use external ratings-based risk weights, consisting of separate schedules for sovereigns/central banks, commercial banks and the corporate sector. To assess the health of banks, Basel II replaces the CAMELS (capital adequacy, asset quality, management, earnings, liquidity and market-risk sensitivity) with a simple pre-commitment approach. This approach requires a continuous dialogue between banks and the regulatory agency, and for regulators to be more proactive and to carry out frequent examinations to detect problems and to take prompt corrective action to address them.

Table 2.5 Selected indicators of financial health of the banking system 2005–10 (in per cent)

	2005	2006	2007	2008	2009	2010
A. Commercial Banks						
1. Risk-based capital adequacy ratio (CAR)	19.30	21.27	19.30	16.76	17.42	17.18
2. Earnings:						
2.1 Classified earning assets	4.70	3.91	3.03	2.95	2.83	2.36
2.2 Reserve/mandatory asset earningasset write-off reserve	127.25	128.86	191.95	168.12	157.55	130.69
3. Profitability:						
3.1 Return on assets (ROA)	2.55	2.64	2.78	2.33	2.80	2.96
3.2 Operating expenses/ operating income	89.50	86.98	84.05	88.59	86.63	86.74
4. Liquidity:						
4.1 Liquid asset to liquid liabilities ratio	2.64	3.06	3.55	4.49	4.03	3.99
4.2 Loan-to-deposit ratio (LDR)	59.66	61.56	66.32	74.59	72.89	75.21
B. Sharia Banks						
1. CAR	-	-	-	-	-	16.70
2. Earnings:						
Classified earning assets to earning assets	-	-	-	-	-	96.84
3. Profitability:						
3.1 Net operating margin (NOM)	-	-	-	-	-	1,77
3.2 Return on assets (ROA)	-	-	-	-	-	1,59
3.3 Operating expenses/ operating income	-	-	-	-	-	82.38
4. Liquidity:						
4.1 Short-term mismatch	-	-	-	-	-	16.76
4.4 Financing-to-deposit ratio	-	-	-	-	-	87.80
C. Rural Banks						
1. Loan-to-deposit ratio (LDR)	82.00	87.37	80.03	82.54	79.61	79.02
2. Non-performing loans	7.97	9.73	7.98	9.88	6.90	6.12
3. Return on assets	2.96	2.12	2.39	2.61	3.08	3.16
4. Return on equity	26.23	19.25	20.98	22.67	25.08	26.71

Source: *Indonesian Banking Statistics*, Vol. 10, Nr 1, December 2011. www.bi.go.id.

IX.   Financial infrastructure

The objectives of the banking reforms of 1988 were mainly to promote financial deepening and free entry and exit of financial institutions. However, the reforms were not accompanied by stronger financial surveillance, or a suitable framework for preventing and handling banking crises. As a result, a combination of failures in bank regulation and supervision, as well as weak corporate governance and risk management, were key causes of the financial crisis of 1997. One can argue that against a background of weak market infrastructure, related lending to affiliated companies helps overcome the problem of information asymmetry. It improves credit efficiency as bankers have more information on affiliates compared with non-affiliates. Banks can also use internal information to assess the ex-ante risks of investment projects or persuade borrowers to cancel risky projects. On the other hand, the Asian experience during the financial crisis of 1997 indicates that related lending is prone to insider trading and principal-agency problems. Banks tended to evaluate loan applications from affiliates less rigorously than they would in the case of unaffiliated credit applicants.

Indonesia's recent Bank Century scandal, which erupted in October 2008, revealed that the bank lent money under favorable terms to affiliated companies controlled by the bank's principal's owners and family members. These affiliated companies were shells that siphoned cash to the personal offshore accounts of the owners. Their related lending to affiliated companies was also used to loot both public funds as well as deposit insurance funds. One of the affiliated companies of Bank Century was PT Antaboga, which acted as a management company that invested the funds of clients, including some state-owned enterprises. The company had neither a license to operate as a mutual fund nor as an investment management company. Further, PT Bank Century, which held the portfolio of PT Antaboga, was not licensed as a custodian bank (Kenward, 2011).

The financial crisis in Indonesia in 1997 also came about because of violations of the net open position (NOP) regulations. As a result, banks and non-bank corporations borrowed heavily in the short term from international markets, with loans denominated in foreign currencies, to finance long-term loans denominated in Rupiah, mainly extended to affiliates. At the time, foreign borrowing was attractive as it allowed borrowers to take advantage of the low interest rates prevailing on the international market under the pegged exchange rate system. It was perceived that there was no exchange rate risk under such an exchange rate system. Some of the external borrowings were used to finance long-term investment projects in the non-traded sector of the economy, such as real estate. Such practices resulted in maturity and currency mismatches. The experience gained from the 1997 financial crisis indicates that the poor quality of bank assets was partly due to conflicts of interest between different businesses within the same business groups.

As pointed out earlier, in rebuilding the banking system following its collapse in 1997, the government has created the basis for a sound financial system, including reform of the legal and judicial infrastructure and the accounting system to comply with the 25 Basel core principles and international standards to improve the functioning, stability and governance of the financial system. New institutions were established between 2000 and 2008 to modernize the payment system, protect small depositors and stabilize the financial system.

The basic ingredients of market infrastructure are, however, still in the making, including adequate legal and accounting systems to protect private property rights at least cost and to obtain high-quality information so as to minimize market asymmetries. All these things are necessary for the development of an efficient market with low transaction costs. The legal reforms introduced to date have not significantly improved things as regards the enforcement of business contracts and protection of property and creditor rights, or to make it possible to define, pledge and quickly execute collateral. The World Bank (2010c), in a report on the Observance of Standards and Codes (ROSC) on implementation of Corporate Government in Indonesia, makes it clear that Indonesia still lags in some key areas. Recovery rate is below 15 per cent, the cost of bankruptcy procedure is about 18 per cent of the estate, enforcement of contracts takes about 570 days and the costs are about 123 per cent of the claim. It takes between 5 to 6 years to resolve bankruptcies in Indonesia. As economic agents cannot rely on the legal system to execute contracts and enforce seizure of collateral pledged by defaulters, even reputable, world-class institutions, such as Citibank N.A., allegedly resort to use of debt collectors to recover overdue loans. The high cost of gathering information results in an adverse selection of bank customers and raises net interest margins and lending rates.

There have been some improvements in the regulation and supervision of the financial sector, including banks, so as to correct market failures. But, scandals and failures of financial institutions, including banks, continue to occur, such as the Bank Bali case in 2000 and the Bank Century scandal in 2008, as well as successive scandals in the mutual funds industry between 2003 and 2008. These scandals indicate that the enforcement capacity of bank regulators remains weak and still strongly influenced by the government for not strictly applying the rules and regulations for certain troubled banks. In an environment of weak financial supervision, banks developed a variety of risky new products, many of them denominated in foreign currencies, which made financial institutions more vulnerable to short-term capital flows. The social and fiscal costs of such crises and scandals are high.

Adoption of Basel core principles and standards

To some extent, the revised regulatory framework has strengthened the capitalization of the banking system, reduced the level of state intervention in the financial system, and facilitated market-based regulation. On capital adequacy, the country uses risk-based-capital guidelines for all banks as suggested by the Basel standards. The capital adequacy ratio is the key indicator of a bank's solvency and resilience. As pointed out earlier, at present, the Indonesian banking system is on Basel I. Basel II requires a bank's risk assets ratio to be 8 per cent.

At this level of equity, bank debt is 92 per cent, giving a gearing/leverage ratio of 92/8 or 11.5. At the same time, Basel II changes the practice of bank supervision from compliance-checking towards risk-oriented procedures. On 12 September 2010, the Basel Committee on Banking Supervision announced a new package, known as Basel III, to strengthen the regulation, supervision and risk management of the banking system (BCBS, 2010). Basel III will gradually introduce a new solvency measure, the leverage ratio, defined as Tier I capital over weighted on and off balance sheet assets.

Building on three principles, Basel III is more comprehensive than Basel I and II. The first principle is to reduce the pro-cyclicality problem, the second to ensure the soundness of not only individual banks but also the entire financial system, and the third to mitigate the 'too-big-to-fail' problem by forcing banks to bear the costs of the failures they impose on society. To achieve these objectives, Basel III introduces a combination of new micro – and macro – prudential reforms to address both institutions and system-level risks. To minimize transition costs, the Basel III requirements will be phased in gradually between 1 January 2013 and 1 January 2019.

Basel III was endorsed by the Meetings of Heads of State of the G20 countries in Seoul on 11–12 November 2010. It is, however, mainly designed for banks in advanced industrial economies with mature and well-developed financial markets and good legal system. It primarily covers standards and regulations on shadow banks and complicated derivatives which do not exist in the emerging economies. Rules on complex securitization, such as collateralized debt obligations (CDO), are irrelevant to Indonesia as the financial system in this country is still centered on banks that continue to rely on traditional, less sophisticated deposits and loans. To build effective and efficient financial markets, Basel III strongly recommends the use of credit rating and credit scoring systems and stress testing. These, however, are difficult to implement in emerging economies. This is because of weaknesses in market infrastructure arising from a combination of relatively weak legal and accounting systems, limitations on data availability and the dominant role of state-owned enterprises, including in the financial system. State-owned banks and enterprises in these countries are implicitly guaranteed by their owners as they are the implementers of government industrial policies. Meanwhile, private banks are intertwined with their business affiliates. Laws and regulations are difficult to enforce against state banks and state-owned enterprises, as well as politically well-connected business groups.

According to Walter (2011), in the micro prudential sphere Basel III significantly increases risk coverage with a focus on areas that were most problematic during the global financial crisis in 2008.[7] To mitigate the 'too-big-to-fail' problem, Basel III tightens the definition of capital with a strong focus on common equity, the highest quality component of a bank's capital. This forces banks to bear the costs of the failures they impose on society. The regulation intrudes a leverage ratio to serve as a backdrop to the risk-based framework and global liquidity standards to address short-term and long-term liquidity mismatches. At the same time micro-regulation enhances the Pillar 2 supervisory review process and Pillar 3's market discipline, particularly for trading and securitization activities.

Table 2.6 shows that there are three components of bank capital under Basel III, namely: (1)minimum common equity requirement, (2) a conservative buffer and (3) a countercyclical buffer. The countercyclical buffer promotes the build-up of capital in good times that can be drawn down in periods of stress. This partly corrects the inherently pro-cyclical capital regulation and mark-to-market accounting ruling. The requirement for a conservative buffer has system-wide benefits by preventing the excessive build-up of debt across the banking system during boom times. The new micro and macro prudential rules of Basel III will significantly raise banking capital requirements. The three components of bank capital should be raised from a combination of raising capital on the financial markets and restricting discretionary payments, such as dividends, share buybacks and bonuses to shareholders, employees and other capital providers. The restriction of discretionary distributions of bank earnings will shift the risks as much as possible from depositors to shareholders and employees of the banks.

Basel III raises the minimum common equity requirement to 4.5 per cent of risk-weighted assets (RWA) from 2 per cent under Basel II. In addition, banks are required to hold another 2.5 per cent of RWA as a capital conservation buffer to face economic stresses. Further, Basel III requires banks to create a countercyclical buffer of between 0 per cent and 2.5 per cent of RWA during periods of excess credit growth. In total, therefore, banks need to maintain a common minimum required equity ratio of 7 per cent of RWA. The Tier 1 minimum capital requirement is increased from 4 per cent to 6 per cent of RWA to improve the solvency of commercial banks. The total Tier 1 capital that must be maintained by a bank is, therefore, equal to 8.5 per cent of RWA. The total capital requirement of banks increased from 8 per cent of RWA under Basel II to 10.5 per cent under Basel III (Table 2.6). But, 'there remains the more difficult (if not impossible job) of setting accurate risk weight against which to measure capital' (Scott, 2011).

The countercyclical capital buffer under Basel III results in capital adequacy ratio (CAR) being high during a boom period and low during a sluggish period. The capital buffer, therefore, should be built during times of economic growth to be used as a cushion to absorb losses in times of stress. This ruling corrects the inherently pro-cyclicality of the capital regulation and mark-to-market accounting of Basel II that could precipitate an unnecessary crisis. The countercyclical capital buffer serves two purposes. First, to allow banks to grant credit during periods of stress, therefore preventing a sudden drop in bank lending and the amplification of economic cycle through the banking system, thereby pushing the real economy deeper into recession. The second purpose is to dampen credit growth or to act as a brake on bank lending that can cause asset price bubbles as its accumulation raises cost to the banking system. In reaction to capital shortages, banks can also reduce investment in risky assets in favor of safer investments, rather than raising additional capital.

Table 2.6 Strengthening capital framework: From Basel II to Basel III

In percentage of risk-weighted assets	Capital Requirements							Additional Macroprudential Overlay	
	Common equity			Tier 1 Capital		Total capital		Countercyclical buffer	Additional loss-absorbing capacity for SIFIs*
	Minimum	Conservation buffer	Required	Minimum	Required	Minimum	Required	Range	
Basel II Memo:	2 Equivalent to around 1% for an average international bank under the new definition			4 Equivalent to around 2% for an average international bank under the new definition		8			
Basel III New definition and calibration	4.5	2.5	7.0	6.0	8.5	8	10.5	0–2.5	Capital surcharge for SIFIs?

Source: Caruana, J. 2010. 'Basel III: towards a safer financial system'. A paper delivered at the Third Santander InternationalBanking Conference. Madrid 15 September.

Note: *Modalities to be defined.

The countercyclical capital buffer is relevant to an open and export-oriented emerging economy, such as Indonesia. Being located on the ring of fire and the Asia-Australia plate, Indonesia is also prone to natural calamities such as the devastating tsunami of December 2004 and regular volcanic eruptions. Indonesia is a recipient of large short-term capital inflows, which are prone to sudden stops and reversals. Indonesia's export of raw materials and labor-intensive manufactured products are inherently sensitive to the global business cycle. The effects can be positive and negative through the goods market (exports and imports), labor market and international capital market. When industrial countries grow rapidly, emerging economies experience favorable shocks from the rise in demand and international prices of their exports of energy, raw materials and foodstuffs, as well as labor remittances. The cost of overseas borrowing falls in line with improvements in the rating of sovereign bonds and during times marked by low interest rate policy in the advanced countries. For example, prior to the global financial crisis of 2007–09, and when the advanced countries adopted quantitative easing monetary policy to overcome the crisis. Currency realignments or movements in exchange rates of leading convertible currencies can have important effects on the prices of exports and imports, and the balance sheets of economic units, including the public sector and financial institutions in emerging economies.

A combination of higher capital ratios and tighter regulations under Basel III will reduce the capacity of the banking system to supply credit to the economy. This is particularly true for emerging economies with higher risks resulting from less sophisticated information and legal systems.

Reducing insider trading

The transfer of ownership of domestic private banks from conglomerates to foreign investors and the removal of controlling shareholders and managers found to be 'unfit and improper' have improved the human resources of Indonesia's banks, their corporate culture and the image of domestic private banks, as well as the use of their loans. Bank managers are now under pressure to adhere to strict norms of internal risk management and earnings. Lending to affiliated companies in the same group is now being replaced by credit expansion to non-group borrowers, including small and medium enterprises. Household indebtedness has increased markedly with the rapid expansion of consumer credit, including the use of credit cards, car and motorcycle loans and housing loans.

The improvements that have taken place in the implementation of prudential rules and regulations have helped reduce the risk of (1) uncompensated wealth transfers, particularly fraud and outright theft, (2) incompetence and (3) negligence on the part of bank owners and managers. However, the preference for Indonesian nationals for management and key positions in state-owned banks limits the mobilization of highly qualified bankers. CEO positions in these banks are reserved for political appointees, often without any knowledge of the banking business. A new bankruptcy law was passed in 2000 to replace the antiquated law inherited from the colonial era. The Banking Law of 1998 also addressed the connected lending of domestic private banks, which was one of the causes of the crisis in 1997–98, and imposed strong liquidity management rules. Gradually, Indonesia has developed a prudential framework for the financial sector that, among other things, includes disclosure standards, stringent rules for loan classification and provisioning, stricter application of rules on connected lending and on banks' exposure to foreign-exchange rate risks and clear procedures for correction of liquidity solvency problems.

The adoption of the Basel core principles and standards to a radically different regulatory framework is not sufficient to build effective bank supervision. Implementation and enforcement of the new prudential rules and regulations required by the new institutional environment are the most critical and difficult parts of the reforms. Implementing the new Basel II and Basel III standards requires new technology, innovation and skilled personnel and expertise in both the regulatory agencies as well as the banks. The relaxed credit culture of the borrowers as regards the timely repayment of loans has to be changed. The culture became relaxed partly because of relatively easy access to debt rescheduling and forgiveness during the past, heavily politicized era of financial repression. The legal and accounting systems in Indonesia continue to be underdeveloped as regards the proper application of the laws and regulations, enforcement of contracts and the punishing of defaulting borrowers. Without a strong legal system and reliable, up-to-date and comprehensive information, the market cannot work effectively and efficiently. Given such a system, it will also be impossible to mitigate certain types of banking crisis as it is difficult to enforce the seizure of collateral pledged by defaulters. Because of this, pledged collateral is unable to perform its role as a guarantor of the credit.

A combination of weaknesses in the market infrastructure, credit programs and the ownership structure of the banks makes it more difficult to change banking practices that arose from the long era of financial repression and connected lending. As responsibility for risks under credit programs was assumed by the government, there was no incentive for managers of the lending banks to monitor and manage risk, to encourage transparency in corporate reporting or to provide economically relevant information. Both the lending banks and the supervisors were more interested in verifying credit delivery based on the intended purpose according to Bank Indonesia regulations. As credits were allocated based on non-interest rate criteria and not always on economic considerations, the supervisors classified loans based on repayment of the credit rather than on the creditworthiness of the borrowers or the market value of the pledged collateral. Such inefficient non-price allocation of financial resources resulted in poor asset quality and a high level of non-performing loans. State-owned banks frequently have to provide a large volume of loans to non-bank, state-owned enterprises operating under soft budget constraints. Banks owned by large business conglomerates only lend to themselves and their business associates. State-owned banks and those owned by well-connected business groups use their political clout to escape regulatory and market discipline. Distorted, unreliable and incomplete information that only becomes available following a time lag means that the market cannot work effectively and efficiently.

The handling of the PT Bank Century collapse in October 2008 shows that the quality of bank supervision is still relatively weak and the legal lending limit regulations are not stringently enforced. This case also indicates that the authorities lack operating procedures for handling problem banks. CAMEL-style sets of indicators for individual institutions are not available. Both the FSSF (the Financial System Stability Forum) and LPS (the Deposit Insurance Company) rely solely on stress tests designed by the central bank based on incomplete and outdated information and unrealistic scenarios. Before Bank Century was transferred to the LPS in October 2008, Bank Indonesia provided lender-of-last resort facilities to Bank Century against collateral of questionable quality. This violates the Bagehot principle: 'lend freely at a high rate against good collateral'. Neither the FSSF nor the LPS have supervisory power over banks and they rely solely on Bank Indonesia for information on the financial circumstances of insured banks. The LPS has no direct access to the computer systems of insured banks or to the detailed structure of their deposits. So, if something goes wrong, it cannot act rapidly to transfer insured deposits to bridge banks or to other institutions.

Successive booms, busts, frauds and scandals in the newly developed mutual funds industry between 2003 and 2009 indicate weakness in regulation and supervision as well as in interagency coordination, particularly between Bank Indonesia and Bapepam-LK (Capital Markets and Financial Institutions Supervisory Board). First introduced to Indonesia in June 1996, the mutual fund industry began to flourish in 2002thanks to the selling of its holding of recap bonds by Bank Danamon to an investment manager and Citibank, which actively acted as sales agent. Fixed-income mutual funds that invest at least 80 per cent of their asset in debt securities are the major market-makers for the Indonesian mutual fund industry. They are attractive to investors because of an exemption from 20 per cent withholding tax on interest income for newly created funds.

The bust occurred in November 2003 following rumors of massive redemptions from one of the leading mutual funds because of a lack of clarity in asset pricing and mark-to-market. The frauds and scandals that have since occurred include the selling of fictitious mutual funds to investors by Bank Global in 2004, while PT SarijayaPernama misused client accounts and falsified reports on its net adjusted working capital in 2008. As noted earlier, without permission from Bank Indonesia, Bank Century acted as custodian bank and marketer of mutual fund products for its affiliate, PT Antaboga Delta Sekuritas. It turned out that the Bapepam-LKhad never granted approval for Antaboga's products and the money went directly to the owners of Bank Century (Kenward, 2011).

To further prevent insider trading and to upgrade the financial soundness of the banks and improve their corporate governance, Bank Indonesia issued a regulation on 13 July 2012 that introduces bank ownership restrictions. The regulation sets a limit of 40 per cent ownership of the share capital of a bank by a corporate entity, including banks and NBFIs. The maximum limits for non-financial corporate entities, individual *shariah* banks and individuals in conventional banks are, respectively, 30 per cent, 25 per cent and 20 per cent. An individual investor can own 25 per cent of the share capital of a *sharia* bank. Bank Indonesia can provide a special exemption for qualified investors (domestic and foreign) to own up to 99 per cent of an Indonesian bank. The exemption will only be given to those that have attained adequate bank health ratings (BHR) and adequate good corporate governance (GCG) ratings. The ratings, based on a scale of one to five, will be conducted annually starting from December 2013. Those in Tiers 1 or 2 (the healthiest ratings) will be exempted until the next rating period. The healthy banks must, among other things, have been publicly listed for at least 5 years and have sold at least 20 per cent of their share capital, and have a minimum 6 per cent of Tier 1 capital. Such banks must also receive a good recommendation from the supervisory authority. Banks in Tier 3 or lower must divest their stake according to the new regulation with a transition period of up to 2019. Public sector banks (state-owned and Regional Development Banks) and LPS (the Deposit Insurance Company) are exempt from this ownership regulation.

Accounting standards

To comply with international standards, new accounting standards for the banking industry were introduced in 2001 and revised in 2008. To upgrade the relatively underdeveloped auditing profession, the government liberalized accounting services by allowing greater penetration of international accounting firms and foreign accountants in the domestic market. At present the accounting standard has not captured information on legal lending limits to internal parties and others related to party transactions, consolidated financial statements, employee benefit and derivative transactions. Due diligence and forensic auditing of the collapsed banks in 1997 was mainly done by internationally reputable accounting firms. The new standards upgrade the quality of information, governance and prompt delivery of information to all stakeholders to promote market development, market discipline and prudential lending, and to avoid adverse selection of borrowers. As noted earlier, up-to-date and accurate information required by Basel II includes capacity, character and disclosure of asset quality to assess the financial positions of borrowers and therefore the loan portfolios of banks.

A credit bureau was established in 2006 to encourage growth in consumer finance, including the credit card market, which grew rapidly following the banking reforms. As market competition is so fierce, many individuals obtain credit cards from more than one bank, with the credit limit extended by each bank being typically 4 times monthly income. At the same time, consumer lending for durable goods, including motor car, motorcycles and cell phones, is also booming. Credit information helps mitigate an 'adverse selection' problem so as to reduce the cost of credit that arises when financial institutions make credit decisions without full information on consumer credit: character, willingness of borrowers to repay, capacity of borrowers to repay and the quality of debt collateral. The sharing of information validates the 4 C's of consumer credit as a basis for credit extension.

Financial sector supervisory authority (OJK – Otoritas Jasa Keuangan)

Financial regulation and supervision are designed to correct market failures, with the objective being to ensure the soundness of individual institutions against the risk of losses on their assets. Regulation and supervision of the financial industry can be divided into four segments, namely: (1) macro-prudential to avoid systemic instability or macroeconomic fragility so as to limit the probability of crisis; (2) micro-prudential supervision of individual institutions to mitigate the problem of asymmetric information, (3) business supervision/consumer protection to correct market misconduct and (4) the rules of the game to encourage healthier competition and avoid anticompetitive behavior. Traditionally, Indonesia has adopted a sector-by-sector approach to regulation and supervision: banking industry supervised by the central bank, while non-bank financial institutions, including insurance and pension funds, are supervised by the Ministry of Finance (Bapepam-LK).

As noted earlier, Article 24 of the Bank Indonesia Law (No. 23 of 1999) calls for the establishment of the OJK (*OtoritasJasaKeuangan*) to integrate the existing segmented financial supervision so as to anticipate the increasing integration of the banking, securities and insurance markets, and their respective products and instruments. The OJK has been given over (micro) prudential supervision of the three key segments of the financial sector, namely, banking, insurance and pension funds. After a long delay, the OJK was formally established in July 2012 and has taken over supervision and regulation of non-bank financial institutions (NBFI) and the capital markets on 1 January 2013, and of the banking industry by the end of 2013 and became fully functional on 1 January 2014. At present, Bank Indonesia has signed two Memorandums of Understanding on cross-border banking supervision with the Australian

Table 2.7 Summary of pros and cons of integrating financial sector supervision

Potential Pros	Potential Cons
Easier to achieve efficiency in supervising financial conglomerates	If objectives not clearly specified, may be less effective than sectoral supervisors
Possible economies of scale	Possible diseconomies of scale if organization is too large and difficult to manage
Possibly improved accountability	If objectives not clearly communicated, moral hazard problem could be extended across the entire financial sector
Easier to eliminate duplicities, turf wars	Process of integration may lead to politically or special-interest motivated changes in supervisory framework
Easier to ensure level playing field across market segments	Process of integration, if not managed properly, may lead to loss of key staff or to other problems

Source: Cihak, Martin and Richard Podpiera. 2006. 'Is one watchdog better than three? international experience with integrated financial sector supervision', *IMF Working Paper No. WP/06/57*. March. Table 3, p. 13.

Prudential Regulation Authority (APRA) and the Financial Services Commission of South Korea.

Cihak and Podpiera (2006) have summarized the potential pros and cons of integrating financial sector supervision in 67 countries (Table 2.7). The table identifies five benefits from integration, namely (1) increases efficiency in supervising financial conglomerates, (2) increases economies of scale, (3) improves accountability, (4) eliminates duplication and avoids turf wars among supervisors and (5) ensures the same level playing field across market segments. On the other hand, there are also potential cons to integration, particularly if (1) objectives are not clearly specified, (2) the organization is too large so as to make it difficult to manage, thereby creating diseconomies of scale, (3) moral hazard results if objectives are not clearly communicated, (4) political influence and interests may lead to changes in the regulatory framework and (5) key professional staff may leave institutions if the process of integration is not managed properly.

There is general agreement that the central bank should be involved in macroeconomic surveillance to preserve macroeconomic stability. There are synergies between banking supervision and monetary policy. First, through its daily transactions with market participants as part of its core function of implementing monetary policy, the central bank gathers information about the liquidity needs, solvency and the creditworthiness of individual banks and their clients. Second, the economies of scale and commonalities between banking supervision and other functions of the central bank are substantial and strong. The central bank attracts and retains high-quality personnel as required by its banking supervision function and other central banking tasks. The central bank is also equipped with adequate resources for hiring highly qualified staff.

The Cihak and Podpiera study suggests that full integration of financial supervision will improve the quality of supervision in insurance, pension funds and securities, and critical interaction between these institutions, as well as greater consistency of supervision across sectors. The study also shows that fully integrated supervision is not associated with a significant reduction in supervisory staff. The single agency responsible for financial supervision reduces the need for close coordination among financial authorities, as shown by the Financial Stability Forum. To avoid politicization and interagency rivalry, Kawai and Pomerleano (2011) recommend the appointment of a renowned expert to chair the systemic stability regulatory 'council' that coordinates between the finance minister, the central bank governor and the heads of all the financial supervisors.

For four reasons, 15 leading financial economists of the Squam Lake Group (French et al., 2010, chapter 2) in the United States suggest that the central bank is the natural choice to serve as systemic regulator overseeing the health and stability of the overall financial system. First, through its daily trading activities, the central bank has access to broad flows in the financial system so as to allow it to monitor market events and recognize looming problems in the system. Second, the central bank's mandate to preserve macroeconomic stability is closely connected with the stability of financial system. This requires the provision of an explicit mandate to the central bank. Third, central bank independency allows it to focus on the long-run stability of the financial system. Fourth, through its role as the lender of last resort, the central bank can use its balance sheet as a tool to address systemic financial crises and limit systemic shocks that arise from other financial institutions. To act as systemic regulator, the central bank should be given adequate resources. Along these lines, the United Kingdom has handed bank supervision back to the Bank of England in 2013.

The recommendation of the Squam Lake Group is relevant to Indonesia because of the leading role of the banks in the financial system. As pointed out earlier, pension funds, insurance companies and mutual funds are growing fast, but their share of the financial industry remains small. Investment patterns among institutional investors are mainly focused on short-term assets because their obligations are mainly short term, while the yields on long-term sovereign bonds are relatively low. Meanwhile, pension funds mainly offer short-term defined benefits. In addition, the primary market instruments are still SBI and long-term government bonds.

Deposit insurance

As pointed out earlier, the LPS, a state-owned deposit insurance company, was established in 2004 to protect small depositors and help to insulate the money stock from credit market disruption. This replaced the blanket guarantee that was introduced in January 1998. The scheme covered all deposits with all domestic banks (excluding shareholders' capital, subordinated debt and deposits of insiders and related parties). This guarantee scheme, along with the liquidity supports from the central bank and capital injections from the government, was aimed at restoring public confidence in the banking system so as to reduce the likelihood of deposit withdrawals and bank runs and thereby lead to a reduction in the need for recapitalization. The fiscal cost of the blanket guarantee was expensive as the scheme paid off depositors of financially distressed banks, and supported the absorption of their assets and liabilities. At the same time, the guarantee scheme encouraged moral hazard as with the backing of a blanket guarantee, banks were able to engage in risky activities. The existence of the blanket guarantee eliminated the need for depositors to screen their banks.

A limited level of deposit insurance (coverage up to Rp20 million) was introduced in November 1997 when Bank Indonesia liquidated 16 domestic private banks. This was insufficient to restore public confidence, partly due to the political uncertainty arising from the strong pressure on President Suharto to step down, as well as the reopening of an already closed bank owned by his son. The blanket guarantee scheme introduced on 1 January 1998 gave full protection for all banks' liabilities, raising deposit insurance limits and extended guarantees to non-deposit domestic and foreign liabilities. The scheme was replaced by a limited deposit insurance scheme in 2004, at which time the financial stability forum was also established to address bank resolution in case of crisis. The guarantee on bank liabilities creates contingent liabilities for the government. Liquidity support in the form of placement of government deposits is only available to state-owned banks and Regional Development Banks that have a monopoly over such deposits.

Prior to the crisis in 1997, state-owned banks and some private domestic banks owned by politically well-connected groups (such as PT Bank Summa International and PT Bank Duta, which failed in 1991) enjoyed implicit guarantee from the government. Explicit and implicit government guarantees are akin to deposit insurance. During the global financial crisis of 2008–09, the amount of deposit per depositor guaranteed by the LPS was raised from Rp100 million to Rp2 billion in October 2008. The scheme is mainly financed by deposit-taking institutions.

To further increase market discipline the central bank sets the upper limit on interest rates on deposits offered by banks that are eligible for deposit insurance. The cap prevents competition to attract deposits by offering extremely high deposit rates.

Financial System Stability Forum

To monitor, evaluate and prevent systemic risks, the government established the Financial System Stability Forum (FSSF) on 31 December 2005. The FSSF is a dedicated inter-agency committee to support the development of a macro-prudential function to prevent the build-up of systemic financial risks that could endanger financial system stability. The FSSF coordinates policy through information sharing and discussions, but responsibility for policy decisions and implementation is retained by the individual agencies. The BIS and IMF define macro-prudential policies as 'those policies that use primarily prudential tools to limit systemic or system-wide financial risks'.[8] At the ministerial level, the FSSF is chaired by the Minister of Finance (fiscal authority), while its membership includes the Governor of Bank Indonesia (monetary authority), the Chairman of OJK (*OtoritasJasaKeuangan*) and the Head of the Deposit Insurance Company. On 1 January 2014, the banking departments of Bank Indonesia and Bapepam-LK merged in the newly established OJK.

There are forums at the management level and the operational level below the ministerial level. The layers coordinate various supervisory agencies and institutions that are relevant to preserving financial stability. The forums are expected to speed up the handling of financial sector crises so as to ensure the provision of extensive liquidity, support, guarantees on bank liabilities, takeover of non-performing assets and recapitalization of financially distressed institutions. The handling of the Bank Century case in October 2008 indicates that the FSSF failed to facilitate coordination between the various regulators, and was ineffective in monitoring systemic risks. Bank Century was a small and not systemically important bank that failed not because of its dealing in derivatives or US subprime mortgages, but rather because it was continuously allowed by the central bank to violate prudential rules and regulations, and ended up being looted by its owners. The Minister of Finance openly complained that she had not been provided with complete information on the financial problems of the failed Bank Century from the central bank.

Conclusion

In terms of assets and branch networks, the commercial banking industry constitutes the core of the financial system in Indonesia. Despite the rapid growth in their assets, the role of non-bank financial institutions is still relatively small and only beginning to pose a competitive challenge to the banks. The leading NBFIs consist of insurance companies, pension funds and mutual funds. Indonesia has no postal saving bank that can mobilize the savings of small savers at least cost. Bank operations are mainly concentrating in traditional deposit taking and short-term lending and less involved with the capital and bond markets and derivatives. The banking market is segmented because of government rules designed to protect public sector banks, and the interlocking ownership, management and businesses of privately owned domestic banks. The public sector banks consist of 5 state-owned banks and 26 Regional Development Banks that are jointly owned by provincial and regency (county) governments. The role of the public sector banks is still dominant, both in the deposit and credit markets, because of their extensive branch networks, broad geographical coverage and exclusive monopoly on public sector financial transactions.

The government adopted a restructuring strategy consisting of eight components for the commercial bank industry. The first component was to restore public confidence and stop destabilizing bank runs by introducing a blanket guarantee for both bank deposits and liabilities. Second, addressing the illiquidity and solvency problems of the banks by injecting massive liquidity credits from Bank Indonesia, the takeover of dud assets and injecting large amounts of sovereign bonds to allow banks to reduce NPLs and meet the CAR of 8 per cent. Third, ending financial repression and government-directed lending policy. Fourth, establishing an independent and integrated financial sector supervisor and upgrading banking regulations and supervision in line with Basel standards. Fifth, changing the culture and image of the banks by improving their governance, hiring highly qualified management and professionals, and increasing market competition through greater penetration by foreign investors in Indonesian banks. Sixth, developing the secondary bond market. Seventh, creating a bank safety net and the financial stability forum. Eight, limiting shareholding in banks, encouraging mergers and acquisitions. The selling to new owners of taken-over ailing banks during the crisis reduced the family-controlled ownership of the private banks.

Public infrastructure reforms have been introduced since the Asian financial crisis in 1997. Nevertheless, the system remains very weak. Transaction cost is still relatively high as the legal system cannot properly enforce contract and creditor rights and quickly recover collaterals. Enforcement of prudential rules and regulations is insufficient and can cause market failures. The unreliable legal system and lengthy court proceedings have encouraged creditors to the use of thugs and debt collectors. The long bankruptcy process delays the takeover of assets away from inefficient users, write them down to a fair market value and reintroduce them to the productive economy. The inefficiencies of state-owned banks and regional development banks indicate the public sector failures.

Notes

1 Earlier direct government controlled banking, monetary and credit policies are discussed in Nasution (1983) and Woo, Glassburner and Nasution (1994).
2 Bank Indonesia's Regulation (PBI) No. 14/22/PBI/2012 concerning Credit or Financing and Technical Assistance for Developing Micro, Small, and Medium Enterprises.
3 The Monetary and Capital Markets Department of the IMF. 2009. *Evaluation of technical assistance on bank supervision by long-term experts in Asia*. Washington, D.C.: IMF. June 1.
4 Bank Indonesia Regulation No. 14/26/PBI/2012 on Core Capital Requirement for Banks Based on Business Activity and Branch Network.
5 In 2000, the Province of East Timor seceded to become the independent Republic of Timor-Leste. The number of provinces in Indonesia has since increased to 33

but the number of RDBs remains the same as the newly established provinces share ownership of the banks with their former 'mother' provinces.

6 Such as Carbo-Valverde et al. (2005), Demirguc-Kuntand Huizinga (1999), Saunders and Schumacher (2000) and Tatum (2012).

7 Such as trading book exposures, counter-party credit risk and securitization activities.

8 FSB, IMF and BIS. 2011. *Macroprudentialtools and frameworks.* Update to G-20 Finance Ministers and Central Bank Governors. February.

3 Developing Indonesia's mutual fund industry

A tale of booms, busts, frauds and scandals

Lloyd R. Kenward

I. Introduction and overview of developments

Indonesia's mutual fund industry is a small, but fascinating microcosm of the country's entire financial sector. Since legal inception in 1995, it has proven to be highly innovative and very popular with investors, with net assets growing at roughly 40 per cent per annum during the past decade or so. But the boom has also been subject to busts, scandals and outright fraud, often with the regulators struggling to catch up. Booms and busts seem to be normal market developments in Indonesia, but the scandals and fraud are a different matter. They get to the heart of the problems of financial sector development in Indonesia, and their high international profile has re-enforced the country's image as a risky place to do business. This chapter looks at this industry with a view to policies that would contribute to the development of a strong, sustainable financial sector.

Mutual funds are an important investment vehicle in the diversification of a financial system, allowing relatively small investors to hold diversified portfolios of financial assets.[1] The investor buys 'units' in a fund comprising various financial assets, the range of which is determined by the fund's charter (or prospectus). Normally, the assets are re-priced daily in accordance with market movements, and costs are deducted to obtain the fund's 'Net Asset Value' (NAV or NAB in Bahasa Indonesia), which determines the price when the investor wishes to sell.

The Capital Market Law of 1995 provides the legal basis for mutual funds (*reksa dana*) in Indonesia. They were first introduced in June 1996 by PT Danareksa, but remained a minor financial instrument through 2001 (Figure 3.1). Business began to boom in 2002 when mobilized funds soared from less than Rp8 trillion at end-2001 to almost Rp86 trillion in 2003, just before the industry's first crisis. Important catalysts for the rapid expansion appear to have been: Citibank, which originated banks' acting as sales agents in 2000; and Bank Danamon, which introduced the innovation of selling bank recap bonds (used to recapitalize banks during the 1997–98 crisis) to an investment manager. PANIN Bank, BNI and several others quickly followed suit and the industry was launched.

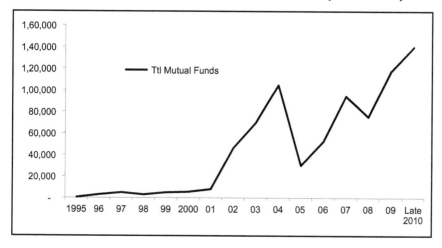

Figure 3.1 Total net asset value of mutual funds (in billions of Rupiah)

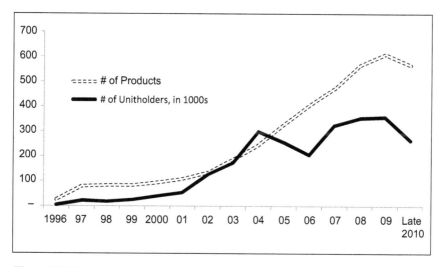

Figure 3.2 Number of products and unit holders

Since inception, the industry has been popular and innovative, despite being highly cyclical.[2] The number of funds increased significantly through 2009 (Figure 3.2); new types of funds have developed rapidly (Figures 3.3 and 3.4); and the number of investment managers expanded markedly, at least through 2007.

Nevertheless, the industry remains small by global and regional standards. As pointed out in World Bank 2006 (pp. 89–90), East Asia accounts for a small portion (5 per cent) of the global market for mutual funds and East Asia's contribution is highly concentrated in Hong Kong and Korea. Indonesia's market share is a tiny fraction of Hong Kong or Korea's, and well behind

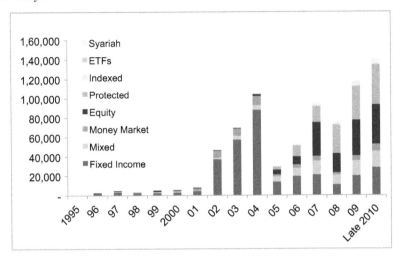

Figure 3.3 NAV of mutual funds, by type of fund (in billions of Rupiah)

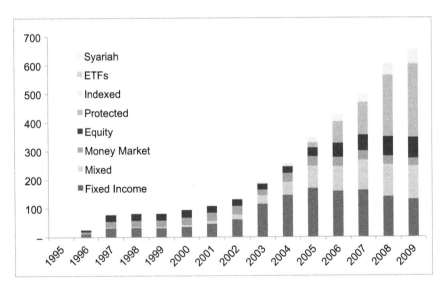

Figure 3.4 Number of products, by type of fund

Malaysia and Thailand. It is also a small component of the Indonesian financial system.[3] As of mid-2010, total net assets in Indonesia were equivalent to only 5½ per cent of M2, which is widely believed to be the main source of funds that have migrated into *reksa dana*. In itself, this shift of funds from M2 to *reksa dana* has important implications for financial sector development in Indonesia; it represents a welcome broadening of the financial system away from its traditional heavy dependence upon commercial banks.

II.   The booms and busts

After a strong expansion in 2002, the industry had its first crisis in the second half of 2003. In September of that year,[4] a major foreign-owned investment management company began voluntarily to price its bond portfolios at market prices. Inevitably, NAVs of some fixed income funds (which accounted for about 90 per cent of all mutual funds at the time) began to fluctuate. Investors were spooked, having grown accustomed to steadily rising asset values (see Box 3.1).[5] The value of assets under management fell precipitously through year-end,[6] although stability was restored in short order by means reported in Box 3.1. To put the overall magnitude of the crisis in perspective, the drop in NAVs and shareholders was barely enough to be visible in annual data (see Figures 3.1 and 3.2).

But the market was again thrown into turmoil in March 2005. On this occasion, the event was driven essentially by the market, not by the technicalities of pricing practices. Rising interest rates during the first half of 2005 depressed bond prices, which drove down NAVs. Investors became nervous and their redemptions of fixed income assets into a thin market further weakened bond prices. The situation was complicated by the abrupt collapse of a fund managed by Bank Negara Indonesia (BNI) and by some investment managers still not using mark-to-market valuations, especially for corporate bonds. The resulting confusion caused massive redemptions, on a scale roughly 10 times as large as in 2003.[7] By late 2005, the situation had stabilized, owing in part to actions by the capital market supervisor, Bapepam-LK,[8] and by purchases of government bonds by Bank Indonesia, in April in the amount of Rp6.5 trillion. For its part, in June Bapepam-LK required the use of price ranges for securities traded over-the-counter (i.e. corporate bonds) and this helped to reduce uncertainty in pricing. In July, Bapepam-LK ruled on protected funds, and in December Bapepam-LK sanctioned four investment managers for failing to use reference prices in calculating NAVs (World Bank 2006, p. 98).

Scandals and frauds

Indonesia's mutual fund industry has been rocked by several scandals in the past several years. The first was sizable, but looked like an isolated incident at the time. In the second half of 2004, the officers of a small bank, Bank Global, reportedly mobilized Rp600 billion (US$60 million) by selling fictitious mutual funds to depositors.[9]

The second,[10] around the end of 2008, featured the Royal Bank of Scotland (RBS; formerly ABN AMRO), PNM Investment Management and PT Bakri Capital Indonesia (BCI). RBS stood accused of fraud worth about Rp1.4 trillion concerning the sale of protected mutual funds to PNM, which used them to buy repos from BCI. According to industry sources, these were actually a cascading series of repos that eventually collapsed. In early 2009, a debt restructuring agreement was reached between PNM and BCI and, reportedly included principal repayments by PNM to RBS.

The third, also near the end of 2008, was a string of alleged frauds by the President Commissioner, Herman Ramli,[11] of one of the country's larger security houses, Sarijaya Pernama ('Sarijaya Named In Securities Scam'. Jakarta Post 8 January 2009). Bapepam-LK alleged misuse of client accounts by Herman.

Box 3.1   An Industry Bust in Late 2003

On 11 November 2003, a story broke in the Singapore press ('Indo Mutual Funds Face Huge Redemptions'. *The Business Times*) that Indonesia's mutual fund industry was faced with 'massive redemptions' and 'in danger of a meltdown'. The story reported that the country's largest fund manager (Prima Investa, a joint product of Bank Danamon and Mees Pierson Finas Investment Management) had received an emergency loan to cover massive redemptions. Reportedly, Bank Indonesia had instructed banks to drop guaranteed returns on mutual funds, before year-end. In separate reports, fund managers were alarmed by the possibility of plunging bond prices and lack of clarity in asset pricing and mark-to-market practices.

Calming the markets. The response from Jakarta was all by way of damage control, but it was fast and well orchestrated ('Danamon Rebuts Shaking Mutual Fund Industry'. *Bisnis Indonesia*, 12 November). Bapepam-LK quickly affirmed that that the underlying assets of the mutual fund (i.e. its government and corporate bonds) were strong. Bank Danamon's management confirmed large redemptions (that funds under management had fallen from Rp11.4 trillion in September to Rp2.5 trillion in November), but pointed out that all redeemed funds had returned to Bank Danamon. Also, they denied that the redemptions were the result of outside pressure; in June, new bank management had placed the product under review and come to the conclusion that changes were necessary in the relationship with Prima Investa. For his part, the President Director of Mees Pierson denied dumping any bonds, but acknowledged bond sales back to Danamon. The Bapepam-LK Chairman issued calming words, while Bank Lippo expressed interest in buying the underlying assets, if they were commercially profitable.

As further damage control ('Capital Market Watchdog Moves to Calm Mutual Fund Industry'. *The Jakarta Post*, 14 November), the Bapepam-LK Chairman denied reports of massive (Rp30 trillion) redemptions, citing outflows of only Rp4–5 trillion in past weeks. Wisely, he reminded investors of the risks of investing in mutual funds and pointed to the importance of mark-to-market valuations, which he announced would be one part of Bapepam-LK's plan to tighten regulation of the industry. In further support, the Bank Indonesia Governor announced that Bank Mandiri and Deutsche Bank stood ready to buy bonds in the event of redemptions by mutual fund customers ('Mandiri & Deutsche to Become Standby Buyers of Bonds'. *Bisnis Indonesia*, 15 November).

The markets responded well. During the last 2 months of 2003, outstanding amounts of mutual funds dropped by Rp13 trillion (7%), but rebounded immediately in early 2004. All in all, the authorities' response was an impressive public relations victory, but only as a near-term step to stabilize the situation. The root problems were not addressed, and would return to haunt the industry repeatedly over the next several years.

Consequently, it requested that the Indonesia Stock Exchange suspend Sarijaya activities and that PT Kliring Penjaminan Efek Indonesia and central custodian PT Kustodian Sentral Efek Indonesia freeze all assets belonging to the broker and its clients. In its statement, Bapepam-LK said Sarijaya had falsified reports on its net adjusted working capital, in the amount of at least Rp245 billion

(US$22.5 million) of investors' money. Top executives of the company claimed that the fraud had been solely committed by the owner-broker. The Bapepam-LK chairman responded that company management were at fault for being controlled by the owner. Herman was taken into custody on 24 December 2008 and several employees were subsequently arrested ('Police Arrest More Suspects in Massive Sarijaya Scandal'. Jakarta Globe, March 20, 2009).

Box 3.2 Still more scandals and fraud in the mutual funds industry

In late 2009, Indonesia's mutual fund industry suffered its second major scandal in two years. This one was associated with the controversial—and highly politicized—bailout of Bank Century by Bank Indonesia (see Patunru and von Luebke, 2010). As background, in 1989 Robert Tantular founded Bank Century Intervest Corporation (Bank CIC), and in December 2004 it merged with Bank Danpac and Bank Pikko to form Bank Century. Somehow Mr. Tantular managed to become majority owner of Bank Century despite having failed Bank Indonesia's fit and proper test.

Apparently after several years of shaky operations, Bank Century began to encounter more serious financial problems in 2008. In response, Bank Indonesia summoned Mr. Tantular on 15 September 2008, and asked him to take personal responsibility for Bank Century's operations. This included signing a Letter of Commitment (with two other majority owners) to ensure the bank would pay its debts. Nevertheless, around the end of November, Bank Century encountered serious liquidity problems. It quickly became insolvent, resulting in effective nationalization and eventually a large (US$750 million) bailout from the central bank.[a] Around the same time, BI reported Robert Tantular and two other co-owners to the National Police for alleged financial crimes.

These banking problems spilled over into the mutual funds industry in a strange way. According to press reports, Bank Century was marketing mutual funds for PT Antaboga Delta Sekuritas Indonesia,[b] a mid-sized securities company with offices in Jakarta, Medan, North Sumatra and Bali. However, according to the Head of Bapepam-LK, that institution never granted approval of Antaboga's mutual fund products,[c] and the money went directly to the owners of Bank Century. In total, the alleged fraud is reported to have involved some Rp1.4 trillion (US$137.37 million).

In January 2010, the Jakarta High Court sentenced Mr. Tantular to 5 years in prison and Rp50 billion in fines. In May 2010, the Supreme Court added another 4 years to Mr. Tantular's term and ordered him to pay Rp100 billion (US$11 million) in fines. Antaboga's president director, Hendro Wiryanto, and two other executives (director Anton Tantular and commissioner Hartawan Aluwi) were questioned by police and announced as suspects in the case. However, the three escaped, reportedly to Singapore. Anton is the brother of Robert, and Robert and Hartawan are sons-in-law of Sukanta Tanudjaja, the former owner of textile giant PT Great River International.

The other two co-owners of Bank Century were Hesham al Warraq (a citizen of Saudi Arabia) and Rafat Ali Rizvi (a British citizen of Pakistani origin).

Both successfully eluded the authorities, despite an Interpol arrest warrant. On 24 November 2009, British newspaper *The Telegraph* reported that the two were not fighting claims of fraud. Rather, they argued that they were not the beneficiaries, and they blamed Robert Tantular. Mr. Rivzi (who was then living in the UK) claimed to be the victim of a 'xenophobic campaign to put the blame for the collapse onto the bank's foreign owners'. On 9 February 2010, *The Telegraph* reported that Interpol had issued an arrest warrant for the two at Indonesia's request. In the same article, *The Telegraph* reported that Mr. Rivzi was splitting his time between the UK and Singapore, noting that neither country has an extradition treaty with Indonesia. In April, lawyers for Mr. Rivzi threatened to sue Interpol for millions in reputational damages unless the 'red notice' issued against him was removed. Press reports indicate that Mr. Rivzi is a multi-millionaire, believed to be worth around $600 million.

In mid-December 2010, the Central Jakarta District Court found the two guilty of corruption, money laundering and looting their bank. They were sentenced to 15 years in absentia and ordered to return Rp3.1 trillion (some US$310 million) or face seizure of their personal assets; the court warned that failure to repay could result in an additional 5 years ('Briton, Saudi Get 15 Years For Bank Century Saga'. *Jakarta Globe*, 16 December 2010).

[a]/In October 2009, Bank Century was re-named Bank Mutiara.
[b]/The symbolism is striking. 'Antaboga' is the serpent god in Balinese Hindu mythology.
[c]/The President of the Indonesian Mutual Fund Managers Association (APRDI) stated that Antaboga is not registered with that Association (vivanews.com, 3 December 2008).

Source: various press reports.

In late 2010, another scandal may have been headed off at an early stage in an encouraging display of cooperation between Bank Indonesia and Bapepam-LK. Press reports indicate that Bank Bumiputera was acting as a selling agent for questionable financial instruments known collectively as Kontrak Pengelolaan Dana (KPD; Fund Management Contracts) for a company called Natpac Asset Management.[12] BI threatened sanctions because Bank Bumiputera was selling these capital market products without the permission of the central bank. At the same time, Bapepam-LK threatened to revoke Natpac's business license for failure to meet a deadline for placement of counterpart assets into a custodian bank. Allegedly, some Rp200 billion (US$20 million) was involved.

III.   The legal and supervisory structure of the mutual funds industry

Historically Bapepam-LK's responsibility

The highest legal authority for Indonesia's mutual fund industry is the Capital Market Law (No. 8 of 1995), especially Chapter 4 (Articles 18 to 29) which governs the creation and management of mutual funds.[13] Other forms of regulation governing the industry include: government regulations; Minister of Finance decrees; and Bapepam-LK rules. Prior to the introduction of consolidated supervision (see below), Bapepam-LK had responsibility for supervision, and the Chairman of Bapepam-LK reported to the Minister of Finance. Inside Bapepam-LK, the Investment Management Bureau had responsibility for day-to-day monitoring of the mutual funds industry; fraud was handled by the Enforcement Bureau. The Heads of Bureaus reported to the Chairman.

Bank Indonesia's role[14]

Although Bank Indonesia has no responsibility for supervision of mutual funds, it became involved in the process, essentially through the back door. As described above, recent frauds have involved banks, and Bank Indonesia (which had responsibility for bank supervision prior to 2014) has been widely criticized for not preventing mutual fund fraud that involves banks. In reaction, Bank Indonesia responded by tighter supervision of banks' association with capital market instruments. For example, banks cannot market a capital market product without BI's permission. Also and in the specific case of bank-linked products, BI has to clear the bank's selling of any underlying financial instrument whenever there is any change to the bank's risk profile.[15] These developments triggered old institutional rivalries between Bank Indonesia and the Ministry of Finance which made for slow process in regulatory improvements, notwithstanding favourable, top-level relations in recent years. OJK (see below) is one obvious example, but there are others, too. For instance, custodian banks were a point of intersection between the two regulators, and slow negotiations of an MoU were needed before BI could get access to custodian banks data to verify the existence of certain underlying assets of mutual funds.[16]

Traditionally, supervision of Indonesia's mutual funds has reflected Bapepam-LK's general philosophy of emphasizing disclosure and self-regulation. For example, a *reksa dana*'s prospectus contains a great deal of information about its operation, and inspections have tended to focus on compliance with this prospectus. In support, the custodian is expected to report rule violations to Bapepam, with companies' regular reports being the primary monitoring device. In normal circumstances, on-site inspections have been targeted at once every year or so, although this seems to be a difficult target to hit. For large companies, inspections also focus on internal controls, management and sampling the investment manager's portfolio management. Between 2000 and 2005, paid-up capital of investment managers was raised significantly to bring capital requirements more in line with risk;[17] in 2010, it was raised significantly again. As enforcement, Bapepam-LK has imposed sanctions of one form or another,[18] and it has closed sizable numbers of funds over the years.[19]

The transition to OJK

Originally to be established by end-2002, Law No. 3 of 2004 (amending Law No. 23 of 1999 concerning Bank Indonesia) mandated the establishment of a

Consolidated Supervision Authority (*Otoritas Jasa Keuangan*, OJK) by end-2010. This included moving Bapepam-LK from MoF into OJK. In late 2010, Parliamentary Committee XI (on Finance and Banking) agreed that OJK's Board of Commissioners would be vested with their full powers by 1 January 2013. In the event, the non-banking aspects of OJK became operational on that date, and banking supervision was added one year later. At finalization of this paper, it remains to be seen how effective OJK will be, especially in light of experience with the 2008/09 global financial crisis; controversy over the advisability of consolidated supervision;[20] and the magnitude of OJK's challenges, including merging divergent, pre-existing bureaucratic cultures into one new institution. Still, the step has been taken and OJK is the way forward for the indefinite future. Hopefully, OJK will provide the institutional arrangements for better coordination between bank and non-bank supervision, thereby minimizing crises like Bank Century-Antaboga in 2008 (Box 3.2).

IV.   The players in the industry

Investors

Data from Bapepam-LK for end-2009[21] indicate that the vast majority (95 per cent) of *numbers of account holders* are individuals, and virtually all of these are domestic investors. There were over 300,000 unit holders at end-2009, of which almost 290,000 were domestic individuals. Many of these individuals are believed to be high-worth persons, often served through banks' private banking departments; overall, the average holding was around Rp200 million (roughly US$25,000).

Domestic institutions, which have much larger average holdings (almost US$1,000,000), account for most *funds*, approximately 58 per cent of the total. Their total funds are about 50 per cent more than domestic individuals. Foreign institutions are negligible in numbers of funds.

Investment managers

Mutual funds are managed by *Manajer Investasi* (investment management companies), which are securities firms specially licensed by Bapepam-LK for this service. Fund managers work for these investment companies and must be licensed by Bapepam-LK. As of August 2010, there were 94 licensed investment managers, down from a peak of 99 earlier in the year. It's notable that not all investment management companies manage mutual funds, and not all licensed fund managers are 'active'; industry sources indicate 72 companies as of early 2011. These investment managers were offering 604 products, down from 617 early in the year.[22] The fund managers are represented by the Indonesian Mutual Fund Managers Association (*Asosiasi Pengelola Reksa Dana Indonesia*, APRDI). Management of mutual funds is a highly concentrated business in Indonesia. The top 10 managers account for about 80 per cent of the market; among these, the top three (two foreign and one domestic company) account for almost

Table 3.1 Indonesia's 10 largest mutual fund investment managers (ranked by net asset value, as of end-April 2010, in Rp trillions)

Fund manager	No. of Funds	NAV	Market share (%)
Schroder Investment Mgmt Indonesia (UK)	38	27.34	22.9
BNP Paribas Investment Partnersa/ᵃ/ (France)	42	16.26	13.6
Mandiri Investment Mgmt	84	15.31	12.8
Bahana TCW Investment Mgmt	57	9.06	7.6
Manulife Asset Mgmt Indonesia (Canada)	23	8.46	7.1
Batavia Prosperindo Asset Mgmt	66	4.98	4.2
Danareksa Investment Mgmt	69	4.68	3.9
Mega Capital Indonesia	14	4.06	3.4
Panin Securities	33	2.97	2.5
Trimegah Securities	14	2.93	2.5
Total market	1,042	119.30	100.0

Source: Bapepam-LK, cited by the Economist Intelligence Unit.

half (see Table 3.1). At the opposite end of the spectrum, some 20–30 companies are quite small, managing average portfolios of roughly Rp50 billion.

It's notable that the regulator, Bapepam-LK, regularly revokes licenses of investment managers. For example, during 2009 seven licenses were revoked,[23] and there was further consolidation among investment managers in 2010.[24]

Investment managers market their products themselves and indirectly through multiple channels, for example: commercial banks; insurance companies; and brokers. Within the network are Investment Fund Selling Agents (*Agen Penjual Efek Reksa Dana*, APERD) and their sales representatives (*Wakil Agen Penjual Efek Reksa Dana*, WAPERD). The former operate on the basis of a contract with the Investment Manager, and they comprised 26 banks as of end-2009. As for WAPERD, Bapapem-LK granted 2,657 WAPERD licenses in 2009, bringing the total number of WAPERD to 21,152.[25]

The APERD/WAPERD arrangements have come under various criticisms from the World Bank (World Bank 2009, p. 105). First, the Bank notes that there are issues as to who is the regulatory authority. In particular, the sales activity is usually concentrated in a single unit within the bank and that part of the bank – not the entity regulated by Bapepam-LK – supervises the sales activity. As for Bank Indonesia – which supervises the banks – it is unlikely to focus on this peripheral banking business. Issues like this were behind the Bank Global and Bank Century-Antaboga frauds. Second, the World Bank criticized licensing standards for WAPERD as being too lenient, but this criticism has been overtaken by subsequent regulatory changes (see Annex 3.1).

Custodians

A custodial bank acts as a third-party watchdog, providing a first line of defense for investor's assets from illegal activities by a fund manager. Custodial services are provided by strictly licensed banks, with the services including administration; reporting; transfer services; and safekeeping. In Indonesia, the custodian banks are required to be unaffiliated with the investment manager, and they are expected to issue warnings to the investment managers and to report violations to the supervisory authority.[26] As of end-2009, 21 banks were providing custodial services, including for mutual funds, down 1 from a year earlier.[27] Of these, 4 seem to dominate the market for mutual funds. The list of custodian banks in Indonesia includes some well-known names, for example: Deutsche Bank; Niaga CIMB; HSBC; Standard Chartered; and Bank Mandiri. The supervisory authority conducts compliance audits of the custodian banks, for example, 10 of them in 2009.

Securities price valuation institution

Lembaga Penilaian Harga Efek (LPHE) values debt securities and *sukuk* to determine a fair market price. This price serves as a benchmark in the fixed income market, and it provides a valuation price for calculation of daily net asset values. This is important for day-to-day valuation of thinly traded securities, especially corporate bonds and *sukuk*. Without LPHE, these would have no benchmark for pricing, which opens the door to abuse, fraud and crisis as in 2003 and 2005. The Agency was set up in September 2007, and appears to be modeled on the Bond Pricing Agency of Malaysia.

V.   The industry's products

There are eight types of mutual funds available in Indonesia, including three (Indexed, ETFs and Protected) that have only been developed since 2005.[28] The popularity of funds has changed markedly over the past decade, as discussed below (also see Figures 3.2, 3.3 and 3.4).

Fixed income: the original market-maker

This is a mutual fund that invests at least 80 per cent of its assets in debt securities. It proved to be the major market-maker for mutual funds, partly because it offered banks the opportunity to move sizable amounts of recap bonds off their balance sheets and into mutual fund accounts. The most rapid expansion was in the period 2004/05, which was marked by the crisis of 2003 and the crash of 2005. Subsequent expansion has been much more measured, and there was a setback during the global financial crisis of 2007/08. Consequently, fixed income gave up its lead position among mutual funds, having been overtaken by equity funds in 2007 and by protected funds in 2008. The number of fixed income funds peaked in 2005, and has declined substantially (by almost ¼) since then (see Figure 3.3). In late 2010, mutual funds held roughly 5 per cent of total tradable government securities.[29]

Money market

This fund invests only in debt securities with initial maturity of less than 1 year. Its characteristics (like cyclical fluctuations) are very similar to those of fixed income funds, but maturities are shorter-term and their instruments are generally Bank Indonesia Certificates (SBIs). Overall, it is the smallest of the four 'original' funds (fixed, money market, equity and balanced). It's notable that yields are less market-determined than for fixed income funds, being more directly affected by Bank Indonesia's policies on interest rates. In late 2010, mutual funds held about 3 per cent of total outstanding SBIs.[30]

Equity: a late bloomer

This fund invests at least 80 per cent of its assets in equities. It accounted for a small market share until 2003 (Figure 3.3). Since then, it has boomed, increasing by a factor of about 100, notwithstanding a pronounced cyclical downswing during the global crisis of 2007/08. As of late 2010, it was the second-largest type of fund, running just a little behind Protected Funds.

Balanced (mixed): the oldest

This fund invests in equities *and* securities in proportion other than the 80 per cent, mentioned immediately above. It was the first type of mutual fund developed in Indonesia, and has generally expanded at a measured pace, avoiding the boom and bust pattern of most other accounts.

Shariah

These are mutual funds that operate according to Islamic principles of finance, their portfolios comprising only *shariah*-compliant securities (equity and *sukuk*). The instrument was introduced in 2003, and it was the first product innovation after 1996. Initially, it appears to have benefitted from the general wave of popularity in Islamic financing in Indonesia. However, by 2010 the NAB flattened out, at a level that accounts for a small proportion (about 3½ per cent) of the total mutual fund market. Nevertheless, the number of products continued to increase in 2010.

The main special problem posed by *shariah* mutual funds mainly relates to the regulator. Namely, what are the eligible financial products? Periodically, the supervisor authority publishes a list of *shariah*-compliant securities, typically adding new issuances recently available in the market. This list serves as guidance for *shariah* fund managers (and for other investors wishing to invest selectively in these instruments). The supervisor is assisted in this regard by the National Shariah Board of the Indonesian Ulama Council, which is involved in the drafting of the relevant *fatwas*. There is also a program of public education concerning the *shariah* capital market as well as a cooperation program with the Securities Commission of Malaysia to develop *shariah*-based investment funds in both countries.

Protected: a popular newcomer with a short shelf life

This type of fund invests in investment grade debt securities, with an underlying financial transaction ensuring that the capital value at maturity is no less than a specified value.[31] It was introduced in 2005 and initially proved enormously popular, because it combines some upside potential with full protection of capital value. Within 3 years, it became the largest type of fund; it expanded rapidly even during the general downswing of 2007/08.

However, protected funds have a fixed tenor (usually about 3 years, because of the maturity of the underlying financial instrument), and there have been very few new entrants recently. Historically, the main reason for the limited number of new entrants has been the need for Bank Indonesia to clear a bank's involvement in the underlying transactions,[32] and Bank Indonesia's clearance often came only slowly. Effectively, market opportunities could slip away before BI clearance could be obtained. Analysts report some progress in resolution of these problems,[33] but more consolidation in this sub-sector looks likely unless OJK proves more agile than Bank Indonesia.

Indexed: a slow, late starter

This is a portfolio of securities with a composition that reflects movements in some well-known index.[34] These were introduced in 2006 and they have been very slow to get off the ground. At end-2009, only 2 Indexed products were offered, and by late 2010 these accounted for a tiny market share (less than ¼ of 1 per cent), NABs having declined by about 15 per cent during that year. Progress continued slow through early 2013, by which time only 5 products were available (OJK Quarterly Report for 1Q2013, p. 19).

ETFs: still to prove itself[35]

These are a fund whose units are traded on the stock exchange, and they can comprise either shares or fixed income instruments, although fixed income dominated as of late 2010. Like Indexed funds, they have been slow to gain popularity. Indeed, total NAB decreased during 2009 and through late 2010. At end-2009, only 2 ETFs were on offer and they accounted for less than 1/2 of 1 per cent of total mutual funds.[36] Demand for this product is low, apparently for two reasons: (i) belief that an actively managed portfolio will produce better returns; and (ii) lack of liquidity for the ETF on the JSX.

Other related products

These go by various names, for example: discretionary funds;[37] *Kontrak Pengelolaan Dana* (KPDs); unit linked products;[38] bank assurances; and *reksadana terbatas* (RDPT or limited mutual funds). Their common characteristic is that they resemble mutual funds, but they are separately regulated and usually only lightly regulated until a problem surfaces.[39] Also, for some (e.g. discretionary funds), there has been only infrequent (monthly) reporting.

VI. The industry's taxes, fees and pricing

Taxation issues

During the early years, a large contributing factor to the success of fixed income mutual funds was an exemption from withholding tax on the interest (or discount) received on bonds traded or listed on the Jakarta Stock Exchange(s).[40] In 2009, this exemption was put on a phase-out schedule. Tax considerations are:

- Cash distributions (dividends) are subject to regular tax rates, but normally they are not distributed to shareholders. They re-invested in the fund and are used to increase the NAV;
- Interest on bank deposits and SBIs (the main alternative financial instruments) is subject to withholding tax;
- Redemptions by the unit holder are not subject to a capital gains tax;
- Redemptions are subject to a sales transaction tax of 0.1 per cent.

Fee structures

Fees charged by the industry are presented in Table 3.2. Fees charged directly to the mutual fund (and deducted to obtain the NAV) range from about 1 to 3¼ per cent per annum, depending upon the type of mutual fund. This range is surprisingly wide and the upper end is definitely on the high side,[41] with the management fee accounting for the great bulk. By contrast, the redemption fee, which is payable by the investor only if the units are redeemed before a fixed minimum period (typically 1 year), is often low; an up-front subscription fee of 1 per cent is in line with standards.[42] It is notable that the custodian fee has been cut roughly in half in recent years by the entry of an aggressive new custodian bank. Auditor fees are very small.

Table 3.2 Indicative fee structure for mutual funds

	Cost (in %)
Fees charged to the mutual fund (annual)	
Management fee[i]	½ to 3
Custodian fee	< ¼
Auditor fee (fixed amount)	US$4000–8000
Fees charged to the investor (per transaction)	
Subscription (up-front) fee; negotiable[ii]	0 to 2
Redemption (back-end) fee	
If held less than minimum period (usually 1 year)	½ to 2½
If held more than minimum period	0
Transfer (between funds) fee; negotiable	¼ to 1

Source: Field interviews.

Note: i) Lower-end fees are for money market funds; upper end is for equity funds. Fixed income funds are mid-range, roughly 1 to 1¼ per cent.
ii) The lower end is for money market funds; the upper end for equity funds.

Pricing issues

As mentioned elsewhere, pricing of thinly traded securities was an early thorn in the side of fixed income mutual funds. It triggered the crisis of 2003, but it has been largely resolved, among others, by creation of the LPHE. Fund managers say that pricing for equity funds is not an issue because it is fully transparent, including as regards participants (noting the advent of electronic trading). However, there is still some room for slippage in the fixed income market, because transactions are not 'live', that is, there are delays between the agreement with the mutual fund customer and the official transaction.[43] This said, remaining problems appear minor relative to those of fixed income funds early in that product's lifetime.

Prior to 2008, there were also issues in the frequency of pricing (that is, monthly versus daily), but these now seem to be behind the industry owing to (daily) E-Reporting. In the days of monthly pricing, fund managers were able to pursue higher returns by following relatively risky investment practices during the month. At month-end, their portfolios would be brought back into line with their prospectus.

VII.   Other notable matters

Restrictions on portfolios

There are numerous limits on holdings of financial instruments, which are spelled out in funds' prospectus, and which vary by type of fund. By way of a few examples, *reksa dana* cannot engage in short-selling or buying on-margin; use of credit and types of credit is restricted; a tight ceiling (10 per cent) is specified on the percentage of a listed firm's shares that can be purchased; there is a minimum size of assets under management (Rp25 billion); there is a minimum time (90 days after registration) to achieve that size; and activities are limited to investment and trading of securities.

Liquidity management

At drafting of this paper, there were no official liquidity requirements of mutual fund managers, and practice appears to vary widely across Investment Managers and products. For example, big cap equity funds have relatively low liquidity needs, whereas small caps have larger liquidity needs, which increase with the size of the fund. Fund managers report that the liquid instruments vary among cash; deposits; SBIs; and some government bonds.

Settlement period

Redemptions normally have a 4- or 5-day settlement period, but there is provision for up to 7 bourse-days (i.e. when the Indonesian Stock Exchange is open). The extra days seem to be intended to provide portfolio managers with flexibility as regards illiquid assets, that is, corporate bonds and many equities on the JSX. Also, bond trading is often over-the-counter, making timing somewhat unpredictable. Less than 7 days is regarded as a 'service' on the part of the investment manager.

VIII.   Notable regulatory improvements[44]

Bapepam-LK is constantly adjusting its regulatory framework, with the changes usually reported by press releases; loaded on its website; and consolidated in its Annual Report. In recent years, there have been four important steps forward:

1. *Taxation.* As mentioned above, Indonesia's mutual fund initially benefitted from a 5-year exemption from a 20 per cent withholding tax on interest (or discount) on bonds traded or listed on the Jakarta Stock Exchange(s) and received by registered mutual funds. This exemption, which was subject to abuse,[45] was terminated in stepwise fashion by Government Regulation 16/2009 (dated 9 Feb. 2009).[46] The tax rate was set at 5 per cent for 2011–13 and at 15 per cent beginning 2014. Despite the long phase-out period, this was a commendable step that recognized the progress to date in developing bond markets and that leveled the playing field among competing financial instruments.
2. *Daily Pricing and E-Reporting.* In 2008, Bapepam-LK required fund managers to provide daily valuations of their portfolios by electronic reporting. This was important because it ensures that the composition of portfolios is kept on-track with the mutual fund's prospectus.[47] This prevents risky intra-month distortions in portfolios, which are only cleaned-up using

end-of-month window-dressing. Clearly, it provides Bapepam-LK with a powerful tool to monitor fund managers' compliance.

3. *Minimum Capital Requirements.* There have been major increases in minimum capital requirements in the past decade. In 2000, it was increased in a (slow) stepwise fashion by a factor of 10; the final step was effective (for existing license holders) only in 2005, when minimum paid-up capital was raised to Rp5 billion (roughly US$500,000). Bapepam-LK took another commendable step in August 2010 by raising it by another factor of 5, to Rp25 billion (US$2.5 million) by end-2012. This step taken, it will now be important to ensure that good, small companies are not closed simply because they are small. Consolidation needs to happen in a way that ensures that the cream of the smaller companies rises to the top, and they are not pulled under by well-intentioned attempts to close the weakest.

4. *Separating Brokerage from Fund Management.* As of early 2011, this step had not officially been taken, but it looked as though it was being implemented.[48] In principle, it will significantly reduce conflicts of interest between investment managers providing objective advice to clients and selling in-house products.

Other steps represent improvements that appear more marginal in nature (see Annex 3.1).[49] By way of overview of these changes, in 2007 Bapepam-LK struggled to re-gain some control and credibility in the wake of scandals and fraud. To this end, Bapepam-LK commissioned a Task Force to investigate allegations of illegal fund marketing and management;[50] it would increase public awareness of potential fraud and improve the authorities' effectiveness in responding to fraud. Bapepam-LK also revised several regulations (whose aim was to improve the governance of mutual funds and the professionalism of fund managers). It also introduced the Bond Pricing Agency, mentioned previously. In addition, Bapepam-LK emphasized its new focus on risk-based supervision of investment management.

The year 2008 marked a shift in Bapepam-LK's focus from micro-regulation to broader, more strategic issues affecting mutual funds (Annex 3.1). These mainly involved the draft OJK Law, including alternative forms of supervision and amendments to the Capital Market Law to harmonize them with the OJK Law. There was also an extension of the lifetime of 2007 Task Force and the appointment of a second task force, this one to look into allegations of illegal acts associated with the global financial crisis of 2008.[51] The global financial crisis also initiated a 'relaxation policy' (officially promulgated in 2009), which temporarily eased certain regulations to maintain continuity in the industry (see Annex 3.1). Revisions to Bapepam-LK Rules also laid the basis for E-Reporting.

In 2009, Bapepam-LK continued its strategic focus, adding a coordination role (on behalf of the Ministry of Finance) for the IMF/World Bank Financial Sector Assessment Program (FSAP).[52] There was little by way of regulatory changes that directly impacted the mutual fund industry until very late in the year.

On 31 December 2009, Bapepam-LK promulgated regulations that placed new requirements on Investment Managers, intended to increase their professionalism (See Annex 3.1). It's particularly notable that investment managers were also required to screen staff during recruitment and reject any applicants with a criminal background, or who have been directly responsible for a firm's bankruptcy. These various steps provide a useful complement to minimum capital as a means to weed out companies without serious long-term commitment to the industry. Existing firms were given 1 year to adjust to the new regulations; if they fail to comply, Bapepam-LK could revoke their business license.

In 2010, the main regulatory change concerned higher capital requirements discussed above. This was a commendable step, but questions remain whether minimum capital of Rp25 billion (less than US$2½ million) is commensurate with the risks being taken with third-party funds. Even US$2½ million pales in comparison with the alleged fraud of US$137 million in the Antaboga case (see Box 3.2). Since 2010, the emphasis has been on the transition to OJK, as described above.

Bapepam-LK has an extensive program of international cooperation that is summarized in a section towards the end of each Annual Report. Especially notable in the current context is technical assistance from the Government of Australia delivered via various arms of that country's bilateral assistance. Most important, the Australian Securities and Investments Commission (ASIC) has been cooperating with a sizable program of capacity building since 2005. In 2010, this included a technical review of aspects of the local mutual fund industry. For its part, the Australian Prudential Regulation Authority (APRA) contributed with, for example, bilateral visits and a secondment program, beginning in 2008 with emphasis on risk-based supervision.

IX. The developmental issues

Mutual funds have an important role to play in a country's financial development, and the market in Indonesia appears to be far from saturated, as industry proponents are quick to point out. However, the risks to investors are high, stemming from several fundamental local weaknesses. For example, the main supervisor looks under-resourced, including with weak human resources; there are on-going problems of coordination among various arms of the regulator; there are grey areas in products and supervision; and there is a pre-existing culture of corporate corruption, which has proven to be sufficiently innovative to stay at least one step ahead of the regulators. In these circumstances, the developmental challenge is to regulate the industry in a way that minimizes fraud, without killing its innovation.

Given the magnitude of this challenge, it's difficult to see how it can be met any time soon, especially when some of the best regulatory agencies in the developed world are unable to prevent enormous frauds.[53] Many local stakeholders are pinning their hopes on OJK and, indeed, a well-functioning OJK would be a significant step forward. However, other steps are also needed, for example, tighter on-site supervision by the regulator and more aggressive, downstream criminal prosecution of fraud (that is, by the police and the attorney general). Moreover, a well-functioning OJK certainly cannot be taken for granted, considering the delays to date; well-known cross-institutional difficulties between the pre-OJK regulators; and the prospects for quick progress any time soon. Realistic near-term policy recommendations should aim lower.

Stated in a general way, the developmental problems of this industry – like much of the rest of Indonesia's financial system – are not so much a matter of insufficient regulation. Indeed, Bapepam-LK made significant improvements after 2008 and OJK stands to benefit. Rather the remaining problems are more a matter of lax enforcement, and improvements along these lines would go a considerable distance to improving the situation, as discussed below. Also, consumer education has a role to play, to ensure that investors better understand the risks they are taking.

Strengthen the Supervisor's capacity to supervise effectively

The supervisor needs to change Indonesia's traditional approach, by becoming more pro-active with tighter supervision and emphasizing early intervention. This could begin with a public announcement of a 'get-tough' policy, followed by active implementation of:

- An expansion of the quality and quantity of resources devoted to supervision.
- Lower tolerance levels for violations, including more use of sanctions that are consistent with the size of the offense and sufficient to deter others. This includes administrative sanctions by OJK and criminal prosecutions by the National Police and the Attorney General.
- More on-site supervisions, of once per year.
- Hire local, private sector analysts to assist, especially with on-site supervision.
- Engage international experts to assist with supervisions, operating behind the scenes as necessary. And
- Negotiating/concluding extradition agreements with key countries, like Singapore and the UK.

Better risk-based supervision

The author was unable to discuss with Bapepam-LK (or OJK) their processes for on- and off-site supervision. Still, there appear to be possibilities for better indicators of risk used by the supervisor,[54] based upon discussions with other stakeholders. By way of examples:

- More focus on the medium and smaller funds, which is where most of the fraud has occurred in recent years;
- Greater reliance upon pre-existing indicators of weak corporate governance;[55]
- Greater attention to the potential for abuse by new products and processes, e.g. on-line trading;[56]

- Comparisons against benchmark rates of return as a preliminary indicator of well-hidden fraud;
- Better tracking of insider trading on the JSX (or market manipulation) and links to mutual funds;
- More imaginative, indirect indicators of fraud. For example, pronounced shifts of personnel from a company's Board of Directors (which has legal responsibility) to its Board of Commissioners (which does not have legal responsibility). Or, large and/or timely transactions among related companies having the potential for transfer pricing.

Shorter phasing periods for policies

As a narrow technical instrument, the supervisor could have shorter phasing periods for new policies. For example, 5 years to phase-out a tax exemption looks excessively long, especially for an exemption that was intended only to get the industry off-the-ground. Likewise, 3–6 years to raise capital requirements, even significantly, seems very generous. Long phasing periods look very much like preference to narrow industry interests over higher-level public policies.

Better cooperation among the main players

There have been well-known problems of coordination between the two (formerly) main regulators, Bapepam-LK and Bank Indonesia. But the problems go much further, including downstream to the police (which has limited expertise in this area) and the attorney general. Finally, there are still some corners of the financial sector outside OJK's authority (for example, cooperatives), and supervisory responsibility in some areas, like pensions, is shared with other authorities. A few other areas, like the Indonesian Stock Exchange, are self-regulating. It would be helpful if these areas could eventually be brought under a wider, stronger OJK umbrella, and be supported by enhanced coordination in the meantime.

Annex 3.1 Principal regulatory changes affecting mutual funds, 2007–10[57]

Year	Regulation	Key Features
2010	Ministry of Finance Decree No.153/PMP/010/2010 dated 31 August 2010.	Minimum paid-up capital of investment mangers raised to Rp10 billion by 31 December 2011; to Rp20 by 31 December 2011; and to Rp25 billion by 31 December 2012.
2009	Bapepam-LK Chairman Decree # Kep-479/BL/2009 dated 31 December 2009 regarding Licensing of Securities Companies Performing as Investment Manager.	Requires Investment Managers to apply risk management and compliance strategies, and to have a business unit or officer with Investment Manager functions.

(*Continued*)

Year	*Regulation*	*Key Features*
	Bapepam-LK Regulation #V.D.11, Attachment of Bapepam-LK Chairman Decree #Kep-480/BL/2009 dated 31 December 2009, regarding Guidelines for the Performance of Investment Manager Functions.	Requires Investment Manager to perform the following functions: Investment; Risk Management; Compliance; Marketing; Trading (dealing); Securities Transaction Settlements; Investor Complaint Management; Research & Information Technology; Human Resource Development; Accounting; and Finance.
	Circulation Letter Number SE-03/BL/2009 dated 16 April 2009.	This 'relaxation policy' officially eased several policies temporarily, including: asset pricing; redemption times; size limitations; minimum assets values; and the advanced education program. Policy was begun in 2008.
2008	Bapepam-LK Chairman Decision #KEP-78/BL/2008, dated 27 March 2008.	
	Ministry of Finance Decision #KEP 353/KMK.010/2008, dated 28 November 2008.	
	Rule # IV.B.1 concerning Guidelines for Contract of CIC Mutual Funds.	The 30 days, mandated under ii) below, is increased to 90 days.
	Revisions to Rule #X.N.1 concerning Mutual Fund Managers' monthly reports.	Changes to reporting requirements, including requirement for digital submissions.
2007	Bapepam-LK Chairman Decision #KEP-208/BL/2007, dated 20 June 2007.	Creates a Task Force for Handling of Alleged Illegal Acts in Public Funds Raising and Management.
	Bapepam-LK Rule # V.D.3 concerning a Bond Pricing Agency, with attachment of Bapepam-LK Chairman Decision # Kep-329/BL/2007, 19 September 2007.	Provides the legal framework for the Bond Pricing Agency.
	Revision to Rule # IV.B.1 concerning Guidelines for the Management of Mutual Funds in the Form of Collective Investment Contracts (CIC)	i) Obliges mutual funds to apply Know-Your-Customer principles. ii) Requires minimum collection of Rp25 billion within 30 working days of effective registration of mutual fund. iii) Changes certain limitations on participation of 2%. iv) Clarifies definitions and processes for handling liquidations.

Year	Regulation	Key Features
	Rule # IV.B.2 concerning Guidelines for Contract of CIC Mutual Funds.	Concerns conditions under which existing mutual funds can start new funds.
	Rule # IV.C. 4 concerning Guidelines for Protected Mutual Funds, Guaranteed Mutual Funds and Exchange Trade Funds.	Harmonizes this Rule with changes to others.
	Rule # IX.C.5 concerning Registration Statement for a Public Offering of an CIC Mutual Fund.	Minor changes to documentation requirements.

Source: Bapapem-LK Annual Reports.

Notes

1 Mutual funds appear to have originated in the Netherlands in the second half of the 18th century (see Rouwenhorst 2004). In the English-speaking world, Scottish Widows Fund and Life Assurance Society brought them to market in 1815, to provide for widows, sisters and other female relatives of fund holders on the death of the fund holder around the Napoleonic wars. They were only popularized worldwide in the 1980s and 90s. For a primer in Bahasa Indonesia, see http://id.wikipedia.org/wiki/Reksadana

2 In the view of some industry analysts, another important factor promoting expansion during this period was Bapepam-LK's removal in 2005 of limits on individual customer's holdings in individual mutual funds.

3 World Bank estimates about 1 1/2 per cent of the total financial sector (World Bank 2006, Table 4.2).

4 The crisis appeared unrelated to a coincident US mutual fund scandal (Putnam Investment Fund) in October 2003 (see www.sptimes.com/2003/10/29/ Business/Putnam_Investments__t.shtml).

5 Bapepam-LK blamed the redemptions on the issuance of a Circular letter by Bank Indonesia that tightened banks' involvement with mutual funds. To promote stability, Bapepam-LK formulated its 'Grand Strategy for the Investment Fund Industry', which would provide investor protection by guarding against transaction failures in the industry (see pp. 2–4 of the chapter entitled 'Reksa Dana' of the 2003 Bapepam-LK Annual Report).

6 Bapepam-LK put net redemptions at Rp4.5 trillion, but private estimates ran as high as Rp30 trillion ('Warning on mutual funds'. Jakarta Post 12/02/2003). The World Bank estimated Rp6 trillion by December (World Bank 2006, p. 97).

7 Redemptions peaked in September 2005 when NAVs dropped to Rp32.9 trillion versus Rp113.6 in February (World Bank 2006, p. 98).

8 Bapepam-LK stands for *Badan Pengawas Pasar Modal Lembaga Keuangan*. It was formed in 2005 by the merger of Bapepam with the pensions and insurance Directorates of the old DG Financial Institutions/MoF during a much larger re-organization of the Ministry of Finance.

9 See World Bank 2006, footnote 41 to Chapter 4.
10 See http://janganserakah.wordpress.com/2009/03/07/lagi-lagi-pelajaran-bagi-investor-kasus-rbs/
11 Herman Ramli is the younger brother of Rudy Ramli, head of the Ramli family. The family was the founder and controller of the now-defunct Bank Bali, which merged with four other mid-sized banks to form Bank Permata in 2002. (At drafting of this paper, Bank Permata was jointly controlled by PT Astra International and Standard Chartered Bank, with no stake left for the family.) The Ramli family made headlines from 1999 to 2000 when Rudy was implicated in a scandal involving irregular payments worth US$80 million from a Bank Bali account to a company controlled by Golkar Party deputy treasurer Setya Novanto. The payment was reportedly aimed at supporting the re-election efforts of former President B.J. Habibie. In late 2000, the court acquitted Rudy of all charges.
12 See 'Jual KPD Natpac, Bank Bumiputera Terancam Sanksi BI', detik Finance, 3 November 2010. According to a senior Bank Indonesia official, the transactions in the Natpac affair were executed in two separate stages in a blatant attempt to circumvent BI regulations. In the first stage, the customer withdrew his deposit from Bank Bumiputera; in the second stage, the customer contracted to transfer his cash to Natpac. Because no bank deposits were involved in the second stage, the transaction was technically outside BI's jurisdiction. To BI's great credit, the technicalities did not prevent BI from imposing sanctions on Bank Bumiputera.
13 Under the Capital Market Law, there are two types of legal mutual funds: (i) a corporate mutual fund (*Perseroan*); and (ii) a contractual-collective fund (*Kontrak Investasi Kolekfif*, KIK). The KIK is the dominant form. For the main distinctions between the two, see World Bank 2006, pp. 95–96.
14 Another potential regulator is the Ministry of Trade (*Bappebti*), which would become involved in commodity-based products.
15 It's notable that this includes the launching of relevant new products (like bank assurances); because BI's clearance is likely to come only slowly, development of this corner of the industry stalled. Effectively, the development of bank-linked new products is being delayed for the sake of some consumer protection.
16 See source: http://en.vivanews.com/news/read/147767bapepam_to_gain_acces_to_bank_ customers__data. Indeed, it's curious that Bank Indonesia – and not Bapepam-LK – was verifying the existence of the mutual fund assets.
17 Prior to 1999/2000, minimum paid-up capital was exceedingly low, only Rp500,000,000 (very roughly US$50,000). In that year it was raised to Rp2 billion for new licenses, and to Rp5 billion in May 2003. For existing licenses, the schedule was more extended, to Rp2.5 billion by December 2003; to Rp3 billion by December 2004; and to Rp5 billion by end-2005.
18 These include: letters of written warnings (admonitions); fines; and revocation of license.
19 For example, 60 and 120 were closed in 2007 and 2008, respectively.
20 Despite extended debate, there is no consensus on 'best practice' concerning the respective responsibilities for financial supervision as among central banks, ministries of finance, other agencies and consolidated financial supervision authorities. The most definitive study, commissioned by the G-30, concludes that 'No simple correlation exists between the supervisory approach adopted in a jurisdiction and that approach's effectiveness during a financial crisis, nor does one model appear to be clearly superior to the others in responding to crises' ('The Structure of Financial Supervision; Approaches and Challenges in a Global Marketplace', Deloitte, Center for Banking Solutions, 2008, p. 1.)

21 Table 21 in *Statistik Pasar Modal.*

22 At end-2009, there were also 1,831 Investment Manager Representatives (*Wakil Manajer Investasi*, WMI), who are individual portfolio managers. They act on behalf of the investment manager and are licensed by Bapepam-LK.

23 Of these, two were due to non-compliance and one (Antaboga) was due to violation of regulations (Bapepam-LK Annual Report for 2009, p. 50).

24 For instance, late in the year, Deutsche Bank relinquished its license to sell mutual funds, having failed to achieve a sufficiently large scale of operations ('Deutsche Bank PWM shutters Indonesia mutual-funds business'. *Asian Investor*, 22 November 2010).

25 Bapepam-LK Annual Report for 2009, pp. 51–52.

26 Portfolio managers report that the custodians do monitor portfolio limits carefully. Breaches of these limits trigger a warning from the custodian, and normally three warnings (for the same offense) are given before the case is referred to Bapepam-LK. Each warning typically allows 1 week for rectification of the problem.

27 This decline was due to the effective merger of the services of Bank Lippo with Bank CIMB Niaga.

28 This excludes products like Private Equity Funds (*Penyertaan Terbatas*) and Asset Backed Security Dealers (KIK-EBA). The former is a vehicle used by an Investment Fund Manager to gather funds from Professional Investors to be invested in securities portfolio. (A 'Professional Investor' is defined as an investor that can purchase Participation Units and perform risk analysis of the Equity Fund as regulated by Bapepam-LK.) A Private Equity Fund is sometimes referred to as *reksa dana* in Bapepam-LK documentation, but it is fundamentally different because the investment manager deals with a limited number of investors, not many individuals. At end-2009, there were 64 Private Equity Funds, holding Rp16.6 trillion in assets which is less than 15 per cent of the total for the eight products described in the main text. For their part, KIK-EBA comprise financial assets with some real or financial asset as implicit collateral, like commercial paper, housing or apartment mortgages and debt securities guaranteed by the government. They were introduced in early 2009; at the end of that year, there were two EBA Investment Managers with total assets of about Rp1/2 trillion.

29 This compares the total of Fixed Income Funds (from Figure 3.3) with total Rupiah-denominated tradable government securities (SUN) as presented by Bank Indonesia.

30 This compares the total of Money Market Funds (from Figure 3.3) with total SBIs as presented by Bank Indonesia.

31 This model works in the following way. A mutual fund will take, say US$100, of an investor's income and buy, say a bond, for US$80 that will be worth US$100 at maturity, thereby guaranteeing the investor's capital at maturity. The portfolio manager will then use the remaining US$20 to obtain some upside for the client, possibly by investing in options, which have very limited downside (basically, the cost of the option).

32 Bank Indonesia became involved because banks sell the options. Business has been further handicapped because (according to analysts) Bapepam-LK has ruled that portfolio managers can only invest in *listed* options, which don't exist in Indonesia.

33 Historically, the process required that a proposed Protected Fund go to Bapepam-LK for approval, which takes roughly 45 days. After that, Bank Indonesia clearance required another 60 days or so. To accelerate the process, Bapepam-LK and BI agreed to proceed in parallel (not sequentially), which was a significant improvement. However, other problems remained. For example, if a proposed

fund involved multiple banks and one bank was not approved, development of the product encountered significant setbacks.

34 For example, the MSCI Indonesia Market which tracks the performance of equities in the top 99 per cent of market capitalization on the Indonesian Stock Exchange (IDX). See www.mscibarra.com/products/indices/

35 Another new product that has encountered problems is Real Estate Income Trusts (REITs). These appear to have become so bogged down in taxation issues that one large player moved its business to Singapore. See, for example, http://www.singaporepropertywatch.com/property/lippo-launches-retail-reit-ipo-aims-to-treble-size-by-end-09

36 The two ETFs were: the 'Asian Bond Fund Indonesia B', a fixed income fund; and 'Premier ETF LWQ-45', an equity fund that comprises 45 of the largest and most liquid companies on the IDX. As of early 2013, only 3 ETFs were available (OJK Quarterly Report for 1Q2013, p. 19).

37 These are also called 'mandated portfolio management agreements'. They are direct contractual arrangements whereby a client entrusts his funds to an investment manager.

38 These are a combination of insurance and mutual funds, based upon a contract between a policyholder and an insurance company. See http://www.cea.eu/index.php?page=asset-management

39 A case in point is discretionary funds. Apparently as a result of the Antaboga case (see Box 3.1), regulations were tightened on discretionary funds, to serve only single clients versus a maximum of 49 previously. Also, a minimum portfolio size was introduced, and a copy of the contract needs to be provided to the supervisory authority.

40 This exemption was provided under Government Regulation No. 6 of 2002.

41 As a benchmark, the World Bank 2006 (p. 93) cites an average expense ratio of 1½ per cent for US fund managers. This is in line with other readily available information (for instance, www.investopedia.com/university/mutualfunds/mutualfunds.asp) but a bit low relative to Canadian funds which typically charge around 2½ per cent (http://wheredoesallmymoneygo.com/how-mutual-funds-are-compensated-in-canada/)

42 Up-front and redemption fees are discussed in http://wheredoesallmymoneygo.com/how-mutual-funds-are-compensated-in-canada/

43 In theory, agile traders can take advantage of this delay to trade on their own account, appropriating any interim gains for themselves and consigning any losses to the client.

44 See Annex A of World Bank 2006 for a list of the main regulations as of 2006.

45 As mutual funds reached their 5-year terminal horizon, they would be closed, but then re-started as a new fund with a new 5-year exemption.

46 The same Regulation also reduced the general withholding tax on bond interest from 20 per cent to 15 per cent.

47 A fund's prospectus defines how much can be invested in different types of assets, effectively defining the risk limits of the fund. Prior to daily E-Reporting, aggressive fund managers could invest in more risky assets during the month to achieve higher rates of return, as mentioned in the main text.

48 Fund managers were told that these functions had to be separated by end-2011, perhaps with the possibility of a 1-year grace period. In addition, it appears that in separating the functions, companies will need to put up minimum capital requirements for the new entity.

49 As mentioned previously, Bapepam-LK was not available to discuss these issues. Consequently, this section relies heavily upon Bapepam-LK's Annual Reports; press releases; and field interviews with other stakeholders.

50 The Task Force included representation from: Bapepam-LK; Bank Indonesia; the National Police; PPATK; and the Ministry of Trade. The Task Force had two programs: preventative and handling. See p. 69 of the 2008 Bapepam-LK Annual Report for a description of the two programs and a terse statement of their accomplishments.

51 Institutional representation overlapped with the 2007 Task Force (see previous footnote). It included: Bapepam-LK; Bank Indonesia; the National Police; the Attorney General; and PPATK. As reported in the 2008 Bapepam-LK Annual Report (p. 68), the Task Force attended workshops for members; shared information; and held regular and incidental meetings to discuss cases.

52 Curiously, there is no reference in Bapepam-LK's Annual Reports to the views of the FSAP, which were received badly by the Minister.

53 By way of a few examples, Bank of Credit and Commerce International (BCCI) in the 1980s; Bernie Madoff in New York in the 1990s; Globalstar in Dubai in 2007; Northern Rock in the UK in 2008; and Istituto per le Opere Religiose (the Vatican's Bank) in 2010.

54 During the field work for this chapter, fund managers expressed the view that Bapepam-LK relied excessively upon size as an indicator of risk. This is questionable on two grounds. First, larger funds are more concerned with reputational risk and therefore take regulatory compliance more seriously than smaller funds. And second, the scandals and fraud of recent years have been concentrated in small- and medium-sized funds, not the largest ones.

55 Bank Century and Robert Tantular is an obvious case in point.

56 For instance, an on-line trader can use multiple accounts to disguise manipulative trading.

57 For regulations prior to 2007, see Annex A to Chapter IV of World Bank 2006.

4 Are emerging Asia's reserves really too high?

Marta Ruiz-Arranz and Milan Zavadjil

I. Introduction

This chapter looks at whether foreign exchange reserves in emerging Asia have grown to beyond what is needed to support financial stability.[1] In assessing global foreign exchange reserve levels in September 2003, the World Economic Outlook concluded that reserves in some Asian emerging market economies were approaching a point where a slowdown in the rate of accumulation was desirable. Since then, however, reserves in these economies have continued to surge in nominal terms. The rapid accumulation of reserves is often seen as the by-product of a development strategy based on boosting exports and growth through maintaining undervalued exchange rates, and thus a reflection of growing global imbalances. Green and Torgerson (2007) state that the largest reserve holders among emerging markets far exceed needed precautionary levels and that the marginal precautionary return to additional reserve accumulation is now low; they see most reserve accumulation as an attempt to limit exchange rate flexibility. Summers (2006) sees excessive reserves as wasteful given the large infrastructure and social needs in emerging markets.

Why have reserve holdings in Asia increased so sharply over the past decade? Fundamentally, reserves are held to provide liquidity in case of temporary shortfalls in exports or capital inflows, and thus avoid disruptive changes in the exchange rate, or investment and consumption. In addition, reserves can protect the domestic banking system – and more broadly domestic credit markets – from outflows of domestic or external resources (Obstfeld, Shambaugh, and Taylor, 2010).

Based on such motivation, there appears to have been plenty of cause for Asian economies to increase their reserves over the past decade. Much of the recent increase in reserves can be explained by the precautionary motive, and has paralleled the sharp expansion of trade and capital flows, as well as the increase in the volatility of gross capital flows to Asian economies. These factors have increased the disruptive potential of sudden stops. In addition, accelerated financial intermediation including the development of local bond and equity markets, have raised the stakes in case of outflows from the domestic financial system. Finally, the build-up of reserves in Asia was a natural response to the disruptions and the disastrous impact of the 1997–99 crises on the economic, political and social fabric, which has understandably increased risk aversion. Thus, despite moves towards more flexible exchange rates and better capital market access, many emerging market central banks have used the opportunities provided by large current account surpluses and capital inflows since the 1997–99 crises to build reserves. Indeed, the high level of reserves could be a major help in maintaining financial stability in Asian economies during the current global credit crunch when the possibility of a sudden stop and/or capital outflows from these economies has risen significantly.

Of course, it could be claimed that with the shift to inflation targeting and floating exchange rates, Asian economies need less reserves than before. In our view, this is wishful thinking. Sudden stops in a financially increasingly integrated world can cause even greater volatility in nominal and real exchange rates, especially in relatively thin and institutionally less developed financial markets. Thus, in addition to less political tolerance for volatility, the level of financial development may explain why Asian economies have had a tendency to hold increased reserves compared with small open industrial economies such as Australia and New Zealand.

Empirical analysis does not suggest that reserves are 'too high' in the majority of Asian economies, though China may be a special case. After recovering following the crisis, reserve adequacy indicators have leveled off in Asia (excluding China). In fact, in Asian economies with very high indicators of reserve adequacy, these indicators have begun to decline, as some of these economies have moved further towards exchange rate flexibility and have accumulated reserves at a slower pace in the past few years. On the other hand, economies with relatively lower reserves continue to increase reserve holdings, resulting in some convergence. Reserve adequacy indicators for emerging Asia (outside of China), at least in the aggregate, can no longer be considered as significantly out of line with other emerging economies. Moreover, much, though not all, of the reserve increase in Asia can be explained by an optimal insurance model under which reserves provide a steady source of liquidity to cushion the impact of a sudden stop in capital inflows on output and consumption. While there is an opportunity cost to holding reserves, which is considered in the insurance model, it does not incorporate the impact of reserves in lowering spreads on an economy's privately held external debt. Using threshold estimation techniques, we show that most of Asia can still benefit from higher reserves in terms of reducing borrowing costs.

This chapter first looks at reserve developments in Asia using traditional adequacy indicators, including the ratios of reserves to imports and short-term debt. However, we argue that the latter is no longer an adequate indicator of vulnerability because of the strong expansion of non-debt cross-border flows, and prefer the ratio of reserves to gross external liabilities for this purpose. We also compare reserves with some broad domestic financial aggregates to assess whether reserves are adequate to protect the financial systems against domestic and internal drains. Subsequently, we assess whether reserves in emerging Asia exceed the optimum level using an existing model (Jeanne, 2007), making changes in parameters to take into account conditions in Asia. Finally, we use a threshold model and assess the benefits of reserves in terms of reduced borrowing spreads.

II. Developments in reserve adequacy indicators

The foreign exchange reserves of Asian economies have quadrupled since the end of the 1997–99 financial crisis. Even after excluding China, reserves more than doubled in nominal terms during 2000–07 (Figure 4.1). Relative to GDP, there has also been an significant increase in reserves, by about 10 percentage points over 2000–07, to 36 per cent of GDP, excluding China (Figure 4.2). Emerging Asia's reserves also reached the equivalent of about 5 per cent of global GDP (in nominal terms) at end 2007.

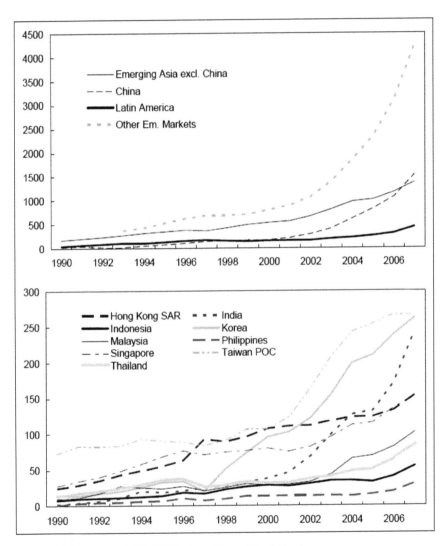

Figure 4.1 Reserves, 1990–2007 (in millions US dollars)

Sources: IMF, *World Economic Outlook*; and Fund staff calculations.

Note: Taiwan POC stands for Taiwan Province of China.

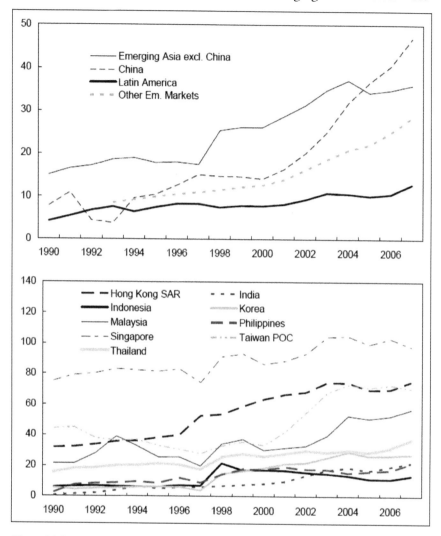

Figure 4.2 Reserves, 1990–2007 (in per cent of GDP)

Sources: IMF, *World Economic Outlook*; and Fund staff calculations.

Note: Taiwan POC stands for Taiwan Province of China.

Traditional reserve adequacy indicators in emerging Asia remain high, but have begun to moderate in recent years because of the acceleration in global trade and capital flows over the past few years. Excluding China, the ratio of reserves to imports has declined modestly since 2003, though it is still significantly higher than the traditional benchmark of 3 months of imports (for which there is little theoretical substantiation) and higher than in the 1990s (Figure 4.3). China's reserve to import ratio, however, continues to rise. There has been some convergence between the economies of the region in terms of the reserves to imports ratio, with the economies with the highest ratios showing

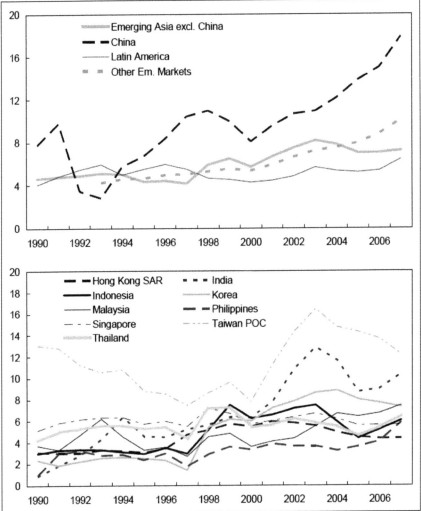

Figure 4.3 Reserves, 1990–2007 (in months of imports of goods and services)

Sources: IMF, *World Economic Outlook*; and Fund staff calculations.

Note: Taiwan POC stands for Taiwan Province of China.

declines in recent years, and the opposite trend evident in economies with lower ratios. Similar trends are evident for many of the other reserve adequacy indicators. Only in Singapore could the decline in reserve ratios have possibly been caused to a significant extent by transfers to sovereign wealth funds. While there is little insistence in economic literature that the equivalent of 3 months of imports (or of 1 year of short-term debt) is an appropriate level of reserves, these indicators remain important in operationally assessing the level of reserves; for example, they are still used in most IMF staff reports.

The ratio of reserves to external debt coming due within the next year has become the standard indicator of vulnerability to capital account crisis, and has found the most empirical support (Bussière and Mulder, 1999). This ratio remains very high in emerging Asia, exceeding the recommended 100 per cent under the Greenspan-Guidotti rule by a wide margin in all economies (Figure 4.4). Nevertheless, it has started to moderate in the past few years, reflecting some increase in short-term debts in some economies, notably India and Korea.

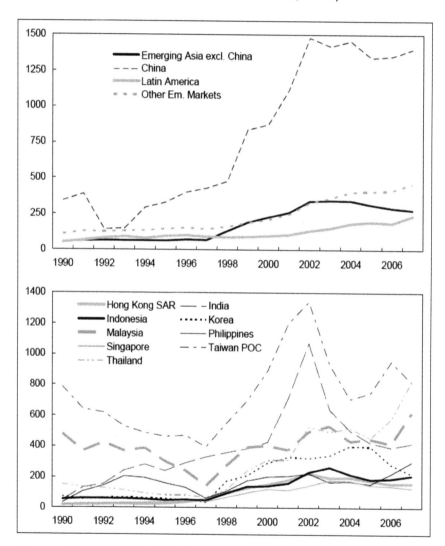

Figure 4.4 Reserves, 1990–2007 (in per cent of short-term debt)[1]

Sources: IMF, *World Economic Outlook*; Bank for International Settlements; and Fund staff calculations.

Notes: Taiwan POC stands for Taiwan Province of China; 1) 2007 data is as of September.

In our view, however, the very high levels of these ratios overstate the extent to which Asian economies are insured against sudden stops, especially in view of the sharp increase in portfolio and direct investment flows to emerging Asia (see Box 4.1).

Reserves currently cover less than one-third of external liabilities in emerging Asia (excluding China) (Figure 4.5).[2] Reflecting greater real and financial integration with the global economy, cross-border capital flows in emerging Asia – both in and out – have grown sharply over the past decade, resulting in a build-up

Box 4.1 Why scale reserves by gross external liabilities?

Over time the nature of balance of payments shocks has evolved. The ratio of reserves to imports was developed to measure resilience to tradexe "Trade" shocks that tended to predominate before the liberalization of financial systemxe "Financial: System"s and capital accounts. Subsequently, with the increase in cross-border capital flowsxe "Capital Flow" and the rising possibility of sudden stops and capital outflows, the ratio of reserves to external debt maturing within a year became a key indicator of reserve adequacy. This reflected in part the nature of the crisisxe "Crisis" in Asia and elsewhere in the 1990s when banks and corporations built-up large short-term foreign exchange liabilities with which they financed long-term investments that did not generate foreign exchange. Foreign exchange reserves were not sufficient to finance outflows of short-term capital when they occurred. The ratio of reserves to short-term debt was thus highly suitable for assessing vulnerability to these types of currency and maturity mismatches and was indeed a good predictor of crisis.

Capital flows to non-emerging Asia have evolved considerably since the crisisxe "Crisis" of the 1990s. The share of debt, including short-term debt, has decreased (Figure 4.6). Moreover, portfolio flows have proved to be the most volatile form of capital flow, and the volatility of both gross inflows and outflows has risen sharply since 2000. Indeed recent episodes of global risk aversion such as May–June 2006 or August 2007 have been most felt in domestic bond and equity markets which have been volatile in many economies. While somewhat more stable, the volatility of direct investmentxe "Direct Investment" flows has also increased. Moreover, long-term liability holders rarely remain passive when balance of payments problems arise. As noted by Wyplosz (2007), speculation mostly takes the form of short-term liabilities, but long-term holders can quickly build up hedges, and the potential for such a build-up is captured by looking at the overall liability position.

Of course, it is not suggested that reserves need to cover external liabilities entirely, as in the case of the Greenspan-Guidotti rulexe "Greenspan-Guidotti rule". The appropriate coverage adequacy ratio should clearly be lower for some components (FDIxe "Foreign Direct Investment", portfolio equity) than for others (short-term debt). It would make little sense to argue that the Greenspan-Guidotti rule of 100 per cent coverage should apply to total gross liabilities (if each dollar of gross capital inflow should be saved in reserves, rather than being invested domestically, why have capital inflows?). So there probably should be different reserve coverage depending on the nature of the liabilities. The appropriate coverage of policies could also depend on the volatility of the particular flow/liability.

In sum, the ratio of reserves to gross external liabilities appears to best capture the vulnerability to sudden stops and capital account reversals, especially in light of the growing complexity of capital market instruments.

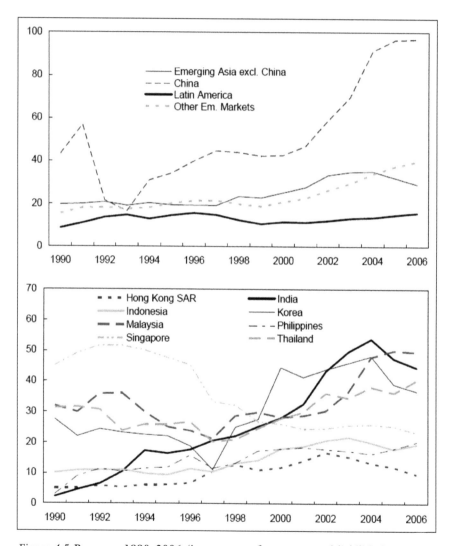

Figure 4.5 Reserves, 1990–2006 (in per cent of gross external liabilities)

Sources: IMF, *World Economic Outlook*; Milesi-Feretti data; and Fund staff calculations.

Note: Taiwan POC stands for Taiwan Province of China.

in external assets and liabilities in all the economies of the region (Figure 4.6). The ratio of reserves to external liabilities increased through 2002 as emerging Asia rebuilt its reserves following the crisis, but has since eased. It has been declining – albeit very gradually – or stable in all economies, except China and Malaysia. In addition to the increase in size, the volatility of gross capital flows has risen (IMF, 2007). According to this work (Table 4.1), the increase in volatilities for gross flows can be explained by their growing size and the increasing share of portfolio and other investments in total flows. On the other hand, the volatility of net inflows has decreased, indicating that gross inflows and

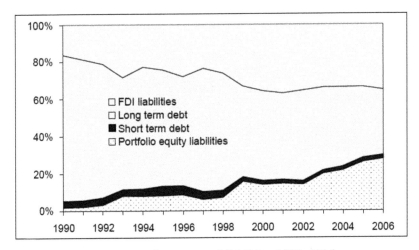

Figure 4.6 Asia emerging markets: external liabilities, 1990–2006

Sources: IMF, *World Economic Outlook*; Milesi-Feretti data; and Fund staff calculations.

Table 4.1 Volatilities of capital flows in Asia-Pacific economies[1]

	Inflows		Outflows		Balance (net inflows)	
	1987–96	*2001–06*	*1987–96*	*2001–06*	*1987–96*	*2001–06*
Emerging Asia (excluding Hong Kong and Singapore)[2]						
Total Capital Flows	2.76	3.48 *[3]	1.29	2.62**	2.95	2.65
Direct Investment Flows	0.55	1.03 **	0.28	0.47*	0.68	0.82
Portfolio Investment Flows	0.79	2.01 **	0.19	1.01**	0.87	2.04**
Other Investment Flows	2.45	1.88	1.08	2.26**	2.52	2.15
ASEAN						
Total Capital Flows	3.31	4.54 *	1.17	2.79**	3.20	3.35
Direct Investment Flows	0.78	1.53 **	0.12	0.68**	0.78	1.24*

Portfolio Investment Flows	1.12	2.23 **	0.23	0.66*	1.23	2.30**
Other Investment Flows	2.91	2.33	1.11	2.64**	2.77	2.10
Korea and Taiwan						
Total Capital Flows	3.16	3.70	2.36	3.23	4.06	2.46
Direct Investment Flows	0.16	0.71**	0.75	0.34	0.70	0.53
Portfolio Investment Flows	0.48	3.11**	0.27	2.10**	0.59	2.59**
Other Investment Flows	3.14	1.87	1.74	1.97	3.67	2.67
Singapore						
Total Capital Flows	10.80	14.57	12.14	15.74	5.95	4.08
Direct Investment Flows	4.29	5.74	2.06	12.10**	4.19	9.94*
Portfolio Investment Flows	2.26	4.15	5.52	4.09	5.43	5.49
Other Investment Flows	12.14	10.84	11.27	13.99	5.46	6.21
China						
Total Capital Flows	1.29	1.24	0.49	2.53**	1.51	1.87
Direct Investment Flows	0.84	0.46	0.26	0.30	0.84	0.37
Portfolio Investment Flows	0.26	0.33	0.04	1.29**	0.24	1.30**
Other Investment Flows	0.81	0.90	0.25	2.85**	0.98	2.29*
Australia and New Zealand						
Total Capital Flows	3.18	5.29	2.52	6.34**	2.92	1.84
Direct Investment Flows	1.09	5.33**	1.78	3.17*	2.22	2.86
Portfolio Investment Flows	1.88	3.93***	0.61	1.59**	1.73	4.34**
Other Investment Flows	2.54	2.98	0.99	3.73**	2.36	2.80

Source: ADB *Regional Economic Outlook*, April 2007.

Notes: 1) Volatility is defined as standard deviations of changes in capital flows relative to nominal GDP; 2) Number for the group of countries are simple averages of the standard deviations calculated for individual countries; 3) ** and * indicate the standard deviation increased with statistical significance at 1% and 5% (based on F-statistics), respectively.

outflows are better synchronized. As the reasons for the better synchronization are not fully understood, there is no guarantee that this trend will continue. In all, while it is not possible to calculate a benchmark for an adequate level of reserves compared with external liabilities, current reserve levels in most Asia economies do not appear excessive against historical levels given the size of gross liabilities and the increased volatility of gross flows.

Reserves on average cover about one-third of broad money in emerging Asia. This ratio can be interpreted to measure resilience to outflows from an economy's banking system. All emerging Asian economies are above the Wijnholds and Kapteyn (2001) recommended holdings of 5–20 per cent, though there is little theoretical substantiation for this threshold (Figure 4.7). The overall number is somewhat

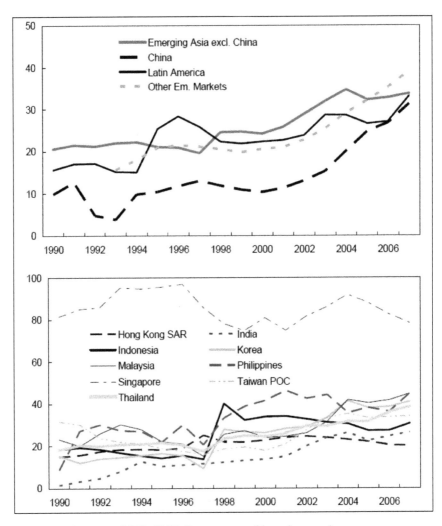

Figure 4.7 Reserves, 1990–2007 (in per cent of broad money)

Sources: IMF, *World Economic Outlook*; Milesi-Ferretti data; and Fund staff calculations.

Note: Taiwan POC stands for Taiwan Province of China.

distorted by Singapore where the ratio is over 80 per cent. There has been little change in the ratio since 2004, as broad money growth has kept pace with reserves.

Financial deepening has outpaced reserve growth in emerging Asia (excluding China) since 2002. To measure the potential for outflows from the domestic financial system in the broadest sense, we tap a World Bank database to derive a series that includes all financial sector deposits (not just the banking system), as well as domestically issued government and corporate bonds and equity market capitalization (Figure 4.8). In 2005 (the latest data available), reserves covered about 15 per cent of financial sector deposits, bonds and equities, according to a World Bank database. The ratio for most economies was around

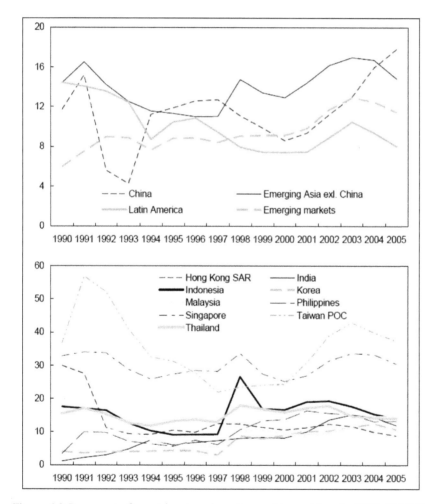

Figure 4.8 Reserves to financial system deposits, equities and bonds, 1990–2005 (in per cent)

Sources: IMF, *World Economic Outlook*; World Bank, *Financial Development and Structure Dataset*; and Fund staff calculations.

Note: Taiwan POC stands for Taiwan Province of China.

10 per cent, with only Singapore and Taiwan Province of China, in the 30–40 per cent range. The ratio has declined for all economies in 2002–05.

Excluding China, emerging Asia's reserve adequacy are not out of line compared with other emerging markets. After their moderation over the past few years, emerging Asia's reserve adequacy, excluding China, are only modestly higher than South America's, but lower than the average for other emerging markets, given the sharp increase in oil producers' reserves. China's reserves, however, have continued to grow rapidly and reserve adequacy indicators are considerably higher than in most other emerging markets.

III.   An insurance model of optimal reserves

This section attempts to explain the recent build-up in international reserves in emerging Asia using an insurance model of optimal reserves based on the work of Jeanne (2007).[3] In the model, reserves enable an economy to cushion the impact of a sudden stop in capital flows on domestic consumption and output by providing a ready source of liquidity. However, holding liquid reserve assets entails an opportunity cost equal to the difference between the return on capital and on reserves. The optimal level of reserves is derived from this cost-benefit analysis and depends on: the probability and size of a sudden stop (or crisis), the output loss in the event of a sudden stop, the opportunity cost of holding reserves and the degree of risk-aversion. The model is calibrated on economy-specific data for 11 emerging market economies in Asia and results compared with actual levels of reserves at the end of 2007.

The model

Jeanne (2007) derives the optimal level of reserves by minimizing a loss function that equals the opportunity cost of reserves plus the expected welfare cost of a crisis:

$$Loss = \delta R + \pi f(R) \tag{1}$$

where δ is the opportunity cost of reserves; R is the reserve holdings; π is the probability of a crisis or sudden stop; and $f(.)$ is the welfare cost of a crisis, which is increasing in the size of the sudden stop and the output loss (L and ΔY). Assuming constant risk aversion (σ) and an exogenous probability of crisis, the optimal level of reserves is given by:

$$R = L + \Delta Y - [1 - [(1 + \delta / \pi)]^{(-1/\sigma)}] \tag{2}$$

That is, the optimal level of reserves is larger the greater the size and output cost of a crisis, the higher the probability of a sudden stop, the lower the cost of holding reserves and the higher the degree of risk aversion.[4]

Estimating output loss

The Asian crisis provides a useful benchmark to assess the size of the output loss in the event of a sudden stop in capital flows, a key parameter in the model. Given its massive impact on the region, it is reasonable to assume that this episode has, to a large extent, motivated the rapid accumulation of international reserves across Asia and that many economies may have accumulated reserves to cushion a potential loss in output of magnitude similar to that experienced a decade ago.

The cost in terms of output during the period 1997–99 is estimated by cumulating the output gap in these years under the assumption that output would have grown at the same rate as the average before the crisis.[5] Results suggest that the cumulative output loss for the six Asian economies most affected by the crisis was 19 per cent of GDP on average (Table 4.2). This was significantly higher in the case of Indonesia and Thailand, where the cumulative cost amounted to around 30 per cent of GDP. These estimates may however underestimate the total output loss of the Asian crisis if the recession lowered the level of output permanently, rather than being a temporary deviation from trend. Indeed, Cerra and Saxena (2005) find evidence of permanent losses in the levels of output in six Asian economies following the 1997–98 crisis. The magnitude of the permanent losses is found to be economically significant for all economies, except perhaps the Philippines. For instance, in the case of Indonesia, the contemporaneous output loss is estimated at 22 per cent of GDP, and the total loss including the losses beyond the crisis period reached 42 per cent of GDP.

In addition, if sudden stops in capital flows trigger banking crisis, the cost could be substantially higher. According to Beim and Calomiris (2001), the resolution costs (bailouts and restructuring) following the Asian crisis reached 50 per cent of GDP in Indonesia, above 40 per cent in Thailand and 20 per cent in Malaysia and Korea. Similarly, Caprio and Klingebiel (2003) estimate the fiscal costs of the

Table 4.2 Output loss in Asian crisis

	Average Growth	Difference between Actual Growth and Average Growth			Cumulative Output Loss
	1970–96[1]	1997	1998	1999	1997–99
Hong Kong SAR	7.4	–2.2	–12.8	–3.4	18.4
Indonesia	6.9	–2.2	–20.0	–6.1	28.2
Korea	8.1	–3.5	–15.0	1.4	17.1
Malaysia	7.6	–0.3	–14.9	–1.4	16.6
Philippines	3.6	1.6	–4.2	–0.2	4.4
Thailand	7.6	–9.0	–18.1	–3.2	30.3
Average	*6.9*	*–2.6*	*–14.2*	*–2.2*	*19.2*

Note: Real GDP series have been detrended using Hodrik Prescott filter. Results are robust to different time period averages.

banking crisis at 55 per cent of GDP in Indonesia, 35 per cent of GDP in Thailand, 28 per cent of GDP in Korea and 16 per cent of GDP in Malaysia.

Based on these results, the assumption of 10 per cent of GDP output loss in the benchmark calibration in Jeanne (2007) appears too low. The exercise in this chapter assumes a potential output loss of 19 per cent of GDP, in line with the average output loss estimate from the Asian crisis experience, although a higher estimate would also be reasonable.

Estimating the probability and size of a sudden stop

Consistent with the benchmark calibrations in Jeanne and Rancière (2006) and Jeanne (2007), the average probability of crisis is set to 10 per cent, equal to the unconditional frequency of sudden stops in a large sample of emerging economies during the period 1975–2003.[6] In this exercise, the probability of crisis is assumed to be exogenous and thus independent of the level of reserves. It is, however, plausible that reserves could have a crisis prevention role by reducing the likelihood of crises. If this were the case, the optimal level of reserves could be significantly larger.

During the historical sudden stop episodes, the average size of the capital outflows is estimated at around 10 per cent of GDP. This estimate is relatively close to the weighted average short-term external debt in our sample and could, therefore, be a good predictor of the potential immediate rollover needs. The calibrations in this chapter use this estimate, except for Hong Kong SAR and Singapore (where short-term liabilities significantly exceed 10 per cent of GDP) and for Indonesia (where short-term debt is estimated at around 6.5 per cent of GDP). In these cases, the actual ratio of short-term external debt to GDP is used instead.

Nevertheless, it is worth noting that the potential size of a capital flight in Asia could be significantly larger than 10 per cent of GDP or the level of short-term external debt. In some economies, such as Hong Kong SAR and Singapore, gross external liabilities exceed 700 per cent and 400 per cent of GDP, respectively. As discussed earlier, total foreign liabilities could capture Asia's vulnerability to reversals in capital flows better than short-term debt.

Estimating the opportunity cost of holding reserves

The opportunity cost of reserves is the difference between the return on reserves and the return on capital or an alternative investment. In absence of a broad consensus over how to best capture this cost, several measures have been used in the literature, as noted below.

The spread between private foreign borrowing costs and yields on reserve assets

Rodrik (2006), Levy Yeyati (2008) and others have argued that the alternative use of one dollar of reserves is one less dollar of foreign debt or, alternatively,

Table 4.3 Interest rate spreads (basis points)[1]

China	71
Hong Kong SAR	−44
India	332
Indonesia	197
Korea	73
Malaysia	87
Philippines	178
Singapore	−175
Taiwan Province of China	−230
Thailand	−4

Note: 1) Average for 2007. EMBI spreads for Indonesia, Malaysia, Philippines. Ten-year government bond spreads for others.

reserves can be accumulated by issuing foreign debt. The opportunity cost of reserves can, therefore, be viewed as the return that the government has to pay in excess of the return on liquid foreign assets to finance the purchase of reserves. This is proxied in our chapter by the sovereign risk premium (as measured by EMBI or the 10-year government bond spreads). Since the sovereign risk premium reflects also the probability of default, and hence of less than full repayment, these spreads are likely to overstate the real opportunity cost of holding reserves. Moreover, as discussed in the next section of the chapter, increases in reserves reduce the spread paid on the stock of foreign debt, thereby reducing the marginal cost of reserve accumulation and increasing the propensity to hold reserves. As shown in Table 4.3, sovereign interest rate spreads for foreign debt have averaged less than 4 per cent during 2007 in emerging Asia, and in some economies (e.g. Singapore, Hong Kong SAR and Taiwan Province of China) the risk premia has been negative.

The term premium

Assuming a zero probability of default, the opportunity cost of reserves is simply the difference between a long-term foreign rate (such as the US 10-year Treasury rate) and a short-term foreign rate (such as the 3-month US T-bill rate or the Federal Funds rate). Based on this measure, the financial cost of accumulating reserves does not appear to have been large: the average term premium in the United States during 2007 was less than ¼ per cent, reflecting the flattening of the yield curve over the past two years.

The fiscal cost of sterilizing reserves

This is computed as the difference between the domestic financing rate the central bank pays to withdraw liquidity from the local market as a result of reserve

Table 4.4 Estimated sterilization financing costs[1]

	Domestic Financing Costs (Serilization Rate)	Net Carry (Interest on Foreign Reserves Minus Sterilization Rate)[2]	Carry Income on Total Reserves (% GDP)[3]
China	3.24	0.10	0.05
India	6.00	–2.66	–0.7
Indonesia	8.00	–4.66	–0.6
Korea	5.00	–1.66	–0.5
Malaysia	3.50	–0.16	–0.1
Philippines	5.25	–1.91	–0.4
Singapore	0.98	2.36	2.5
Taiwan Province of China	3.38	–0.04	0.0
Hong Kong SAR	5.75	–2.41	–1.8
Thailand	3.25	0.09	0.0

Sources: Country authorities; IMF, APDCORE database and *World Economic Outlook*; Fund staff calculations.

Note: 1) As of December 2007; 2) The rate on foreign reserve holdings is assumed to be the yield on the 1-year US Treasury note (3.34 per cent at the end of 2007).

accumulation and the interest in the foreign reserves (assumed to be the yield on the 1-year US Treasury bill or other short-term foreign rate). On average, the opportunity cost did not seem too high over the last year, except perhaps in Indonesia, where the sterilization rate exceeded by more than 4 per cent the return on reserves. Other economies, such as China and Singapore, experienced a positive income gain (net positive carry) during 2007, as the cost of domestic financing was lower than the rate earned on foreign reserves (Table 4.4).

Our baseline scenario assumes the opportunity cost of reserves is equal to the interest spread on foreign debt. The other two measures are used as robustness tests.

Calibration results

The findings of the chapter suggest that a simple insurance model performs relatively well in explaining the stock of reserves in emerging Asia. Except in China and possibly Malaysia, reserves in emerging Asia cannot be considered excessive, when compared to what would be optimal from a precautionary motive standpoint. Figure 4.9 shows the optimal level of reserves (in nominal terms) predicted by the model against the actual level at the end of 2007 in each of the Asian economies. The current level of reserves in Hong Kong SAR, Korea, the Philippines and Singapore appear to be at or very close to optimal levels. Furthermore, the model can explain about 80 per cent of current reserves in Thailand, 70 per cent of total reserves in India and 60 per cent of the reserves

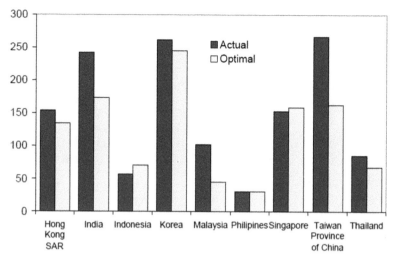

Figure 4.9 The optimal level of international reserves, 2007 (in billions US dollars)

in Taiwan Province of China. There are, however, notable exceptions: the model can only explain about half of the reserve accumulation that has taken place in China. Similarly, reserve levels in Malaysia at the end of 2007 had exceeded by more than twice the optimal levels predicted by the model. This suggests that factors other than insurance motives may be at play in these economies. On the other hand, the current level of reserves in Indonesia seems to be lower than predicted by the model, suggesting scope for further accumulation from an insurance motive point of view alone.

These results contrast with those in Jeanne and Rancière (2006) and Jeanne (2007) that find reserves in Asia to be significantly above optimal. The choice of the model parameters is crucial in delivering our results: by acknowledging that the potential size of the output loss in the event of a crisis may be larger than 10 per cent of GDP and that the opportunity cost of reserves in Asia does not appear to have been very elevated in the recent period, we can go a long way in explaining the current stock of reserves. Furthermore, for some of the newly industrialized emerging economies (NIEs), the size of the potential capital flight might be larger than 10 per cent of GDP, as assumed in the original authors' model.

Notwithstanding the power of the model, we cannot explain the entire build-up in Asia, particularly in the most recent period. Table 4.5 shows the year where the optimal threshold level was breached in those economies with relative high levels of reserves, in most cases, this took place between 2002 and 2005. For instance, China's reserves before 2004 had not reached the optimal level predicted by the model, and India breached the threshold in 2003. Our results suggest that most economies in Asia were closer to their optimal levels in 2003 than they were at the end of 2007. This is depicted graphically in Figure 4.10,

Table 4.5 Foreign reserves levels: optimal vs. actual (in per cent of GDP)

	Optimal	*2007*	*2006*	*Above optimal since*
China	26	47	40	2004
Hong Kong SAR	66	75	70	2001
India	16	22	20	2003
Indonesia	17	14	11	
Korea	26	28	27	2004
Malaysia	25	57	53	1998
Philippines	21	22	17	
Singapore	102	98	103	
Taiwan POC	43	71	73	2002
Thailand	29	37	32	2005

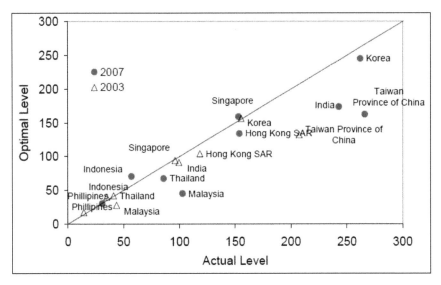

Figure 4.10 Optimal vs. actual levels of international reserves in Asia (in billions US dollars)

which shows a smaller dispersion around the 45 degree line (where actual reserves equal optimal reserves) in 2003 than in 2007. This could to some extent explain the pattern described in the introduction, which suggests that the accumulation of reserves in emerging Asia (excluding China) has started to decelerate recently. In few economies where the level of reserves had overshot recommended levels (e.g. Taiwan Province of China, Korea) the trend has started to reverse, which is a rational response from the cost-benefit analysis discussed before. Another indication that some economies have reached adequate levels is the emergence of sovereign wealth funds (SWFs). This trend would be in line with the recommendations in IMF (2003) that concluded that a slow-down in the pace of accumulation was desirable.

The discussion of the findings of the model is more meaningful when reserves are presented in terms of adequacy ratios rather than in dollar terms or in per cent of GDP. Several conclusions emerge from Figure 4.11. First, the optimal

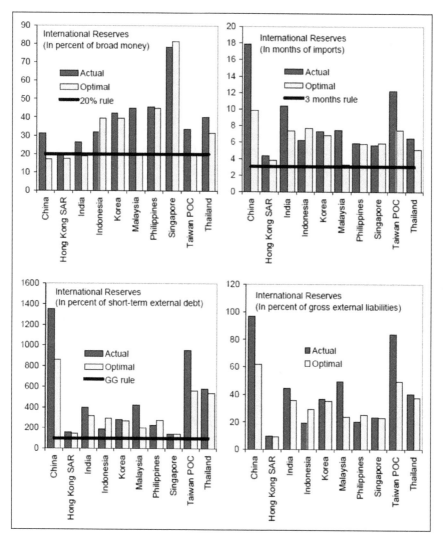

Figure 4.11 The optimal level of international reserves and traditional reserve adequacy indicators

Sources: IMF, *World Economic Outlook*, Milessi-Feretti data; BIS; and Fund staff calculations.

Note: Taiwan POC stands for Taiwan Province of China.

levels predicted by the model are above the standard rules of thumb in most economies. For instance, the average optimal level of reserves for Asia is estimated at around 6 months of imports, twice as large as the traditional benchmark. Estimated optimal ratios for Indonesia, India, China and Taiwan Province of China are above 6 months. With regards to short-term external debt, all economies' optimal reserve levels are above the 100 per cent Greenspan-Guidotti rule. Indeed, the average optimal level in Asia is more than three times this level. Similarly, the average optimal level of reserves to broad money is around 30 per cent, above the 5–20 per cent range usually proposed in the literature. This suggests that these rules of thumb may no longer be relevant and that economy-specific indicators that account for economy-specific vulnerabilities and opportunity costs may be preferable to standardized rules.

Second, actual reserve ratios are not substantially above adequate levels, except in the economies discussed above (e.g. China, Malaysia, Taiwan Province of China). The difference seems to be smaller when expressed in terms of months of imports, broad money, short-term debt or gross external liabilities than when presented in nominal terms or in per cent of GDP. This suggests that the evolution of reserves cannot be assessed independently of the trade and capital account flows against which reserve provide an insurance. In light of these results, we can conclude that much of the recent increase in reserves can be explained by the precautionary motive, and has paralleled the sharp expansion of trade and capital flows, as well as the increase in the volatility of gross capital flows.

Third, the model tends to perform better in terms of explanatory power when the ratio of reserves to total external liabilities is used as the indicator of reserve adequacy. In particular, a higher fraction of the current reserves in China, Taiwan Province of China and Malaysia can be explained and the dispersion of excess reserves, defined as the difference between actual reserves and optimal reserves, around the mean is smaller when reserves are measured against total external liabilities than when measured against any other metric.

IV.   A threshold model of spreads-reserves elasticity

To the extent that reserves lower the spreads on the economy's privately held external debt, the opportunity cost of holding reserves is reduced and the incentives to accumulate reserves become higher (Levy Yeyati, 2008). This prevention aspect has been neglected in the model presented in the previous section as well as in other theoretical models on optimal reserve holdings. Alternatively, one could argue that holding reserves reduces the probability of a sudden stop. In either case, this would increase the desired level of reserve holdings. This section estimates how significant this 'prevention' effect is and whether the current stock levels can be justified in terms of the benefits of reduced borrowing costs.

We estimate spreads-reserves elasticities for a panel of 34 emerging economies for the period 1997–2006. Because the marginal effect of reserves on spreads might be different at different levels of reserves, we look for a non-linear relation between spreads and international reserves applying threshold estimation as in Hansen (2000). By applying this methodology, we can endogenously determine the threshold level(s) of reserves (and confidence intervals) at which the relation between reserves and spreads changes. In particular, these threshold levels will provide information about the maximum level of reserves where no further gains from lower spreads could be realized. We will then be able to compare them with the optimal levels found in the previous section as well as with the traditional rules of thumb.

Methodology

Threshold estimation takes the form:

$$S_{it} = \beta_1' X_{it-1} + \beta_2 R_{it-1} + \varepsilon_{it} R_{it-1} \leq \gamma \tag{3}$$

$$S_{it} = \alpha_1' X_{it-1} + \alpha_2 R_{it-1} + \varepsilon_{it} R_{it-1} \leq \gamma \tag{4}$$

where S is JP Morgan's EMBI spreads; R is a reserve ratio indicator, which is used both as a regressor and as the threshold variable that splits the sample into two groups; γ is the endogenously determined threshold level; and X is a vector of control variables. The vector of control variables includes: (i) two exogenous global factors: the international risk-free asset (proxied by the 10-year US Treasury rate) and global risk aversion (proxied by the Credit Swiss First Boston's High Yield spread); and (ii) the country's GDP growth rate and the ratio of debt to GDP to control for country-specific and time varying characteristics. All the variables are estimated in logs and are lagged one period to reduce potential endogeneity concerns. The regressions also include country-specific fixed effects. A description of the variables and their sources can be found in the Annex.

The main feature of the model is that it allows the regression parameters to differ depending on the value of R. We are interested in estimating the threshold level beyond which the marginal impact of reserves on spreads stops being significant. If needed, we perform multiple threshold regressions proceeding in a sequential way. First, we fit a threshold model to the data to estimate a first reserve ratio threshold level and the least square coefficients of each subsample. We compute confidence intervals for the parameters, including the reserve threshold coefficient, and provide an asymptotic simulation test of the null hypothesis of linearity against the alternative of a threshold. If the spreads-reserves elasticity beyond the threshold is not statistically significant, the procedure stops. If we find evidence of a first threshold, we proceed to the second stage (provided the number of observations allows doing so): drop the subsample below the threshold and repeat the procedure just described but applying it to the rest of the sample in search for a second threshold. This allows us to compute estimates for the two remaining subsamples and test the null hypothesis of no second reserve threshold. In all cases there is no need to proceed beyond the second stage.

Empirical results

To summarize, holding reserves has a significant impact in reducing spreads, and hence in lowering the economies' interest rate bills. This effect continues to be important even at relatively high levels of reserves. The estimated thresholds beyond which there are no gains in holding reserves in terms of reduced cost of borrowing are significantly above the levels implied by the standard rules of thumb and closer to the optimal reserve levels. This, together with the insurance motive discussed earlier, further contributes to explain the levels of reserves currently observed in emerging Asia and other emerging economies.

The findings for six different reserve adequacy indicators are presented in Figure 4.12.[7] A first set of indicators includes the traditional measures, but other liability metrics are also explored. As discussed earlier, given the extent of financial globalization and the potential for both internal and external drains, reserves as ratio of total foreign liabilities or as ratio of financial system deposits and stock market capitalization may be better determinants of reserve holdings than more traditional reserve adequacy indicators. What follows is a more detailed description of the results for each of the reserve indicators.

Reserves to GDP

There is only one relevant threshold at 49 per cent of GDP.[8] Below this level, the elasticity of spreads with respect to reserves is 43 per cent. That is, a 1 per cent increase in the ratio of reserves to GDP leads to a 0.43 per cent decline in spreads. Reserves in excess of 49 per cent of GDP do not longer have an impact on spreads. It is worth noting that most observations in the sample fall below this threshold (except Hong Kong SAR, Malaysia, Lebanon and Algeria for some recent years). This means that most economies continue to benefit from reserve accumulation, even at current levels.

Reserves to months of imports

The threshold level of reserves above which they no longer reduce spreads is estimated at 6.3 months of imports, twice as large as the traditional rule of thumb. This threshold is very close to the average optimal level of reserves. The spreads-reserves elasticity below 6 months of imports is 33 per cent. In 2006, the level of reserves of some important Asian economies (e.g. Indonesia, Thailand, the Philippines and Hong Kong SAR) fell short of the estimated threshold, which provides a rationale for continued accumulation of reserves.

Reserves to broad money

For economies with reserves to broad money below 28 per cent, the elasticity of spreads is 46 per cent. Beyond this level, there is no evidence that further reserve accumulation contributes to reduce spreads. Again, the estimated

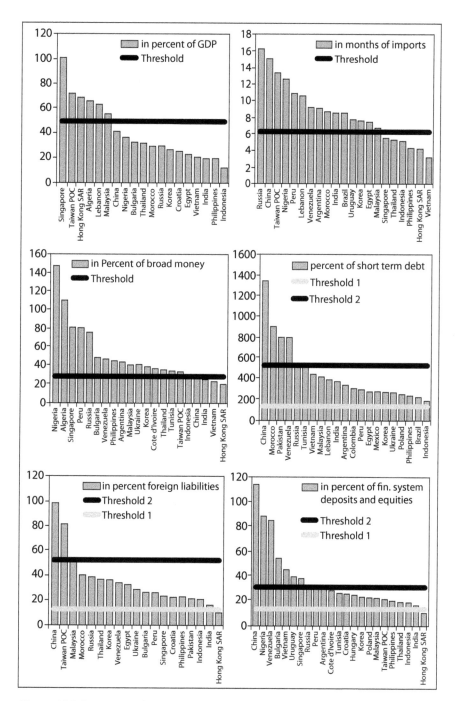

Figure 4.12 International reserves and threshold estimates

Sources: IMFWEO; Milessi-Feretti data; BIS; and Fund staff calculations.

Note: Taiwan POC stands for Taiwan Province of China.

Table 4.6 Thresholds in the spreads-reserves relation

Reserves to	Threshold 1		Threshold 2		Reserve Adequacy Benchmark
	Estimate	Confidence Inerval	Estimate	Confidence Interval	
GDP[1]	49	[23, 51]			
Months of imports[2]	6	[2, 9]			3
Broad money[2]	28	[6, 85]			5–20
Short-term debt[3]	125	[112, 692]	534	[534, 535]	100
Foreign liabilities[3]	12	[12, 12.4]	52	[52, 66]	
Fin. system deposits and equities[3]	13	[12, 14]	30	[14, 40]	

Note: 1) The marginal impact of reserves is negative and significant below threshold 1; there are insufficient observations to estimate the impact above the threshold; 2) The marginal impact is negative below threshold 1 and not significant above the threshold; 3) The marginal impact is not significant below threshold 1, negative between threshold 1 and 2 and insignificant above threshold 2.

threshold level is close to the average optimal level for Asia (32 per cent of broad money) and is above the current reserve levels of many Asian economies, including China, Indonesia, India, Hong Kong SAR and Vietnam.

Reserves to short-term debt

As shown in Table 4.6, we find two significant thresholds using reserves in terms of short-term debt, both of them higher than the Guidotti rule. The estimates of the first and second reserve thresholds are 125 and 534 per cent of short-term debt, respectively. The effect of the reserve ratio on spreads is found to be negative for the intermediate regime (elasticity of 31 per cent) and insignificant for the first and third regimes. In other words, reserves need to be sufficiently high in order to find a significant effect in terms of reduced cost of borrowings. However, beyond the second threshold, there are no additional gains. In Asia, only China's reserves are above the second threshold level.

Reserves to total foreign liabilities

In Table 4.7, a sample split based on the level of reserves to total external liabilities produces a first threshold at 12 per cent, and a second threshold at 52 per cent. The middle point of this range coincides with the average optimal level found in the previous section. We find a very negative and significant impact of reserves on spreads in the intermediate range (elasticity of 42 per cent). Under the first and third regimes the debt coefficients are not statistically different from zero. It is worth noting that the thresholds are estimated with a higher level of precision than the previous indicators, as evidenced by the narrow

Table 4.7 Threshold estimates of the elasticity of EMBI spreads with respect to international reserves. Traditional indicators

Thresholds	GDP	Months of Imports		Broad Money		Short-term Debt		
	< 49	< 6.3	> 6.3	< 28.3	> 28.3	< 125	[125, 534]	> 534
Spreads-reserves elasticity	− 0.425***	− 0.329***	− 0.004	− 0.463	0.167	− 0.31	− 0.311*	− 0.531*
	(− 0.11)	(0.12)	(0.37)	(0.17)	(0.25)	(0.20)	(0.19)	(0.37)
Observations	286	176	112	151	144	80	169	38
R-squared	0.53	0.5	0.46	0.42	0.46	0.24	0.6	0.7

Note: Robust standard errors in parentheses; *significant at 10%; **significant at 5%; ***significant at 1%.

95 per cent confidence intervals. Under this indicator, only the current levels of reserves in China and Taiwan Province of China cannot be explained in terms of their benefits in reducing spreads.

Reserves to financial system deposits and stock market capitalization

Two relevant thresholds are found, at 13 per cent and 30 per cent, respectively. The elasticity in the intermediate regime is 61 per cent and is not statistically significant from zero in the other two. As before, the coefficients are estimated with great precision, as indicated by the thresholds' confidence intervals.

A word of caution regards the use of some of the threshold point estimates as benchmark values for policy purposes: the confidence intervals for some of the threshold parameters are sufficiently large that there is considerably uncertainty regarding their true values. However, the estimates using the new reserve adequacy indicators are estimated with much higher precision than the more traditional ones, especially in terms of gross foreign liabilities.

This exercise has analyzed the impact of the accumulation of reserves on the service costs of the stock of sovereign debt. Therefore, it provides a lower bound estimate of the benefits of reserves in terms of lower financing costs, since it does not incorporate similar gains in the private sector.

V. Conclusions

The chapter has presented evidence that to a large extent explains Asia's large reserve accumulation since the 1997–98 crisis through the precautionary motive. Current reserve holdings in most of Asia (excluding China) are not seen as excessive when compared with levels predicted by a simple model of optimal reserves applied to specific country and regional characteristics. By mitigating the potentially large welfare costs of crises, reserves provide benefits in terms of insurance that more than compensates economies for the opportunity cost of holding liquid assets. The reserve accumulation observed so far in Asia (excluding China) reflects largely (though not entirely) this favorable trade-off, which has continued even at relatively high levels of reserves as a result of moderate opportunity costs.

When the large increase in the size and volatility of foreign liabilities – against which reserves provide insurance – is taken into consideration, the case for a precautionary motive behind the reserve accumulation over the last decade is reinforced. Furthermore, the benefits of reserves in terms of reduced spreads on privately held external debt, and thus borrowing costs, further justifies most of the observed growth in reserves. The chapter finds that a majority of economies in Asia continue to benefit from reduced spreads, as evidenced by the high estimated threshold levels beyond which no further gains are realized.

Notwithstanding these results, the chapter concurs with the conclusions in World Economic Outlook (IMF, 2003) that a slowdown in the pace of accumulation in Asia is now desirable. Even though current reserves are not 'too high' in most economies, they are close to or have recently reached optimal reserves levels as predicted by the insurance model, suggesting that going forward accumulation at the same rapid pace could result in excess reserves. Nevertheless, there is some indication that a deceleration has already started to take place, as evidenced by the leveling off of some reserve indicators and the decline in some others since 2003–04, which makes reserves in Asia (excluding China) in line with emerging markets in the rest of the world. To the extent that capital flows and economies' foreign liabilities continue to increase we should expect reserves to continue to mount in nominal terms. However, assuming an optimal response according to the predictions of the model, we are likely to see stabilization or even a moderate decline in reserve ratios going forward.

The chapter casts doubt on the use of the traditional rules of thumb to assess reserve adequacy. The reason is three-fold: first, country-specific optimal reserve ratios are found to be significantly above 3 months of imports, 100 per cent of external short-term debt or 20 per cent of broad money. In light of these findings, the traditional rules of thumb appear more arbitrary than ever. Second, these indicators fail to capture recent developments in financial markets, namely: increased vulnerability to large capital flows and the different nature of the potential balance of payments shocks against which reserves provide insurance. We have argued that the precautionary aspect of reserves is better captured by measuring reserves against total foreign liabilities. Finally, country-tailored reserve adequacy indicators seem more appropriate than standardized rules of thumb, in particular given the different country exposure and vulnerability to sudden stops as well as the heterogeneity in opportunity costs (as measured by external spreads or sterilization costs) across Asian economies.

As other papers before, our analysis cannot fully explain the large stock of reserves in China, neither from an insurance standpoint nor when accounting for the benefits of reserves in terms of reduced spreads. This chapter has attempted to differentiate China from the rest of emerging Asia, usually lumped together in the literature, and has largely focused on explaining reserve accumulation in the latter. The motivations, other than precautionary, behind the reserve build-up in China are to be explored in future research.

A word of caution regards the use of the estimated country-specific optimal reserve ratios or the threshold point estimates as benchmark values for policy purposes: the results of the calculation are sensitive to the choice of model parameters and the confidence intervals for threshold estimates are often sufficiently large that there is uncertainty about their true value. Moreover, in some cases regional averages, rather than country-specific estimates, were used for consistency purposes or data limitation reasons.

An aspect not discussed in the chapter, but with potential implications for the current global credit crunch, is the positive spillover dimension of reserve accumulation. The reserve build-up has contributed to reduce external vulnerabilities in all emerging market economies in Asia and, as a result, is helping to maintain financial stability in the region as a whole. Not only are individual economies better prepared to weather a sudden stop of capital flows, but the risk of financial contagion in the region may have decreased as a result of the reserve accumulation.

Finally, this chapter has abstracted from addressing issues surrounding the emergence of sovereign wealth funds (SWFs). However, the fact that the largest funds in Asia are China, Singapore and Malaysia is not surprising in view of our results that suggest that these economies have just reached or exceeded recommended reserves levels. Our chapter has also implications for the near future

Annex 4.1 Variable Definitions and Sources

Variable	Description	Source
Spread	JP Morgan EMBI spread in bps	Bloomberg, Datastream
10Y US T-bond	US Treasury note, 10-year maturity	US Treasury
Risk aversion	CSFB high yield spread	Bloomberg
Reserves	International reserves	IMF, WEO
GDP growth	GDP growth	IMF, WEO
Debt	Sovereign debt stock	IMF, WEO
Imports	Imports of goods and services	IMF, WEO
Broad money	M2	IMF, WEO
Short-term external debt	External debt maturing within 1 year	BIS
Foreign external liabilities	Gross external liabilities	Milessi-Feretti IIP Database
Fin. system deposits and equity	Total deposits and market capitalization	World Bank

Annex 4.2 Summary statistics

	Obs.	Mean	Std. Dev.	Min	Max
Sovereign spread	320	514.9	823.8	−260.9	6182.0
US 10Y bond rate	320	4.7	0.7	4.0	6.3
High yield spread	320	584.7	240.6	329.2	950.8
GDP growth	320	4.1	3.9	−11.0	18.3
Debt to GDP	310	93.5	265.5	4.9	2101.7
Reserves to GDP	320	22.0	19.9	1.5	104.5
Reserves to months of imports	320	6.4	4.1	0.3	35.3
Reserves to short-term debt	320	395.4	659.4	6.5	7530.8
Reserves to broad money	320	35.5	22.9	2.9	146.3
Reserves to foreign liabilitis	298	25.8	36.8	2.0	490.5
Reserves to fin. system deposits and equities	248	28.5	22.2	1.6	113.9

growth of these funds. Since other Asian economies are close to their optimality thresholds, the same rapid pace of accumulation observed so far could result in a very large growth in the pool of assets managed by SWFs, assuming excess reserves are directed to SWFs. The potential impact of this trend for the global economy and global financial stability is an aspect to be explored in future research.

Notes

1 © International Monetary Fund. Reprinted with permission. The views expressed in this chapter belong solely to the authors. Nothing contained in this chapter should be reported as representing IMF policy or the views of the IMF, its Executive Board, member governments, or any other entity mentioned herein.
2 Data from Lane and Milesi-Feretti (2007).
3 In an earlier paper, Jeanne and Rancière (2006) present a similar model of optimal reserves. We calibrate both models and obtain similar results. This chapter presents calibration results of the 2007 model; results using the 2006 model are available upon request.
4 Risk aversion is assumed to be equal to 2, in line with the previous literature.
5 Results are robust to using averages corresponding to different time periods. The real GDP series are detrended with a Hodrik Prescott filter.
6 Jeanne identifies sudden stops as those years in which net capital inflows fell by more than 5 per cent of GDP.
7 For the sake of simplicity and presentation, only the economies with the highest reserve ratios are presented in the figure. Results for the remaining emerging economies in the analysis are available upon request.
8 The test of the null hypothesis of no threshold against the alternative of threshold is performed using a Wald test under the assumption of homoskedastic errors. Using 1,000 bootstrap replications, the p-value for the threshold model was 0. This suggests that there is evidence of a regime change at the specified level of reserves.

5 Tax administration reform and fiscal adjustment

The case of Indonesia (2001–7)

John Brondolo, Carlos Silvani,
Eric Le Borgne, and Frank Bosch

I. Introduction

This chapter analyzes the role of tax administration reform in supporting fiscal adjustment based on the recent experiences in Indonesia.[1] The study draws on an extensive set of tax administration reforms that Indonesia's Directorate General of Taxation (DGT) initiated in 2001 and has continued to implement through 2008, with refinements, under the country's broader economic reform program. The chapter sets out the key objectives of Indonesia's fiscal adjustment strategy, describes the tax administration reforms that were introduced to help achieve these objectives and assesses the results of the reforms in terms of both their quality of implementation and impact on the fiscal objectives.

Fiscal adjustment involves the use of public revenue and expenditure measures to help achieve key economic objectives (Daniel et al., 2006). These objectives commonly include promoting economic growth, achieving macroeconomic stability, alleviating poverty and reducing fiscal vulnerability. Fiscal adjustment has been an integral part of Indonesia's economic reform efforts over the last several years.

A central objective of tax administration is to collect the full amount of taxes due under the tax laws in a cost-effective manner and according to a high standard of integrity. In pursuing this objective, tax agencies apply a mixture of measures to help taxpayers comply with the requirements of the tax laws and to enforce compliance when taxpayers fail to do so voluntarily. Both sets of measures have played a role in Indonesia's tax administration reform strategy in recent years.

Tax administration and fiscal adjustment intersect when the implementation of a fiscal adjustment program requires the strengthening of a country's tax agency. In the case of Indonesia, the Indonesian authorities have, over the last several years, viewed the DGT's modernization as being critical to the advancement of two key fiscal objectives: (1) increasing the tax yield and (2) promoting the investment climate. Indeed, these two objectives have anchored Indonesia's tax administration reforms since 2001.

Against this background, the chapter consists of several sections. The second section describes the broad context for the tax administration reforms in Indonesia. The section reviews Indonesia's macroeconomic situation in 2000 as the country emerged from the Asian financial crisis and describes the key elements of the fiscal adjustment strategy. In addition, the main features of Indonesia's tax regime are described, at the outset of the reforms, including the low tax yield, the complexities in the tax laws and weaknesses in tax administration.

The next section presents a framework for analyzing the linkages between tax administration and the tax yield, which is elaborated on in mathematical terms in Annex 5.1. The framework shows that a tax agency collects revenue through two channels: voluntary payments by compliant taxpayers and enforced collections from noncompliant taxpayers. While enforced collections may, under some circumstances, provide a potentially large source of tax revenue in the short term, the framework demonstrates that a tax agency's ability to sustain and increase the tax yield over the medium term depends critically on expanding voluntary collections by raising taxpayers' compliance rates. This section also provides an overview of the DGT's short- and medium-term reform strategies.

The fourth and fifth sections describe the details of the DGT's short- and medium-term reforms, respectively, and review the extent and quality of their implementation. The short-term strategy, which was formulated in late 2001, comprised a small number of initiatives designed to generate quick gains in fiscal adjustment and also to jump-start the process of modernizing the DGT. The medium-term strategy, which was developed in 2003 and refined in subsequent years, provided a more comprehensive set of reforms aimed at addressing the DGT's most fundamental weaknesses. Overall, implementation of the reforms was good although the highly positive results of the short-term reforms are balanced against the more varied progress that has been made in implementing the medium-term strategy (notwithstanding their ongoing nature thanks to the adoption, in 2006, of a new medium-term modernization program backed by senior DGT officials and the Minister of Finance).

The sixth section assesses the impact that the tax administration reforms have had on the key objectives in Indonesia's fiscal adjustment program: increasing tax collection through tax compliance improvements and bettering the investment climate. With respect to the revenue objective, the evidence suggests that the tax administration measures accounted for over half of the 1.1 percentage points of GDP increase in tax collection over the reform period (2002 to 2006, the last year for which actual data is available) – preliminary revenue estimates for 2007 indicate that the good revenue performance is continuing. Regarding the investment climate objective, a number of surveys have indicated that tax administration reforms have had (and continue to have) strong positive effects on investors' perceptions at the pilot tax offices but these necessary but not sufficient reforms need to be (1) broadened to cover a wider range of tax administration issues (in particular the administration's audit and appeals processes); (2) extended beyond the pilot tax offices; and (3) sustained over time before they can be expected to have a material impact on the investment climate.

The section afterhand discusses Indonesia's unfinished reform agenda for tax administration. Despite the good progress that has been achieved since 2001, much work still remains to be done to transform the DGT into a modern and highly effective revenue collection agency. Key reform priorities for the future include: further strengthening the legal framework for tax administration and simplifying the tax system; enhancing the capacity of the DGT's recently reorganized headquarters to manage a national tax administration; refining the strategies for administering different taxpayer segments that have been intro-duced at the pilot tax offices; continuing the modernization of all field offices based on the experiences of the pilot tax offices; introducing a balanced set of performance measures for evaluating core tax administration processes; further developing new human resources management policies that create incentives for high performance and noncorrupt behavior among tax officers; and continuing to improve the DGT's enforcement programs, particularly in the audit area. Reforms in many of these areas have been adopted by the DGT's new man-agement in 2006 and continue to be implemented through today with strong support from the Ministry of Finance.

Finally, the last section presents the main conclusions that may be drawn from Indonesia's experience with tax administration reform. Some conclusions reaffirm lessons in tax administration reform that the IMF has learned in other countries while other conclusions offer insights into new areas. These include:

- Since 2002, Indonesia's tax administration reforms have been successful in advancing the country's fiscal adjustment program. The improvements in tax administration had (and continue to have) a strong, positive impact on the tax yield and a positive, though difficult to quantify, effect on the investment climate.
- Linking tax administration reform to a government's wider fiscal adjustment program can both assist fiscal adjustment and improve tax administration. Given the gestation period for designing and implementing tax administra-tion reforms, the sooner such reforms can be incorporated into an adjust-ment program the better.
- Tax administration reform can help raise the tax yield by increasing enforced and voluntary tax collections. Programming these gains should be based on a coherent framework, such as that set out in section II and Annex 5.1 with realistic estimates for increasing collections that are linked to concrete administrative measures for bringing about the targeted increases.
- In the short term, enforced collections may provide a substantial source of additional tax revenue. However, because these collections typically account for a relatively small share of tax revenue, very high growth rates are required to have an appreciable impact on the tax yield. The Indonesian experience demonstrates the practical difficulties of achieving high growth rates in enforced collections year after year.
- Over the medium term, increasing voluntary collections (by raising taxpay-ers' compliance rates) is the key way that tax administration can help sustain and expand the tax yield. Therefore, tax agencies should be encouraged to measure tax compliance, identify reasons for noncompliance and develop appropriate compliance-enhancing strategies.

- Tax administration reform can be a necessary (but not a sufficient) condition for improving a country's investment climate. A tax agency can help boost the investment climate through measures that lower compliance costs faced by taxpayers and promote integrity among tax officers. Indonesia achieved promising results in this area through the careful vetting of tax officers, providing sufficiently high salaries, establishing clear standards of conduct that were effectively communicated to taxpayers and tax offices and accelerating the processing of tax refunds.

- The good results that have been achieved in improving Indonesia's tax administration were due, in part, to a reform strategy that focused initially on a few key initiatives. This approach allowed early successes to be registered in the short term and helped build confidence within the DGT to take on increasingly more challenging reforms over the medium term.

- Strong political commitment was critical to the success of Indonesia's tax administration reforms. This commitment was most evidenced by the government's willingness to place tax administration reform high on its reform agenda, allocate resources (staff, budgetary and technical assistance) to support the reforms and appoint capable staff to lead the reform effort.

- Technical assistance and policy conditionality can play an important role in helping tax agencies to design and implement reform programs. However, ownership of the reform process by a country's tax agency is indispensable for sustaining the reforms over time.

- There remains ample scope for Indonesia to increase the tax yield and stimulate the investment climate through further improvements in tax administration. In this regard, the strategic plan that the DGT's new management formulated in 2006 provides a sound basis for strengthening revenue collection and promoting fiscal adjustment over the coming years. Preliminary estimates for 2007 revenue collection point to a successful start.

II.   The context for tax administration reform in Indonesia

Indonesia's fiscal adjustment and tax administration reform strategies emerged in the early 2000s against the backdrop of the East Asian financial crisis. Three factors had a significant role in shaping the tax administration reforms: the macro-fiscal situation, the structure of the tax regime and the weak state of the DGT's operations.

The macro-fiscal situation

The 1997 Asian financial crisis afflicted Indonesia more severely than most economies and served as a major catalyst for reforming Indonesia's tax administration. Real GDP contracted by 13 per cent in 1998, and by July 1998 the Rupiah had depreciated by about 80 per cent from the previous year, while inflation had accelerated to about 70 per cent per annum. The situation deteriorated further as a run on the banking system left many banks insolvent. While progress had been made in restoring macroeconomic stability by mid-1999, the early gains began to unravel in 2000 and 2001. Slippages in reforms and an increasingly uncertain political climate contributed to renew downward pressure on the Rupiah, and new inflationary pressures emerged.

To achieve economic stability and growth, the Indonesian authorities formulated an economic reform program in 2000 which was supported by IMF financial and technical assistance. The program envisaged restoring the growth rate to 5–6 per cent over the medium term, restricting inflation to below 5 per cent annually and achieving fiscal sustainability. Under this program, public debt – which had shot up from 25 per cent of GDP before the crisis to about 100 per cent of GDP in 2000[2] – was to be reduced to 65 per cent of GDP by 2004.

In this context, the authorities designed a fiscal adjustment program that aimed at achieving a balance between supporting economic recovery and making progress toward the public debt objective. Given the fragility of the emerging recovery in early 2000, it was considered important to maintain fiscal stimulus in 2000 while planning for early fiscal consolidation. Hence, the government's medium-term macroeconomic framework targeted a gradual reduction in the central government deficit.

With oil production projected to decline, increasing the buoyancy of non-oil and gas tax revenue was to become a key element in Indonesia's fiscal adjustment strategy.[3] With the economy slowly recovering from a major economic and financial crisis, the authorities sought to generate as much revenue as possible through improvements in tax administration rather than to rely exclusively or mainly on tax changes for increasing the tax yield (see Table 5.1 and Table 5.3).

The year 2002 would become a pivotal one for tax administration reform in Indonesia. That year's budget targeted a sizable reduction in the deficit which would require, among other things, increasing non-oil tax revenue by 1.2 percentage point of GDP. About one-half of the revenue increase was to be generated through tax administration improvements. To achieve the targeted increase, the government called upon the DGT to identify specific administrative measures for increasing tax collections. Linking the tax administration reforms to higher-order economic objectives would prove crucial for locking in the political commitment needed to implement the DGT's reform agenda.

The government's economic reform program during the early 2000s also attached great importance to improving the investment climate as a key to achieving its growth and employment objectives. With a number of studies and surveys indicating that problems in tax administration were among the top impediments to doing business in Indonesia, tax administration reform came to be seen as crucial for reasons beyond its potential for generating revenue (see the sixth section for details). As a result, the DGT's reform strategy was eventually broadened to include measures aimed at simplifying the compliance requirements of the tax system, promoting integrity among tax officers, accelerating refunds to taxpayers and a number of other investment-enhancing initiatives.

Table 5.1 Indonesia: total revenue collections FY1993/94–FY1999/00

	FY93/94	FY94/95	FY95/96	FY96/97	FY97/98	FY98/99	FY99/00
	Act.	Act.	Act.	Act.	Act.	Act.	Act.
	(Rp. trillions)						
Total Revenue and grants	55.4	63.1	70.8	82.7	106.9	152.3	188.4
Oil and gas revenue	14.8	15.5	16.5	20.1	30.6	41.2	58.5
Nin-oil and gas revenue	40.2	47.1	53.8	62.0	76.3	111.0	129.9
Tax revenue	36.7	42.7	49.2	57.2	70.0	100.7	112.8
Directorate General of Taxes	30.5	35.6	42.4	50.1	61.8	87.6	97.4
Income tax	14.8	18.4	21.6	27.0	34.0	55.9	59.7
VAT & luxury sales tax	13.9	15.3	18.5	20.1	24.5	27.7	33.1
VAT	…	13.4	16.5	18.0	22.0	26.6	30.7
Load tax	1.5	1.6	1.9	2.5	2.7	3.6	4.1
Other taxes	0.3	0.3	0.5	0.5	0.6	0.4	0.6
Directorate General of Customs	6.2	7.2	6.8	7.1	8.2	13.1	15.4
Non-tax revenue	3.5	4.3	4.5	4.9	6.3	10.3	17.1
Grants	0.4	0.5	0.5	0.5	0.0	0.0	0.0
	(per cent of GDP)						
Total Revenue and grants	16.3	15.8	15.1	14.9	15.4	14.9	16.6
Oil and gas revenue	4.4	3.9	3.5	3.6	4.4	4.0	5.2
Nin-oil and gas revenue	11.8	11.7	11.5	11.2	11.0	10.9	11.5

(Continued)

Table 5.1 (Continued)

	FY93/94	FY94/95	FY95/96	FY96/97	FY97/98	FY98/99	FY99/00
	Act.	Act.	Act.	Act.	Act.	Act.	Act.
Tax revenue	10.8	10.7	10.5	10.3	10.1	9.9	9.9
Directorate General of Taxes	9.0	8.9	9.0	9.0	8.9	8.6	8.6
Income tax	4.3	4.6	4.6	4.9	4.9	5.5	5.3
VAT & luxury sales tax	4.1	3.8	3.9	3.6	3.5	2.7	2.9
VAT	...	3.3	3.5	3.2	3.2	2.6	2.7
Load tax	0.1	0.4	0.4	0.4	0.4	0.3	0.4
Other taxes	0.1	0.1	0.1	0.1	0.1	0.0	0.1
Directortae General of Customs	1.8	1.8	1.5	1.3	1.2	1.3	1.4
Non-tax revenue	1.0	1.1	1.0	0.9	0.9	1.0	1.5
Grants	0.1	0.1	0.1	0.1	0.0	0.0	0.0
			(per cent of non-oil GDP)				
Total Revenue and Grants	18.6	18.0	17.2	17.0	17.6	17.0	18.9
Oil and Gas Revenue	5.0	4.4	4.0	4.1	5.0	4.6	5.9
Nin-oil and gas revenue	13.5	13.4	13.1	12.7	12.6	12.4	13.1
Tax revenue	12.3	12.2	12.0	11.7	11.5	11.2	11.3
Directorate General of Taxes	10.2	10.1	10.3	10.3	10.2	9.8	9.8
Income tax	4.9	5.2	5.2	5.5	5.6	6.2	6.0
VAT & luxury sales tax	4.7	4.3	4.5	4.1	4.0	3.1	3.3

Load tax	0.5	0.5	0.5	0.5	0.4	0.4	0.4
Other taxes	0.1	0.1	0.1	0.1	0.1	0.0	0.1
Directortae General of Customs	2.1	2.0	1.7	1.5	1.4	1.5	1.5
Non-tax revenue	1.2	1.2	1.1	1.0	1.0	1.2	1.7
Grants	0.1	0.1	0.1	0.1	0.0	0.0	0.0
(per cent of total revenue and grants)							
Total Revenue and grants	100.0	100.0	100.0	100.0	100.0	100.0	100.0
Oil and gas revenue	26.7	24.6	23.4	24.4	28.6	27.1	31.0
Non-oil and gas revenue	72.5	74.5	75.9	75.1	71.4	72.9	69.0
Tax revenue	66.1	67.7	69.5	69.2	65.5	66.1	59.9
Directorate General of Taxes	55.0	56.3	59.9	60.6	57.8	57.5	51.7
Income tax	26.6	29.1	30.4	32.6	31.8	36.7	31.7
VAT & luxury sales tax	25.2	24.2	26.1	24.3	22.9	18.2	17.6
Land tax	2.7	2.6	2.7	3.0	2.5	2.3	2.2
Other taxes	0.5	0.4	0.7	0.6	0.5	0.3	0.3
Directorate General of Customs	11.2	11.4	9.6	8.6	7.7	8.6	8.2
Non-tax revenue	6.4	6.8	6.4	5.9	5.9	6.8	9.1
Grants	0.8	0.8	0.7	0.6	0.0	0.0	0.0
Memorandum items							
Nominal non-oil GDP (Rp. trillions)	298	351	412	487	608	896	995
Nominal GDP (Rp. trillions)	340	401	469	556	693	1,022	1,135

Source: IMF staff.

In this way, the government's macro-fiscal objectives propelled tax adminis-tration to a prominent position in Indonesia's economic policy agenda, which triggered a series of tax administration reforms that began in late 2001 and have continued since. Before turning to the details of the tax administration reform strategy, the chapter first describes the state of Indonesia's tax system and tax administration in 2000.

The structure of the tax system

Prior to the Asian financial crisis, Indonesia had taken steps to improve the tax system by introducing a modern VAT and income tax. By 2000, the overall design of the tax system was generally regarded as sound, but its yield was low and the tax laws included a number of features that unnecessarily complicated administration. As such, some aspects of the tax policy regime made the chal-lenges of administering the tax system that much greater for the DGT.

The overall yield of the tax system was low. The overall burden of Indonesia's tax system in 2000 was relatively light compared to that of other countries in the region (Table 5.2). Specifically, the ratio of tax revenue to GDP in Indo-nesia (excluding oil and gas tax revenues) was 9.9 per cent compared to an average of 14.0 per cent among non-OECD countries in the region and 24.9 per cent among Asian OECD countries.[4] Indonesia's low tax burden reflected several weaknesses, including the narrowness of major tax bases, relatively low taxation of petroleum, tobacco and certain forms of income, and a high rate of noncompliance among taxpayers. Correcting these weaknesses would be essential to mobilizing the revenue that Indonesia's fiscal adjustment program required.

Income taxes. Income taxes (both corporate and individual) in Indonesia com-prised 4.3 per cent of GDP (excluding oil and gas income tax revenue) which is noticeably lower than the average of 6.0 per cent of GDP among selected non-OECD Asian countries.[5] In these countries, corporate income tax accounts for about two-thirds of total income tax collections and personal income tax the remainder. In Indonesia, because of the means of presenting the data by nature of collection rather than corporate or personal income taxpayers, it is not possible to determine the relevant breakdown. However, a rough allocation of components of income tax revenue (excluding oil and gas revenues) suggests a similar breakdown (or a somewhat lower reliance on personal income tax) as that of non-OECD regional comparators.

General consumption taxes. General consumption taxes in Indonesia were equivalent to 3.4 per cent of GDP compared to the regional average of 3.2 per cent for non-OECD comparators. In Indonesia, the general consumption tax category includes VAT and luxury tax, with the latter applying to an extensive list of goods. If the luxury taxes were reclassified to the excise tax category, then the general consumption tax would have yielded about 3.0 per cent of GDP, in line with the average for non-OECD regional comparators.

Excise taxes. Excise taxes comprised only 1.1 per cent of GDP in Indonesia, compared to a regional average of 2.7 per cent. The lower share of excises in

Table 5.2 Level and composition of tax revenue in selected Asian/Pacific countries[1]

	Total Tax Revenue	Income Tax			Consumption Taxes			Trade	Property Taxes	Total Revenue
		Total	Corporate	Personal	Total	General	Excises			
					(in per cent of GDP)					
Indonesia	9.9	4.3	...	...	5.0	3.4	1.1	0.5	0.5	18.3
Average all countries	17.6	8.6	3.8	4.9	7.4	3.7	2.6	0.8	1.0	24.8
OECD[2]										
Australia	30.0	18.1	4.9	13.2	7.6	2.5	3.3	0.6	2.9	33.2
Japan	17.7	9.3	3.5	5.7	5.1	2.4	2.0	0.2	2.8	39.7
Korea	15.7	5.7	2.7	3.0	9.6	4.5	4.0	1.1	0.4	30.8
New Zealand	36.2	21.3	4.4	15.3	12.5	8.9	2.1	0.6	2.1	40.8
Average	24.9	13.6	3.9	9.3	8.7	4.6	2.9	0.6	2.1	36.1
Non-OECD[3]										
China	15.9	4.1	2.7	1.0	11.3	9.5	1.0	0.9	0.5	17.1
Hong Kong	10.0	5.7	3.4	2.3	3.9	0.0	3.9	0.0	0.1	16.3
Malaysia	14.3	7.9	5.8	2.1	4.5	2.9	1.7	1.4	0.1	18.3
Philippines	13.1	5.8	2.5	2.3	7.2	2.8	1.8	1.4	0.1	14.8
Singapore[4]	16.3	7.8	5.5	1.3	6.8	1.4	4.0	0.7	1.0	30.5
Thailand	14.1	4.8	3	1.8	8.4	2.8	3.8	1.8	0.1	16.1
Average	14.0	6.0	3.8	2.0	7.0	3.2	2.7	1.0	0.3	18.4

Sources: *Revenue Statistics* (OECD); OECD *Economic Outlook*; and IMF country documents.

Notes: [1]Data from 2001 for either central or general government. Totals do not necessarily add up with their subcomponents as 'other taxes' are not shown.
[2]General government.
[3]Central government.
[4]The breakdown between corporate and personal income tax revenues is estimated to be 70 and 30 per cent, respectively.

Indonesia compared to the region was largely accounted for by the omission of petroleum from Indonesia's excise regime. Indonesia does not impose an excise tax or luxury sales tax on gasoline and other petroleum products, which represents a significant source of revenue for many other countries in the region. Excise taxes, both on domestic and international transactions, are collected by Indonesia's customs administration.

International trade taxes. International trade taxes in Indonesia also yielded less than the regional average. This appears to have reflected a combination of weak enforcement, widespread exemptions and generally low tariff rates.

Property taxes. Property taxes were slightly above the non-OECD regional average. However, compared with OECD countries in the region, this tax yielded little revenue mainly due to its policy design. With a 0.5 per cent tax rate and a standard property assessment at 40 per cent of market value, the effective rate is 0.2 per cent of assessed property value, which is low.

Some features of the tax system were unnecessarily complex. The tax laws included a number of provisions, relating to both income and consumption taxes, that presented difficulties for taxpayers to comply with and for the DGT to enforce. Tax simplification, therefore, offered significant advantages for tax-payers and the DGT alike, and would become a key element in Indonesia's tax administration reform strategy.

Income taxes.[6] The personal income tax had several positive features that sim-plified compliance and tax administration, including the widespread withholding of tax at source and a simplified regime for individual entrepreneurs. However, many of these advantages were offset by the government's decision in 2001 to require most individual taxpayers (even employees with only a single source of income) to file an annual tax return. This requirement dramatically increased the number of tax returns that had to be filed beyond the capacity of the DGT to process and enforce.

The corporate income tax law also had a number of features that complicated administration and provided scope for abuse. Chief among these was the rein-troduction of tax privileges in 1996 (under Government Regulation 45) which provided tax holidays to newly incorporated firms 'operating in certain industries' for up to 10 years. Tax holidays and other tax incentives present serious admin-istrative challenges to a tax agency as they introduce the possibility for taxpayers to transfer profits from operations that do not qualify for the holiday to those that do. Such schemes are also an invitation to corruption as government officials commonly have wide discretion in their administration.

Value-added tax (VAT).[7] The general design of the VAT in 2000 provided a number of advantages for administration. These included a single positive rate of 10 per cent, the limitation of zero-rating to exports, the use of the invoice/credit method (accrual) to calculate the VAT liability and a simpli-fied regime for small taxpayers. Along with these desirable features, however, the VAT also contained a number of undesirable features that significantly complicated administration. The most serious of these problems involved a legal provision that requires all refund claims to be audited, regardless of the taxpayer's compliance history, prior to payment and approved (or disallowed) within 12 months.[8] This requirement led to lengthy delays in processing refund claims which caused major cash flow problems for businesses, particularly to exporters who were regularly in a refund position for the value-added tax. It also created problems for tax administration by requiring the DGT to allocate a disproportionate amount of audit resources to examining refund claims and, as a result, leaving insufficient resources for auditing other, potentially more significant issues.

An additional problem involved the VAT-free status of Batam Island, which was difficult to enforce and created risks of significant revenue leakage. Other complications with the VAT involved the separate registration thresholds for goods and services, separate VAT reporting by each branch of an enterprise and the excessive use of 'collectors' who were required to withhold 100 per cent of the VAT from their suppliers.

Luxury sales tax (LST). The LST added much complexity to the tax system but produced little revenue. The tax provided for approximately 350 tariff codes, which apply to both domestic and imported goods, with more than half of the codes containing either taxable and nontaxable products or products taxable at different rates. The taxable status of a product depended on one of several factors including its price, packaging, quality or output capacity. Distinguishing among these various factors and applying the correct rate made compliance extremely difficult for the DGT to achieve or verify.

The state of tax administration

In 2000, Indonesia's tax administration was beset by many weaknesses. Poor legal and governance frameworks, shortcomings in organizational and staffing arrangements, ineffective taxpayer services and enforcement programs and outdated information systems combined to severely reduce the DGT's effectiveness and efficiency in collecting taxes. These weaknesses resulted in large amounts of foregone tax revenue due to noncompliance by taxpayers[9] and also raised the cost of doing business in Indonesia. Addressing these problems would become central to the DGT's reform strategy and to advancing the government's fiscal adjustment program.

Poor legal and governance frameworks. In Indonesia, the legal framework for tax administration is contained in two sets of laws: the rules that apply to all taxes are set out in the general law on tax administration and arrears collection[10] while the rules that apply to a particular tax are provided for in each substantive tax law. Deficiencies in this framework meant that tax officers lacked many powers common to modern tax agencies while taxpayers lacked a number of basic protections. From the tax officers' perspective, the deficiencies included a weak penalty regime, inadequate access to taxpayers' records (particularly banking records) and the absence of key powers for enforcing the collection of tax debts. From the taxpayer's perspective, the tax laws led to lengthy delays in processing refunds, did not offer sufficient protection from receiving large (unwritten) arbitrary tax assessments (which often became the basis for negotiating the tax liability), the objection and appeals processes was viewed as biased in favor of the DGT and certain tax offences could lead to imprisonment without trial. Together, these problems contributed to an environment of mutual suspicion and distrust between tax officers and taxpayers.

Shortcomings in organizational and staffing arrangements. The DGT's organizational structure suffered from a number of shortcomings.[11] Headquarters was not organized in a manner that would allow it to effectively manage ongoing operations and develop new tax administration programs. The field offices, on the other hand, had separate units for administering different types of taxes along with a parallel network of audit offices and property tax offices, all of which operated largely independently of each other.[12] This organizational set up led to a fragmentation of tax administration programs, both at headquarters and the field offices, resulting in a lack of accountability for results.

In addition to its organizational shortcomings, the DGT also had a number of serious staffing problems. During the 1990s and into the 2000s, the DGT had insufficient numbers of staff assigned to the key functions of strategic planning, audit and taxpayer services. For example, in 1996 the DGT had only about 1,800 skilled auditors, equivalent to about 7 per cent of its staff, whereas effective tax administrations commonly assign up to 30 to 40 per cent of their staff to the audit function. Such misallocations of staff constrained the DGT in carrying out key management and operational functions.

Ineffective enforcement and taxpayer service programs. In 2000, the DGT had considerable difficulty in enforcing taxpayers' basic obligations under the tax laws: only a very small fraction of the taxpayer population was registered with the DGT and, among those who were, many failed to file their tax returns on time, did not fully pay their tax liabilities and underreported substantial amounts of taxes. These problems reflected weaknesses in the DGT's enforcement programs, particularly in the audit and arrears collection areas. Similar problems existed in the directorate's taxpayer services function, which was poorly organized, staffed with tax officers who had little training and lacked a service-oriented attitude and provided taxpayers with only the most basic types of services and assistance.

Outdated information technology systems. While the DGT had introduced computer technology to all levels of the organization by the mid-1990s, the quality of its information systems remained very low in 2000. The main deficiency was that separate, nonintegrated systems were used to administer each tax, thereby making it difficult to get a consolidated picture of taxpayers' overall account status with the DGT. In addition, the information systems provided few automated tools to help front-line staff in carrying out their operational responsibilities and practically no electronic services for taxpayers. Management oversight was severely compromised by the lack of reliable information that could be used to evaluate the effectiveness and efficiency of the DGT's core enforcement and taxpayer services programs.

Summary

As the government developed its economic reform program in 2000, Indonesia's tax system and its administration suffered from serious weaknesses. Non-oil tax receipts were low, certain features of the tax policy regime were unnecessarily complicated and tax administration was both weak and arbitrary. At the same time, it was generally recognized that there existed considerable scope (and need) for increasing non-oil tax revenue and promoting the investment climate by improving tax administration. This constellation of factors would bring tax administration reform into sharp focus beginning in late 2001.

III.   The tax administration reform strategy

This section describes the tax administration reform strategy that the Directorate General of Taxation (DGT) formulated beginning in late 2001 and has continued to implement, with refinements and additions along the way, ever since. The section begins by presenting a framework for analyzing the revenue impact of tax administration reform, and then provides an overview of DGT's short-term and medium-term reforms, which are elaborated on in next section, respectively.

Analytical framework

In designing tax administration reform strategies where increasing revenue is a key objective, it is important to understand the linkages between a tax agency's administrative programs and the tax yield. These linkages are described conceptually below and expressed more precisely in mathematical terms in Annex 5.1.

The 'tax gap' concept. The analysis of how tax administration improvements can increase tax revenue is anchored in the concept of the tax gap. The tax gap is generally defined as the difference between, on the one hand, the amount of tax revenue that would have been collected had all taxpayers fully complied with their obligations under the tax laws and, on the other hand, the amount of tax revenue that was actually collected by the tax administration. The difference, or gap, between potential and actual tax collections consists of taxes that were legally due but not paid by taxpayers as a result of noncompliance.[13]

The tax gap has three main components: nonfiling, underreporting and underpayment. The nonfiling gap represents the amount of taxes not paid by taxpayers who have an obligation to file a tax return, but do not file on time. The underreporting gap is the tax owed by taxpayers who file tax returns on time, but do not report the full amount of tax they owe. The underpayment gap is the amount of foregone revenue resulting from taxpayers who fail to fully pay on time the amount of tax owed.

The tax gap provides a useful organizing principle for designing a tax administration reform strategy within the context of a fiscal adjustment program. A tax agency has at its disposal various measures to increase actual tax collections relative to potential collections and, thereby, reduce the tax gap. Before turning to these measures it is important to first recognize that tax collections take two broad forms.

Forms of tax collection. A tax agency receives revenue in two ways: (1) taxes that are paid voluntarily by taxpayers and (2) taxes that are collected from noncompliance taxpayers through some form of enforcement by the tax authorities. In all countries, these two forms of collection account for vastly different shares of tax revenue and respond differently to a tax agency's administrative programs.

Voluntary collections. Voluntary collections consist of those taxes that are paid by taxpayers without requiring any direct form of enforcement on the part of the tax authorities. These collections commonly occur when taxpayers self-assess a tax return and voluntarily pay the declared tax liability. In all countries, voluntary collections account for a much larger proportion of tax revenue (usually far more than 90 per cent) than enforced collections. A tax administration can increase voluntary collections by putting in place measures that raise the rate of voluntary compliance among taxpayers.[14]

Because of the large share of voluntary collections in tax revenue, relatively small increases in taxpayers' compliance rates can generate substantial increases in tax revenue. However, it may take time for a tax agency's measures to increase voluntary collections since these measures work through changes in taxpayers' compliance rates which often take a while to adjust. The difficulties in measuring compliance rates is one of the reasons why fiscal analysts are often reluctant to program tax administration gains into their revenue projections.

Enforced collections. Enforced collections are those taxes that a tax agency collects through some form of enforcement action that is taken against noncompliant individuals and businesses. Examples include revenue recovered from taxpayers who failed to file a tax return on time, underreported their taxes or owed tax arrears. Revenue from enforced collections normally accounts for a relatively small share of a country's tax revenue (commonly far less than 10 per cent).

Because of its small share in total tax collections, enforced collections must increase at a high rate in order to have a significant impact on the tax yield. *Nevertheless, enforced collections have the potential to increase quickly, since these collections do not require adjustments in taxpayers' compliance patterns, but instead result directly from a tax agency's own enforcement actions.* Since most tax agencies have the capacity to measure the amount of revenue recovered through enforcement, fiscal analysts can estimate more precisely the potential for tax administration measures to increase enforced collections than voluntary collections.

Tax administration instruments and their linkages to the tax yield. A tax agency has two broad sets of instruments for reducing the tax gap: *compliance facilitation and compliance enforcement.* These two sets of instruments affect the tax yield in different ways through their impacts on voluntary collections and enforced collections.

Compliance facilitation affects the tax yield by increasing voluntary collections. Compliance facilitation entails those tax administration measures that make it easier for taxpayers to comply with their obligations under the tax laws. Common examples include simplifying the tax laws, streamlining administrative procedures and information reporting requirements and improving taxpayer services. By reducing the cost of compliance, compliance facilitation creates incentives for taxpayers to voluntarily pay their taxes. To the extent that taxpayers respond positively to these incentives, their voluntary compliance rate will increase and voluntary collections will rise.

Compliance enforcement affects the tax yield by increasing both voluntary collections and enforced collections. Compliance enforcement involves a tax agency's measures for detecting and redressing noncompliance by taxpayers. Common examples include identifying potential registrants, detecting under-reported tax liabilities and recovering delinquent tax returns and late tax payments. Compliance enforcement measures can have a direct effect on the tax yield by increasing enforced collections. They can also have an indirect effect on the tax revenue by discouraging taxpayers from engaging in noncompliance and thereby increasing voluntary collections.[15]

To summarize the discussion, Figure 5.1 below illustrates how the various concepts fit together. As can be seen in the diagram, potential tax collections represent the amount of revenue that would have been collected had taxpayers fully complied with the tax laws. Actual tax collections equal the amount of taxes that taxpayers paid voluntarily plus the amount of taxes that a tax agency recovered through some form of enforcement. The gross tax gap equals the difference between potential tax collections and voluntary tax collections while the net tax gap equals the gross tax gap less the amount of enforced collections. A tax agency can reduce the tax gap (and, thereby, increase the tax yield) through compliance enforcement measures (which can increase both enforced and voluntary collections) and compliance facilitation measures (which can increase voluntary collections).

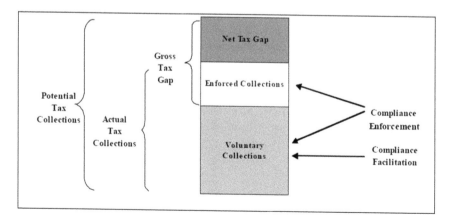

Figure 5.1 The tax gap and tax administration measures

Overview of the reform strategy

Indonesia's tax administration reforms were guided by two primary objectives in the fiscal adjustment strategy: increasing the tax yield and promoting the investment climate. In pursuing these objectives, the DGT formulated both short- and medium-term reform strategies whose main features and their rationale are summarized below.

The short-term reforms

In late 2001, the DGT developed a short-term reform strategy in close coordination with the MOF which, at the time, was formulating the country's fiscal adjustment program. In designing the short-term strategy, priority was given to those tax administration measures that could have an immediate impact on both the tax yield and the investment climate as well as jump-start the process of modernizing the DGT. The latter was seen as crucial for further increasing tax collection and improving the investment climate over the medium term.

The scope of the short-term strategy was constrained by the DGT's limited implementation capacity. At the time, the DGT had little experience in managing a comprehensive reform program and had little time to produce results. Consequently, the short-term strategy was restricted to a small number of reforms that the DGT could effectively manage and which could generate quick results. This approach of focusing on a few major initiatives and piloting their implementation wherever possible has been a constant theme in Indonesia's tax administration reform strategy since 2001.

The DGT's short-term strategy was built around three initiatives: (1) a 'revenue generation program' which included a number of measures aimed at tightening the enforcement of the tax laws. The rationale for this initiative flowed from the analytical framework that was presented in the previous subsection which demonstrated that stepped-up enforcement could yield potentially large increases in tax revenue in the short term; (2) the establishment of a special tax office within the DGT to administer the largest taxpayers. Since these businesses were not only large taxpayers but also large investors, it was felt that this initiative could have significant short-term impacts on both tax revenue and the investment climate; and (3) the introduction of an electronic system for processing tax payments to replace the existing system, which was slow, costly and vulnerable to 'leakage'. This initiative, which was already on the drawing board in 2001, could enhance tax collections by accelerating the processing of tax payments and guarding against illicit paper-based payment advices, a common problem at the time.

The medium-term reforms

As the short-term reforms were being implemented during 2001 and 2002, it became apparent that a broader set of tax administration reforms would be required to further increase tax collections and promote the business climate over the medium term. To achieve these goals, the DGT would have to address its most fundamental weaknesses, including those involving the legal and governance frameworks for tax administration, organizational and staffing arrangements, tax-payer services and enforcement programs, information systems and technologies and human resource management policies. Given the deep-seated nature of these problems, a medium-term perspective was needed for their improvement.

In early 2003, the DGT designed a medium-term reform plan, which was intended to be implemented over the next three years. In broad terms, the plan provided for a continuation of the short-term strategy and added to these reforms several major new initiatives. More specifically, the medium-term plan comprised the foundation statements in Box 5.1 and the following 10 initiatives:

1. Increasing the number of taxpayers administered by the large taxpayer office (LTO) and extending the LTO reforms to another region that also administered large businesses.
2. Establishing model tax offices for administering small and medium-sized taxpayers, and gradually extending these models to all tax offices throughout Indonesia.
3. Continuing the revenue generation initiative.
4. Simplifying each major tax, beginning with the value-added tax.
5. Revising the legal framework for tax administration.
6. Enhancing the capacity of the DGT's audit function.
7. Developing a balanced set of performance measures for the DGT's core tax administration processes.
8. Introducing new human resource management policies.
9. Designing a comprehensive information technology master plan.
10. Creating an internal investigation unit to investigate misconduct by tax officers.

Although the medium-term plan would be refined in subsequent years to include additional measures – such as reorganizing DGT headquarters and creating data processing centers – the 10 above-mentioned initiatives would continue to form the core of the reform strategy through 2007.

Box 5.1 Foundation statements for the DGT's medium-term plan

Mission Statement: To collect the full amount of revenue required under the tax laws at a minimum cost to taxpayers and the government.

Vision Statement: By 2006, the Directorate General of Taxation will become the premier tax administration among developing countries in Asia and a leading institution in Indonesia's public service in terms of taxpayers' compliance with the laws, excellence in service to taxpayers, fairness and integrity in tax administration and the quality of the work environment for tax officials.

Guiding Principles

Simplicity. The tax system and its administration should be easy to comply with.

Predictability. Tax laws and regulations should be clear, accessible and consistently applied.

Effectiveness. Taxpayer services and enforcement programs should be tailored to the specific characteristics of large, medium and small taxpayers.

Integrity. The DGT should adopt a policy of 'zero-tolerance' for corruption.

Performance. There should be incentives for high performance and accountability for results.

Transparency. Actions taken by the tax administration should be subject to scrutiny and results widely publicized.

Efficiency. Paper-based processes should be eliminated through extensive investment in modern technologies.

Quality. Problems should be identified and resolved before they become disputes.

Fairness. Dispute resolution mechanisms should be fast, low-cost and impartial.

Professionalism. Tax officers should be competent and highly motivated.

Goals

1. High level of taxpayers' compliance with the tax laws
2. High level of taxpayers' confidence in tax administration
3. High level of efficiency in administration

IV. The short-term reforms

The DGT launched its tax administration reform strategy in 2001 with an initial set of reforms that was intended to be implemented over the next 12–18 months. The main driving force behind the short-term strategy was the government's 2002 budget which set a target of increasing tax revenue by 0.5 percentage points of GDP through improvements in tax administration. The strategy was also driven by the government's desire to begin removing the impediments to the investment climate, including those related to tax administration.

In this context, the DGT selected three main initiatives to start the reform process: (1) several enforcement measures which were collectively known as the revenue generation initiative; (2) the creation of a special tax office for administering large taxpayers; and (3) the introduction of an electronic payment notification system. As will be seen, these initiatives were successfully implemented in almost all aspects and had a positive impact in advancing the government's fiscal adjustment program. They also created within the DGT a momentum for change that would later help to spawn a broader reform program over the medium term.

The revenue generation initiative

To help achieve the revenue target in the 2002 budget, the DGT implemented four measures aimed at intensifying enforcement: (1) registering additional taxpayers (the 'extensification' program); (2) improving audit performance; (3) intensifying the collection of tax arrears; and (4) enforcing tax return filing requirements. These measures were expected to generate short-term revenue gains mainly by increasing enforced collections. Over the medium term, the reforms were also expected to increase voluntary collections as taxpayers gradually improved their compliance rates in response to the DGT's stepped-up enforcement efforts.

While each of the four enforcement programs had its own distinct features, all four shared a common approach that included the preparation of an annual plan that set targets for the number and types of enforcement actions that were to be undertaken. The plans also included a forecast for the amount of taxes that each enforcement program was expected to generate. The comparison of the actual and estimated amounts of enforced collections provided the authorities with a convenient (but partial) way for measuring the revenue impact of the tax administration reforms.[16] This has important implications for designing fiscal adjustment programs as it demonstrates that the revenue impact for at least some tax administration measures can be measured fairly easily.

The extensification program. This program aimed at identifying and registering those individuals and businesses that were carrying out taxable activities without having registered for taxation with the DGT. Given the large number of businesses and individuals who were thought to be operating outside the tax system, the extensification program was considered fertile ground for expanding the tax net and increasing revenue.

To expand the tax net, the DGT focused on registering high-income earners (both companies and individuals) and securing their future compliance with the tax laws. Specific actions for identifying potential registrants included: (1) exploiting third-party information to identify owners of luxury cars and expensive homes, professional service providers and other indicators of tax potential; (2) canvassing shopping malls, newspapers and the Internet to ensure that all businesses were registered; (3) an aggressive advertising campaign to promote tax registration through television and billboards; (4) implementation of an electronic registration system which allowed taxpayers to register over the Internet; and (5) sending letters to new registrants to remind them of their obligation to file an income tax return.

The extensification program was highly successful in registering large numbers of taxpayers. More than 11 million new taxpayers were registered from 2002 to 2005. However, while searching for high-income registrants, large numbers of low-income taxpayers were also registered. Consequently, while the amount of tax collections that was generated by the extensification program rose steadily from Rp0.5 trillion in 2002 to Rp2.1 trillion in 2005, many of the new registrants contributed little revenue but added significantly to the DGT's administrative costs. From a revenue perspective, future registration efforts would be well advised to focus on registering medium-sized businesses (since it is highly unlikely that large-scale businesses are operating outside the tax net) and higher wealth individuals.

The audit program. The purpose of this program was to increase the DGT's capacity to identify and tax unreported income and sales. By doing so, an intensified audit program was seen as providing a ready source of additional tax revenue, first by recovering underreported taxes (and, hence increasing enforced collections) and second by improving taxpayers' compliance rates (and, thereby, increasing voluntary collections).

The DGT identified five major reforms for strengthening its audit function: (1) a national audit plan that sets targets for the number and types of audits to be conducted by each field office for different categories of taxpayers and economic sectors; (2) increasing audit coverage for large and medium-sized businesses; (3) reducing the excessive amount of audit resources that was allocated to examining refund claims, regardless of the claimants' compliance histories; (4) improving case selection systems by developing computer-based algorithms that would target audits on those taxpayers who had the highest risk of underreporting taxes; and (5) developing management reporting systems that would help DGT headquarters to better monitor the audit activities of the field offices. The strategy purposely excluded improving the methods and techniques that auditors use in examining taxpayers' records, which, while critical, could only be implemented over the medium term because of their extensive training requirements.

Although the results varied among the five audit reforms, the audit program as a whole was successful in recovering substantial amounts of revenue. The initiative generated Rp3.2 trillion in tax collections in 2002 which more than doubled over the next three years, reaching Rp7.8 trillion in 2005. Notwithstanding the impressive revenue results, the continuing weaknesses in key aspects of the DGT's audit program – most notably, in case selection, third-party data matching and the methods used by auditors to examine taxpayers' records – means that this remains an area with substantial, unrealized revenue potential.

The arrears collection program. This program sought to enhance the DGT's ability to recover taxes that were legally due but had not been paid by taxpayers within the statutory payment deadline. In 2001, the stock of tax arrears stood at about Rp17 trillion which was equivalent to about 13 per cent of tax collections for that year. Although this was not excessive by regional standards, tax arrears nevertheless represented another source of potential revenue to support the fiscal adjustment program's revenue objective.[17]

To intensify arrears collection, the DGT implemented the following four measures: (1) immediate assignment of new tax arrears cases to collection officers for action; (2) the close monitoring of the largest 1,000 debt cases; (3) increased use of existing legal provisions to freeze tax debtors' bank accounts; and (4) publicizing the names of tax debtors. These measures could be implemented relatively quickly, as they did not require changes in legislation or significant re-training of staff, and, therefore, could have an immediate impact on revenue.

Despite limitations with some of the measures, the arrears collection program generated more revenue than was originally expected. Under this program, the DGT recovered Rp4.8 trillion in tax arrears in 2002. Over the next three years, the recovery of tax arrears more than doubled, reaching Rp10.5 trillion in 2005. With the stock of tax arrears has continued to rise in recent years – as a result of the increase in the DGT's audit activities and the associated increase in audit assessments – the collection of delinquent taxes continues to be a good source of additional revenue.

The returns filing enforcement program. This program sought to improve taxpayers' compliance with their obligation to file tax returns. In 2001, filing compliance was extremely poor: only about one-third of registered businesses and one-quarter registered of individuals filed an income tax return despite the obligation to do so. This problem was a matter of serious concern as non-compliance with filing obligations not only results in a loss of revenue but also strikes at the very heart of the tax system: in an environment where there are few consequences for failing to file a tax return, compliant taxpayers are also encouraged to opt out of the tax system.

To improve filing compliance, the DGT developed an action plan in 2003 that included increasing the penalty for late filing, introducing systematic procedures for following-up on nonfilers, establishing a special team of tax officers to issue estimated (default) assessments to nonfilers, and commencing prosecution of certain high-profile nonfiler cases. Implementing this plan would require the issuance of several important decrees.

The results of this program were disappointing. Delays in promulgating the required decrees meant that little progress was made in implementing the reforms and, as a consequence, little revenue was generated. With taxpayers' filing rates are still very low, the initiative retains the potential for generating substantial tax revenue in the future.

The large taxpayer initiative

This initiative involved the creation of a special large taxpayer office (LTO) within the DGT to administer the relatively small number of taxpayers who collectively accounted for the largest portion of tax collections. The LTO opened in July 2002 at which time it administered 200 large enterprises and their 300 branches who contributed 23 per cent of total tax collections. In 2004, the LTO was expanded by an additional 100 large corporations, which brought LTO tax receipts up to 27 per cent of total DGT collections.

The large taxpayer initiative offered important advantages for Indonesia's fiscal adjustment program through its potential for: (1) increasing tax revenue by achieving tight control over a large portion of the tax base and (2) improving the investment climate by providing large taxpayers, who were also large investors, with high-quality services and introducing a number of measures to curb malfeasance by tax officers. In addition, the creation of an LTO was viewed as an important stepping stone in modernizing the DGT by providing a controlled environment for testing a wide range of new tax administration processes prior to their roll-out to other tax offices.

The LTO initiative encompassed several major reforms. The LTO was re-organized into units based on tax administration function (e.g. taxpayer services, audit, arrears collection), which facilitated the development of specialized skills among staff. Service to large businesses was improved through the creation of a cadre of service-oriented tax officers who were trained in the complex tax law issues that often arise when dealing with large taxpayers.[18] Refunds were accelerated through the introduction of a 'gold card' program which simplified the refund process for highly compliant businesses. Enforcement was strengthened through the quick identification and rapid treatment of taxpayers who filed their tax returns late, paid their taxes late or committed other forms of noncompliance. Perhaps most notably, the LTO provided for a careful vetting of staff, substantially higher wages, a widely publicized code of conduct and improved IT systems and office facilities. This quality work environment was crucial in promoting productivity and noncorrupt behavior among LTO staff.

The LTO reforms were well implemented and produced excellent results. As described in section VI, the growth rate of LTO tax collections substantially exceeded that for the rest of the DGT. At the same time, large taxpayers reported a high degree of satisfaction with the LTO's services, the integrity of its staff and the measures taken to accelerate refunds. Importantly, the new tax administration features that were introduced at the LTO would later become the standard for the DGT and were gradually rolled-out to additional field offices.

The electronic payment notification initiative

This initiative involved replacing the existing paper-based system for processing tax payments and tax refunds with a modern, electronic system. By allowing tax payments to be processed more quickly and reliably, the electronic system had advantages for the DGT and taxpayers alike. As such, the initiative had the potential for improving both tax collection and the investment climate.

The payment system that had been in place in 2001 was slow, costly and vulnerable to abuse. The paper-based nature of the system resulted in significant time delays before the DGT received confirmation of a tax payment from Directorate General of Budget, which seriously hampered the DGT's capacity to identify delinquent taxpayers on a timely basis and take action to recover tax arrears. The paper-based payment system also created opportunities for unscrupulous taxpayers to submit fake payment advices to the DGT and receive credit for taxes that they had not actually paid.

With the new electronic system, banks, upon receipt of a tax payment from a taxpayer, sent an electronic payment advice to the DGT which was automatically posted to the taxpayer's account with the DGT. The payment information was conveyed over a secure communication line linking the banks to the DGT, and included a number of controls that ensured the authenticity of the payment. Through this system, the DGT received real-time notification of a tax payment from banks.

The new payment system was piloted at the LTO in 2002 and by 2003 was processing nearly 90 per cent of the tax payments received by the DGT. Though difficult to measure, the system had positive effects on both revenue collection and the investment climate. By speeding up the flow and accuracy of tax payment information, the new system helped to increase tax revenue as it virtually eliminated fake payment advices and allowed tax officers to take timely action against those taxpayers who failed to pay their taxes on time. The system also helped improve the business climate by restoring taxpayers' trust in the tax payment system: prior to the introduction of the electronic system, it was purportedly not uncommon for taxpayers to be presented with payment demands for tax liabilities that they had already paid.

Summary

The short-term reform strategy was highly successful in strengthening tax administration. In almost all cases, the short-term reforms were implemented in line with good international practice and achieved a high quality of implementation. The key success factors explaining the good results appear to be that the strategy, while limited in scope, focused on those reforms that were both critical to the fiscal adjustment program and within the DGT's limited implementation capacity. This approach allowed the reforms to be implemented rapidly and the results to be realized quickly. Yet the short-term reform strategy had its limitations: sustaining and further improving the initial results over the medium term would require a broader and more complex set of reforms, as discussed in the next section.

V. The medium-term reforms

Building on the positive results that had been achieved by the short-term reforms in 2001 and 2002, the DGT took a decision in 2003 to develop a more ambitious set of reforms that aimed at sustaining and further advancing Indonesia's fiscal adjustment program over the medium term. As the new strategy was being developed, the central objectives of the fiscal adjustment program remained unchanged: achieve fiscal sustainability and promote the investment climate. However, the authorities recognized that a more intensified and broader set of tax administration reforms would be needed to help achieve these objectives over the medium term.

The DGT's medium-term reform strategy followed a two-tracked approach of: (1) gradually extending the short-term reforms while (2) broadening the scope of reforms to address the tax agency's most fundamental weaknesses. As such, the medium-term strategy included 10 major initiatives, which cut across a wide range of topics, including new legislation, tax administration processes and information systems. The DGT introduced the strategy during the second half of 2003 and continued to implement the reforms, at varying degrees of intensity and with some refinements, through 2007.

In contrast with the short-term reforms, the quality of implementation for the medium-term reforms was more varied: some initiatives were implemented on time and as intended while others were not. These mixed results reflected a number of factors, including the inherent complexity of the reforms and a pause in the reform effort following the election of a new government in 2004 – which wanted to take stock of the existing administrative reforms; the reform drive started anew with the election of a successor government in December 2005. Despite the mixed results, the medium-term reform strategy has still delivered important gains and established the broad direction for the DGT's ongoing reform efforts.

Extending the initial reforms

Rolling out the large taxpayer reforms. By 2003, some of the innovations that had been successfully introduced at the LTO were reaching a level of maturity that signaled their readiness for extension to other tax offices. Accordingly, the DGT took a decision in early 2003 to commence the roll-out of the large taxpayer reforms to its administrative Region VII in Jakarta. This region had a number of similarities with the LTO – including significant numbers of large taxpayers and large investors – which made it an ideal candidate for adopting the large taxpayer reforms.[19]

Planning for the roll-out started in late 2003. By the end of 2004, the LTO reforms had been fully implemented at all of the tax offices in Region VII. These reforms included: (1) reorganization of staff into units based on tax administration function; (2) merging of the field offices and audit offices; (3) the appointment of staff based on merit; (4) enhanced taxpayer services, including the assignment of an account representative to each large taxpayer; (5) more effective enforcement procedures; (6) introduction of higher salary packages linked to a new code of conduct; and (7) refurbishment of office accommodations.

The extension of the LTO reforms to Region VII by end-2004 produced excellent results. The reforms were carefully planned and smoothly implemented. They led to significant increases in tax revenue and overwhelmingly favorable feedback from taxpayers, as described in section VI. As such, the Region VII initiative had a highly positive impact on the fiscal adjustment program and continued to be a key reform driver through 2007.

Improving the administration of small and medium-sized taxpayers. Having established effective arrangements for large taxpayers, the DGT turned its attention to developing new approaches for administering other categories of taxpayers. This initiative aimed at tailoring the DGT's taxpayer services and enforcement programs to the characteristics of small and medium-sized taxpayers. The reforms were to be tested in one region and, if successful, replicated throughout the country.

The DGT's Jakarta Region VI was chosen as the pilot region for designing and testing the reforms. In early 2005, the region created two special tax offices: a Medium Taxpayer Office (MTO) to administer the region's 200 largest taxpayers and a Small Taxpayer Office (STO) for businesses with small amounts of turnover. Although the STO and MTO were originally envisaged to customize their operations for small and medium taxpayers, in actuality the offices mainly implemented the more generic reforms that had been introduced for large taxpayers, with some modifications. These reforms included re-organizing the offices into units based on tax administration function, increasing staff salaries, enhancing communications with taxpayers and introducing modern technology and improved office accommodations.

By the end of 2007, the MTO and STO had achieved highly positive results in terms of improving compliance, revenue collection and taxpayer satisfaction which are evaluated in section VI. However, the positive results were more attributable to the general modernization of the tax offices than to the customization of the DGT's administrative programs for small and medium-taxpayers. Thus, realizing the full potential of the small and medium taxpayer reforms will depend not only on rolling-out the generic reforms to additional tax offices[20] but more important to better tailor the DGT's enforcement and taxpayer services to the requirements of small and medium-sized taxpayers. Such tailored approaches could include simplified bookkeeping methods, volunteer tax return preparers, centralized processing of tax returns, telephone contact centers, industry-specific audit guides and indirect audit methods for examining taxpayers with inadequate books and records.

Continuing the revenue generation initiative. While the medium-term reforms were being designed and implemented, the DGT recognized the continuing importance of protecting ongoing tax collections. For this reason, a decision was taken to continue the revenue generation initiative, which had been first introduced in 2002. As was described in the previous section, this initiative entailed the setting of national targets for each of the DGT's main enforcement programs (e.g. number of new taxpayers to be registered, number of audits to be completed, amount of arrears to be recovered) and the implementation of specific measures to achieve the targets.

Through 2005, the revenue generation initiative continued to generate substantial amounts of revenue and, as such, had a positive impact on the fiscal adjustment program's revenue objective. The initiative demonstrated that good revenue results could be achieved simply by establishing reasonable targets for key enforcement programs and holding staff accountable for their achievement. Unfortunately, the DGT discontinued the systematic tracking of tax collections from each of its four major programs after 2005.

Broadening the scope of reforms

As the medium-term reforms were being formulated, the DGT recognized that further increases in revenue collection and improvements in the investment climate would require more than just extending the initial tax administration reforms to additional tax offices. With this in mind, the medium-term strategy also included a broader set of reforms aimed at addressing some of the most fundamental constraints to the DGT's performance.

Simplifying the tax laws. This initiative envisaged conducting a comprehensive review of each major tax, beginning with the value-added tax (VAT), with a view towards identifying and eliminating those aspects of the tax system that unnecessarily raised the costs of compliance and administration. Tax simplification was expected to advance the fiscal adjustment strategy by: (1) increasing tax revenue through the facilitation of voluntary compliance and (2) improving the investment climate by reducing the complexities and uncertainties that the tax system posed for investors.

The initiative began with the appointment of a joint public sector-private sector *Task Force on VAT Simplification* in May 2003, which submitted its final report and recommendations to the Minister of Finance in December of that year. The report resulted in the adoption of a number of important reforms, the most important of which was the extension of the 'gold card' program beyond large taxpayers. This program accelerated the processing of VAT refund claims, normally within seven days, for highly compliant taxpayers. Other reforms included unifying and raising the VAT registration threshold for goods and services, and restricting the number of VAT withholding agents to government treasuries.

Notwithstanding the improvements that were introduced to the VAT in 2003, many other measures that have a high potential for simplifying the VAT have not been adopted. These include: (1) eliminating the requirement for auditing all refund claims; (2) substantially reducing the numerous lists of purchase and sales invoices required as supplements to the VAT return; (3) discontinuing the requirement for VAT refund claimants to submit the original copies of all purchase and sales invoices; and (4) streamlining the VAT refund process for taxpayers without gold card status.

Thus far, the compliance simplification initiative has yielded limited results. Significant opportunities for simplifying the VAT have not been realized and the work on streamlining other major taxes has not yet been started. Despite the limited results, compliance simplification remains an important and ongoing reform.

Improving the legal framework for tax administration. The main purpose of this initiative was to strengthen the DGT's legal framework by revising the rules and procedures governing tax administration. As mentioned in Section II, these rules are contained in two sets of tax laws: the rules that apply to all taxes are stipulated in the general laws on tax administration and arrears collection while the rules that apply to a particular tax are provided for in each substantive tax law (income tax, VAT, etc.). Critical shortcomings in this legislation weakened the DGT's capacity to enforce the tax laws and reduced taxpayers' confidence in the fairness of the tax system.

To improve this situation, the authorities carried out an extensive consultation process during 2003 on the tax administration laws with tax and legal experts, officials from international organizations (particularly multilateral donors) and members of the business community (both international and domestic). On the basis of these consultations, an initial package of amendments was formulated in early 2004 which were later revised by the new government that came into office in October 2004. Although these packages contained a number of positive proposals, they also omitted other changes that were critical for effective tax administration, including: restructuring the penalty regime; strengthening the DGT's powers to access taxpayers' and third-party information; and providing greater fairness in the appeals process.

After protracted deliberations by Parliament over nearly three years, the amendments were finally enacted in 2007 and are in effect in 2008. However, given the amendments' limited scope, it remains uncertain whether the new legislation will have much of an impact on enhancing the DGT's capacity to enforce the tax laws or promoting taxpayers' rights. In this situation, the authorities will need to closely monitor the operation of the new legislation and consider further amendments in the event that the legislation does not generate the intended improvements in the legal framework for tax administration.

Increasing audit effectiveness. While the tax audit function is one of a tax agency's most important tools for ensuring that taxpayers comply with the tax laws, it has been one of the weakest links among the DGT's enforcement programs for many years. Although some piecemeal reforms had been introduced in this area under the short-term reform strategy, the DGT's audit capabilities in 2003 continued to face difficulties at detecting the large amounts of underreported taxes and foregone revenue. In this connection, strengthening the DGT's audit function was (and continues to be) a major priority for the medium-term reform strategy.

By 2004, the DGT had identified those aspects of its audit program that were in most urgent need of reform. These included: improving the targeting of audits on those taxpayers who are most likely to be underreporting taxes; introducing a broader range of audit types and methods; training auditors to look beyond a taxpayers' accounting statements to examine source documents and third-party information; increasing the number of audits conducted at taxpayers' premises and greatly reducing the large amount of resources allocated to examining refund claims; implementing more stringent controls and quality assurance programs to deter collusion between taxpayers and auditors; and introducing computerized audit tools.

Through 2007, insufficient progress had been made in improving the DGT's audit program. Part of the problem seemed to involve the sheer complexity of the reforms, but there also appeared to be a lack of political will to initiate reforms in this sensitive area. A more vigorous reform effort, therefore, will be required to improve this situation. Given the crucial role that audit plays in a modern tax administration and its potential benefits for fiscal adjustment, strengthening the audit program should be considered a top priority for future reform.

Implementing a performance measurement system. The main purpose of this initiative was to develop a comprehensive set of measures for evaluating the DGT's performance. The idea was to broaden the DGT's narrow focus from achieving an annual revenue collection target – which was thought to create perverse incentives for arbitrary administration – to improving its core tax administration processes. This initiative could contribute to the fiscal adjustment program's revenue collection and investment climate effects by creating greater accountability for results and enhanced transparency in administration.

The DGT commenced work on developing new performance measures in late 2004 by reviewing its existing performance measurement practices in comparison to international best practice. The review led to a consensus within the DGT that a new system was needed which should feature performance measures at: (1) at three levels – strategic, operational and individual and (2) in three broad areas – tax administration programs, taxpayer satisfaction and employee satisfaction. There was also agreement within the DGT that the new performance measures should be implemented gradually as an integral part of the DGT's modernization program.

At the end of 2007, the DGT had formulated an initial set of performance indicators covering key aspects of its operations. The indicators were approved by DGT management in early 2008, although considerable effort will still be required before the measures become operational. The slow progress has resulted, in part, from the difficulties in developing reliable measures for some aspects of the DGT's operations in an environment of limited IT systems. Notwithstanding these challenges, performance measurement is a well-accepted management concept that has been successfully implemented by many tax administrations around the world, even those with limited IT capacities. As such, the implementation of a performance measurement system should be a top priority for the DGT's ongoing reform program.

Reforming human resource management policies. This initiative sought to increase the productivity and integrity of tax officers by providing the DGT with greater flexibilities over its human resource (HR) management policies. The directorate's existing HR regime, which was based on the standard civil service system, was seen as poorly suited for motivating its workforce and establishing accountability for results. For this reason, a more flexible regime was viewed as crucial for providing tax officers with the types of incentives needed to transform the DGT into a high-performance revenue collection agency.

Under the DGT's short-term reform program, the DGT had tested a number of important HR reforms at a few pilot tax offices beginning with the large taxpayer office. These reforms included new procedures for appointing staff, a code of conduct for tax officers, and the issuance of a special allowance that had substantially increased salaries. Building on these initial reforms, the DGT reviewed its HR policies in late 2004, which pointed to the need for more comprehensive reforms. In this connection, priority was to be given to developing a new job classification scheme (that would rank jobs on the basis of the complexity of work, overall responsibilities and specific skills and competencies required), new compensation and promotion policies (that would set salaries at appropriate levels and base raises/promotions on staff members' level of performance), and an improved staff appraisal regime (that would cascade DGT-wide performance measures down to individual tax officers).

By the end of 2007, the DGT was still at a very early stage in reforming its HR regime. The slow progress resulted mainly from the DGT's limited capacity to design the detailed features of the reforms. Consequently, HR reform continues to have considerable potential for improving the DGT's performance, but significant efforts are still needed to realize the potential gains.

Designing an information technology master plan. The key objective of this initiative was to develop an information technology (IT) strategy that was aligned to the directorate's overall medium-term reform plan. In this way, the IT initiative could more effectively support the DGT's taxpayer services and enforcement programs, which were the keys for increasing compliance and revenue. As importantly, advanced information technologies could also help improve the business climate by reducing the need for face-to-face contacts between taxpayers and tax officers, thereby providing taxpayers with greater convenience and limiting the opportunities for rent-seeking behavior by tax officers.

Under the DGT's short-term reform strategy, the directorate had successfully implemented a number of important IT initiatives, the most important of which was to pilot at the large taxpayer office a new computer system that supported core tax administration processes. Over the medium term, the DGT sought to: (1) gradually roll-out the pilot computer system to all tax offices throughout Indonesia and (2) improve the pilot system through various enhancements. The latter would include centralizing the processing and storage of taxpayer data (which had previously been carried out by the hundreds of field offices), creating a data warehouse that could cross-match taxpayer and third-party information as well as carry out other compliance functions, and introducing a broad range of new web-based services (such as electronic registration and taxpayers' online access to their accounts with the DGT). At the end of 2007, the DGT's information technology initiatives had yielded a number of important advances but their full potential for raising tax administration performance had not been realized because the reforms were not underpinned by unified IT strategy. On the positive side, the DGT had, by 2007, deployed the pilot computer system to some 100 field offices, its electronic payment notification system was processing 100 per cent of tax payments, a broad range of new electronic services had been introduced, and the DGT was set to deploy its first centralized processing site. However, in the absence of an IT master plan, the DGT found itself operating four separate IT systems which could neither communicate with each other nor produce reliable national data. Going forward, the DGT needs to develop an IT master plan to guide its future investments in technology.

Creating an internal investigation unit. To improve governance among tax officers and other MoF staff, the Indonesian authorities decided in 2003 to create an internal investigation unit at the MoF with the responsibility for investigating allegations of misconduct and corruption within the ministry's directorates. In light of the widespread complaints among taxpayers about malfeasance by tax officers, this initiative sought to restore taxpayers' confidence in the tax administration which, along with other governance-enhancing initiatives, was seen as essential for boosting Indonesia's investment climate.

The internal investigation unit was established as a special section within the MoF's Inspectorate General in November 2004. During 2005, the unit had achieved a satisfactory level of performance as evidenced by: (1) the fact that the unit had been implemented on time and largely in line with good international practice; (2) the number of investigations that had been initiated (51) and completed (33); (3) the significance of cases selected for investigation, with most cases involving serious abuses of authority; and (4) the overall quality of the investigations. However, the unit's overall impact of the internal investigation unit on reducing corruption was seriously hindered by the fact that no tax officers had been referred for prosecution for corruption and bribery offences as a result of the unit's investigations, and that the DGT had applied administrative sanctions against only 23 of the 111 employees where such sanctions had been recommended.

The creation of the internal investigation unit was one of several important actions that the Indonesian authorities had taken to improve integrity in tax administration under the DGT's medium-term strategy. Others included the increase in salary and introduction of a code of conduct for staff at the DGT's pilot offices. Despite these positive steps, citizens' groups and the business community continued to report, at the end of 2005, misconduct by tax officers remained a major problem, particularly outside of the pilot offices. Improving this situation would require, inter alia, ensuring that the investigations of misconduct by tax officers led to the imposition of appropriate sanctions against corrupt staff, including job termination and imprisonment in cases involving serious offences. The appointment of a new MOF Inspector General in 2006 created an opportunity to move forward in this important area.

Summary

Through 2007, the medium-term reforms reached varying states of implementation, with some initiatives fully implemented and achieving good results while others were still at an early stage of development. On the plus side, good progress had been made in rolling-out the initial pilot reforms to additional tax offices, creating model tax offices for administering small and medium-sized taxpayers, and introducing new technologies. On the negative side, slower progress had been made in implementing some of the more far-reaching reforms such as amending the tax administration law (which was eventually amended in 2007), simplifying the tax laws, overhauling the audit system, designing new human resource management policies and establishing a performance measurement system.

Yet despite the mixed results, the DGT's reform program had (and continues to have), in its totality, a demonstrably positive impact on Indonesia's fiscal adjustment strategy, as described in the next section. As importantly, the initial reforms created the foundation for a new modernization program that the DGT's new management adopted in 2006 and is currently ongoing.

VI. Impacts of the reforms

This section analyzes the impact that the reforms have had on two key objectives in Indonesia's fiscal adjustment strategy: (1) increasing non-oil and gas tax revenue and (2) improving the investment climate. The available evidence suggests that the reforms had a strong, positive impact on the tax yield and a positive, though difficult to quantify, effect on the investment climate.

Impact on revenue

Prior to the 1997–98 Asian crisis, (non-oil) tax collection in Indonesia was on a slow but steady downward trend (see earlier Table 5.1, and Figure 5.2). In the five years prior to the 1997–98 Asian crisis, Indonesia's tax yield averaged 10.5 per cent of GDP and then declined and eventually bottomed out at 9.6 per cent in 2000. A similar downward trend in collection is also observable as a ratio of non-oil GDP. The decline mostly came from lower DGT collections.

In breaking with pre-crisis (and crisis) trends, the tax yield increased over the period of the tax administration reforms. From 2001 – the year preceding the introduction of the reforms – to 2006 the (non-oil and gas) tax-to-GDP ratio rose from 9.9 to 11.0 (Table 5.3).[21] Over this period, DGT collections rose by 1.2 percentage points of GDP while collections from DG Customs decreased by 0.1 percentage points of GDP. The buoyancy in GDT collection was generated by three taxes: income tax (0.6 percentage points of GDP), VAT (0.5 percentage points of GDP), and land tax (0.3 percentage points); luxury and sales tax collection partly offset this good performance, as it declined by 0.2 percentage points of GDP. In the five reform years beginning in 2001, the average tax yield increased to 11 per cent of GDP.

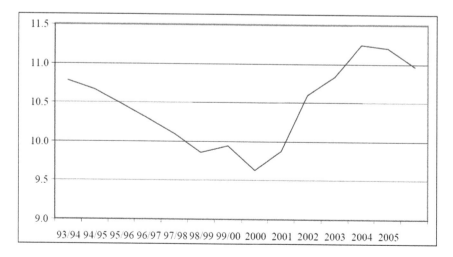

Figure 5.2 Indonesia: tax-to-GDP collection

Table 5.3 Indonesia: summary of central government operations, 2000–07

	2000[a]	2001	2002	2003	2004	2005	2006	2007
	Act.	Act.	Act.	Act.	Act.	Act.	Act.	Est.
	(Rp trillions)							
Total Revenue and grants	228.1	301.2	300.0	336.4	407.9	495.4	634.0	705.9
Oil and gas revenue	85.1	104.1	77.8	80.4	108.2	138.7	201.3	168.5
Non-oil and gas revenue	143.0	196.6	221.9	255.6	299.4	355.4	430.9	535.7
Tax revenue	127.8	162.6	193.1	218.1	258.0	311.8	365.9	447.4
Directorate General of Taxes	109.5	135.6	159.2	180.6	216.1	263.3	314.9	381.9
Income tax	58.3	71.5	84.5	93.8	112.0	140.3	165.6	194.6
VAT & luxury sales tax	44.4	56.0	65.2	74.2	87.6	101.3	123.0	155.0
VAT	39.0	50.2	59.4	71.0	81.0	93.3	117.8	…
Domestic	21.9	30.0	37.3	47.1	46.3	47.5	74.7	…
Imports	17.1	20.2	22.1	23.9	34.7	45.8	43.1	…
Land tax	5.7	6.7	8.0	10.9	14.7	19.6	23.9	29.5
Other taxes	1.1	1.4	1.5	1.7	1.8	2.1	2.3	2.7
Directorate General of Customs	18.3	27.0	33.9	37.5	41.9	48.5	51.0	65.5
Non-tax revenue	15.2	34.0	28.8	37.5	41.4	43.6	65.0	88.3
Grants	0.0	0.5	0.3	0.4	0.3	1.3	1.9	1.7
	(per cent of GDP)							
Total Revenue and grants	19.3	18.3	16.5	16.7	17.8	17.9	19.0	17.8
Oil and gas revenue	8.2	6.3	4.3	4.0	4.7	5.0	6.0	4.3
Non-oil and gas revenue	11.1	11.9	12.2	12.7	13.0	12.8	12.9	13.5
Tax revenue	9.6	9.9	10.6	10.8	11.2	11.2	11.0	11.3

Directorate General of Taxes	7.9	8.2	8.7	9.0	9.4	9.5	9.4	9.6
Income tax	4.2	4.3	4.6	4.7	4.9	5.1	5.0	4.9
VAT & luxury sales tax	3.2	3.4	3.6	3.7	3.8	3.7	3.7	3.9
VAT	2.8	3.0	3.3	3.5	3.5	3.4	3.5	...
Domestic	1.6	1.8	2.0	2.3	2.0	1.7	2.2	...
Imports	1.2	1.2	1.2	1.2	1.5	1.7	1.3	...
Land tax	0.4	0.4	0.4	0.5	0.6	0.7	0.7	0.7
Other taxes	0.1	0.1	0.1	0.1	0.1	0.1	0.1	0.1
Directorate General of Customs	1.8	1.6	1.9	1.9	1.8	1.7	1.5	1.7
Non-tax revenue	1.5	2.1	1.6	1.9	1.8	1.6	1.9	2.2
Grants	0.0	0.0	0.0	0.0	0.0	0.0	0.1	0.0
(per cent of non-oil GDP)								
Total Revenue and grants	22.0	20.9	18.8	19.1	20.3	20.4	21.7	20.3
Oil and gas revenue	9.3	7.2	4.9	4.6	5.4	5.7	6.9	4.9
Non-oil and gas revenue	12.7	13.6	13.9	14.5	14.9	14.6	14.7	15.4
Tax revenue	11.0	11.3	12.1	12.4	12.8	12.8	12.5	12.9
Directorate General of Taxes	9.0	9.4	10.0	10.2	10.7	10.8	10.8	11.0
Income tax	4.8	5.0	5.3	5.3	5.6	5.8	5.7	5.6
VAT & luxury sales tax	3.6	3.9	4.1	4.2	4.4	4.2	4.2	4.5
Land tax	0.5	0.5	0.5	0.6	0.7	0.8	0.8	0.8
Other taxes	0.1	0.1	0.1	0.1	0.1	0.1	0.1	0.1

(*Continued*)

Table 5.3 (Continued)

	2000¹	2001	2002	2003	2004	2005	2006	2007
	Act.	Act.	Act.	Act.	Act.	Act.	Act.	Est.
Directorate General of Customs	2.0	1.9	2.1	2.1	2.1	2.0	1.7	1.9
Non-tax revenue	1.7	2.4	1.8	2.1	2.1	1.8	2.2	2.5
Grants	0.0	0.0	0.0	0.0	0.0	0.1	0.1	0.0
	(per cent of total revenue and grants)							
Total Revenue and grants	100.0	100.0	100.0	100.0	100.0	100.0	100.0	100.0
Oil and gas revenue	37.3	34.6	25.9	23.9	26.5	28.0	31.7	23.9
Non-oil and gas revenue	62.7	65.3	74.0	76.0	73.4	71.7	68.0	75.9
Tax revenue	56.0	54.0	64.4	64.8	63.3	62.9	57.7	63.4
Directorate General of Taxes	48.0	45.0	53.1	53.7	53.0	53.1	49.7	54.1
Income tax	25.6	23.7	28.2	27.9	27.5	28.3	26.1	27.6
VAT & luxury sales tax	19.5	18.6	21.7	22.1	21.5	20.4	19.4	22.0
Land tax	2.5	2.2	2.7	3.2	3.6	4.0	3.8	4.2
Other taxes	0.5	0.5	0.5	0.5	0.4	0.4	0.4	0.4
Directorate General of Customs	8.0	9.0	11.3	11.1	10.3	9.8	8.0	9.3
Non-tax revenue	6.7	11.3	9.6	11.1	10.1	8.8	10.3	12.5
Grants	0.0	0.2	0.1	0.1	0.1	0.3	0.3	0.2
Memorandum items								
Nominal non-oil GDP (Rp. trillions)	1,218	1,443	1,597	1,765	2,013	2,432	2,928	3,469
Nominal GDP (Rp. trillions)	1,390	1,646	1,822	2,014	2,296	2,774	3,339	3,957

Source: Country authorities and IMF staff calculations.

Note: ¹The fiscal year changed in 2000 from previously April to March to January to December so FY2000 is from April to December. For comparison purposes with other outer years, data for 2000 present the full calendar year (January to December) except for oil and gas revenues, DG customs revenues and non-tax revenues for which data were not available. For these latter three revenue sources, their revenues in per cent of GDP and in per cent of non-oil GDP has been scaled to the April–December GDP and non-oil GDP, respectively.

The increased tax buoyancy could have resulted from a mix of: (1) tax policy changes, (2) structural economic changes and (3) tax administration improvements. Before assessing the likely revenue impact of the latter, we briefly review the revenue impact that the former two factors could have had.

Tax policy effects. Changes in tax policy over the 2002–06 period were relatively limited and concerned a few taxes only. On the income tax front, no major taxes changes occurred during the reform period – a tax reform package was drafted in 2004 but has not yet been passed by Parliament. Income tax changes, however, did take place on 1 January 2001, with some of revenue impact of these measures falling in 2002; the impact of these measures seems to be slightly negative for revenue.[22] The VAT was not subject to any significant tax policy changes during the period.[23] The luxury sales tax was subject to numerous base and rate changes[24] (rates now range from 10 to 75 per cent, the list of goods subject to the tax is fairly extensive) so that the revenue impact of those tax changes is unclear ex ante. The land and building tax bases and rates were not significantly modified during the reform period.

Structural economic effects. Changes in Indonesia's economic structure were more significant since the economy was recovering from a major economic and financial crisis. This is likely to have affected tax collection through several channels. For CIT, the Asian crisis is likely to have materially impacted revenue collection up to 2002 due to the slow winding down of loss carry-forward provisions and of tax relief for the restructuring of businesses completed in the tax years 2000 to 2002. For PIT, the labor market strengthened significantly from its trough during the Asian crisis which impacted both the base (less unemployed individuals) and the salary of each worker. Hence, an improved income tax buoyancy is expected. Similarly, VAT buoyancy should also be up due to a recovery in domestic consumption. The land and building taxes rely heavily on collections from mining resources and other natural resources rather than developed real estate. Due to booming commodity prices over the reform period, an improved tax elasticity is expected.

Tax administration effects. In light of the above tax policy and structural changes, isolating the revenue impact of tax administration reforms involves a number of methodological and data challenges. The approach adopted here is to focus on analyzing the factors that accounted for the increase in VAT collections, where the availability of data makes the analysis more tractable. In doing so, the analysis derives the tax administration effects on VAT collections as the residual between actual and projected VAT revenue, with the latter controlling for changes in economic structure (as previously mentioned, there were no significant VAT policy changes since 2001 that need to be controlled). A simple macro-based estimation of the VAT revenue collection is conducted using a GDP decomposition to estimate aggregate final consumption, which is the taxable base for VAT (see Annex 5.2 for details of the methodology).[25]

The analysis of VAT collection reveals that more than half of the VAT revenue buoyancy is due to tax administration improvement. Based on the changes in the economic structure from 2001 to 2006, VAT revenue collection was projected

Table 5.4 Indonesia: VAT revenue projections based on GDP decomposition, 2000–06

	2000	2001	2002	2003	2004	2005	2006
	Act.	Act.	Act.	Act.	Act.	Act.	Prel. Act.
	(In trillion Rp. Unless otherwise specified)						
Nominal GDP	1,390	1,646	1,822	2,014	2,296	2,785	3,338
Imports (cif)	366	385	357	632	490	731	734
Export (fob)	−549	−588	−551	−550	−632	−844	−949
Final base consumption	1,207	1,443	1,628	1,826	2,154	2,671	3,123
Exemption rate (per cent)[1]	34.2%	34.2%	34.2%	34.2%	34.2%	34.2%	34.2%
Consumption subject to VAT	794	950	1,071	1,202	1,417	1,758	2,055
Statutory tax rate (per cent)	10.0%	10.0%	10.0%	10.0%	10.0%	10.0%	10.0%
Potential VAT collection	79	95	107	120	142	176	206
Compliance rate (per cent of potential VAT)	49.1%	52.9%	52.9%	52.9%	52.9%	52.9%	52.9%
Estimated VAT revenue (assuming unchanged compliance)	39.0	50.2	56.7	63.6	75.0	93.0	108.7
Actual VAT revenue	39.0	50.2	59.4	71.0	81.0	93.3	117.8
Implicit compliance rate (per cent of potential VAT) 2/	49.1%	52.9%	55.4%	59.1%	57.2%	53.1%	57.3%
	(In per cent of GDP)						
Estimated VAT revenue (assuming unchanged compliance)	2.81	3.05	3.11	3.16	3.27	3.34	3.26
Actual VAT revenue	2.80	3.05	3.26	3.53	3.53	3.35	3.53
Domestic	1.58	1.82	2.05	2.34	2.02	1.71	2.24
Imports	1.22	1.23	1.21	1.19	1.51	1.65	1.29
Memo items							
VAT efficiency ration	28.0%	30.5%	32.6%	35.3%	35.3%	33.5%	35.3%
VAT C-efficiency ration (total consumption)	32.3%	34.8%	36.5%	38.9%	37.6%	34.9%	37.7%
VAT C-efficiency ration (private consumption)	39.0%	46.1%	45.6%	48.8%	47.2%	43.4%	48.0%

Source: Authors' calculations.

Notes: [1]Derived as a residual from Marks (2005).

to increase by 0.21 percentage points of GDP. Actual collection, however, increased by 0.48 percentage points of GDP. Since there were no tax policy changes during that period that could explain the remaining increase in VAT collections, it can be concluded that the DGT's comprehensive tax administration reforms described in the previous sections and reflected in an increasing implicit compliance rate account for the residual 0.27 percentage points of GDP in over-performance (more than half of the increased tax yield). Consistent with the above conclusion, various productivity indicators (VAT efficiency; VAT C-efficiency out of total and private consumptions – see details in Annex 5.2) also report an improvement in the efficiency of the value-added tax. Consistent with the revenue over-performance linked to administrative reforms, VAT compliance increased from 52.9 per cent in 2001 to 57.3 per cent in 2006 – an increase of 8.3 per cent over the pre-reform compliance level.

Conducting a similar analysis for CIT and PIT collections is particularly difficult in Indonesia since only aggregate income tax data are available. This is because the data are presented by nature of collection rather than corporate or personal income taxpayer. Without this breakdown, modeling the (different) corporate and individual income tax bases and their evolution over the reform period would be futile since one cannot compare these projections with actual CIT and PIT collections. Despite this, and the expected positive revenue impact that the termination of tax relief after 2002 had on revenue collection, it is worth noting that the income tax yield continued to increase from 2003 to 2006 (by 0.3 percentage points of GDP or 0.4 percentage points of non-oil GDP). Given the comprehensive nature of the DGT's reform program, it is not unreasonable to conclude that tax administration improvements likely had a similar significant impact on the increase in income tax collections as has been shown for VAT collections.

Data that also point to a significant revenue impact of the tax administration reforms can be seen from the compliance control indicators established by the DGT during 2002–05.[26] These indicators include tax arrears collection, the proportion of taxpayers that are late filers and the proportion of late payers. As described in the section before, improved DGT efficiency could be expected to lead to the following pattern in the data. First, in the initial phase of reforms – when the tax administration improves its enforcement capacity – the share of revenue collection stemming from enforced collection to total DGT collection should increase. Second, as taxpayers increase their voluntary compliance rates in response to the tax agency's stepped up enforcement efforts, the share of enforced collection to total collection should gradually decline. DGT data (shown in Table 5.5) reveal that:

- The share of both late filers and late payers has decreased over time in the pilot DGT offices that went through the reform program.
- The trend in arrears collection data is consistent with improved tax compliance in the economy (the share of enforced to total DGT collection first rises then declines over time).

Table 5.5 Indonesia: selected DGT performance indicators, 2002–05

	2001	2002	2003	2004	2005
	(In per cent of GDP unless otherwise specified)				
Total DGT collections	8.23	8.74	8.97	9.41	9.45
Enforced collection	...	0.47	0.54	0.94	0.73
Voluntary collection	...	8.27	8.43	8.48	8.73
Enforced collection (per cent of DGT collection)		5.4	6.0	9.9	7.7
Total DGT collections	8.23	8.74	8.97	9.41	9.45
Non-modernized offices	8.23	7.20	7.17	4.56	4.12
Modernized offices[1]	–	1.54	1.80	4.85	5.33
of which:					
Large Taxpayer Office					
Total taxes collected	...	1.54	1.80	2.17	2.34
Enforced	...	0.02	0.04	0.05	0.10
Voluntary	...	1.52	1.76	2.12	2.24
Number taxpayers	...	200	200	297	296
Late filers (per cent)	...	9.0	34.0	20.9	16.6
Late payers (per cent)	...	13.5	32.5	25.3	17.6
Special Region					
Total taxes collected	...	...	...	2.51	2.80
Enforced	...	...	...	0.57	0.37
Voluntary	...	...	...	1.94	2.43
Number taxpayers	...	...	...	27,575	32,445
Late filers (per cent)	...	...	...	15.0	6.2
Late payers (per cent)	...	...	...	4.6	3.6

Source: GDT and authors' calculations.

Note: [1]Data for the Medium Tax Offices and the Small Tax Offices are not reported but available from the authors.

A more compelling analysis of the tax compliance impact of the DGT reforms arises from the comparison in voluntary tax collections at the pilot tax offices relative to nonpilot tax offices. This approach treats the nonpilot tax offices as a 'control group'. Interestingly, for our control group analysis, the DGT administrative reforms were introduced in a staggered manner beginning with four pilot tax offices. Specifically, the reforms were first introduced in July 2002 with the Large Taxpayer Office (LTO), and then extended 2004 to three additional tax offices: (1) the Special Region Office (SRO) which also administers large taxpayers;

(2) the Medium Taxpayer Office (MTO); and (3) the Small Taxpayer Office (STO). While some of the pilot reforms were subsequently introduced to all tax offices nationwide, the most far-reaching reforms have been implemented only at these four pilot offices.[27] With the LTO and the SRO together accounting for about half of DGT's total collection, tax-administration-induced increases in compliance, if successful, should have a noticeable revenue impact.

The data reveal a striking and consistent increase in voluntary collections at each of the pilot offices, while nonpilot offices experienced no such increase. For instance, the LTO in 2002 and 2003 had the same number of large tax-payers (200) but voluntary tax collection jumped from 1.5 to 1.8 per cent of GDP between these two years, while the rest of DGT's collection remains flat at 7.2 per cent of GDP. The same pattern emerged between 2004 and 2005: voluntary collection at both the LTO and the MTO grew faster (again, holding the number of taxpayers constant) than the rest of DGT's tax collection. The Special Region also witnessed a much faster increase in revenue collection than observed in the rest of the DGT. However, since the number of taxpayers in this region also increased, a proper benchmark is to compare revenue growth per taxpayer at the SRO with overall DGT revenue growth. The result is also quite stark: SRO revenue per taxpayer rose by 29 per cent between 2004 and 2005, while nonmodernized DGT offices saw revenue increases of 10 per cent (and overall DGT growth rose by 22 per cent).[28]

Significant improvements in compliance indicators at the DGT pilot offices offer further evidence that the better performance of the pilot offices is linked to improved tax administration. Specifically, the strong revenue performance at the pilot offices was accompanied by a dramatic increase in two key compliance indicators: the timely filing of tax returns and the timely payment of taxes. One could indeed argue that, although unlikely, a recovery in corporate profits, wage bill growth, and value added of firms could have fortuitously coincided with the modernization of DGT's offices. The fact that the DGT modernization effort (1) has been staggered over several years; and (2) concerned a representative sample of small, medium and large taxpayers make such a series of coincidences a low probability event.

Taken together, these data provide evidence that the DGT's reforms led to an improvement in taxpayers' compliance rates at the pilot offices, which was in turn associated with significantly higher increases in voluntary collections compared to the national trend.

Summary

The DGT's tax administration reforms are estimated to have accounted for over half of the 1.2 percentage points of GDP increase in tax collection over the reform period. The evolution of the above compliance indicators confirms the results stemming from the analysis of VAT collection, namely that DGT's reforms improved overall tax compliance which led to a significant boost in tax buoyancy. Assuming that the impact of DGT reforms on revenue collection is the same for income tax and the VAT, then tax administration reform would account for 0.35 percentage points of GDP out of the 0.6 percentage points of GDP increase in income tax from 2001 to 2006. Combined with the revenue improvement in the VAT, the revenue generated by the DGT reforms would be over 0.6 percentage points of GDP.

From this perspective, the contribution of the tax administration reforms to the overall fiscal adjustment effort during 2001–06 was significant. The overall fiscal balance improved by 2.2 percentage points of GDP over the period, of which 0.7 percentage points stemmed from revenue and grants (Table 5.6). Tax revenue was the only revenue category that did not decline over the period and tax administration reforms are estimated to have increased tax revenue by 0.6 percentage points. Without this tax administration-induced increase in tax revenue, total revenue and grants would have been flat over the period and only about two-thirds of the improvement in the overall fiscal balance would have been realized. The improvement in the government's balance was critical in helping Indonesia to attain a more sustainable fiscal position, as gross government debt was sharply reduced from 77.0 per cent of GDP in 2001 to 39 per cent of GDP in 2006.

Preliminary estimates for 2007 point to a continued positive impact of tax administrative reforms on tax revenue collection. The (non-oil and gas) tax yield increased to an all-time high of 11.3 per cent of GDP, which was mainly due to a record high collection from the DGT (9.6 per cent of GDP). This strong performance occurred in an environment with no tax policy changes but with the implementation of a new round of tax administration reforms (that was designed in 2006 and took hold in 2007).

Table 5.6 Indonesia: sources of the fiscal consolidation, 2001–06

	2001	2002	2003	2004	2005	2006
	Act.	Act.	Act.	Act.	Act.	Prel. Act.
	(In per cent of GDP)					
Revenue and grants	18.3	16.5	16.7	17.8	17.8	19.0
Oil and gas revenues	6.3	4.3	4.0	4.7	5.0	6.0
Non-oil and gas revenues	11.9	12.2	12.8	13.0	12.8	12.9
Tax revenues	9.9	10.6	10.8	11.2	11.2	11.0
Nontax revenues	2.1	1.6	2.0	1.8	1.6	1.9
Grants	0.0	0.0	0.0	0.0	0.0	0.1
Expenditure and net lending	21.5	18.0	18.7	19.1	18.1	20.0
Overall balance 3/	−3.2	−1.6	−2.0	−1.4	−0.3	−1.0
Memorandum items:						
Public debt	77.0	65.4	58.3	55.2	45.6	38.8

Sources: Data provided by the Indonesian authorities and Fund staff estimates.

Impact on the investment climate

Indonesia's investment rate dropped sharply during the Asian crisis and has only partly recovered since. Prior to the Asian crisis, Indonesia's gross fixed investment as percentage of GDP averaged 27 per cent from 1994–97 (Table 5.7). During this time, Indonesia was one of the region's favored destinations for foreign direct investment (FDI), as FDI inflows reached USD 6.2 billion in 1996. As Indonesia was hit by the economic and financial crisis, the investment share dropped sharply in 1998 to 22.3 per cent before eventually bottoming out at 18.1 per cent in 1999. Investment has since rebounded but only to a level of around 22 per cent of GDP in 2006. Similarly, FDI inflows turned negative in 1998 and then dropped sharply in each of the next three years only to recover from 2004 onwards.

Indonesia's investment climate and competitiveness is poor compared to emerging regional economies although some improvement has occurred recently. In terms of competitiveness, Indonesia ranks in the lowest quartiles when comparing with other emerging regional economies (and globally), a situation that has been relatively stable from 2001 to 2007 (Table 5.8). However, the investment climate, as assessed by the International Country Risk Guide's overall country ranking, showed a marked improvement over the past few years; whereas Indonesia ranked last among regional countries in 2000, it out-ranked both Thailand and the Philippines and was close to both India and Vietnam by 2007.

Table 5.7 Indonesia: trends in investment performance, 1994–2006

Year	Gross Fixed Investment	Net FDI Inflows
	(Per cent of GDP)	(US$ billions)
1994	24.9	2.1
1995	26.2	4.3
1996	27.9	6.2
1997	28.9	4.7
1998	22.3	–0.2
1999	18.1	–1.9
2000	19.9	–4.6
2001	20.4	–3.0
2002	20.4	0.1
2003	19.6	–0.6
2004	21.4	1.9
2005	22.5	8.3
2006	21.9	5.6

Source: IMF staff.

Table 5.8 Indonesia: investment climate indicator, 2000–07

Countries	International Country Risk Guide				IMD World Competitiveness Yearbook			
	Overall Rangking				Overall Rangking			
	2000	2002	2005	2007	2001	2002	2005	2007
Indonesia	118	122	109	77	45	47	60	54
China	47	49	52	30	35	23	21	15
India	77	85	65	73	43	34	39	27
Malaysia	36	35	32	23	26	26	31	23
Philippines	59	61	81	82	37	19	26	45
Singapore	3	4	6	6	1	2	2	2
South Korea	23	26	23	29	31	32	47	29
Thailand	45	52	62	89	39	20	14	33
Vietnam	74	77	77	68	. . .	. . .	. . .	. . .
Number countries	140	140	140	140	49	49	60	55

Source: Internal Capital Generation Rate (ICGR), International Institute for Management Development (IMD).

Business surveys reveal that tax administration was perceived as, and remains, one of the top impediments to investment (Figure 5.3). A joint study by the Asian Development Bank and World Bank in 2003 revealed that firms in Indonesia perceived the most critical investment obstacles to be macroeconomic instability and economic and regulatory policy uncertainty, followed by corruption, taxation, financing, labor issues and infrastructure; 47 per cent of surveyed firms viewed tax administration as a moderate to very severe business obstacle (Asian Development Bank and World Bank [ADB-WB], 2005). Improving tax administration was therefore expected to favorably impact the investment climate in Indonesia. The 2003 ADB-WB study was updated by these institutions in 2005 and in 2007. The updates reveal that, at the national level, tax administration is still seen as a key obstacle to investment, with no perceived improvement since 2003 (however, as detailed below, several factors can reconcile the overall negative perception of the tax administration for the investment climate with the numerous taxpayers' surveys that reveal high satisfaction with the DGT pilot offices).

Despite the overall negative perception of the tax administration, several surveys of taxpayers reveal that satisfaction with the DGT pilot offices is very high. One such study was undertaken in June 2005 by AC Nielsen. That survey entailed a comprehensive assessment of taxpayer satisfaction with the DGT's Large Taxpayers Office.[29] Based on Nielson's eQ method for measuring customer satisfaction, the LTO scored an overall performance rating of 81 per cent, indicating an exceptionally high level of taxpayer satisfaction. Among the survey's

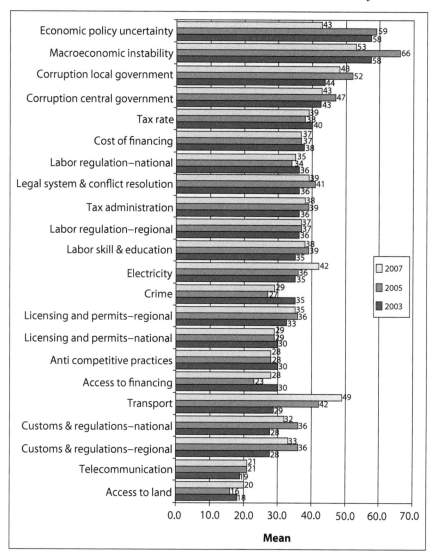

Figure 5.3 Indonesia: obstacles to investment 2003, 2005, 2007

Source: ADB and WB, Investment Climate and Productivity Study (2003, 2005, and 2007).

respondents, about 85 per cent reported that the LTO reforms dramatically simplified their tax obligations and nearly 80 per cent reported positive changes in tax officer behavior.

Detailed questions from the Nielsen survey revealed the comparative strengths of the LTO lies in its professional integrity as well as its taxpayer services, simplicity and efficiency, and information resources. These findings are noteworthy since they provide evidence that the DGT's governance framework (involving a careful vetting of staff, higher wages and a rigorously applied code of conduct) helped promote integrity among tax officers – a major concern among investors in Indonesia.

An assessment of the LTO's performance for each core tax administration function also revealed that satisfaction was the highest with the filing/payment and refund management functions, and lowest with audit and objections. These findings are encouraging in that they suggest the LTO's gold card program has been effective at accelerating the processing of refunds, another major investor concern. But they still point to significant investor concerns over the fairness of the audit and appeals processes. International comparisons, based on Nielsen's eQ surveys, show that the LTO's score stands out well above the average (Table 5.9). AC Nielsen attributes the positive results partly to large taxpayers' perceptions that the LTO represented a major improvement over what had been in place before. If true, this would suggest that the challenge for the LTO going forward would be to maintain this level of satisfaction once the 'novelty' has worn off. Similar positive results emerged from a later Nielsen survey of the DGT's Special Region Office (SRO), which like the LTO, administers many large businesses and was among the original four pilot tax offices (Table 5.9). In 2004, the SRO adopted many of the reforms that were first piloted at the LTO, including its governance framework and accelerated refunds program. The results of the SRO survey, which was conducted in 2005 after the LTO survey, were very similar to those achieved at the LTO in terms of taxpayer satisfaction with the reforms. With the LTO and SRO administering Indonesia's largest taxpayers, who also tend to be the largest investors, the Nielsen surveys suggest that the DGT has made important progress in addressing some of the concerns of major investors. A more recent eQ survey of the STO also showed similarly encouraging results.

Other studies have confirmed the findings that taxpayers' satisfaction is high at the DGT's pilot offices, but that overall taxpayer perception is far less sanguine. For example, the CGI Investment Climate Working Group prepared reports in 2004 and 2005 that looked into the principal investment challenges facing

Table 5.9 Comparison of Nielsen's eQ satisfaction ratings for selected Asian economies

Country	Pilot Offices	Overall	Public Sector
Indonesia (LTO, SRO, STO)	81, 78, 74	. . .	. . .
Australia	. . .	66	74
Hong Kong	. . .	75	71
Singapore	. . .	76	76

Source: AC Nielsen LTO, SRO and STO Surveys.

Notes: 'Overall' refers to the average rating for all entities that AC Nielsen evaluated in each country; 'Public Sector' refers to the average rating for public sector entities only. In Indonesia the sample is as follows: SRO in central Jakarta and in Batham, STO concerns 15 pilot offices in Jakarta Pusat.

Indonesia.[30] While acknowledging the many positive results of the LTO and its 'customer-friendly' approach to tax administration, the reports found that taxation continued to be among investors' chief concerns. Within the tax area, the major obstacles for business still include several tax administration factors.[31]

Several hypotheses can reconcile the overall negative perception of the tax administration for the investment climate with the numerous taxpayers' surveys that reveal high satisfaction with the DGT pilot offices. These include: (1) incomplete reform of the pilot offices – the pilot offices have introduced a number of changes that are important to investors (better services, electronic filing, quicker refunds, less corruption) but large taxpayers continue to be concerned with other important aspects of the pilot offices' operations (audit, appeals) and with the slow progress in strengthening the Ministry of Finance's internal investigation capacity; (2) it takes time for recent administrative reforms to filter through companies' perceptions of tax administration (e.g. improved perceptions by a company's finance department of DGT might take time to filter through to the CEO or other parties in charge of investment plans); and (3) even if information flows within a corporation are frictionless, given that investment decisions take a long perspective, recent changes in tax administration performance – though welcome – would need to be sustained over time to alter investment behavior (e.g. a Bayesian updating process starting with a sufficiently strong negative prior belief).

Summary

The tax administration reforms appear to be a necessary but not sufficient factor in improving the investment climate in Indonesia. Although tax administration has been, and continues to be, a major impediment to investment in Indonesia, taxpayers' satisfaction with the pilot DGT offices is very high. Reforms that achieved particularly good results, as perceived by large taxpayers, are the governance framework and the accelerated refunds. Reforms that remain incomplete include tax simplification and revisions to the tax administration laws. Those that are not functioning as originally intended include the DGT's audit and appeals processes and the Ministry of Finance's internal investigation unit.

Improving the investment climate remains crucial to meeting Indonesia's poverty reduction and employment objectives. Since investors continue to view tax administration as a major obstacle to the business environment, the DGT will need to make further progress in this area. A judicious strategy would be for the DGT to extend nationally those investor-friendly reforms that have proven to work well at the pilot offices and to redouble efforts on those reforms that so far have fallen short of expectations.

VII.   The unfinished reform agenda

Through 2007, a great deal had been achieved in improving Indonesia's tax administration. The DGT had made good, albeit uneven, progress in implementing its reform agenda and, as a consequence, the tax-to-GDP ratio had steadily increased and governance had improved at the pilot tax offices. However, a great deal remained to be done before the DGT would become a modern and highly effective tax agency. This section sets out the critical initiatives that remain to be completed and summarizes the next phase in the DGT's evolving reform strategy.

Although a pause in the tax administration reforms occurred during 2005 as a new government took stock of the DGT's progress, a cabinet reshuffle in December 2005 brought about renewed momentum to the reforms. This new momentum is largely driven by the efforts of the Minister of Finance and the DGT's new management team. By the summer of 2006, the DGT had updated its reform plans, which included many pending initiatives from the earlier reform program. Through 2007, the reform strategy has proceeded in three directions with varying degrees of success:

1. Continuing to expand the pilot tax offices in a carefully phased, step-by-step manner;
2. Further enhancing the DGT's institutional capacity by addressing the remaining, fundamental weaknesses in its headquarters' organizational structure, performance measurement systems, taxpayer services and enforcement programs, human resource management policies, governance controls, and information systems; and,
3. Putting in place measures to ensure normal operations continue, services to taxpayers do not decline and revenue is protected as the modernization strategy is implemented.

Rolling out the pilot tax office

The establishment of the LTO and the modernized offices in both the Jakarta Special Region and Jakarta Region I were high-profile events that proved to be greatly successful, as described in earlier sections. The introduction of a functional organizational structure, significantly enhanced taxpayer services activities, an integrated tax administration computer system, and modern office accommodations have substantially boosted the DGT's performance and professional image at those sites.

The LTO has now been operational for more than five years and has yielded good results in terms of revenue collection, service to taxpayers and governance.[32] Going forward, the key challenge will be to provide large taxpayers with increasingly better services and to further strengthen the LTO's enforcement capacity in dealing with the more complex compliance risks common to large taxpayers such as international tax issues, aggressive interpretations of the tax laws, and sophisticated tax evasion schemes. In this context, the audit methods used by LTO auditors need to be substantially upgraded.

Given the initial success with piloting a medium-taxpayer office (MTO) in Jakarta, the DGT took a decision in 2006 to roll-out the pilot office to additional regions and by April 2007, 19 MTOs had been established across the country. But along with increasing the number of MTOs, greater efforts are needed to identify those taxpayers that make up the medium-sized taxpayers segment and to tailor the MTO's service and enforcement programs to this group. From this perspective, consideration could be given to expanding the size of each MTO beyond the largest 200 taxpayers in each region. Moreover, the DGT needs to redouble its efforts at custom-izing its taxpayer services and enforcement programs to the needs and risks of medium-sized taxpayers.

After an initial review of the model small taxpayer office (STO) in September 2006, the DGT commenced the first phase of the STO roll-out in mid-June 2007 by extending the STO reforms to 15 tax offices in south Jakarta. By 31 December 2007 the DGT had established 171 new STOs with another 128 planned for implementation in 2008. While the initial results of the STO pilot have been broadly favorable, the STO has not sufficiently customized its tax-payer services and enforcement programs to the specific characteristics of small taxpayers. Therefore, the expansion of the STO reforms to additional tax offices should be accompanied by the development of more appropriate approaches for administering small taxpayers.

Further enhancing institutional capacity

In addition to deploying the pilot tax offices throughout the country, the DGT's ongoing reform strategy also provides for fundamental reforms in a number of key areas of tax administration. Such reforms include (or should include):

- *Strengthening the legal framework for tax administration.* Although the law on tax administration procedures was amended in May 2007, the legal framework for tax administration still requires further improvement in several important areas, including: (1) strengthening the DGT's enforcement pow-ers,[33] (2) creating a more even-handed system for resolving tax disputes;[34] (3) eliminating the legal requirement to audit every refund claim; and (4) intro-ducing a more appropriate penalty regime.[35]These improvements are essential if Indonesia's legal framework for tax administration is to achieve an appropriate balance between the powers of the tax authorities and the rights of taxpayers, which is critical for good tax administration.
- *Reorganizing the DGT's headquarters.* DGT management assigned high priority to strengthening its head office, given the critical role that a strong headquarters plays in both managing ongoing operations and designing reform programs. In recent years, the headquarters' organizational structure – which was based partly on tax administration function and partly on tax types – had become increasingly out of step with the DGT's emerging network of functionally organized field offices for large, medium and small taxpayers. With this in mind, the DGT reorganized its head office on 1 Janu-ary 2007.[36] To leverage the new organizational structure, it will now become

essential to train senior headquarters' staff in the modern methods for managing a national tax administration.

- **Simplifying the tax system.** Although some progress had been made in simplifying the value-added tax, the business community continues to voice its concerns about the excessive demands and high compliance costs that the tax system imposes on taxpayers. In this connection, there remains considerable scope for simplifying the policy and administrative provisions for each tax, beginning with a redoubling of efforts to further simplify the VAT[37] and then extending the effort to the other major taxes. In this regard, tax simplification continues to have substantial potential for both reducing taxpayers' compliance costs and increasing the DGT's administrative efficiency.

- **Implementing a balanced set of performance measures.** Reliance on the revenue collection target as the main measure of the DGT's performance has damaged integrity and good tax administration practice by creating perverse incentives for arbitrary and inflated audit assessments, delayed refund payments, delays in reaching decisions on objections and other inappropriate actions. The development of a more balanced set of performance measures would help the DGT to focus on improving the full scope of its tax administration programs and not just on achieving an arbitrary revenue target. To this end, the DGT has drafted a set of key performance indicators to underpin its strategic plan and now needs to take steps to put these indicators into operation.

- **Designing a new human resource (HR) management regime.** Such a system is critical for creating incentives for improved performance and appropriate behavior by managers and staff. Under current arrangements, salary increases and promotions for DGT staff are linked to performance to only a very limited extent, even at the modernized offices. This situation seriously hampers the DGT's ability to reward top performers and create incentives for high performance and noncorrupt behavior. In this context, fundamental changes need to be made to the DGT's HR management policies in job classification, remuneration, promotion and staff evaluation. Importantly, policies for increasing staff remuneration need to be linked to efforts at 'right-sizing' the DGT's work-force.

- **Enhancing governance controls.** Some positive steps have been taken in recent years to improve governance, including the introduction of a code of conduct at the LTO and the other pilot tax offices as well as the establishment of an internal investigations unit within the MoF's Inspectorate General. The pilot office reforms are integral to Indonesia's business climate and should be rolled-out nationally as quickly as possible. Similarly, the good progress that has been made in creating the MoF's internal investigation unit needs to be capitalized on by ensuring that serious cases of misconduct by tax officers result in severe administrative penalties and, where appropriate, are referred for prosecution. As part of this effort, the authorities need to monitor and publicize the numbers of investigations that have been conducted and their results.

- *Further strengthening the DGT's enforcement programs.* While the DGT has introduced some improvements in the enforcement area, its core enforcement programs still require substantial upgrading. In particular, major improvements are needed to the DGT's programs for cleaning up the taxpayer register, identifying potential registrants, controlling nonfilers, collecting tax arrears, and, most important, auditing taxpayers. In each of these areas, the DGT needs to overhaul its approach to setting operational targets, risk assessment systems (including the cross-matching of information on tax returns to information reported by third parties) and the methods and techniques used by front-line enforcement staff.[38]

- *Modernizing information systems.* Over the last several years, the DGT's efforts at strengthening its IT systems have helped to improve compliance and increase tax collection. However, the lack of a unified IT system is a major impediment to further improvements. Other priority areas include the need to expand electronic filing and other electronic services, automate risk assessment systems and third-party information matching, develop telephone contact centers and centralized sites for processing paper tax returns and improve management information on core tax administration processes. The establishment of the DGT's first data processing center, which was scheduled to be implemented in 2008, is an important step forward. However, the DGT urgently needs to develop a comprehensive information technology strategy to guide its future IT reforms.

Safeguarding revenue

The DGT's ongoing tax administration reforms pose some risks to revenue collection as existing forms of administration are replaced by new and less familiar ones. To mitigate these risks, the DGT needs to implement measures that ensure revenue collection is not adversely affected as the reforms take hold. For this purpose, the DGT may consider reviving the revenue generation initiative, which it had introduced successfully in 2002.

Under the revenue generation initiative, DGT headquarters set operational targets for the number and type of enforcement actions (audit, arrears collection, etc.) that were to be taken by each of its core enforcement programs (audit, arrears collection, etc.) along with forecasts for the amount of revenue that would be recovered through these actions. It then carefully monitored performance against targets, and held staff accountable for results.

This initiative proved highly effective in mobilizing substantial amounts of tax revenue through 2005. After 2005, however, the DGT discontinued the systematic reporting on the amount of revenue that was generated by each of its enforcement programs. Re-establishing the revenue generation initiative may provide the DGT with an effective option for safeguarding revenue as its modernization program continues to unfold.[39]

VIII.   Lessons and conclusions

Since 2002, Indonesia's tax administration reforms have made significant contributions to the country's fiscal adjustment program and have also placed the DGT on a reform path that has continued through 2007. From this perspective, the reforms can be considered to have been successful in achieving their objectives. Yet despite the broadly positive results, it is nevertheless clear that some reforms have been implemented more fully than others and, in a number of important areas, much further progress is still needed. In this final section, the chapter identifies the key success factors and major impediments to reform along with the main conclusions that may be drawn from Indonesia's experience in reforming tax administration within the context of a fiscal adjustment program.

Key success factors

Several factors have contributed significantly to the success of the tax administration reforms over the last several years. As the DGT continues to move forward with its reform agenda, it will be important to preserve these key success factors, which have included:

Direct linkages with the fiscal adjustment program. Strong pressure to increase revenue from non-oil and gas sources, coupled with the limited agenda for tax policy reform, focused the government's attention on tax administration reform as an integral element in its strategy for achieving fiscal sustainability. The linkage of the tax administration reforms to the government's high-level policy objectives was crucial for ensuring that sufficient amounts of resources (political, budgetary and staffing) were made available to support the reform effort. It also made the reforms more consequential to DGT officials, who initially were not necessarily convinced of the reform program's benefits.

Strong political support. From the outset, the reforms received strong support from the Minister of Finance and other senior government officials. This support was manifested in a number of ways, both big and small. Most important, the finance minister allocated adequate resources to the reforms, monitored developments to ensure that the reforms remained on track and intervened in a timely manner to overcome obstacles. Less obviously, but equally important, the minister and other senior government officials made significant efforts at explaining the reforms to the media and taxpayer population, encouraging the DGT staff to implement the reform agenda, and recognized and rewarded good performance. These efforts are continuing.

Appointment of capable staff to lead the reforms. Among the most important decisions that the authorities had taken at the beginning of the reform program was to appoint a capable group of DGT officials to lead the reforms. These staff were highly motivated, open to new approaches in tax administration and possessed strong leadership skills. They worked long hours on designing and implementing the reforms while at the same time holding down their regular operational positions. Their dedicated efforts were truly impressive and provide yet another example of the close relationship that exists between efforts and results in tax administration reform.

Achievable targets to deliver early results. To avoid the DGT from becoming overwhelmed by a comprehensive reform program that exceeded its implementation capacity, the initial phase of reforms in 2002 was purposely restricted to a relatively small number of priority initiatives that the DGT could effectively manage. This approach allowed early successes to be registered, which built confidence within the DGT to take on increasingly more challenging reforms. In this way, the modestly ambitious reforms that commenced in 2002 catalyzed commitment and enthusiasm for the more ambitious reform program that was to follow.

Phased implementation. Wherever possible, new initiatives were tested at one or more pilot sites before being rolled out nationally. For example, new organizational structures, human resource management policies and IT initiatives were first piloted in the LTO. This approach facilitated better control and monitoring during the implementation stages and allowed teething problems to be dealt with more expediently. Once the success of these initiatives had been confirmed, including through feedback from taxpayers, the reforms were duplicated at the medium-taxpayer office and are now being extended to all small taxpayer offices as an integral part of the DGT's modernization strategy.

Private sector stakeholders involvement. From time to time, the DGT met with representatives of the business community to update them on progress with the tax administration reforms and to solicit feedback on proposals. The DGT also made great effort to invite business representatives to significant events, such as new office openings offices or new initiative launches. Apart from providing valuable feedback that assisted in the design and implementation of modernization initiatives, involving the private sector business community also secured its support for the reforms, which had further positive impacts on the political support for the project.

Appropriate use of policy conditionality and technical assistance. The policy conditionality that accompanied the financial assistance from international agencies helped to catalyze Indonesia's tax administration reforms. Similarly, the Indonesian authorities made excellent use of technical assistance from these agencies at each stage in the reform process. When combined with strong political commitment for reform by governments, the experience from Indonesia shows that policy conditionality and technical assistance can play an important role in advancing tax administration reform.

Major impediments

In addition to factors that helped the tax administration reforms succeed, there were also a number of constraints that have impeded the reform effort over the years. The success of the reforms going forward depends critically on the steps that the Indonesian authorities take to ease these constraints, which include:

Political constraints. Despite strong political support for the reforms from some key officials, there were a number of critical areas where interests at both the executive and administrative levels within government, as well as powerful interests outside government, were not always aligned with the reforms and inhibited, at times, the implementation of some key initiatives. This was particularly the case with the efforts at overhauling the DGT's audit program, which to date have produced few results despite being crucial to the tax administration reform strategy. Similarly, the initiative to register additional numbers of high-income taxpayers was hindered by the refusal of many third parties, such as professional associations, to provide details about their members to the DGT. When faced with this situation, the DGT itself was reluctant to adopt a firm stance, instead opting to seek legal clarification that was rarely decisive.

Legal and procedural constraints. Legal constraints sometimes obstructed progress on the implementation of reforms. Some reforms required legislative amendment, which inevitably caused long delays. Other delays resulted from the requirement for the DGT to issue a formal decree, signed by the Director General, to effect changes in instructions regarding operational methods and procedures. For example, the introduction of the 'gold card scheme', which was designed to speed up the VAT refund process, not only required decrees for operational instructions, but also required each taxpayer to be named in a decree as being awarded gold card status. The extensive requirement for issuing DGT decrees and the lack of managerial empowerment severely restricted the pace at which detailed operational matters could be reformed.

Organizational constraints. Operational pressures meant that most key players responsible for designing the reforms were also expected to continue carrying out their regular operational duties, which made it difficult to maintain enthusiasm for the reform program over a prolonged period. From this perspective, a more productive arrangement may have been to create a full-time modernization team and to relieve the staff assigned to this team from other responsibilities. Similarly, the DGT's policy of mandatory rotation of staff and managers every two years – though largely an anti-corruption measure – greatly impedes the development of expertise as managers are frequently rotated into areas in which they have little or no experience. Finally, the reform effort was further complicated by fragmented implementation responsibilities at headquarters: for example, despite the establishment of a dedicated headquarters team to improve compliance with tax filing obligations, little progress was achieved on this initiative because critical elements were also required to be performed by other departments at headquarters.

Measurement and incentive constraints. Traditionally, the DGT had relied on the annual revenue collection target as the main measure for judging and rewarding the performance of its regional and district directors. This reliance on a narrow measure of performance, however, created perverse incentives for all sorts of inappropriate practices – including arbitrary audit assessments and delaying the processing of refunds – in order to achieve the assigned collection target. On the other hand, the positive results that were achieved by the revenue generation program – which established targets for each of the DGT's enforcement programs – demonstrates that substantial gains in tax administration can be realized by setting meaningful and reasonably ambitious performance measures, and holding staff accountable for their achievement.

Conclusions

Several conclusions may be drawn from Indonesia's experience in reforming tax administration. Some conclusions reaffirm lessons learned from tax administration reform in other countries, while other conclusions offer new insights. These include:

- Since 2002, Indonesia's tax administration reforms have been successful in advancing the country's fiscal adjustment program. The tax administration reforms had a strong, positive impact on the tax yield and a positive, though difficult to quantify, effect on the investment climate.
- Linking tax administration reform to a government's wider fiscal adjustment program can both assist fiscal adjustment and improve tax administration. Given the gestation period for designing and implementing tax administration reforms, the sooner such reforms can be incorporated into an adjustment program the better.
- Tax administration reform can help increase the tax yield by raising additional amounts of enforced and voluntary tax collections. Programming these gains should be based on a coherent framework, such as that set out in third section and Annex 5.1, with realistic estimates for increasing collections that are linked to concrete administrative measures for bringing about the targeted increases.
- In the short term, enforced collections may provide a substantial source of additional tax revenue. However, because these collections typically account for a relatively small share of tax revenue, very high growth rates are required to have an appreciable impact on the tax yield. The Indonesian experience demonstrates the practical difficulties of achieving high growth rates in enforced collections year after year.
- Over the medium term, increasing voluntary collections (by raising taxpayers' compliance rates) is the key way that tax administration can help sustain and expand the tax yield. Therefore, tax agencies should be encouraged to measure tax compliance, identify reasons for noncompliance and develop appropriate compliance-enhancing strategies.
- Tax administration reform can be a necessary (but not a sufficient) condition for improving a country's investment climate. A tax agency can help boost the investment climate through measures that lower compliance costs faced by taxpayers and promote integrity among tax officers. Indonesia achieved promising, initial results by piloting the careful vetting of tax officers, providing sufficiently high salaries, establishing clear standards of conduct that were effectively communicated to taxpayers and tax offices, and accelerating the processing of tax refunds.

- The good results that have been achieved in improving Indonesia's tax administration were due, in part, to a reform strategy that focused initially on a few key initiatives. This approach allowed early successes to be registered in the short term and helped build confidence within the DGT to take on increasingly more challenging reforms over the medium term.
- Strong political commitment was critical to the success of Indonesia's tax administration reforms. This commitment was most evidenced by the government's willingness to place tax administration reform high on its reform agenda, allocate resources (staff, budgetary and technical assistance) to support the reforms and appoint capable staff to lead the reform effort.
- Technical assistance and policy conditionality can play an important role in helping tax agencies to design and implement reform programs. However, ownership of the reform process by a country's tax agency is indispensable for sustaining the reforms over time.
- There remains ample scope for Indonesia to increase the tax yield and stimulate the investment climate through further improvements in tax administration. In this regard, the strategic plan that the DGT's new management formulated in 2006 provides a sound basis for strengthening revenue collection and promoting fiscal adjustment over the coming years. The 2007 tax collection estimates vindicate these reform efforts.

Annex 5.1. Analytical framework: tax administration and the tax yield

The linkages between tax administration and the tax yield that were described qualitatively in Section II are now presented more precisely in mathematical terms.[40] To isolate the role of tax administration, the discussion assumes no changes in tax policy, structural shifts in the economy that affect relative tax burdens, or changes in any factors that affect the tax yield other than those involving tax administration.

Defining the tax yield. The tax yield is commonly defined as the ratio of tax revenue to GDP. With tax revenue consisting of both voluntary payments by taxpayers and enforced collections by the tax agency, the tax yield may be expressed as follows:

$$\frac{T}{GDP} = \frac{TV + TE}{GDP} \tag{1}$$

where:

T = total tax collection
TV = taxes collected voluntarily from taxpayers
TE = taxes collected through enforcement by the tax agency
GDP = gross domestic product

Accounting for changes in the tax yield. By manipulating equation (1), the sources of change in the tax-to-GDP ratio can be expressed by the following equation:

$$\frac{\dot{T}}{GDP} = \alpha\dot{TV} + (1-\alpha)\dot{TE} - \dot{GDP} \tag{2}$$

where:

α = the proportion of voluntary tax collection to total tax collections

or $\dfrac{TE}{TV+TE}$

$(1 - \alpha)$ = the proportion of enforced collection to total tax collections or

$\dfrac{TE}{TP(1-v)}$

• = percentage change in a variable

Equation (2) demonstrates that changes in the tax-to-GDP ratio are accounted for by changes in the growth rates of voluntary and enforced collections, weighted by their relative shares in total tax collection (α and $1 - \alpha$), and the growth rate of GDP. The equation clarifies an important point made in the body of the chapter that the small share of enforced collections (typically less than 10 per cent) implies that a relatively large increase in the growth rate of enforced collection is required to produce a significant impact on total collections.[41] Conversely, the large share of voluntary collections (commonly greater than 90 per cent) means that a relatively small increase in their growth rate will have a significant impact on the tax yield.

This point has important implications for the design of tax administration reforms that are strongly focused on increasing tax revenue. While it may be possible to raise the tax yield in the short term through large increases in enforced collections, it is not realistic to expect a tax agency to achieve high growth rates in these collections year after year that would be required to continuously increase the tax yield. Over the medium term, therefore, increasing the tax yield through tax administration improvements depends critically on the tax agency's capacity to increase voluntary collections.

Expressing changes in voluntary collections. Voluntary collections (*TV*) can be defined as the product of the total amount of taxes that taxpayers are required to pay under the tax laws (potential tax collections, *TP*) and the proportion of potential taxes that taxpayers actually pay (i.e. the voluntary compliance ratio, *v*). As such, voluntary collections are expressed as follows:

$$TV = v \cdot TP \tag{3}$$

where:

TV = taxes collected voluntarily from taxpayers
TP = amount of (potential) tax collections if taxpayers fully comply with tax laws
v = TV/TP

As indicated in equation (3), an increase (decrease) in the voluntary compliance ratio (v) will lead to an increase (decrease) in the amount of voluntary collections as taxpayers come to pay a larger (smaller) share of their true tax liability. A tax agency can raise the voluntary compliance ratio, and, hence, increase voluntary collections, by enhancing the effectiveness of its compliance facilitation and compliance enforcement programs. As taxpayers improve their compliance rates in response to these programs, voluntary collections will increase. Turning to the second element in equation (2), potential tax collections (TP) are responsive to changes in GDP as increases in income and sales give rise to higher tax liabilities. The degree of responsiveness is referred to as the revenue elasticity of the tax system, which is defined here as the percentage change in voluntary tax collections divided by the percentage change in GDP,[42] or:

$$\varepsilon = \frac{\left(\dfrac{\Delta TV}{TV}\right)}{\left(\dfrac{\Delta GDP}{GDP}\right)}$$

where:

TV = taxes collected voluntarily from taxpayers
GDP = gross domestic product

If the elasticity (ε) is greater than 1, then the tax system is said to be 'revenue elastic' and taxes will rise proportionally more than national income. For example, if ε equals 1.2, then for every 10 per cent increase in GDP tax collections rise by 12 per cent. In contrast, if the elasticity is less than 1, then the tax system is 'revenue inelastic'. Hence, if ε equals 0.8 then a 10 per cent increase in GDP will yield only an 8 per cent increase in taxes.

Now, the growth rate of voluntary collections can be expressed as:

$$(\dot{T}V) = (\dot{v} + \varepsilon \cdot G\dot{D}P) \tag{4}$$

By substituting equation (4) into equation (2), changes in the tax yield can then be expressed as:

$$\left(\frac{\dot{T}}{GDP}\right) = \alpha(\dot{v} + \varepsilon \cdot G\dot{D}P) + (1+\alpha)\dot{T}E - G\dot{D}P \tag{5}$$

The first term on the right-hand side of equation (5) shows that voluntary collections increase with increases in both the voluntary compliance ratio (v) and GDP. For example, if the voluntary compliance ratio were to increase by 5 per cent (e.g. from 60 per cent of potential collections to 63 per cent of potential collections) and GDP were to increase by 10 per cent with an elasticity of unity (1) then voluntary collections would increase by 15 per cent. We now turn to the second term on the right-hand side, enforced collections (TE).

Expressing changes in enforced collections. Enforced tax collections (TE) are determined by two variables: the total amount of foregone revenue resulting from noncompliant taxpayers and the rate at which the tax agency recovers the foregone revenue. The first of these two variables, foregone revenue, is the product of the total amount of taxes due according to the tax laws (potential tax collections, TP) and the rate of noncompliance among taxpayers ($1 - v$, the complement to the rate of compliance, v). The second variable, the revenue recovery ratio (r), can be defined as the proportion of foregone revenue that a tax agency actually recovers each year. Taken together, the amount of enforced collections can be expressed as[43]:

$$TE = r \cdot (1 - v) \cdot TP \tag{6}$$

where:

$$r \qquad = \text{revenue recovery ratio} = TE/(TP - TV) = \frac{TE}{TP(1-v)}$$
$$(1 - v) \quad = \text{noncompliance ratio} = 1 - (TV/TP)$$
$$TP \qquad = \text{potential tax revenue}$$

Based on equation (6) and recalling that potential tax revenue grows in line with the elasticity of the tax system and changes in GDP, the growth rate of enforced collections can then be expressed as:

$$(\dot{TE}) = \dot{r} + (1 - \dot{v}) + \varepsilon \cdot \dot{GDP} \tag{7}$$

An interesting implication of equation (7) is that the growth rate of enforced collections will decrease with increases in the voluntary compliance ratio (v) for a given elasticity and a given amount of GDP. This results from the fact that as taxpayers increase their compliance rates, the 'supply' of foregone revenue that a tax agency can potentially recover will decrease.

Before closing the discussion of enforced collections, it is important to point out that changes in the voluntary compliance ratio (v) and its complement the noncompliance ratio ($1 - v$) are not independent of each other: as the voluntary compliance ratio increases, the noncompliance ratio necessarily decreases and vice versa. The precise relationship between the two can be shown to be:

$$(\dot{1 - v}) = -\dot{v} \cdot \left(\frac{v}{1 - v} \right) \tag{8}$$

This relationship means that the noncompliance ratio $(1 - v)$ will decrease at the rate that the compliance ratio increases adjusted for by the proportion of the compliance ratio (v) to the noncompliance ratio $(1 - v)$. When the compliance ratio is greater than the noncompliance ratio $(v > 0.5)$, the noncompliance ratio will decrease at a faster rate than the compliance ratio increases. Conversely, when the compliance ratio is less than the noncompliance ratio $(v < 0.5)$ then the noncompliance ratio will decrease at a slower rate than compliance ratio increases. Taking this into account, the growth in enforced collections can be more precisely stated as:

$$\dot{TE} = \dot{r} - \dot{v} \cdot \left(\frac{v}{1-v} \right) + \varepsilon \cdot \dot{GDP} \tag{9}$$

Equation (9) shows that a tax agency's ability to increase the growth rate of enforced collections depends on the capacity of its compliance enforcement programs to raise the revenue recovery ratio (r). This ratio will increase to the extent that a tax agency can collect a larger proportion of foregone tax revenue owed by noncompliant taxpayers. As described earlier, identifying and recovering taxes from businesses and individuals who fail to register for taxation, do not file their tax returns and pay their taxes on time, or underreport their tax liabilities are all ways in which a tax agency can increase the revenue recovery ratio (r).

The full expression. Now, by substituting equation (9) into equation (5) and re-arranging terms, the factors accounting for changes in the tax yield can be expressed as:

$$\left(\frac{\dot{T}}{GDP} \right) = \alpha \cdot \dot{v} + (1-\alpha) \cdot \dot{r} - (1-\alpha) \cdot \dot{v} \cdot \left(\frac{v}{1-v} \right) - (1-\varepsilon) \cdot \dot{GDP} \tag{10}$$

Equation (10) provides the full framework for analyzing the impact of tax administration on the tax yield. It shows that a tax agency can affect the tax yield through the four terms on the right hand side of the equation. The meaning of each of these terms is summarized below along with a simple example to drive home the analysis.

The first term on the right-hand side of equation (10) represents the impact that changes in voluntary compliance (v, weighted by the share of voluntary collections in total tax revenue) have on the tax yield. The tax agency can influence the voluntary compliance ratio by improving the effectiveness of its compliance facilitation and compliance enforcement programs. To the extent that taxpayers adjust their compliance patterns in response to these programs, the voluntary compliance ratio (v) will increase and voluntary collections will grow (the indirect effect of compliance enforcement).

The second term illustrates how the tax yield is affected by changes in the tax agency's capacity to recover taxes that were legally due but not voluntarily paid by taxpayers. As a tax agency strengthens its compliance enforcement programs, the recovered revenue ratio (r) will rise and the amount of enforced collections will increase.

The third term shows that increases in the voluntary compliance ratio (v) can, to some degree, diminish the revenue impact of a tax agency's compliance enforcement programs by reducing the total amount of foregone revenue that the tax agency could potentially recover. The magnitude of this 'dampen ing' effect will depend on the proportion of compliance to noncompliance ratios $\frac{v}{1-v}$ and the share of enforced collections in total collections ($1 - \alpha$).

The final term shows the impact that increases in GDP have on the tax yield. Growth in GDP will increase (decrease) the tax-to-GDP ratio to the extent that the elasticity of the tax system is greater (less) than 1.

To bring all the pieces together, consider the case where a government seeks to increase the tax yield from 10.0 per cent of GDP to 10.5 per cent of GDP (i.e. a 5 per cent increase) strictly through improvements in tax administration. As with the earlier examples, assume that the share of voluntary collections in total tax collections (α) is 90 per cent (and, therefore, enforced collections ($1 - \alpha$) equals 10 per cent), the voluntary compliance ratio (v) is 0.60 (and, consequently, the noncompliance ratio ($1 - v$) is 0.40), and that the elasticity of the tax system equals 1. Inserting these figures into equation (10) would yield:

$$.05 = 0.9 \cdot \dot{v} + 0.1 \cdot \dot{r} + 0.1 \cdot \dot{v} \cdot 1.5 - 0$$

Using this framework, fiscal economists and tax administration specialists could determine the feasibility of achieving the targeted increase in the tax yield by assessing the extent to which a tax agency could increase the voluntary compliance ratio (v) and the revenue recovery ratio (r) through improvements to its compliance facilitation and compliance enforcement measures.

So if it were to be determined that a tax agency's measures could increase both the voluntary compliance ratio by, say, 4.5 per cent (0.045) and the revenue recovery ratio by 17 per cent (0.17) then the framework would suggest that the tax yield would rise by about 5.1 per cent, thereby exceeding the target. If, on the other hand, it were to be determined that a tax agency could only increase the voluntary compliance ratio by, say, 3 per cent and the revenue recovery ratio by, say, 10 per cent then the framework would indicate that the tax yield would rise by only 3.5 per cent, thereby falling short of the target. In this situation, the authorities would either need to reduce the targeted increase in the tax yield or introduce a more ambitious set of tax administration measures.

Annex 5.2 VAT revenue projections

This appendix details the methodology used to derive the impact of tax administration reform on VAT collection. As detailed in Section VI, changes in VAT collection can arise from three sources: (1) changes to the nature of the tax itself (tax policy changes); (2) structural economic changes that affect the VAT base; and (3) tax compliance changes – which are primarily the result of the tax administration effectiveness (actual or perceived).

With no tax policy changes occurring over the reform period, VAT buoyancy can only stem from the remaining two sources. The revenue impact of tax administration reforms is derived as a residual between actual VAT collected and VAT that should have been collected based on the observed structural economic changes. More specifically, the methodology, which is based around a GDP-decomposition of the VAT base (Zee, 1995), involves the following steps:

1. Calibrate VAT projections for 2001 to actual revenue collection for that year.

    a) Private final consumption in the economy is estimated (in a simple macro-based model).
    b) The economy-wide rate of activities exempted from VAT is applied to the estimated final consumption base; this provides the taxable base for the VAT.
    c) The statutory VAT tax rate is applied to that base; this provides an estimate of potential VAT collection.
    d) The VAT tax gap is calculated. The tax gap is the difference between potential VAT and actual VAT collection; it measures the degree of tax compliance/leakage.

2. Project VAT collection for 2002 to 2006 assuming an unchanged compliance behavior (i.e. holding the tax gap constant as the 2001 level). These projected VAT revenue take into account changes in the GDP composition (e.g. import growth exceeding that of export, which is revenue positive for VAT collection) but do not allow for improved compliance due to tax administration efforts, and also assume that the share of exempted sector is unchanged (which is a realistic first-order assumption since no changes to the VAT base and rate took place during the period).
3. Calculate the revenue impact of tax administration reforms by taking the difference between actual VAT collection and VAT collection projected based on changes in the economic structure. (This also allows to calculate the reduction in the tax gap/improvement in tax compliance.)

A complication in the above methodology is to calculate the aggregate VAT exemption rate. A standard methodology to estimate this exemption rate is to use a GDP decomposition framework and make several adjustments to the taxable base depending on exemptions and threshold included in the VAT law (Zee, 1995). This requires a comprehensive and detailed analysis of economic sectors and their interactions. Information is mainly obtained from national income accounts, input-output tables, and CPI. Fortunately, such a detailed analysis was undertaken by Marks (2005) for the year 2000. Marks finds the revenue potential of the VAT was 5.7 per cent of GDP; whereas actual collection was 2.8 per cent of GDP which gives an estimated VAT tax gap of 51 per cent or 2.9 per cent of GDP.

Using the compliance rate obtained by Marks (2005) and actual revenue collection, the economy's exemption rate can then easily be calculated as a residual for the year 2000.[44] Assuming the exemption rate is unchanged from 2000 onwards (which is a reasonable first- order assumption, as argued above), a compliance rate is derived (by matching projected and actual VAT collection) for 2001, the year prior to the tax administration reforms. This provides the computations needed for step 1; steps 2 and 3 are straightforward. Table 5.4 (main text) presents the results of these computations, and reveal that tax administration reform efforts account for 0.27 percentage points of GDP in revenue over performance (more than half of the increased tax yield).

There are some standard VAT performance indicators, namely VAT efficiency ratios (also productivity ratios). The first one, the VAT efficiency, is defined as the ratio of VAT revenues to GDP divided by the standard VAT rate (expressed as a percentage). It is widely used as a gauge of the extent to which the VAT bears uniformly upon a broad base, with a low ratio taken as evidence of tax erosion often due to a proliferation of exemptions or to weak tax compliance and enforcement. In Indonesia, the efficiency ratio was 30.5 per cent in 2001, which is lower than the 35 per cent average ratio reported in Ebrill et al. (2001) for Asia and Pacific countries (the world-wide average ratio they computed is 34 per cent). This ratio implies that a 1 point increase in the VAT rate is associated in Indonesia with a 0.305 percentage point of GDP increase in VAT revenue. Thanks to improved compliance linked to the tax administration reforms, by 2006, the impact of 1 point of VAT increased to 0.353 percentage point of GDP – a 16 per cent increase in the productivity of the VAT in Indonesia.

Although widely used, VAT efficiency ratios have important limitations, as detailed in Ebrill et al. (2001). For this reason, two other VAT performance diagnostic tools are also presented, namely VAT 'C-efficiency' (out of total and private consumptions). The 'C-efficiency' ratio is defined as the ratio of the share of VAT revenues in (total or private) consumption (rather than GDP) to the standard rate. The advantage is that this ratio is normalized at 100 per cent (i.e. 100 represents a uniform tax on consumption; zero rating would reduce that number, however, a break in the VAT chain due to exemptions – and cascading – could generate a ratio over 100 per cent). In Indonesia, all VAT performance indicators point to a significant increase over the reform period.

Notes

1 © International Monetary Fund. Reprinted with permission. The views expressed in this chapter belong solely to the authors. Nothing contained in this chapter should be reported as representing IMF policy or the views of the IMF, its Executive Board, member governments, or any other entity mentioned herein.
2 The large increase in public debt did not reflect expansionary fiscal policies but rather a large recapitalization of the banking system and a significant exchange rate depreciation.
3 Another key component of the fiscal adjustment program was a rationalization of spending including through the elimination of untargeted subsidies.

4   However, thanks to relatively large oil and gas revenue total revenue in Indonesia was similar to other non-OECD countries in the region (18.3 and 18.4 per cent of GDP, respectively).

5   In Indonesia, income tax revenue from the oil and gas sector is classified as oil and gas revenue instead of tax revenue. In 2001, oil and gas income tax collections is estimated to have been around 1.1 per cent of GDP.

6   The main income tax legislation is Law No. 17 of 2000, which included provisions applying to both corporate and individual income tax.

7   Indonesia's VAT is legally defined under Law No. 18 of 2000.

8   These requirements are stipulated in Article 17 of Law No. 16 of 2000 on General Rules and Procedures of Taxation.

9   Statistics from 2000 indicated that 60 per cent of corporate taxpayers, accounting for nearly half of turnover, reported no net income while estimates from 2002 revealed that only about 40 per cent of potential personal income tax collections was being paid. See Strengthening Tax Policy Through Tax Reform, Indonesia-Japan Economic Working Team, 2004 (pp. 15–16).

10   Specifically, the Law on General Provisions and Tax Procedures (Law No. 6 of 1983) as last amended by Law No. 16 of 2000 (commonly referred to as the 'general law on tax administration') and the Law Concerning Tax Collection with Coerce Warrants as last amended by Law No. 19 of 2000 (also known as the 'law on arrears collection').

11   In 1996, the DGT was a three-tiered organization (which included headquarters, regional and field offices) with about 26,300 staff. In addition to a headquarters in Jakarta, the DGT comprised 15 regional tax offices and a network of 303 field offices consisting of 141 district tax offices, 55 audit offices and 107 property tax offices. This organization was responsible for collecting the following national taxes: income tax applying to corporations (366,000) and individual entrepreneurs (998,000), income tax on wage earners (9,765,000) withheld by their employers (final withholding), value-added tax and sales tax on luxury goods (280,000), and property tax (75 million properties owned by 40 million taxpayers).

12   District offices had also separate sections that carried out registration, taxpayer services and debt collection for all taxpayers.

13   The tax gap can be measured on both a gross and net basis. The gross tax gap equals the difference between potential and actual tax collections. The net tax gap equals the gross tax gap in any particular year less any tax revenue that the tax agency recovers through enforcement (see Toder, 2007).

14   The rate of voluntary compliance is defined as the ratio of voluntary collections to potential collections.

15   For example, economists have estimated that in the United States, the audit program's indirect effects on voluntary collections are from 6 to 12 times greater than the audit program's direct effects on enforced collections. See Plumley (1996), Dubin et al. (1990) and Dubin (2004).

16   Increases in enforced collections capture only the direct effects that tax administration can have on the tax yield. It excludes the potentially large indirect effects that tax administration reform can have on the tax yield by increasing voluntary collections. This article provides a fuller analysis of the effects that Indonesia's tax administration reforms have had on the tax yield.

17   By comparison, in 2001 tax arrears as a per cent of tax collections was 15.5 per cent in Thailand and 20 per cent in the Philippines.

18   A key feature of the LTO's taxpayer services function was the assignment of an 'account representative' (AR) officer to each large taxpayer. For his assigned set of large taxpayers, the AR served as the first point of contact into the LTO for answering questions on the tax law, straightening out problems involving a

taxpayer's account with the DGT, and following up on such issues as delays in issuing refunds. The AR also closely monitored the taxpayer's filing and payment obligations, and was authorized to undertake some initial enforcement actions such as calling a taxpayer who filed a late tax return or did not pay tax on time.

19 Region VII comprised about 1,050 staff across 1 regional office, 8 field offices and 2 audit offices. These offices were responsible for administering about 15,000 companies and 2,500 individuals who accounted for about 22 per cent of DGT collections. The companies include state-owned companies, local government enterprises, enterprises with foreign investment, foreign-owned companies and foreign resident individuals, and domestic public companies.

20 As of December 2007, the DGT had established a total of 19 MTOs and 171 STOs.

21 Preliminary estimates of 2007 budgetary execution point to a strong improvement in the non-oil and gas tax to GDP ratio (see Table 5.3). Since these are subject to revision, they are not included in the analysis but their inclusion would only reinforce the conclusion reached in the chapter.

22 Regarding the personal income tax (PIT), both the tax brackets and rates were modified, which resulted in a decrease in the effective tax rate for all but the wealthiest tax payers (the top marginal rate was increased from 30 to 35 per cent but the threshold for this top marginal rate was increased four-fold). On the corporate income tax (CIT) front, only the tax brackets were changed (the three rates of 10, 15 and 30 per cent remain). This resulted in a lower effective tax rate for corporations.

23 In 2003, VAT exemptions were granted for goods traded in bonded zones as long as these goods, including those imported, are used in the production of exported goods (Government Regulation 60). Other recent changes, but that pre-date the administration reforms, took place in 2000 and concerned the VAT base (Law No. 18 and Government Regulation 144 detailed the exempted sectors), and, to a lower extent in 2001 (Government Regulation 21 added some 'strategic' products to the 2000 list).

24 The list of goods subject to the luxury sales tax is extensive; it includes alcoholic beverages (which are also subject to excises), motor vehicles, soft drinks, household appliances, cosmetics, electronics and carpets. Rates range between 10 and 75 per cent. It is a final tax, which is not creditable for VAT purposes.

25 A summary of the methodology is the following. The projections are calibrated for the year 2000 based on the tax gap obtained by Marks (2005), with the economy's exemption rate backed up from the compliance rate and actual revenue collection for that year. Holding the nonexemption rate constant for the remaining years (as no significant tax policy changes occurred), a compliance rate is derived (by matching projected and actual VAT collection) for 2001, the year prior to the tax administration reforms. The projected revenue for 2002 to 2006 takes into account changes in the GDP composition (e.g. import growth exceeding that of export, which is revenue positive for VAT collection), while holding tax compliance at the 2001 (pre-reform) level of 52.9 per cent.

26 DGT started to measure enforced collections only in 2002, the first year of the tax administration reform program. Without a base for comparison in 2001, it is not possible to measure the increase in enforced collections from 2001 to 2002. Given the weakness in the DGT's enforcement programs prior to 2002 (as revealed by the steadily declining DGT tax-to-GDP collection ratio since FY1993/94), the pattern of improved compliance shown from 2002 to 2005 is likely to understate the true revenue impact of the tax administration improvements (i.e. compared to 2001).

27 These include the reorganization of staff into units based on tax administration function, the vetting of managers and staff, increased salaries, application of a code of conduct and better taxpayer services.

28 The LTO and SR represented about half of the DGT's voluntary collections in 2004 but accounted for 75 per cent of the Rp48 trillion increase in these collections from 2004–05.

29 The survey involved 126 of the LTO's 300 taxpayers of which 60 per cent were multinational companies and 40 per cent were local companies; 93 per cent of the respondents had dealt with the LTO for 2–3 years.

30 See the following papers by the Consultative Group for Indonesia, Investment Climate Working Group: (1) Creating Jobs Through Investment: Suggestions from the Donor Community on Improving Indonesia's Investment Climate, October 2005; and (2) Creating Jobs Through Investment: An Update on Efforts to Improve Indonesia's Investment Climate, December 2003.

31 These include: (1) arbitrary implementation of tax regulations by tax officers, leading to additional assessment of taxes; (2) excessively complex procedures for tax filing and excessive delays in issuing refunds; (3) a lack of balance in the dispute resolution process and the consequent long periods for resolving tax assessment appeals; and (4) poor governance among tax officers.

32 Reforms that would help improve the administration of small taxpayers include: centralizing the processing of tax returns; developing a start-up guide for new businesses with instructions on how to comply with the basic obligations under the tax laws; introducing a program of advisory visits to the premises of new businesses; creating modern telephone contact centers; ensuring tight control over the timely filing of tax returns and payment of taxes; developing better risk management systems; and designing indirect methods for establishing a tax liability that can be applied to taxpayers who do not maintain proper books of account.

33 The DGT's enforcement powers could be strengthened by: (1) extending the administrative summons power, which is currently limited to criminal tax investigation, to civil tax audits; (2) authorizing DGT staff (not just auditors) to issue an estimated (default) assessment in cases where a taxpayer fails to submit a tax return on time; (3) enhancing the DGT's access to information (particularly banking information); and (4) authorizing the DGT to seize, and not just freeze, bank deposits and accounts receivable of tax debtors without requiring the prior approval of the tax debtor.

34 The system for resolving tax disputes can be made to be more fair by amending the relevant legislation or introducing other institutional changes that would: (1) defer payment of a disputed tax and suspend its collection while the case is under objection or appeal; (2) allow a judge, under prescribed conditions, to waive the requirement for taxpayers to pay 50 per cent of a disputed tax in order to the Tax Tribunal to hear the case; (3) allow taxpayers to appeal an assessment to the Tax Tribunal if the DGT has not issued a decision on the case within, say, 3 months for individuals and 6 months for companies; and (4) establish a full-time objections section in each of the DGT's regional offices that reports directly to the head of the appeals section at DGT headquarters (instead of to the head of the regional office).

35 Indonesia's tax sanctions regime needs to be aligned with international good practice in respect to late payment, underreporting, fraud and voluntary disclosures.

36 Among other things, the new headquarters structure provides for three new directorates to manage the modernization reforms, a strategic planning unit and a criminal investigation unit to investigate criminal violations of the tax laws in cooperation with the MOF's Inspector General.

37 As mentioned in section IV, VAT administration could be further simplified by: (1) eliminating the requirement that all refund claims must be audited; (2) substantially reducing the numerous lists of purchase and sales invoices required as supplements to the VAT return; (3) discontinuing the requirement for VAT refund claimants to submit the original copies of all purchase and sales invoices; and (4) streamlining the VAT refund process for taxpayers without gold card status.

38 In this context, the DGT's VAT refund audit process is in particular need of modernization. Under a modern refund audit program, the entire stock of refund claims is ranked according to risk and, to the extent resources are allocated to refund audits, those with the greatest risk would be audited prior to payment while those with less risk would be audited after a refund has been paid or not at all. This arrangement coupled with the development of modern refund audit procedures would permit the DGT to perform VAT audit refunds more effectively. Such reforms could also have a major impact on the overall audit program as the DGT would be free to assign resources to refund audits and nonrefund audits on the basis of risk as opposed to the current situation where nonrefund audits receive only those resources remaining after refunds are audited.

39 After 2005, the DGT discontinued the systematic reporting on the amount of revenue that was generated from each of its core enforcement programs: registration, arrears collection, audit and late filer programs. Refer to Chapter 4 for details.

40 This section benefited from the guidance provided by Michael Keen and Anthony Pellechio.

41 Assuming 90 per cent of the taxes are paid voluntarily, equation (2) indicates that achieving a 5 per cent increase in the tax yield would require a 5.5 per cent increase in voluntary collections (TV) in the absence of any increase in enforced collections. Achieving the same increase in the tax yield through enforced collections (TE), without any increase in voluntary collections, would require enforced collections to grow at a substantially higher growth rate (i.e. 50 per cent) due to its relatively small share in total revenue.

42 The elasticity of the tax system excludes any legislated changes in tax policy or improvements in tax administration. As such, the elasticity measures only the built-in responsiveness of the tax revenue to GDP growth.

43 To clarify, if the potential amount of taxes is 100 but taxpayers voluntarily pay only 40 ($v = .40$) then the total amount of foregone revenue would be 60. If the tax agency succeeds in recovering 10 per cent of the 60 in foregone revenue ($r = .10$) then enforced collections (TE) would be 6.

44 Marks reports revenue collection of 3.2 per cent of GDP as he includes revenue collected from the luxury and sales tax (since the government does not readily report the breakdown between these two taxes, only their aggregate collection). This generates a lower VAT tax gap in his analysis.

6 Intergovernmental transfers

Effectiveness and response on government

Raksaka Mahi and Riatu Mariatul Qibthiyyah

I. Introduction

Many countries have adopted decentralization in which coverage and designs vary across countries. On the case of decentralization, Indonesia as a country has become a world model of how big countries in terms of population and geographic area have engaged huge reforms on decentralization as response to a crisis.[1]

For the case of Indonesia, the shift to a more decentralized system is characterized by high devolved expenditures to lower-level governments which are mostly financed through intergovernmental transfers from the central government.[2] A strong foundation on an intergovernmental system was laid out in early 2001 by the adoption of Law No. 22 of 1999 on Inter-Government Functional Assignment and Law No. 25 of 1999 on Intergovernmental Transfer.[3] Intergovernmental transfers policy is a major policy, that to some extent, initially supports the devolved expenditures from the central government to subnational (provinces) and local governments. Reviewing the evolution and changes in Decentralization Laws and intergovernmental transfers policies[4], over the years, there seems to be shifts of policies that challenge the effectiveness of the existing transfers. A quest in searching for an effective IGT system may require assessment on each type of transfers.

Provinces or local governments receiving intergovernmental transfers, in the case on lump sum transfers, could use the transfers to increase expenditures or to reduce taxes. As in the case of specific transfers, the associated type of spending is assumed to be affected. Response on government expenditures would likely be different between lump-sum or block grant transfers than transfers that are allocated for a specific type of spending (Fisher 1996). In this case, Dahlby (2009) stated that higher stimulative impact of intergovernmental transfers to government expenditure than impact from personal income may represent relatively higher costs of public funds in that region, implying that allocating the transfers may be a second-best approach than giving higher tax autonomy to relatively inefficient regions.

This study explores the relationship between intergovernmental transfer and various types of spending at the local level. Each type of transfer is believed to have different impacts on local spending behavior; in particular capital spending and current (routine) spending.

II. Intergovernmental transfers in Indonesia: overview

By international standards, the extent of intergovernmental transfer in Indonesia is quite high. For many countries, the share of intergovernmental transfers is generally less than 20 per cent of total central government revenues (Bahl and Wallace 2004). However, as shown in Figure 6.1, the share of intergovernmental transfers of total central government revenues that are allocated to provinces and local governments in Indonesia has reached to 30–35 per cent from previously only around 15–20 per cent prior to 2001.

Policies of fiscal decentralization that heavily use intergovernmental transfer are considered a second-best approach. This is given that the premise of high accountability of a decentralized system required both expenditure autonomy as well as tax autonomy. Thus, the transfers should be only a tool of transition to shape an asymmetric expenditures-revenues assignment. Based on international practices, intergovernmental transfer ideally declines while province and/or local taxes are strengthened. This required devolving a tax base that is buoyant. Province or local taxes refer to policies on the rates structures which are determined by provinces and/or local governments. Nonetheless, Table 6.1 describes composition of own-source revenues in which taxes are generally small especially at the level of local governments. Even at the province level, given own source revenue on average of provinces' total revenues never exceeded 10 per cent of total revenues, provincial taxes are also small. This pattern persisted from conditions prior to 2001 (Mahi 2002, Saad 2001).

Intergovernmental transfer policies are closely watched by the central government as well as provinces and local governments. The pattern on the share of

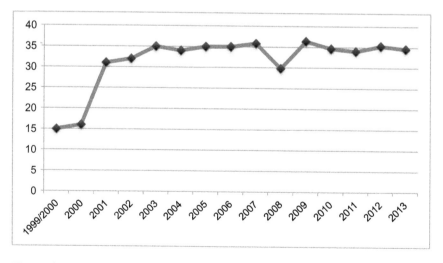

Figure 6.1 Intergovernmental transfers 1999–2013 (as % of total central government revenues)

Source: Calculated from APBN Financial Note (Ministry of Finance 2013).

Table 6.1 Composition of own-source revenues, year 2010: provinces and local governments

Components of Own-Source Revenues	Provinces	Local Governments
Provinces or Local Taxes	83%	33%
User Charges	3%	27%
Profit of Government-Owned Companies	4%	8%
Other Revenues	10%	32%

Source: Calculated from Ministry of Finance (2011).

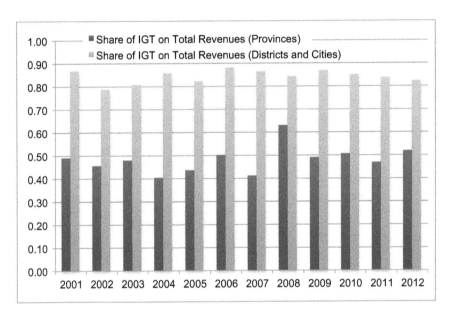

Figure 6.2 Share of intergovernmental transfers on total revenues: provinces and local governments

Source: Calculated from Sistem Informasi Keuangan Daerah (SIKD) Data (Ministry of Finance 2013).

Note: IGT refers to Balancing Funds and Special Autonomy and Adjustment Fund.

intergovernmental transfers to total revenues of provinces as well as local governments as shown in Figure 6.2 implies the importance of intergovernmental transfers to provinces and local governments as a source of revenues. Intergovernmental transfers from the central government to provinces cover around 40–50 per cent of total provinces revenues, while in the case of local governments, the share of intergovernmental transfers on total local government revenues is more than 80 per cent.

Over the years, the intergovernmental transfers have not only become more dominant but also have sprawled to a relatively more ad-hoc than formula-based transfers. There are various new transfers that seem only to cater to ad-hoc policies. Figure 6.3 shows how adjustment funds that pool most of the ad-hoc transfers have increased over the years, while at the same time, balancing funds that consisted mostly of formula-based transfers seem to grow at a moderate level. In this case as shown in Figure 6.4, DAK allocation has even decreased in 2010.

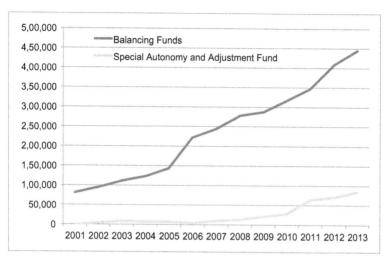

Figure 6.3 Balancing transfer funds and other transfers (Special Autonomy (Otsus) and Adjustment Fund) (in billion IDR)

Source: Calculated from *Anggaran Pendapatan dan Belanja Negara* (APBN) Financial Note (Ministry of Finance 2013).

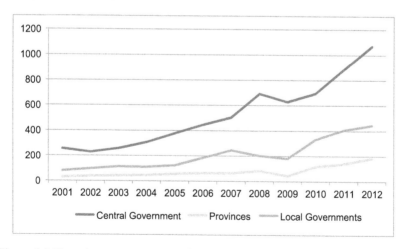

Figure 6.4 Central government, provinces and local governments' expenditures (trillion IDR): 2001–12

Source: Calculated from Ministry of Finance APBN Financial Note and SIKD Data (Ministry of Finance 2011).

Notes: Intergovernmental Transfers are excluded from CG's total expenditures, as well as transfers to local governments from provinces are excluded from provinces' total expenditures.

In regard to the effectiveness of existing transfers, Box 6.1 describes development of intergovernmental transfers in Indonesia and how the system has quite a strong objective on improving equity despite how elusive the terms could be defined. Based on the development of intergovernmental transfers policies under the decentralized regime, the design of the transfers clearly emphasized more on the distributive aspect especially across regions' horizontal income inequality.

Box 6.1 Development of intergovernmental transfers system in Indonesia

2001 Formulation of unconditional grants (DAU) policy; DAU is allocated to equalize the regional disparity, based on a formula adopting fiscal gap concept. There was also a development of sector grants (DAK) to channel funds of reforestation and later on evolve as transfers to cater to technical ministries programs on education, health, infrastructure and administration.

2004 Introducing revenue sharing from central taxes as an addition to the revenue sharing from natural resources. A proliferation of sector grants (DAK) other than education, health, infrastructure and administration.

2008 The proliferation of central government (CG) grants and strong involvement of legislatures on the allocation (i.e. Regional Grant (*Hibah*), Regional Adjustment Fund (*Dana Penyesuaian Daerah*)); Central Government launched a social program fund that matched the characteristics of transfers but it is not 'transfers to region' by legal standing as it does not flow through the local government budget (APBD); the revenue sharing in some contexts are conditional, i.e. to education expenditures.

Source: Updated from Qibthiyyah (2011).

Intergovernmental transfers become a dominant source of revenues to both provinces and local governments given it is a chosen policy following up functional assignments across the level of governments that gives more authority to lower-level governments. High shares of intergovernmental transfers are planned as transition policies following devolution of expenditures assignments to provinces and local governments in 2001, prior to strengthening province and local taxes. Nonetheless, a concern arises on lower-level governments' capacity to raise and collect revenues that are generally still weak (World Bank 2007).

Called a 'Big Bang' decentralization policy, the decentralization policy started with these expenditure assignments. However, as described by Brodjonegoro (2004), functional assignments across the level of governments are far from settled. Various technical ministries are still conducting functions that are supposedly responsibilities of lower-level governments (TADF 2008). There is also use of Deconcentrated and Assistantship Funds, called Dekon/TP – *Dana Dekonsentrasi dan Tugas Pembantuan* (TADF 2008), in which the financing source is treated as the technical ministries spending allocation, although activities are conducted by provinces or local governments. The total funds of Dekon/TP covered around 40–50 trillion IDR, which is much higher than specific grants DAK allocated to provinces and local governments. Table 6.2 shows development of these Deconcentrated Fund and *Tugas Pembantuan*.

Development of consolidated government expenditures in Figure 6.4 shows a soaring of government expenditures in the year 2006 which may or may not associate with the enactment of Law No. 32 and No. 33 of 2004 that amended previous laws on regional government and intergovernmental transfers. Comparing type of expenditures at the provinces as well as local governments, the pattern of expenditures is quite similar. A high share of government expenditures is allocated for routine or operational expenditures.

As shown in Table 6.3, the share of routine expenditures on provinces is around 50–60 per cent and 60–70 per cent for local governments, and growth

Table 6.2 Deconcentrated Fund and *Tugas Pembantuan*

Year	Deconcentrated Fund		Tugas Pembantuan	
	Number of Ps and LGs	*Total Funds (Billion IDR)*	*Number of Ps and LGs*	*Total Funds (Billion IDR)*
2008	60	24,814	474	11,935
2009	89	36,497	484	16,328
2010	169	28,946	474	7,720

Source: Calculated from Ministry of Finance Data (Ministry of Finance 2011).

Table 6.3 Share of routine expenditure and its growth: provinces and local governments

Year	*Share of Routine Expenditures (Provinces)*	*Share of Routine Expenditures (Local Governments)*
2001	0.64	0.69
2002	0.55	0.66
2003	0.54	0.67
2004	0.53	0.72
2005	0.51	0.63
2006	0.50	0.63
2007	0.56	0.59
2008	0.45	0.63
2009	0.49	0.65
2010	0.51	0.69
2011	0.28	0.50
Annual Growth of Routine Expenditures (2001–11)	**30.30**	**34.39**

Source: Calculated from Ministry of Finance (2011).

of routine expenditures on average is also quite high (around 30 per cent); that may signal regions tend to expand their bureaucracy. A constant increase of government size especially in the case of routine expenditures may be caused by the formula of general grants, DAU (*Dana Alokasi Umum*).

III. Provinces and local governments expenditures response

Unlike other countries, decentralization in Indonesia put more weight on local governments, a second tier of governments. Evaluating the impact of intergovernmental transfers should always take into account a likely different institution between provinces and local governments. Therefore in our study, in trying to evaluate the impact of intergovernmental transfers, we separate estimation model for the provinces and local governments level.

Province level estimation

Table 6.4 shows regression results for the province level. Our finding shows that impact of intergovernmental transfers on government expenditures depend on type of transfers. The specific grants, DAK as well as adjustment funds, have not been able to influence government expenditures. In contrast, revenue sharing in the form of DBH as well as DAU has influence on government spending. Both types of transfers have a lump-sum form.

Table 6.4 Regression results on government expenditure (2005–07): provinces

Dependent Variable (Outcome)/ Explanatory Variables	Total Expenditure	Capital Expenditure	Routine Expenditures
General Allocation Fund (DAU)	1.482***	0.133	0.262***
Specific Allocation Fund (DAK)	10.453	–17.491	0.014
Tax Sharing *(DBH Pajak)*	1.863***	0.540***	1.321***
Natural Resource Sharing *(DBH SDA)*	0.711***	0.338***	0.105***
Own-Source Revenues (OSR)	0.079	–0.017	–0.415***
Adjustment Funds	0.254	0.062	0.078
Population	0.026	–0.014	0.020***
GRDP	0.007	0.003*	0.004***
Area	2.717**	0.139	–0.625**
Constant	–266479.600**	37106.100	7966.356
Number of observations	*61*	*61*	*61*
Overall R-Square	*0.98*	*0.96*	*0.99*

Notes: ***1% significance level, **5% significance level, *10% significance level.

Further exploring across type of province expenditures, the response tends to be different by type of transfers. We find that DAU tends to correspond only to provinces routine expenditures, while it is revenue sharing in the form of tax and natural resource sharing that induces capital expenditures. In the case of specific grants, contrary to the popular belief, our results do not find evidence of DAK affecting provincial expenditures. We also do not find that adjustment funds influence government spending at the province level.

The case of own-source revenues in influencing government spending is also not strong. We do not find evidence that own-source revenues, as shown in Table 6.3, have a positive effect on government spending. Instead, our results show that higher own-source revenues associates with lower routine expenditures. At least at the province level, a view that lower-level governments' effort on increasing own-source revenues to fund routine expenditures is weakly supported by our results. This may and may not associate with the characteristics of provincial taxes. Although provinces taxes are relatively more buoyant that local government taxes, most of those taxes are subject to taxes sharing that should partly be allocated to local governments.

In general, based on the province-level estimation results, we only find that block grants which characterized revenue sharing in the form of DAU and DBH have a stimulative effect on spending. Meanwhile, there is no evidence that specific grants, irrespective of whether it is formula-based grants such as DAK or more ad-hoc grants (as in the case of Adjustment Funds), stimulate government spending.

Local government estimation

As shown in the previous section, intergovernmental transfers are the more dominant source of revenues for local governments than for the provinces. In this case, Table 6.5 presents estimation results using local governments as units of observations. Overall, intergovernmental transfers have a positive stimulative effect on local government spending. However, the impact is contrastly different across type of the transfers when the spending is further disaggregated.

DAU have positive effect both on capital and routine expenditures. However, given the magnitude of the impact that is much larger in the case of routine expenditures, the result seems to confirm a popular belief that local governments would mainly use DAU for routine expenditures, and this case refers to salary spending.

DAK seems to be more stimulative than DAU on the case of capital spending, while on routine expenditures, the higher amount of specific grants of DAK associate with lower routine expenditures of local government. This result is in contrast to the regression results of the province level, and thus it appears that DAK tends to be stimulative at local level but not on the province level.

There are also somewhat different results of tax-sharing impact on government spending between the provinces level and local governments. For the case of local governments, tax sharing (*DBH Pajak*) tends to stimulate capital expenditures but not routine expenditures. Meanwhile, revenue sharing from

Table 6.5 Regression results on government expenditure (2005–07): local governments

Dependent Variable (Outcome)/Explanatory Variables	Total Expenditure	Capital Expenditure	Routine Expenditures
General Allocation Fund (DAU)	0.932***	0.055**	0.481***
Specific Allocation Fund (DAK)	1.315***	1.229***	–0.726***
Tax Sharing *(DBH Pajak)*	1.008***	0.329***	0.034
Natural Resource Sharing (DBH SDA)	1.011***	0.395***	0.138***
Own Source Revenues (OSR)	1.498***	0.389***	0.502***
Population	0.038***	0.019***	0.047***
GRDP	–0.001**	–0.002***	0.001
Area	0.035	–0.023	–0.032
LGs received Adjustment Funds	11539.860**	32612.780***	19650.830***
LGs received Transfers from Provinces	22804.370***	–15457.020**	–6672.032
Constant	–12207.940***	28368.830***	23425.860***
Number of observations	*1107*	*1107*	*1107*
Overall R-Square	*0.98*	*0.64*	*0.77*

Notes: ***1% significance level, **5% significance level, *10% significance level.

natural resources (DBH SDA) has a positive influence on both capital and routine expenditures.

On the case of adjustment funds, adjustment fund also have a positive impact on both capital and routine expenditures. Local governments that received adjustment funds tend to have higher spending on capital and routine expenditures. In comparison to regression results for the province level, it seems that adjustment funds are stimulative only for the case of local governments.

Other than transfers from the central government, local governments could also receive transfers from the province. The result shows that local governments receiving transfers from the province tend to have both lower capital and routine expenditures. The results may suggest there is no evidence that province transfers are stimulative.

IV. Exploring effectiveness of intergovernmental transfers

As stated in the previous section, based on the development of intergovernmental transfers policies under decentralization, the design of the transfers clearly emphasized more on the distributive aspect especially across regions' horizontal

Table 6.6 Regression results of economic and welfare outcome: province level

Dependent Variable (Outcome)/ Explanatory Variables	GRDP[1]	HDI[2]	Poverty Rate[3]	Unemployment Rate[2]
Population	+***	+NS	+NS	+***
Area	−***	+NS	+**	−NS
Government Expenditure	+***	+*	−NS	+**
Score of DID	+***	−*	−NS	+NS
KPPOD index	−*	+*	−*	−NS
Intergovernmental Transfer (*Dana Perimbangan*)	+NS	+NS	−***	−NS
GRDP		+NS	−*	+***
Number of observations	*70*	*70*	*70*	*64*
Overall R-Square	*0.9528*	*0.1077*	*0.3476*	*0.9385*

Notes: 1) Explanatory variables are set at *t*; 2) Explanatory variables are set at *t*-1; 3) Explanatory variables are set at *t*-2; ***1% significance level, **5% significance level, *10% significance level.

income inequality. In the case of Indonesia, studies exploring the impact of intergovernmental transfers on outcome remain in void.[5] Although the shifting to more conditional transfers signals the necessity to conduct such study. Most previous studies do not necessarily focus on the impact of intergovernmental transfers, but rather to the extent or the presence of decentralization, which in this case refers to fiscal decentralization (Fauziah 2008, Simatupang 2009).[6]

The following regression results as shown in Table 6.6 are based on provinces-level government as units of observations using the period of 2004–08. The effectiveness of intergovernmental transfers is still inconclusive in the case of efficiency and on impact to economic growth. Nonetheless, the result of this study that intergovernmental transfers tend to affect the poverty rate seems to align with the objective and the design of most of the transfers, referring to *Dana Perimbangan* as central governmental transfers.

V. Conclusions and recommendation: moving to a coherent framework

In the initiation of the 2001 decentralization, Indonesia adopted decentralization policies without a white-paper of the policies. There is a sense that they are flip-of-coin policies considering that repairing the existing centralization management remained a no-option policy at that time. Basically, broader authority is given to local governments to manage their own economic and financial strategy toward a better growth and prosperity.

Fiscal decentralization, primarily using intergovernmental transfer, has been the instrument to empower local financial capability. The policy comes with a high expectation that local governments would allocate their spending effectively for a better public service and capital spending to foster economic growth. And now, after more than a decade of decentralization, having issued and amended the decentralization law in 2004, and the existing laws are also currently under review, the policies framework on intergovernmental transfers as one instrument in the implementation of fiscal decentralization are overdue.

Our study evaluates the impact of intergovernmental transfers on various types of local government expenditures. There are some contradictory results related to the effectiveness of intergovernmental grants in stimulating local spending. In the case of specific grants, contrary to popular belief, our results do not find evidence of DAK affecting provincial expenditures. On the other hand, DAU, which is designed to finance general purpose needs, tends to correspond only to routine expenditures. Finally, it is only revenue sharing in the form of tax and natural resource sharing that induces capital expenditures. Regressions on local governments give different results, where all types of transfers induce positively government expenditure. Beyond DAU, DAK and revenue sharing, there are also adjustment funds, which also tend to stimulate local governments rather than provinces.

The results of this study lead to some recommendations to improve the current fiscal decentralization scheme:

1. DAU seems to be a trigger of increased local personnel spending, at the expense of the capital spending. A policy should be enacted to reduce the stimulative effect of DAU on personnel spending. This could be done, among others, by removing the variable of personnel spending on the DAU formula and instead link the allocation to government output.
2. Revenue sharing has indicated to induce positively capital formation at the province level. This shows that the revenue sharing scheme may be effective in stimulating capital expenditure. This is in line with the perspective that streams of revenue sharing, especially for resource-rich regions that come from non-renewable natural resources, should be carefully used for investment-type of expenditures rather than consumption-type expenditures.
3. DAK is more effective to stimulate capital expenditure for districts and municipalities rather than for provinces. This suggests that DAK could be used effectively to stimulate the economic growth of the districts/municipalities rather than to the provinces.
4. There is a trend of proliferation on the type of transfers, indicating that the government has moved toward adopting soft budget constraints. Proliferation of types of transfers (such as found in DAK sectoral categories) needs to end. Some types of transfers could be regrouped into fewer categories that reflect provision of basic services on education, health and infrastructure given those specific transfers are mostly channeled to these three sectors.
5. A view that lower-level governments' effort on increasing own-source revenues to fund routine expenditures is weakly supported by our results. Instead, our results show that higher own-source revenues associates with

lower routine expenditures. Unfortunately, we also do not find evidence that own-source revenues have a positive effect on government spending. Given this result, we need further elaboration to what extent we could utilize and optimize own-source revenues for stimulating capital expenditure at the local level.

Notes

1 The 1997 financial crisis has led to an economic crisis that put pressure in a change of regime. The change of regime also brought a choice to adopt a full range of decentralization. This decentralization model to a large extent may be only mimicked by South Africa that also undertook huge reforms as part of re-building after apartheid.

2 From what is called the first-generation theory of decentralization by Oates (1972), the choice to decentralize (expenditure) lays out on the premise of how giving more functions to lower-level governments is justified as it assumes a similar efficiency across level of governments; lower-level governments by their close proximity to residents tend to be more accountable and thus they could better match their spending program with their residents' preferences on public service delivery. Challenges for this theory of decentralization mostly lie on the assumption of efficiency across level of governments that generate a strand of literature of what is currently called the second generation of decentralization (Weingast 2007).

3 Law No. 22 of 1999 and Law No. 25 of 1999 are amended by Law No. 32 of 2004 and Law No. 33, respectively.

4 In the period from 2004 and up to now, after the enactment of Law No. 33 of 2004, the intergovernmental transfers policies are also influenced by the central government policy on national budget (APBN) and sectoral laws.

5 Although there are studies exploring the impact of intergovernmental transfers, in the case of Indonesia, the scope of those studies remains limited, focusing only on case studies in some regions or specific level of governments. Also, many of the previous studies misinterpret by easily interchanging the impact of intergovernmental transfers as the impact of fiscal decentralization. While fiscal decentralization is measured more on the extent of either revenues or expenditures across level of government or number of government units, intergovernmental transfers by itself associate to fiscal decentralization only as a means of financing to obtain the objective of fiscal decentralization, and thus not a per se measure of decentralization.

6 Empirical papers exploring the effectiveness of decentralization policies on country-specific situations, as in the case of Indonesia, to some extent create a stock of studies that could help predict how instruments that are taken, and in this case is intergovernmental transfers, may actually work.

7 Managing Indonesia's trade policy

How to remove the agenda?

Lili Yan Ing, Mari Elka Pangestu, and Sjamsu Rahardja

I. Introduction

Managing trade policy and needed reforms in Indonesia have become more challenging as policy makers are faced with increasingly complex issues. The experience from the 1980s and early 1990s suggest trade reforms brought down costs of doing businesses that subsequently boosted economic growth and generated millions of jobs. Indonesia's experiences also suggest that reforming trade and investment procedures are effective measures to increase and diversify exports. But the task for trade policy makers has become more complex compared with periods before the Asian economic crisis due to changes in domestic and external environments. The challenges of the post-global financial crisis have made it even more challenging to deal with keeping protectionism, whether the traditional form or otherwise, at bay. Furthermore, as tariffs have come down, trade-related issues have shifted to non-tariff measures and behind the border issues.

There are significant challenges in policy making in the 'new' Indonesia. Democratization after deep economic and political crises ('twin crises') in 1998 until 2000 distributed political power to wider stakeholders and reduced the role of central government in determining the allocation of resources for economic activities. Before the twin crises, Suharto's growth-oriented government established strong inter-linkages between bureaucratic posture and the political machine that allowed the government to conduct effective decision making and in a centralized way. Of course there were excesses and lack of cross-check mechanisms, but in instances when the decision and political will was in the direction of deregulation and reforms, it worked effectively.

The process of decision making is considerably more complex today. There is no mutual relationship between the government and a single-party majority and with democracy economic policies are subject to a political contest. Policy making now must go through public scrutiny and often must gauge support with the public and Parliament in the equation. Decentralization also delegated and transferred many authorities to local government, including delegating execution of development projects and setting regional regulations. Meanwhile, technical capacity to understand economics and economic reforms varies dramatically among actors involved in economic policies.

So how do those changes affect managing trade policy and the priorities for reforms?

The purpose of this chapter is to provide an analysis and thus an understanding of the management of trade policy and needed reforms in Indonesia over three different phases of recent Indonesian economic development. At the outset we should of course be reminded of the obvious. Trade and related policies that affect the real sector is obviously a means to development as translated into sustainable growth by ensuring efficiency and competitiveness, creation of jobs and spreading the benefits of growth. Trade policy is not an end to itself. The analysis is undertaken by looking at the factors that influence trade and related policy as well as the process of policy and institutional reforms that take place. The factors accounted for are internal and domestic, as it pertains to economic conditions such as a crisis as well as the political and institutional setting spanning from the top down and centralized period under President Soeharto to the democratic and decentralized setting of today. Of course trade policy cannot be undertaken in isolation from the regional and international setting because of the reality of competition between nations, peer pressure in being compared with other nations, and best practices and commitments undertaken through regional and multilateral frameworks and agreements. The chapter ends with the current period which has become even more challenging post-global financial crisis of 2008–09 and continued global economic uncertainties, as well as the continued need to remain competitive, balancing domestic and international roles and the greater role and responsibilities of emerging economies as developed nations struggle with their domestic recovery agenda. How should Indonesia navigate the dynamic changing world and regional order while ensuring a balanced and equitable economic development for its own nation?

II. Managing trade policy reform

The main catalyst for reforms in the 1980s and 1990s in the case of Indonesia was a combination of economic crisis, slowdown in domestic and international economic growth, and commitments under regional and multilateral cooperation, while reforms in the 2000s were driven more by competition and Indonesia being more integrated to the world economy (see Figure 7.1).

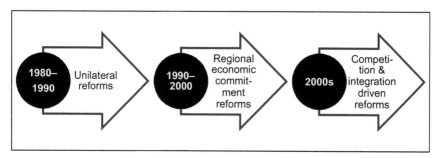

Figure 7.1 Phases of trade policy reforms

The roaring 1980s and 1990s – sweeping reforms to diversify sources of economic growth

Like other countries, crisis and economic shocks were the catalysts for the implementation of unilateral economic reforms in the 1980s. Indonesia was a perfect example in which heavy dependency on oil industries and revenues, coupled with a fixed exchange rate, resulted in episodes of balance of payment crises. The drop in oil price from average USD 36 per barrel in 1980 to USD 14.3 per barrel in 1986 caused a severe shock on Indonesia's trade balance and led to the decision to devalue the Rupiah. Revenues from oil were an important source of government revenue and pro-cyclical nature of government spending, so that the sharp drop in oil prices caused the government to scale down many import-intensive and large government projects (mega projects).

The response from the Soeharto government was to immediately launch a series of deregulations intended to diversify the structure of government revenues and foreign exchange earnings away from oil to non-oil, and increase the efficiency of the overall economy. At the time, the dependence on oil revenues and exports were around 70–80 per cent of total revenues and exports.

The deregulations also involved dramatic institutional changes to reduce the 'high cost economy' which constrained businesses to expand. To increase non-oil tax revenues, in 1985 the government simplified the tax code to reduce corruption and inefficiencies in the tax system. However, one of the boldest reforms was the total overhaul of customs, known at the time for inefficiency and corruption. It was bold because rather than trying to reform the institution, which would have taken time, it was decided to outsource customs clearance processes from *Bea dan Cukai* to a professional surveyor firm, SGS. To boost growth in non-oil exports, the government complemented the improved customs clearance process with a duty draw-back system that allowed Indonesian manufacturers to access inputs at world prices by being able to reimburse duty and value-added taxes paid on imported inputs used in the production of exports. The system was also conducted under good governance with arms-length transactions and efficient processing of applications. In 1987 and 1988 the government also simplified investment procedures by reducing the number of permits and moving from a positive to a negative list approach.

Indonesia was also responding to the increasing competition for investment in the region that took place in the late 1980s and the 1990s. Competitive deregulation took place as countries in East Asia were increasingly looking outward for pushing for higher economic growth. This recognition and the increased confidence due to the process of deregulation and opening up that took place since the mid-1980s also paved the way for Indonesia to begin playing a greater leadership role in the region. In turn this provided additional momentum and peer pressure to continue the process of reforms, and given the importance of Indonesia in the region, marked a new beginning in regionalism in ASEAN as well as Asia Pacific.

After many years of slow progress in economic cooperation within ASEAN, starting with the limited PTA (Preferential Trade Agreement), AICO (ASEAN

Industrial Cooperation) scheme and ASEAN projects in the 1970s and 1980s, Indonesia was finally ready to sign up to the comprehensive ASEAN Free-Trade Area (AFTA) in 1991. In the early 1990s the world again went through a cycle of economic recession and there was the stalling of the Uruguay Round of multilateral trade negotiations. These circumstances led to a new momentum to ensure the growth of the world economy and led to the first APEC Economic Leaders Meeting in Seattle and also the breakthrough in the WTO negotiations, which was completed in 1994 – and the creation of the WTO on 1 January 1995.

This was the setting of Indonesia's year as the host of the APEC meeting in 1994 and which led to the famous APEC Bogor Goals of free trade and investment in the region by 2010 for industrial countries and 2020 for developing countries. Given the recognition that further reforms were needed to improve the competitiveness of the domestic economy to face increased competition in the region, the technocrats managing economic policy at the time also used this setting and the momentum of being host to APEC to put in place a number of important reforms. A number of important trade and investment reforms were undertaken in 1993 and 1994, such as the reduction of tariffs in 1993 and the removal of a number of foreign ownership restrictions in 1993 and 1994, including the sensitive issue of 100 per cent foreign ownership and divestment requirements.

This was followed by a number of regulatory and legal changes, which were adopted after the formation of the WTO in 1995, including the elimination of domestic content regulations, which were linked to investment. It also provided an important check on the national car policy, which would have violated the MFN clause of the WTO agreement whereby a joint venture with a car maker from one country was given special preferences over other countries and domestic producers.[1]

The series of reforms in the mid-1980s through to 1995 brought down the level of protection and led to rapid industrialization. The effects of protection were to raise domestic prices to consumers, shield the protected industry from international competition, reduce incentives for more efficient or innovative production, and also protect the supporting industries whose outputs were used as inputs. Of course it also created groups of vested interests who were the main proponents of continuing protection.

The effective protection escalated in the 1970s to mid-1980s. Hence tariff reduction in the late 1980s and early 1990s brought down the level of protection and the high cost economy associated with it and the decline of the effective protection rate previously enjoyed by the food and beverage industry and manufacturing industries in general (Fane and Condon, 1996). Interestingly, reforms in those periods also included dismantling several non-tariff barriers in the Indonesian manufacturing sector that were sources for rent-seeking activities. Indonesia continued to implement tariff reform until 2003 as part of the tariff reduction schedule in the ASEAN free-trade agreement.

These episodes of reforms were regarded as highly successful in boosting economic growth and diversifying the economy away from oil and gas. Between 1986 and 1996 the Indonesian economy grew at the rate of 12.8 per cent per year. The reforms were followed by a strong growth in non-oil manufacturing GDP of 15.2 per cent per year in the same period. That process was the main driving force behind diversification of Indonesia's exports away from the oil sector from 85 per cent dependent on oil in the early 1980s to just 25 per cent by the 1990s until today. The impact of trade reforms was felt significantly in the labor-intensive and relatively footloose industries and commodity-based manufacturing. The value of exports of textiles, clothing and footwear (TCF) and other manufactures, such as furniture, rubber products and wood products, increased rapidly since the mid-1980s (Figures 7.2 and 7.3). Taking advantage of low labor costs and the quotas under the Multi Fiber Arrangement (MFA) that governed the global trading for textiles and garments, the value of Indonesian exports of textiles, clothing and footwear (TCF) in 1990 increased 10-fold in only 7 years. Because of the labor-intensive process, the Indonesian garment

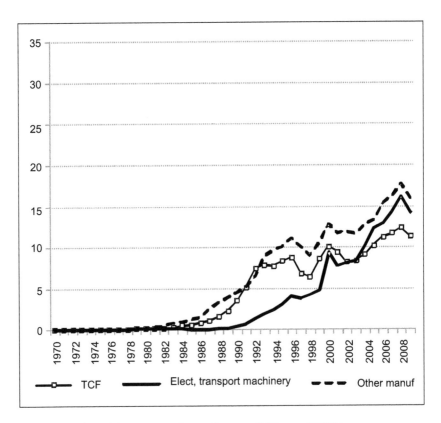

Figure 7.2 Indonesia's exports of manufactures (billions of USD)

Source: Calculated from *Indonesia Statitics*.

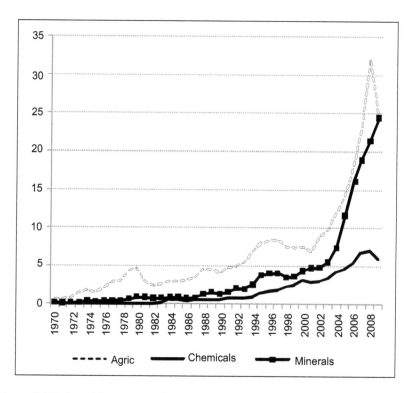

Figure 7.3 Indonesia's exports of commodities and chemicals (billions of USD)
Source: Calculated from *Indonesia Statitics.*

industry in particular emerged as one of the most important export-orientated industries, generating job opportunities for low-skilled, mostly women, workers (Thee, 2009).

The next wave of deeper and broader trade reforms in the 1990s came in the aftermath of the Asian financial crisis. Indonesia undertook major structural policies as part of the IMF assistance package designed to bring market confidence on the currency and subsequently bring growth back on track. The program encompassed a wide range of macroeconomic 'hard' measures to reduce domestic absorption such as trimming fiscal spending and government-sponsored 'mega projects'. But the program also pushed for microeconomic reforms that would raise involvement of private investment. A handful of numbers of non-tariff barriers, monopolies by state-owned enterprises and restrictions over investments were removed. Significant numbers of non-tariff barriers to trade in products considered as 'strategic commodities', such as garlic, rice, wheat and soybeans, were removed, allowing any domestic company with general import licenses to import those products. Monopoly power of the state food agency, BULOG, in distributing strategic food commodities was scrapped and for several years Indonesia fully relied on the world market to make up for any shortages in domestic food production. Domestic arrangements in marketing cement and paper as well as special fiscal facilities for a National Car project were scrapped. For several years after the Asian crisis, Indonesia embraced a freer regime in international and domestic trade.

One could argue that the economic crisis led Indonesia to dismantle protection against investment and trade reform that otherwise would have never been taken away under normal economic and political circumstances. Indonesia also introduced a roadmap to liberalize its retail, fuel distribution, air transport and telecommunication services by abolishing monopoly by SOEs or allowing entry for foreign investment.

A number of studies have discussed why reforms in the 1980s and 1990s worked effectively. The late Soesastro (1989) clearly pointed out that economic deregulation in Indonesia was a political-economic process and historically had been largely driven by necessity to ensure economic survival, such as diversifying the economy out of the oil sector after the free fall in global oil prices. In turn studies by Basri and Hill (2004) and Aswicahyono et al. (2009) shed some light on the political economic forces that made reforms in the late 1980s and 1990s relatively successful. These studies highlighted the shift in the political landscape that affected actors behind economic reforms. More important, those studies highlight the fact that support for trade reform comes from groupings of stakeholders, whether they come from the private sector who benefited or potentially benefited from the reforms or champions within the political establishment – or a combination thereof. The regional and international context also played an important influencing role.

Basri and Hill (2004) provided interesting *fiscal and macroeconomic* arguments as to why reforms in the 1980s received support from domestic constituencies. They argued that from a political economy viewpoint, the decision to devalue the currency increased the border parity price of imported goods and increased price competitiveness of Indonesian exports, which in turn provided a conducive setting for lowering the import tariff. They also argued that, in addition, tax reforms and the lower tariffs on intermediate inputs benefited the private sector and thus they lent their support to the reforms. Meanwhile, as mentioned above, the government also undertook measures, which were 'business friendly' such as deregulated procedures on trade and investment, introduced an effective duty draw-back system and overhauled customs clearance to facilitate exports. In sum, using the words of Soesastro (1989), the reformers' camp, both in and outside the government, could explain to the rest of bureaucracy and other stakeholders the importance of deregulations using simple economic logic and concrete results as evidenced by the increase in exports, growth and jobs. The policy of depreciation of the exchange rate under a managed exchange rate regime probably contributed to exporters' needs. However, the 'predictable' exchange rate regime, combined with other factors, led to overexposure to foreign borrowing without hedging by corporations and banks, and led to the vulnerabilities which were exposed during the financial crisis of 1997–98.

The 2000s reforms – competition and integration-driven reforms

The current situation is different from that in the 1980s or 1990s. Significant increases in competition and an Indonesia more integrated to the world economy push trade reforms to focus more on the competitiveness issue. The deteriorated competitiveness has been partly driven by macroeconomic conditions such as the relatively strengthened Rupiah and commodity boom and partly driven by microeconomic conditions such as infrastructure, cost of finance and labor issues.

Not only the strengthened Rupiah and commodity boom put pressure on competitiveness . . .

The sharp depreciation of the Rupiah after the crisis and low labor cost since then have offset these disadvantages, but currently there are symptoms that Indonesia is facing the competitiveness issue again. Indonesia no longer has a managed exchange rate regime and Indonesia has a regime of free capital movement and independent monetary policy, which make it impossible to dictate a fixed exchange rate regime.[2] Since 1998 the Rupiah has floated freely (Figure 7.4), and has been relatively volatile compared with regional currencies. Volatile exchange rates and relatively immature capital markets expose Indonesian companies to great uncertainties that could affect their investment decision.[3]

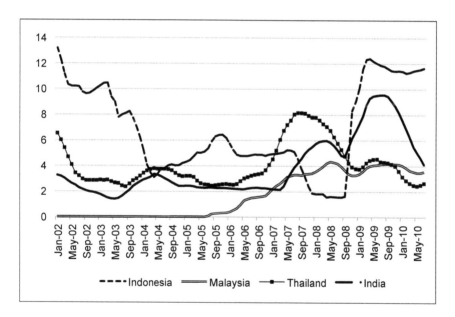

Figure 7.4 Twenty-four months rolling standard deviation of USD exchange rate index (2000 = 100). The Rupiah is relatively volatile compared to other currencies in the region

Source: Calculated from Census and Economic Information Center (CEIC) data.

Real effective exchange rates also show that the Rupiah has experienced steady appreciation. Compared to 2000, the real exchange rate in 2010 has appreciated approximately by 46 per cent while the Malaysian Ringgit appreciated only 3 per cent. Figure 7.4 also suggests that the Rupiah has appreciated beyond the level prior to 1997 crisis. For many firms, such a level of real appreciation could have an adverse implication on their product competitiveness at home or foreign markets. Along with real appreciation of the Rupiah, the relative price of traded to non-traded goods has also been declining (Figure 7.5). This could indicate that increasing demand in the non-traded sector (mostly services) might have pushed up wages in the non-traded sector relative to the traded sector, which in turn can drive resource allocation to the non-traded sector.

At the same time, Indonesia made significant gains from exporting natural resources-based commodities. Indonesia has taken advantage of the global commodity boom and significantly increased its world market share in exports of natural resources-based commodities. The value of total exports of goods in 2010 was largely contributed to by natural resources-based commodities, particularly agriculture commodities and mining and mineral commodities (Figure 7.6). The contribution of the value of exports of agriculture commodities and mining and mineral commodities to the total value of exports of goods has increased from 29 per cent in 2000 to 47 per cent in 2010, while that of exports of manufactured goods to the total value of exports of goods has decreased from 49 per cent to 34 per cent during the same period. Based on this observation,

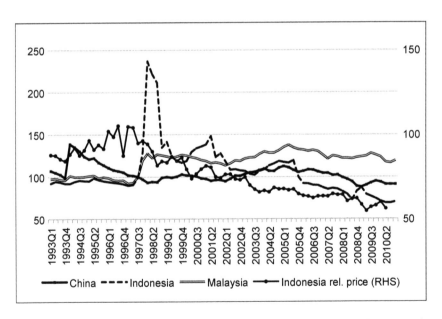

Figure 7.5 Real effective exchange rate index (1997 = 100). The Rupiah has strengthened in real terms

Source: Calculated from Economist Intelligence Unit.

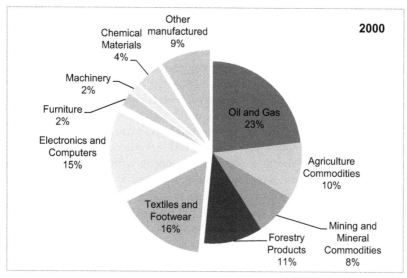

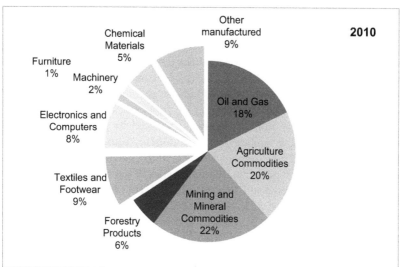

Figure 7.6 Share of exports by major commodities shows transformation of Indonesia's exports. Manufactured goods contributed 49 per cent to total exports of goods in 2000 and contributed 34 per cent to total exports of goods in 2010

Source: Calculated from *Indonesia Statistics*.

we could see there is indeed a need to revitalize its high-value-added sector (i.e. manufacturing sector) as excessive concentration on resource-based sectors could increase exposure to the costly boom-and-bust cycles associated with commodities prices and stocks and thus could lead to volatile growth.

*... But infrastructure, cost of finance and labor issues
also contribute to competitiveness deterioration*

We also argue that the lagging development in infrastructure, cost of finance and labor issues in Indonesia have made the supply response rather inelastic and therefore causing prices to increase faster in response to increased demand for goods and services. First, logistics issues have been highlighted as a major constraint to businesses in Indonesia by numerous recent studies on competitiveness issues including by a study conducted by LPEM (2005), which indicates that the logistics cost in Indonesia reached 14 per cent of the total production cost, much higher than the cost in Japan, for example which only reached 4.9 per cent. Basri and Patunru (2008) argue that, due to the decline in real public spending and the cancellations of numerous private infrastructure projects after the crisis, deteriorating infrastructure quality in Indonesia has been restraining economic growth from reaching its full potential. Benchmarking the state of Indonesia's logistics provides a clearer picture of one of the most pressing problems in the supply side. The World Bank Logistics Performance Indicators, a worldwide survey among logistics providers, also identified Indonesia as an economy with the highest domestic cost of transporting goods to ports, more so than any other countries in the region. Indonesia ranked 75th, which was the highest compared to its main peer countries such as China (27th), Malaysia (29th), the Philippines (44th), Thailand (35th) and Vietnam (53rd). Poor logistics would already have an adverse impact on competitiveness of the manufacturing sector since transport and communication represents 31 per cent of intermediate input, much higher than that in other sectors.[4]

Second, relatively high transaction costs due to asymmetric information in credit and relatively low contract enforcement in Indonesia's domestic market also contribute to the higher nominal lending rate faced by Indonesian firms. The average commercial bank lending rate of Indonesia from 2005–10 was 14 per cent, which was the highest compared to that of its peer countries such as China (6 per cent), Malaysia (6 per cent), the Philippines (9 per cent), Singapore (5 per cent), Thailand (7 per cent) and Vietnam (12 per cent) (CEIC Database, 2010). The slide from the rank of 121 in 2011 to 129 in 2012 was mainly attributed to worsened access to credit (World Bank and International Finance Corporation, 2009). Compared to other major economies in East Asia, Indonesia still does not have a well-functioning private credit bureau as an information exchange and sorting mechanism for lenders. Legal rights to protect borrowers and lenders in loan agreements in Indonesia are also perceived as the weakest in the region. As the result, domestic firms perceive access to finance as a main constraint for business (World Bank and International Finance Corporation, 2009).

Third, labor issues have also been a concern for the private sector in Indonesia. In 2003 Indonesia introduced a new Labor Law with the objective to provide better protection for workers and provide clarity on contracts between employees and employers. But the law also introduced a 'hiring tax' for employers because it significantly increased severance payment and added a gratuity payment for dismissed workers with more than 3 years of service. Although a recent study suggests that the law does not actually protect workers, since significant numbers of dismissed workers did not get their severance payment (World Bank, 2010a) and has also led to the hiring of more temporary rather than permanent workers, the perceived 'hiring tax' has been mentioned as providing uncertainties for investors. Another problematic issue is the increasing tendency to use regional minimum wages as an instrument to gather political support in regional elections by raising the minimum wage, sometimes way above the inflation rate. The problem with labor regulations seem to be more acute among larger firms. This could also indicate large firms are in general prone to regulatory issues because they are visible. Around 18.4 per cent of large firms in Indonesia identified labor regulations as major constraints for businesses and this can have an effect on labor absorption, as larger firms were mostly responsible for expansion in the Indonesian manufacturing sector after the Asian crisis[5].

While trade has become more open . . .

For trade policy indicators, Indonesia is in a rather different situation. Indonesia took unilateral tariff reform by reducing its tariff level and disparity across tariff lines (Table 7.1). The World Bank Tariff Trade Restrictiveness Index suggests

Table 7.1 Enabling environment for trade

	Indonesia	China	Malaysia	Philippines	Thailand	Vietnam
Ranking in Logistics Performance Indicator (2008)						
Domestic logistics cost	93	73	37	19	28	17
Quality of logistics infrastructure	44	30	28	87	31	60
Timeliness	58	36	26	69	28	65
Trade Policy Indicators (2006–2008, latest)[b]						
Trade Tariff Restrictiveness Index	4.47	5.06	3.01	3.80	6.65	N.A.
Overall Tariff Restrictiveness Index (applied tariff and NTMs)[a]	7.63	9.84	24.77	18.99	8.64	N.A.
Simple MFN	6.93	9.67	8.37	6.27	9.94	16.81
Applied tariff	6.73	13.63	8.10	6.10	N.A.	19.31
Ability to Access Foreign Markets – Overall Trade Restrictiveness Index (non-agriculture goods)[b]	9.63	8.33	8.73	10.47	8.37	N.A.

Sources: Basri and Rahardja (2010);[a,b] World Trade Organization (2010).

Note: [a] The level of uniform tariff schedule and non-tariff measures that keeps the import level constant.

that, based on average import tariff levels, the Indonesian trade regime is as open as most of countries in the region. The gap between average MFN tariff and applied tariff, which includes preference, is also smaller for Indonesia than for most other countries in the region. However, in terms of export market access, Indonesian exports of non-agriculture products seem to face slightly more restrictions than most exports from other countries in the region.

With lagging infrastructure development and regulatory uncertainty in the labor market, resistance for more opening up is likely to come from local manufacturers. Despite continued increases in the value of Indonesian manufactured exports, Indonesian manufacturers appear to be wary about competition at home and in international markets. It would seem that Indonesian manufacturers have not fully taken advantage of the shift in global sourcing of manufacturing products towards East Asia. Growth in exports of Indonesian 'traditional' manufacturing products, such as apparel and footwear, were lower than the period before the Asian crisis. Between 1990 and 1996, Indonesian exports of apparel and footwear grew by 14 per cent and 24.9 per cent per year, respectively, whereas in 2004 and 2008, annual growth of exports in those products reached 8.9 and 10 per cent, respectively (lower than the average growth of exports of those products by East Asia of 15.1 per cent and 16.4 per cent).

The external situation in global trade is also changing rapidly. At this stage, the multilateral Doha Round of WTO negotiations remain stalled and regional trade arrangements continue to proliferate. Whilst tariffs have declined significantly due to unilateral reductions as well as regional commitments, the use of other measures that can impede trade is proliferating. Some of those measures are even initiatives from the private sector such as retailers or consumer groups and therefore not part of multilateral agreements on non-tariff measures. Developing countries' exports, including Indonesia, are facing increasing numbers of certification, product standards and technical barriers of developed countries that cause significant costs for small producers.

Whilst the great recession from the global financial crisis has been avoided, prospects for a sustained recovery remain thwarted with downside risks. The recovery has progressed at different speeds, with emerging economies rebounding faster and having higher rates of growth, and therefore the sources of growth have shifted. At the same time, developed countries are experiencing continued high unemployment. Macro imbalances, especially current account imbalances, also mean continued tensions. At the start of the global crisis one of the fears was a rise of protectionism. However, fortunately there was only 'benign' protectionism and a rise in the use of trade remedies. Some countries also used the opportunity of the crisis to undertake reforms, especially in opening up to more investments.

Nevertheless, internal constraints and external development will continue to affect public support in undertaking reforms all over the world. Pushing for more trade and other reforms, and continuing the process of opening up, without addressing internal constraints and concerns are likely not going to get wide support and will be difficult to manage by any government. Indonesia is no exception.

. . . Can a preferential trade agreement help move the reform agenda?

Trade economists have divided opinions on the impact of bilateral or regional trade agreements. Free trade agreements can be building blocks for greater trade liberalization as more countries join the club. However, they can also act as stumbling blocks, raising trade among member countries at the expense of diverting trade from non-member countries. Even within a region with strong ties of intra-regional trade, administrative costs and complying to rules of multiple bilateral agreements can be costly (Casario, 1996; Jin et al., 2006). The dynamics of trade agreements could also result in a hub-and-spoke configuration in which bigger countries in the region will have a higher chance to be the hubs, retain the attractiveness for investment location, while smaller countries are running risk of being marginalized (Horaguchi, 2007). Proponents for trade agreements are also making a case as to why regional trade agreements may not be so bad after all. In the case of ASEAN Free Trade Agreement (AFTA), Calvo Pardo et al. (2009) claim that tariff reductions among members significantly increase trade among members at no expenses of trade with outsiders. Furthermore, Bergstern (1997) also considers that an Asia Pacific trade agreement could generate more gains for the member countries than losses to some non-members. Some studies suggested that an economy will gain from reciprocal treatment from trade, yet it is correlated to the size of an economy. An economy with relatively small-share-trade like Indonesia may only enjoy little gain from free trade agreements.[6]

In East Asia, intra-regional trade has increased over the last two decades and the main drivers have been a combination of opening up and what was termed as market-driven regionalism. That is the integration in the 1990s happened in the absence of a regional free trade agreement connecting these economies, but has occurred because of pull and push factors and technological developments in production processes, telecommunication and logistics. Push factors are rising costs (labor, land and exchange rates) and pull factors include supply of labor and skill sets, degree of opening up and investment climate. Japan initiated greater intra-regional trade which later on was followed by South Korea and Taiwan, then Singapore and Hong Kong participated in the trade network. Malaysia and the Philippines have also emerged into the regional production network in telecommunication and Thailand in automotive since the last decade and, thus, have experienced rising trade. The arrival of China further solidifies trade in East Asia. Machinery parts and components play an important role in the web of the production network in East Asia (Ando and Kimura, 2003). To get a sense of the magnitude of this phenomenon, East Asia's intra-regional trade increased from 37 per cent of total trade to 52 per cent between 1980 and 2008, mainly driven by parts and components (Asian Development Bank [ADB], 2008) at the same time as waves of tariff reductions and free trade agreements (FTA) occurred.

No doubt that as the number of trade agreements in East Asia has increased, trade in the region has expanded. Up to a decade ago, in 2000 East Asia had

3 FTAs concluded and implemented and 1 signed but not yet implemented, and 5 under negotiations and 4 proposed. In just a decade, the number of FTAs increased more than 10-fold. By October 2010, East Asia had emerged to the global FTA, with 41 FTAs in effect and another 48 FTAs under negotiations and 36 proposed (Asian Development Bank Institute [ADBI], 2010). Some of the trade agreements are bilateral agreements, while others are multilateral agreements. By looking at the number of FTAs in effect that the countries have engaged by 2010, Japan (11), China (10), Malaysia (8), Thailand (11), Indonesia (7), the Philippines (7) and Vietnam (7) (ADBI, 2010), it indicates that the more a country engaged in a trade agreement, the more likelihood it will experience rising trade. Kawai and Wignaraja (2010) claim that factor endowments, favorable initial conditions, national policies and firm-level strategies contributed to East Asia's emergence as a global producer.

How would trade agreements affect decisions for economic reform? Economic cooperation and trade agreements, such as AFTA, will lower overall import tariffs as required by regional commitment (Table 7.2). Ornelas (2005) asserts that even though FTAs generally cannot enhance trade between FTA members and non-members, FTAs could induce their member governments to lower their external tariffs which introduce the competition effect for domestic firms to be able to compete with international players. Tariff reductions on intermediate goods or inputs will lower costs of production and have contributed to productivity gains to Indonesian firms (Amiti and Konings, 2007).[7] Trade agreements could also reduce investment barriers to facilitate business expansion that could induce economies of scale.

In 1991 Indonesia took an important step in supporting the ASEAN Free Trade Agreement (AFTA) with the other five original ASEAN member states and started implementing the Common Effective Preferential Tariff (CEPT). Tariffs on agreed products will be reduced from 20 per cent to only 0–5 per cent

Table 7.2 Comparative tariffs on manufactured goods

Country	Tariff (%)			Tariff, MFN (%)		
	1995–1999	2000–2004	2005–2009	1995–1999	2000–2004	2005–2009
China	17.8	13.0	9.1	18.6	13.3	9.6
India	30.9	30.3	17.7	32.7	32.2	17.6
Indonesia	11.6	6.4	5.9	13.3	7.4	7.1
Malaysia	8.7	8.0	7.2	9.9	9.8	8.6
Philippines	12.9	5.6	5.1	13.2	6.0	6.0
Thailand	20.1	14.6	10.3	20.7	15.1	10.7
Vietnam	15.0	13.7	12.1	16.3	16.5	16.6

Source: World Bank, 2010a.

within a time-frame of 5 years to 8 years starting from January 1993, and make the agreement in effect in January 2010. However, it was only in 2004 that Indonesia adopted a multi-track strategy of multilateral, regional and bilateral agreements to pursue a policy approach of market opening, increasing competitiveness and at the same time ensuring that there was also the process of timing and scheduling to give time for adjustment as well as capacity building and economic and technical cooperation built in – especially in the case of agreements with more developed trading partners.

The first bilateral trade agreement Indonesia negotiated and completed was with its largest trade, investment and overseas development partner, Japan. The Indonesia Japan Economic Partnership Agreement (IJEPA) was signed in 2007 and has been implemented since, and beginning with the name alone it was not just a traditional trade agreement confined to goods and liberalization only. In terms of regional agreement, the focus has been to seek agreements with the dialog partners of ASEAN (Table 7.3). Indonesia supported the ASEAN-China FTA, ASEAN-Korea FTA, ASEAN-India FTA and ASEAN-Australia-New Zealand FTA. Moreover, Indonesia also prepares for more comprehensive agreements in the future with the European Free Trade Agreement Council (Iceland, Liechtenstein, Norway and Switzerland) as a training ground for similar comprehensive agreements with the EU in the future (joint study completed), and also complementary top ups of bilateral agreements with its dialog ASEAN partners, namely, Australia and India. Joint studies have been completed with Chile and Turkey, and ongoing study is being completed with Korea.

Starting early on, commitments of multilateral and regional trade have brought some impact on the agenda for domestic policy reform in Indonesia. Since early

Table 7.3 Indonesia in Free Trade Agreement – in effect January 2010

Free Trade Agreements	Signing period	Implementation starting period*
Association of South East Asian Nation FTA (AFTA)	Jan 1992	Jan 1993
ASEAN-China FTA (ACFTA)	Nov 2002	Jul 2003
ASEAN-Korea FTA (AKFTA)	Jul 2006	Jul 2006
Indonesia -Japan Economic Partnership Agreement (IJEPA)	Jul 2008	Jul 2008
ASEAN-Japan Comprehensive Economic Partnership (AJCEP)	Apr 2008	Apr 2008
ASEAN-India Free Trade Agreement (AIFTA)	Aug 2009	Jan 2010
ASEAN-Australia-New Zealand (AANZFTA)	Feb 2009	Jan 2010

Source: Ministry of Trade, 2011 and ASEAN Secretariat, 2011.

Note: *ACFTA, AKFTA, AJCEP, AIFTA and AANZFTA are in effect starting from January 2010.

1990, trade between developing countries has increased significantly and reached 39 per cent of their total trade in 2009 and the rise of trade of China with the rest of the world, which is expected to reach about 50 per cent by 2020, have sharpened the idea ASEAN can also be a trade hub and production platform. The idea has been translated into further reduction of trade and investment barriers. The government launched a deregulation package in May 1995 (dubbed as 'Pakmei') to improve economic efficiency and strengthen industrial competitiveness by clarifying procedures for investment, reducing import tariff of machinery, and removing some non-tariff barriers in some products. After the reform, import duties in excess of 40 per cent were left on motor vehicles and their components and alcoholic beverages. Effective rate of protection for the manufacturing industry was also down from an estimated 86 per cent in 1987 to 24 per cent in 1995 (Fane and Condon, 1996), suggesting that industries were subject to increasing competition. Subsequent after the start of gradual implementation of CEPT, Indonesia also extended reduction of tariff rates and simplified its import tariff structure to minimize trade diversion from non-ASEAN countries. The deregulation package certainly provided Indonesia with credibility in fulfilling commitments of Uruguay Round and as a supporter of Bogor Declaration of Asia-Pacific Economic Cooperation (APEC).

Another push for economic reforms to facilitate economic integration under a democratic environment started in 2004. As a part of commitments in Blueprint of ASEAN Economic Community, Indonesia passed Investment Law No. 25 of 2007 with provision for national treatment for all investors as one of its hallmarks. The Investment Law clarified that all sectors in the Indonesian economy are open for private investment, except those listed in the Negative List of investments, which is an executive order by the president on certain restrictions, including location and foreign equity. Both the Investment Law and the Negative List are meant to give transparency to investors and have been discussed involving stakeholders in private sector. On trade facilitation, the government launched a significant effort to develop a national single window (NSW) for customs clearance involving at least 25 government agencies. The intention of NSW is to facilitate trade by making it easier, faster, as well as less costly.

So far as Indonesian businesses in using the opportunities of trade agreements are concerned, the data suggests that there has been a dramatic uptake in the use of tariff preference by Indonesian exporters. As illustrated by Table 7.4, the use of Certificate of Origin (CoO) among Indonesian firms to enter markets with preferential access has increased followed by increases in the value of exports. The total number of CoO issued by Indonesia has increased from 26,085 certificates in 2007 to 205,775 certificates in 2010, which has been accompanied by an increase in the value of exports using CoO facilities from USD 1.9 billion in 2007 (2 per cent of total exports of non-oil and gas) to USD 19.9 billion (16 per cent of total non-oil and gas exports) in 2010. The increase of the use of CoO – one of free trade agreement facilities – shows efficacies of trade agreements and that the Indonesian private sector is also taking benefit from trade agreements.

Table 7.4 The use of certificate of origin in Indonesia, 2007–10

FTA	2007		2010	
	Total CoO	*Value of Exports using CoO (USD mn)*	*Total CoO*	*Value of Exports using CoO (USD mn)*
AFTA	2,332	1,360	103,334	8,710
ACFTA	19,491	2,04	24,235	5,287
AKFTA	4,262	3,43	28,662	2,776
IJEPA	–	–	48,571	2,642
AIFTA	–	–	1,013	452
Total	26,085	1,907	205,775	19,867

Source: Authors' calculations based on data from the Ministry of Trade of Republic of Indonesia, 2011.

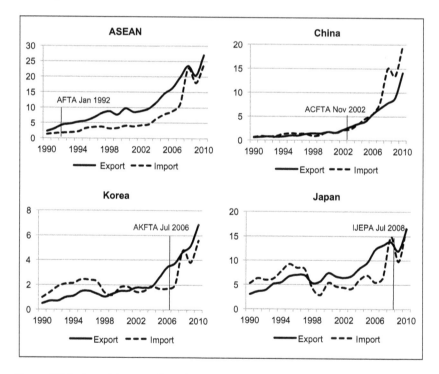

Figure 7.7 Indonesia's non-oil and gas trade with FTA partners (billions of USD)

Note: Export (import) means Indonesia's non-oil and gas exports (imports) to (from) FTA partners.

From the import side, visual inspection of the data suggests that FTAs did not cause an immediate jump in Indonesia's import. Figure 7.7 shows that imports from FTA partners have increased gradually, rather than instantly, suggesting that there are complex economic reasons behind the increasing imports, such as appreciating currency, rising investment and rising income per-capita.

However, there would be internal hurdles for undertaking more FTAs that require changes in domestic policy. First, there has been resistance for Indonesia to take up more FTAs particularly from certain sectors who fear Indonesia will lose from competition with FTA partners. Despite many success stories from Indonesia's FTAs, this concern remains valid given Indonesia's weak infrastructure, low human resource capacity, high costs of logistics and high transaction cost which affects cost of finance; all these are constraining the Indonesian private sector to respond to opportunities of FTAs. Second, like in other democratic societies, nationalist sentiment against the interests of foreigners in domestic policy is more visible and can be politically sensitive for the government to engage. Third, demand from pressure groups to limit foreign investment are gaining ground and this could be driven by interest to extract rents or preserve as much business opportunities as possible for domestic players. The last one, Indonesia still needs to strengthen its internal coordination to translate commitments made in bilateral or regional FTAs into policy and reform. Policy coordination remains a huge problem in Indonesia and currently there is lack of clarity in a mandate to coordinate efforts to implement and inquire commitments from FTAs.

III.   Conclusion and next challenges – gaining public support and managing the process

In the period before the Asian crisis, Indonesia demonstrated determination to engage in a series of unilateral reforms on trade and investment. Reforms were typically swift because of Suharto's authoritarian regime, which saw that reforms were necessary to respond to a series of mini-economic crisis. At the same time, Indonesian firms enjoyed the benefit of reforms in lower transaction costs while they had access to low-cost labor resources and enjoyed protection from a relatively weak real exchange rate.

The Indonesian economy has performed remarkably well in recent years with significant increases in the role of exports of non-oil and gas in driving economic growth. The increases in exports have been mainly driven by significant trade, investment and custom reforms. The share of natural resources-based products in driving Indonesia's exports has also been increasing significantly. Nonetheless, there is no doubt that there have been at least certain portions of the export increases that have been attributed to regional cooperation and trade agreements. Even in the worst story line that free trade agreements may not have brought any significant effect to trade, trade agreements somehow pushes national reforms as well as internal reform at the firm level to be able to compete with international players.

Given the current political circumstances and decentralization of authority, it is important for the government to maintain momentum for reform in trade and investment. Indeed, the path for engaging those reforms, particularly sweeping reforms, is increasingly challenging. Reforms and increasing openness to trade does not always translate to immediate gains and improvement in income equality while risk of losing from competition is always there. For various reasons, political resistance for more trade and investment liberalization is also mounting. But sooner or later Indonesia will have to compete with other countries in providing jobs and a future for millions of its population. Hence, there needs to be a strong leadership and political commitment in implementing gradual but steadfast economic reforms while at the same time demonstrating significant progress in building up infrastructure and setting up social protection programs. Meanwhile, it is important for Indonesia to start institutionalizing the following elements to sustain economic reform in the long run:

a) Improving responsiveness and transparency in the decision-making process: The current political set-up requires the government to have the ability to defend its economic policy, particularly trade reform, to be pro-poor. Meanwhile, the government would also need to put in place a mechanism for reviewing policy, such as in trade licenses and non-tariff measures that incorporate input from wider stakeholders. These challenges would require bureaucratic reform programs that can increase the capacity of bureaucracy in designing and implementing public policy.

b) Strengthening coordination in policy making across relevant agencies: Lack of coordination presents great uncertainties for investment, both domestic and foreign. Indonesia would need to come up with an effective mechanism to address coordination failure in economic policies. So far the government has not fully utilized a prototype mechanism to facilitate high-level decision-making processes (such the National Team for the Enhancement of Exports and Investment). Consolidating coordination in policy making that can have an impact on trade is crucial to ensure certainty of regulations for investors. Consolidating coordination is also crucial for Indonesia to implement necessary follow-ups from commitments made in international economic forums.

c) Prioritizing development in public infrastructure in education and logistics to improve competitiveness. Development is a process that involves success and failures and government can help minimize the costs and uncertainties for the Indonesian private sector in expanding businesses and improving productivity. Public investment in education to improve human capacity and skills and in logistics does not only deliver high social returns but also improves economic competitiveness. Implementing quick wins in those areas also sends a strong signal that the government is committed to improve competitiveness.

Notes

1 This led to a dispute settlement process in the WTO from Japan, the US and the EU, which Indonesia ultimately lost, and provided an important precedent to the role of international commitments vis-à-vis national vested interests.
2 Popularly known as the *trilemma* in macroeconomics. Fixing the Rupiah exchange rate would mean that Indonesia would either need to surrender its monetary policy or to impose control on capital movement. Failure to do the former would

mean that Indonesia could run a risk of having a different inflation rate that would trigger investors to take arbitrage on Indonesian bonds, which under an open capital regime, would force the Rupiah exchange rate to move. A similar argument applies for failure to impose control over capital movement.

3 For example, see Darby et al. (1999) on the negative impact of exchange rate volatility on investment, although it is smaller than the impact of costs of capital or expected earnings.

4 Indonesia Input-Output Table 2005.

5 Aswichayono et al. (2010) showed that industrialization in Indonesia after the Asian crisis has been relying mostly on the performance of large firms, i.e. firms with larger than 500 employees, whereas small firms have been showing lack of dynamism compared to the period before the crisis.

6 See, for example Feridhanusetyawan and Pangestu (2003: 72); and Hartono et al. (2007).

7 Using firm census data from 1991 to 2001, they claim that a 10 per cent point fall in input tariffs leads to a productivity gain of 12 per cent for firms that import their inputs, at least twice as high as any gains from reducing output tariffs. In the same way, by using the North-South trade framework, Xu (2003) and Ing (2009: 1122) also claim that import tariff reductions could actually increase exports of products using imported intermediate goods.

8 Indonesian manufacturing sector

Searching for identity amidst a challenging environment

Dionisius Narjoko and Sjamsu Rahardja

I. Introduction

There are many angles to tell a story about the Indonesian economy. From the success point of view, the Indonesian economy performed remarkably well by demonstrating a relatively quick turn around after the devastating economic and political crises in the late 1990s. Indonesia managed to put its economic growth back on track relatively quickly compared to other countries with similar size struck by economic crisis, such as Brazil and Russia. As consequences, the poverty rate continues to fall and the fiscal position is dramatically improved. While the boom in global commodity prices caused higher import bills in many countries, it lifted Indonesian commodity net exports and reopened vast investment opportunities in Indonesia's natural resource sectors. The Indonesian economy also came relatively unscratched from the global financial crisis.

However, among development issues that Indonesia is facing, slowing down growth of Indonesia's manufacturing sector has become a contentious issue. After the devastating crisis in the late 1990s, Indonesia's manufacturing sector never regained its position as an engine for growth. Now, thanks to deregulation in services and the boom in commodity prices, investors have alternative investment opportunities. Meanwhile, problems with the supply-side are believed to have undermined competitiveness of manufacturing activities in Indonesia. Local manufacturers have to navigate through more open trade regime and regulatory uncertainties coming from the excess impact from a decentralized policy environment. Relatively well organized, several manufacturers associations have been demanding that the government implement more protectionist measures and be aggressive in upgrading public infrastructures. Labor unions from the manufacturing sector are also mounting pressure for social protection.

This chapter intends to raise discussion as to what is going on and why should policy makers be concerned. It draws heavily from recent work by Aswicahyono et al. (2010), on the dynamics of industrialization in Indonesia post the 1997 economic crisis. As with Aswicahyono et al. (2010), we highlight the 'consolidation' process within the manufacturing sector. We complement previous studies by highlighting areas on macroeconomic environment and issues related to institutions that might have an impact on the declining performance of the Indonesian manufacturing sector.

II. Indonesian manufacturing sector since the 1997–98 crisis

The manufacturing sector remains to have a significant share in the Indonesian economy but the ability to lift economic growth has diminished: in 1990–95, 35 per cent of GDP growth came from changes in manufacturing output while in 2003–08 that contribution was only 18.5 per cent.[1]

The 1997–98 crisis severely affected Indonesian manufacturing as it caused deep contraction in 1998 and 1999. Compared to other Asian countries, the Indonesian manufacturing sector was relatively slow to recover from the crisis. As shown in Figure 8.1, it took South Korea 1 year to make a dramatic turn around on its manufacturing sector in 1998 and since then it recorded 7.4 per cent growth per year. Similarly, Malaysian and Thai manufacturing sectors have performed better than their Indonesian counterparts.

Although it recovered quite quickly from the crisis, Indonesian manufacturing was not able to fully recover to its pre-crisis high growth level in the years after the crisis. As shown in Table 8.1, the average growth rate in the period after 2000 was only slightly more than half of the average of pre-1997 growth. This much slower growth rate is recorded in almost all industry groups, except the machinery and equipment industry (ISIC 38). Aswicahyono et al. (2010) attributed the focus on exports of electronics and automotive industry as the explanation for the favorable performance of the machinery and equipment industry; electronics and automotive industries, including their parts and component industries, are the two industry groups that dominate ISIC 38. The subsector electronics has traditionally been export-oriented, and this helped the subsector in weathering the crisis and its post-crisis impact (Aswicahyono et al.

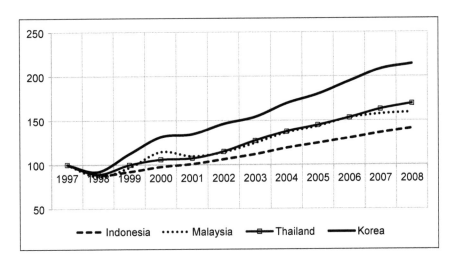

Figure 8.1 Real GDP index of manufacturing (1997 = 100)

Source: Calculated from *World Development Indicator*, World Bank.

Table 8.1 Industrial growth by sector (real value added, % per annum, 1994–2006)

ISIC	Sector	1994–96	1997–99	2000–02	2003–06
31	Food, beverages and tobacco	17.5	5.6	1.6	3.5
32	Textile, clothes and leather industry	8.7	–3.4	4.9	3.2
33	Wood and wood products	4.0	–14.0	2.7	–0.6
34	Paper and paper products	11.4	2.2	1.0	5.1
35	Chemicals and chemical products	10.7	–0.8	4.1	8.2
36	Non-metallic mineral products	16.9	–7.0	10.4	5.2
37	Basic metal industries	11.1	–9.2	3.6	–2.4
38	Fabricated metal, machinery, and eq.	7.3	–21.2	26.3	11.6
39	Other manufacturing industries	10.3	–10.2	4.8	9.2
	Non-oil and gas manufacturing	10.5	–6.3	7.4	6.2

2010: 1090). Meanwhile, the high growth of subsector automotive, including its part and component industries, have been the result of the removal of protection during the crisis – through the IMF programs – and the rationalization during the peak of the crisis as well as implementation of accumulated knowledge and technology from the learning process during the period of high protection (Aswicahyono et al., 2000).

Relatively mild slower growth after the crisis was recorded for mineral-resource industries, chemicals-and-chemical products. Connection to the resilient agriculture sector such as fertilizer partly contributed to this figure (Aswicahyono et al., 2010).

The labor-intensive industry of textile, clothing and footwear (TCF, ISIC 32) grew substantially lower after the crisis. This indicates much lower export growth coming from this industry, which is surprising given the depreciated exchange rate after the crisis. Weak performance was also shown by the post-crisis average growth of resource-based industries, namely, the wood products (ISIC 33) and paper products (ISIC 34). Again, this is in spite of boost in competitiveness from depreciated exchange rate. The slow growth in the resource-based industries, however, may have likely come from the much-limited source of raw materials; the removal of the prohibition on the exports of logs significantly increased the costs for acquiring inputs for firms in these industries (Resosudarmo, 2005).

Rather sharp contraction in post-crisis growth was recorded by the non-metallic industry and food-beverage-and-tobacco industry (ISIC 35 and 31, respectively).

The much-slower growth of ISIC 35 reflects the much slower growth of the construction sector during and after the crisis. It is, however, not clear, and in fact rather surprising, to see the much slower growth in the output of ISIC 31. One potential explanation is due to increased imports from the more opened trade regime after the crisis.

III.   Export performance and competitiveness

The performance of Indonesian manufacturing exports has been rather disappointing after the crisis. As indicated by Figure 8.2, the exports grew rapidly in the 1980s, stagnated in the first half of the 1990s and collapsed during the crisis – but recovered almost immediately, but then they declined in 2000 and continue to decline since then. The 'bounce' in the exports that happened during the crisis was likely due to the sharp exchange rate depreciation during this time; the momentum, however, did not last, which partly may be the result of eroded exchange rate competitiveness coming from higher domestic prices (i.e. stronger real exchange rate after the crisis).

It is important to note that in terms of growth, the export performance had actually begun to decline long before the crisis. The growth trend depicted in Figure 8.2 shows that export has grown slower over time since the early 1990s. This indicates more fundamental issue of declining competitiveness of Indonesian manufacturing exports, a subject to which we return below.

Looking at the export growth across commodity groups defined by factor intensity, Table 8.2 shows that the decline in the growth varies considerably, albeit a generally much slower growth across all groups after the crisis. The commodities coming from resource-based labor-intensive and unskilled labor-intensive

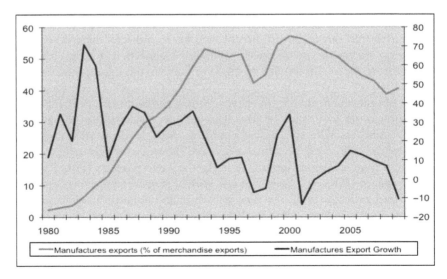

Figure 8.2 Manufacturing export growth and share of total exports, 1980–2009

Table 8.2 Export growth across commodity groups defined by factor intensity

Commodity Group		1990–93	1994–96	1997–99	2000–02	2003–06
1-ULI	Unskilled Labor-Intensive	37.7	6.0	–0.8	0.5	7.9
821	Furniture and parts	44.7	12.1	10.1	7.6	5.6
651	Textile yarn	41.7	35.3	9.7	1.8	10.1
851	Footwear	74.2	9.5	–9.3	–9.5	8.0
843	Women's, girls, infants outerwear, textile, not knitted or crocheted	35.4	–0.8	3.0	4.2	6.8
845	Outerwear knitted or crocheted, not elastic nor rubberized	21.8	–1.6	2.4	3.9	16.8
2-RB-LI	Resource-Based Labor-Intensive	19.9	–1.7	–9.7	–4.6	0.9
634	Veneers, plywood, 'improved' wood and other wood, worked, nes	17.9	–4.4	–12.3	–6.9	–0.9
635	Wood manufactures, nes	53.6	16.8	–2.5	0.7	4.8
663	Mineral manufacture, nes	53.4	18.5	35.5	8.2	5.8
662	Clay and refractory construction materials	74.6	5.6	117.8	10.8	7.8
667	Pearl, precious and semi-precious stones, unworked or worked	27.0	–5.5	19.3	–8.4	32.0
3-RB-CI	Resource-Based Capital-Intensive	8.4	19.0	18.8	4.6	15.6
641	Paper and paperboard	34.1	22.3	38.2	–2.9	18.9
625	Rubber tires, tire cases, inner and flaps, for wheels of all kinds	10.5	45.7	0.9	12.1	23.0
674	Universals, plates, and sheets, of iron or steel	–2.8	38.1	1.6	0.4	61.3
511	Hydrocarbons, nes, and derivatives	205.8	39.8	55.2	31.8	36.6
522	Inorganic chemical elements, oxides and halogen salts	3.0	44.2	–9.3	37.2	34.2
4-ELE	Electronics	93.5	36.9	0.6	37.9	4.7
752	Automatic data processing machines	1,875.6	78.0	–10.2	182.9	16.6
778	Electrical machinery and apparatus, nes	46.6	27.6	3.1	8.7	18.8

(*Continued*)

Table 8.2 (Continued)

Commodity Group		1990–93	1994–96	1997–99	2000–02	2003–06
764	Telecommunication equipment, nes; parts and accessories, nes	81.0	46.2	2.4	29.8	2.5
763	Gramophones, dictating machines and other sound recorders	441.6	36.1	–15.6	49.8	–4.1
772	Electrical apparatus for making and breaking electrical circuits	702.3	27.6	0.1	107.4	14.6
5-FLCI	Footloose Capital-Intensive	42.7	22.1	10.7	8.7	20.0
784	Motor vehicle parts and accessories, nes	50.0	35.9	46.0	27.4	32.6
582	Condensation, polycondensation and polyaddition products	23.7	115.8	18.6	13.2	14.2
583	Polymerization and copolymerization products	29.2	44.1	23.0	1.9	16.9
513	Carboxylic acids, and their derivatives	16.6	64.8	37.8	10.7	13.1
512	Alcohols, phenols, etc., and their derivatives	48.3	56.4	9.9	6.2	19.7
Manufacturing Exports		29.5	9.6	0.8	9.9	7.9

Source: UN Comtrade Database.

experienced the largest decline in the growth rate. The decline in growth of resource-based capital-intensive (RBCI), electronics (ELE), and footloose capital-intensive (FLCI) was relatively mild; in fact, the export growth of RBCI tends to meet its pre-crisis level. The buoyant commodity price in the 2000s is the likely explanation for this. The mild decline in the growth of ELE and FLCI may have been the result of the connection of the exports in these commodity groups to the East Asia production networks (Aswicahyono et al., 2010). As for the FLCI exports, as noted earlier, the ability of firms to adjust quickly and the removal of trade protection during the crisis may have helped firms in these industries to quickly make a favorable export response (Aswicahyono et al., 2000). However, the limited connection of Indonesia in the regional production networks may have been the reason why the increase in the exports in ELE and FLCI was only moderate.

As indicated, we argue that much of the slower growth in the exports might have been due to declining competitiveness. Aswicahyono et al. (2010) support this proposition. Using the Constant Market Share Analysis (CMSA) method, they showed a declining trend was recorded during the 1990s and up to about

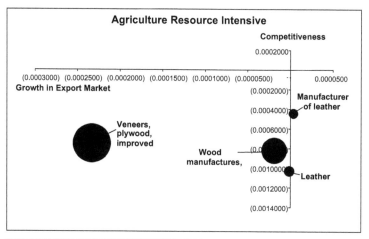

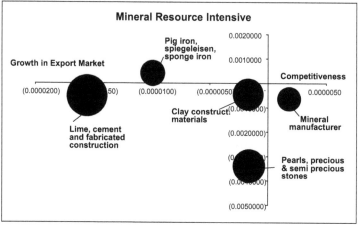

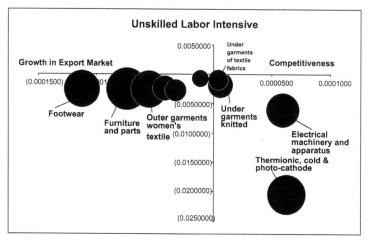

Figure 8.3 Export share, competitiveness, and growth in export market by factor intensity (ARI, MRI, and ULI), 1990–2005

the mid-2000s. They argued that much of the decline comes from the decline in the competitiveness of two broad sectors: natural resource – or unskilled labor – intensive. As Figure 8.3 shows, many of the main products defined by these sectors have either actually lost their export competitiveness or gone to declining export markets. This is in contrast to some exporting goods which can be categorized under technology and capital-intensive sectors. In fact, as Table 8.2 shows, this is quite a paradox for the reason that Indonesia does not have comparative advantage in this sector.

Examining the unit labor cost, or ULC, is another way to assess the competitiveness. It has been widely used for international comparisons of cost competitiveness. ULC can be defined as the cost of labor required to produce one unit of output. The interpretation of ULC might be better understood when expressed in terms of a ratio with the nominator being labor compensation per unit of labor, and the denominator being the productivity of labor. The formula reveals that a country can improve its competitiveness either by decreasing its labor compensation per unit of labor, by improving its labor productivity or optimal combination of both.

Figure 8.4 provides the trend of ULC, labor productivity and wages in Indonesian manufacturing during 1990–2005. We can distinguish three major episodes of a ULC trend during the period: pre-crisis (1990–95), crisis (1995–2001) and post-crisis (2001–05). Wages increased considerably during the crisis compared to pre-crisis, and then moderated post-crisis. Labor productivity shows steady increases during and post-crisis; the growth of labor productivity is even higher during and post-crisis. As a result of those trends, ULC increased

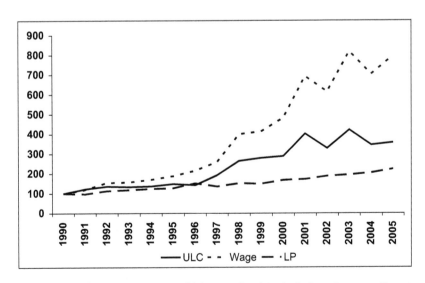

Figure 8.4 Trend in ULC, wages and labor productivity in Indonesian manufacturing (indexed, 1990 = 100), 1990–2005

substantially during the crisis, but was moderated post-crisis. The figure even shows a declining trend of ULC post-crisis.

Figure 8.4 provides ULC trends during 1990–2005 by factor intensities. The ULC for the whole manufacturing sector increased by a factor of 2.4 during the period 1995–2005. Unskilled labor-intensive industry and agriculture resource-intensive industry experienced the highest increase in ULC, that is, by 2.7 and 2.6 times, respectively. The next ones are mineral resource-intensive and technology-intensive industries, which increased by a factor of 2.3. The lowest increased of ULC was found in the human capital-intensive industry (2.1 times).

IV. Insights from firm dynamics

The results presented above give an impression of a rather substantial decline in the output growth and competitiveness of Indonesian manufacturing for the period after the crisis, albeit some variations across industries. This raises a question as to why it happened. Obviously, there can be many answers for this. Nonetheless, as indicated earlier, it can be argued that the decline could be attributed to a less favorable business environment after the crisis. Several contributing factors have been identified, including a rigid labor policy, weak foreign direct investment, deteriorating infrastructure and adjustment to decentralization.

The rest of this section addresses this subject, by an attempt to find some formal support for the general hypothesis (i.e. of the less favorable business environment after the crisis). This is carried on by examining firm dynamics in the manufacturing sector. Formally, this is approached by examining the trend and pattern of firm entry-exit and expansion-contraction rate over the time (period 1993–2004) and across industry groups.[2]

In terms of firm dynamics, the general hypothesis can be translated into a more specific – but still relatively general – hypothesis that the trend of entry and expansion rate should be declining over the years after the crisis. The prediction, obviously, is the other way around for exit and contraction rate; that is, an increasing trend for the post-crisis period.

Figure 8.5 shows the trend of entry and exit rate in terms of number of plants over the period 1993–2004. It provides some support for the hypothesis, that is, the extent of entry has not really recovered after the crisis. The entry rates for the years in the period 2001–04 (post-crisis) were about half of the rates for the years in the period 1993–96 (pre-crisis). As for the exit rates, meanwhile, although they were about the same between pre- and post-crisis, they were higher than the entry rates for the first three years after the crisis (i.e. from 2001–03). This suggests that more firms have been forced to exit, rather than to establish their presence in the industry. The trend in entry and exit rates in terms of employment (not shown here) also reveals a similar picture. It is worth mentioning here that a comparison between the entry-exit rates in terms of the number of plants and employment indicates that the size of firms

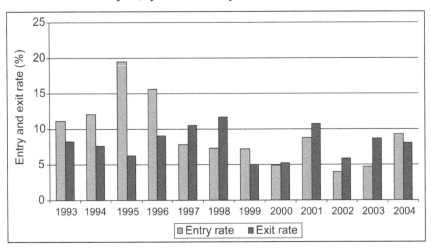

Figure 8.5 Exit and entry rate (% in terms of number of plants), Indonesia, 1993–2004

Source: Statistic of Industry, 1993–2004.

that entered and exited the industry tend to be larger for the period of post-crisis, compared to that of the pre-crisis period.

The picture suggested by Figure 8.5 is consistent with the general perception of an expensive cost for doing business in Indonesia, in comparison to other countries in the region. It might also be the result of a significantly less direct investment after the crisis, for both domestic and foreign direct investment. Thus, potential entrants were likely holding back, and at the same time, observing the exit process and perhaps waiting for a strong demand from the industry – there is likely a high level of excess capacity following the crisis (Aswicahyono et al., 2010). The more unfavorable commercial environment may have increased either the barriers of entry, in terms of increased costs to be borne by the entrants, or shown much less of a profit incentive, which also comes from the increased operational costs that the incumbents have to pay.

Figure 8.6, which shows the trend in expansion and contraction rate over the period 1993–2004, provides more support for the general hypothesis of less favorable business environment after the crisis. The extent of expansion and contraction rate has not really recovered in some years after the crisis (i.e. 2001–03). This situation, however, seems to have started to change in 2004, where the extent of the rates are more or less back to those of the average pre-crisis period. This might suggest that the business environment had actually started to improve in that year. Another important observation is that much of performance of Indonesian manufacturing after the crisis seems to have been contributed by survivors (i.e. firms that have already been inside the industry), and not by newcomers.

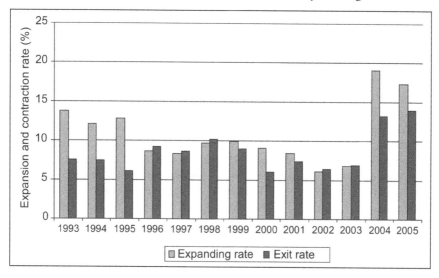

Figure 8.6 Expansion and contraction rate (%, in terms of employment), Indonesia, 1993–2004

Source: SI, various years.

V. Environment for industrialization after a deep economic crisis

Promoting outward orientation has been the dominant feature of economic policies affecting Indonesian manufacturing before the 1997–98 crisis.[3] To reduce dependency on oil and gas economy, the government took a series of comprehensive and bold reforms in the 1980s and 1990s with the objective to encourage foreign direct investment and promote export. Liberalizations in the area of banking, trade and investment policy were at the same time directed to increase the extent of efficiency-seeking and export-oriented direct investment, both from domestic and foreign direct investment (FDI). Policies to provide fiscal incentives for exporters, eliminate tariff and non-tariff barriers (NTBs) and improve trade facilitation were also introduced to reduce export bias. Parallel to all these reforms, the government continuously invested in public infrastructure which evidently supported the expansion of the industry.

The impact of the policy changes in the 1980s and early 1990s on Indonesian manufacturing is apparent. The sector transformed rapidly during this time and had become an important source of growth by the mid-1990s. The share of the sector in GDP increased from 12 per cent in 1975 to 24 per cent in 1995. Accompanying this structural change is the rapid growth of export and the change of the manufacturing export structure, reflecting mostly the comparative advantage of the sector in the 1990s. The share of manufacturing in total exports increased dramatically from 1.2 per cent in 1975 to 50.6 per cent in 1995.[4] At the same time, there was an increasing foreign participation in the sector, coming as a result of the major investment reforms over the first half of the 1990s.

However, policies determining the performance of Indonesian manufacturing have changed quite dramatically since the crisis. First, trade regime has become more opened than before the crisis. Significant trade reforms were undertaken as a part of the IMF's crisis-support program. Included in these reforms are further reduction of tariffs and elimination of NTBs as well as introduction of more export promotion schemes. The removal of NTBs largely captures the World Bank's proposal to continue some elements of trade reforms which were not undertaken in the early 1990s (Soesastro and Basri, 2005). Tariff reduction driven by unilateral initiatives and commitments to regional trade agreements have lowered the overall effective protection rates for the Indonesian manufacturing sector (Marks and Rahardja, 2011). This process of lowering trade barriers, although having had a positive impact on aggregate productivity of the manufacturing sector, also has exposed less productive Indonesian manufacturing firms to more intense competition from emerging low-cost manufactures of other countries.[5] Meanwhile, there is some sense that Indonesia sometimes uses non-tariff measures, such as licenses and technical standards, as additional instruments to protect certain industries from international competition.

Second, the policy framework governing the labor market has become more restrictive after the crisis. The rise of the pro-labor movement after the crisis gives more power to labor unions in setting the regulated minimum wage and introduces rigidities for firms to hire and dismiss workers. The most controversial change is the sky-rocketing severance payment, which is the highest in the region, and the significant increase in the minimum wage, reaching 90 per cent over the period 1999–2002 (Aswicahyono et al., 2010). Firms, therefore, were discouraged from hiring or expanding (Manning and Roesad, 2006) and faced with much higher risk for survival – because of the large amount of cash they have to prepare for severance payment (Narjoko and Jotzo, 2007).

The 'harmony' of policies that support Indonesian manufacturing seems to have broken down after the crisis. Net FDI inflow to Indonesia suffers from a crunch time and has been trailing behind other emerging markets. Net FDI over GDP of Indonesia was similar to China between 1985 to 1991 when Indonesia initiated a series of trade and investment reforms (see Figure 8.7). But the government's slow response to conduct reforms in order to improve the investment climate and to maintain the pre-crisis growth in public infrastructure has made Indonesia a less desirable destination for FDI. Competition from China and other emerging Southeast Asian countries for the location of foreign direct investment seems to have contributed to the slow FDI recovery of Indonesia since the crisis. It was only in 2007, which is about 10 years after the crisis, that the government introduced a new investment law for a hope to boost the declining investment figures and ratings. Meanwhile, infrastructure development has weakened considerably since the crisis, at about half of the pre-crisis level of development.

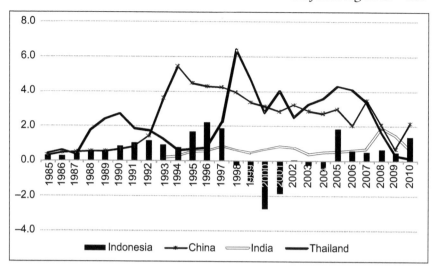

Figure 8.7 Ratio of net FDI over GDP
Source: Calculated from EIU database.

The 'big bang' decentralization program in 2001 that dissolved significant power and resources to second-tier regional government (i.e. district level) seems to have had the unintended impact of lowering the development of public infrastructure, and thereby discouraged investment. There is often a lack of technical capacity to implement infrastructure projects at district level; moreover, fiscal decentralization and the strong authority of the local government poses a problem of effective infrastructure provision, because of the widespread mismatch between the cross-district nature of many types of infrastructure (e.g. ports benefit not just the district they are located in but also the surrounding areas) (Narjoko and Jotzo, 2007: 160–61). The infrastructure problem has become acute and has appeared as an important constraint for business, particularly for Indonesian manufacturers (LPEM, 2005). Without breakthroughs in logistics infrastructure, Indonesia may not be able to take advantage of the increase in output of resource products for industrialization at home (Basri and Rahardja, 2010).

The business environment was much less attractive after the crisis. This is reflected by Indonesia being ranked poorly in the annual World Bank's Doing Business Survey in the past couple of years. As is often argued by many, Aswicahyono et al. (2011) attribute this to the situation where there was greater unpredictability in the business deal in general, which means more expensive corruption, but, at the same time, there was only slow growth. The growth therefore would make the 'return' from the business deal much lower if one compares it to the situation before the crisis. The implication is clear, and that is, investments are holding back; and indeed this is what seems to have happened.

The 1997 crisis also dramatically changed the macroeconomic landscape surrounding the Indonesian manufacturing sector. Indonesia adopted an open capital account and abandoned the regime of fixed exchange rates that allowed the Rupiah to float. After the crisis, the Rupiah sharply depreciated before it appreciated but then it remained relatively volatile compared to exchange rates of regional comparators despite significant improvement in political stability. The 'excess sensitivity' of the Rupiah, from the 1997 crisis until the period of the global financial crisis of 2008, could increase uncertainty for manufactures relying on exports and imports.

The commodity boom has pushed the importance of resource-based and services activities. Indonesia has been a natural resource–rich country and the commodity boom unlocked and renewed investment potential in natural resource sectors, such as minerals and plantation. Income and returns from commodity increased demand for goods in regions off-Java. Meanwhile, there has been significant increases in investment to develop service hubs on finance, legal, telecom, trade and transport in manufacturing areas in Java. The boom in commodity and services has increased demand for goods and services. With bottlenecks in infrastructure, the increase in demand is likely to have raised the cost of labor and costs of other intermediate inputs, which in turn could amplify the real appreciation of the Rupiah.

Without prejudging the policy options, we think real appreciation of the Rupiah subsequently may have contributed to the declining performance of the Indonesian manufacturing sector. Rupiah real appreciation would reduce incentives to expand in 'non-booming' tradable sectors, including many sub-sectors of manufacturing, and increase economic concentration towards primary or natural resources-based product (Basri and Rahardja, 2011). Figure 8.8 suggests

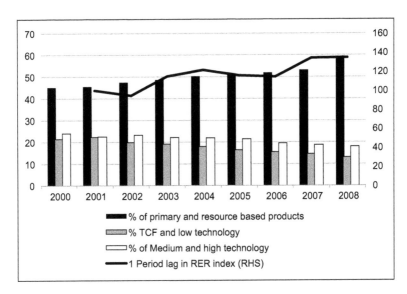

Figure 8.8 Share of products in Indonesian exports (%)

Source: Basri and Rahardja (2011).

Note: TCF: textile, clothing, and footwear.

that there is a certain correlation between real appreciation and a subsequent increase in the share of primary and resources-based products and the declining share of manufactured products in Indonesian exports.

VI. Going forward

Since the 1997–98 crisis we have witnessed a dramatic change in the role of the manufacturing sector in the Indonesian economy. No longer as the main engine to lift economic growth, slow growth in the manufacturing sector could become a drag for long-term growth and economic transformation. In the 1980s and 1990s, manufactures were more likely to be proponents for trade reforms and policies facilitating trade integration. But the slowdown in manufacturing growth has affected sub-sectors that are important for generating jobs, such as clothing and footwear, and sub-sectors with a large presence of small enterprises, such as clothing, furniture and metal work. Declining performance of firms in certain sub-sectors also has increased political pressure for the government to implement protectionist measures to assist local manufactures.

The crisis also left some marks on the dynamics within the Indonesian manufacturing sector. Investors perceived that the crisis increased regulatory uncertainties, red tape, infrastructure bottlenecks, that matter for the decision to operate in the manufacturing sector. Our analysis based on the manufacturing census also suggests some correlation between the worsening business environment with net entry into the manufacturing sector. Unlike before, the contribution of newcomers on growth of output and employment has declined. We also indicated a possibility of a correlation between real appreciation of the exchange rate and a subsequent decline in the role of manufacturing output in exports.

But there are reasons for Indonesia to remain optimistic about the future of its manufacturing sector. The sector could be experiencing adjustment to a new economic landscape and undergoing a consolidation process along with reallocation of resources to fewer but more productive firms. Meanwhile the gravity of global economic growth is shifting towards emerging markets and Indonesia is well positioned to supply increasing demand for consumer products in Asia and at home. A large labor force pool and rising nominal wages in other countries relative to Indonesia has increased the attractiveness of Indonesia as a destination for relocation of manufacturing processes. A large and growing domestic market, well endowed with natural resources for processing manufacturing products, should have a positive effect in facilitating growth in the Indonesian manufacturing sector.

Regardless of the differences of opinions on the significance of the manufacturing sector for driving the Indonesian economy to the future, we believe that we can share the same concern. Sustaining growth in the Indonesian manufacturing sector should be a priority in the policy agenda for creating more jobs. We also believe that targeted policies to improve competitiveness and productivity should be done in stages with a priority to reform the supply side of the Indonesian economy to reduce uncertainties for investors and to lower logistics costs.

But there are lots of remaining unknowns that we think are best answered by other studies with more rigorous analysis. For example, we do not fully know whether Indonesia is experiencing a consolidation in its manufacturing industry or experiencing an impact related to the boom in commodity and services industries. We also have not yet shown whether Indonesia's case is normal compared to what happened to most manufacturing sectors in Latin and South American countries. We also have not looked at specific constraints in the investment climate that might have affected performance in certain manufacturing sub-sectors. Last, but not least, without getting a reasonable grip on this information, we are still short of recommending an agenda for policy actions.

Notes

1 Changes of manufacturing GDP divided by changes of GDP between periods, all in constant prices.
2 Entry (exit) rate is defined as the ratio of firms entering (exiting) an industry at a point of time to the stock of firms in the industry at the previous period of that point of time. It can be measured both in terms of the number of plants and employment. Meanwhile, the expansion (contraction) rate is defined as the ratio of some creation (destruction) in employment at a point of time to the stock of employment in the previous period of that point of time.
3 See Hill (1996) and Pangestu (1996) for the detail of policy reforms affecting industrialization in Indonesia before the 1997–8 crisis.
4 Manufacturing exports classified by SITC rev 1, which is products covered under SITC 5, 6, 7 and 8 but excluding 68. This way of classifying manufacturing exports is rather different than the usual manner done by Indonesian authorities, which typically uses ISIC classification and accounts semi-processed agriculture products, such as crude palm oil, as manufacturing.
5 See Amiti and Konings (2007) that showed liberalizing tariff for input allowed Indonesian manufacturing firms to access input at world prices and have a positive effect on productivity.

9 Globalization and innovation in Indonesian manufacturing

Ari Kuncoro

I. Introduction

With globalization the world has become more integrated through movements of goods, capital, labor and ideas (Bloom, 2002). How it can be transmitted into domestic economy is manifested in many ways, but the usual avenue is via trade and investment liberalization. With decreasing trade barriers countries can now increase exchange of goods and services among them. This process has been sped up by the fast pace of development in information and communication technology. In this new world, fresh ideas are quickly brought to practice, new technologies developed and applied faster than at any other time in history. More important than any other time in the past, knowledge now has become an increasingly important determinant of wealth of nations.

The importance of knowledge has revived attention on innovation systems and research institutions. The process of globalization has made innovation more important than before; even poor countries can no longer neglect the development of innovation systems. Innovation systems as creator, adaptor and disseminator of knowledge can be used as a vital tool for developing countries to benefit from globalization. Firms facing domestic as well as international competition have to adjust quickly to the ever-changing market demand, and for this they need to innovate.

The purpose of the study is to look at the impact of globalization on innovation at the firm level in Indonesian large and medium manufacturing. This study, employing the Indonesian data on large and medium-size manufacturing establishments, tries to provide a contribution to answer at least for the Indonesian case, whether globalization is innovation enhancing or innovation reducing. The most important question is whether government policies to liberalize trade and investment regimes will boost innovations, and afterward whether innovation will improve firms' ability to compete globally. If that is the case, then the policy to open up the economy to global competition is desirable. It will allow developing countries, or more specifically Indonesia, to jump up the learning curve by bypassing expensive processes of invention. The government then after a series of trade and investment liberalization policies could focus on policies to facilitate firms to exploit the benefits of globalization.

The relationship between globalization and innovation is a complicated one. Increasing imports and inward FDI brought by decreasing trade barriers would intensify competition in the domestic market and erode the domestic firms' profitability. This will force domestic firms to produce efficiently (Bertscheck, 1995). To stay competitive in the business one way is to increase innovation activity. So globalization and innovation may be positively related.

On the other hand, others argued that the above relationship may just be the opposite (Braga and Willmore, 1991). Because firms have to spend handsomely on R&D to create new products and new production processes while its return is highly uncertain, they tend to be very conservative on innovation, focusing only on the assimilation of imported technology to local conditions. Hence, the relationship between globalization and innovation may be negative.

Although the term 'globalization' is well understood, translating it into the empirical world is not an easy matter. First, globalization can be considered as a regime change from a relatively highly regulated and protected economy to a more open and deregulated one. Any economic reform that involves trade and/or investment liberalization will fit into this definition. In this respect, the period of analysis will be appropriately divided into before and after liberalization to examine the impact of regime change on any defined outcomes, for example its impact on the number of innovations conducted by firms or on R&D intensity.

The second way is more at the firm or industry level. As a result of the dismantling trade barrier, a firm has options to go to export markets, operating as FDI, licensing or some or all combinations of the above. This applies to all firms irrespective of their countries of origin (Bertscheck, 1995). One implication is that export activities, the presence of FDI and/or licensing can be used to present the extent of globalization at the firm and industry levels, an example is the use of the ratio of exported output at the firm level (Kuncoro, 2002) and the presence of FDI firms to measure the impact of globalization on firms (Kuncoro and Resosudarmo, 2006).

For innovation the measurement is more straightforward provided the data are available. There are two aspects of innovations, namely, product technology or product innovation and process technology or process innovation. Product innovation is substantial improvement of a current product or development and manufacture of a new product. Kraemer and Dedrick (2000), for example used the number of new products introduced over the last three years to capture product innovation. Process innovation on the other hand involves substantially improved or new production processes through the introduction of new process equipment or re-engineering of the operational process. For example if a firm in a specific period of time does the following: to set up a new production line, to put in a new production system and to put in a new computerized system to upgrade production facilities, then they can be categorized as process innovation. This also applies to the purchase of new capital equipment if it involves a new production process or at least if it brings improvement in the production process.

Unfortunately, observing innovations directly, the Indonesian manufacturing data sets are problematic. Both types of innovation are simply not available in the BPS large and medium manufacturing surveys. The only observed outcome from innovation activities is R&D expenditure in which all product and process innovations are lumped together. So relying on the concept of knowledge production function directly is difficult. Fortunately using economic theory one can derive R&D expenditure as a product of cost minimization process where total cost of production, which includes R&D expenditure, is minimized subject to a certain level of targeted output. In other words by relying on the concept of innovation or knowledge production function R&D expenditure can be interpreted as preceding activities prior to actual innovations and thus can be used a proxy for these activities.

II.   Overview of Indonesian manufacturing

In order to be able to get better grasp on the relationship between globalization and innovations at the firm level, first we look at the broader side at the industry level. Structurally the Indonesian economy has undergone transformation during three decades going from an agriculture-dominated economy into a manufacturing-dominated one, signifying transformation to a more modern economy. The share of agriculture sector fell from around 34 per cent in 1971 to around 15 per cent in 2000 while manufacturing has increased its share from around 8 per cent in 1971 to 28 per cent in the same period. The structural transformation has altered the growth dynamic. Now anything that retards growth in manufacturing will be translated to diminished GDP growth despite the fact that other sectors provide some offsetting factors. The slow growth of manufacturing provides some explanation about the modest growth of GDP in the post-crisis period (Table 9.1).

In the post-crisis period manufacturing has gone from the engine of the economy to the one important source of the drag to the GDP growth simply because of its share in the economy (Table 9.1). Along with transportation, manufacturing is the only sector that recorded growth below GDP in the 2004–10 periods. Amid the sluggishness of the other sectors, communication appears to have its own life. The growth is extraordinarily high at around 26 per cent per annum in the 2004–09 periods.

To examine the growth dynamic more closely we look at the graph of GDP growth in the post-crisis period after 2000. Figure 9.1 summarizes the growth dynamic from the output side in this period. Due to its dominating share, the movement of manufacturing over time, for the most part, resembles GDP. After starting with a modest recovery in Q1 2001, it lost its steam in Q1 2005. The peak was reached in Q4 2004 with 8.7 per cent annual growth, thereafter the growth continued to slide gradually. The GFC in 2008 only made matters worse. Beginning in Q4 2008, manufacturing growth in all quarters in 2009 except the last one fell below 2 per cent. This had caused GDP growth to drop

Table 9.1 Sectoral average annual growth

Sector	1994–1996		2000–2003		2004–2009	
	Growth	Share	Growth	Share	Growth	Share
Agriculture	2.7	17.1	3.2	15.2	3.5	14.0
Mining	6.2	8.7	1.4	9.8	1.5	10.6
Mfg	13.0	21.7	5.9	24.5	5.0	22.8
Utilities	14.0	1.2	7.4	0.8	8.6	0.9
Construction	13.7	7.6	5.5	6.0	7.7	7.9
Trade	7.9	16.6	4.9	16.4	6.5	14.8
Transportation	6.8	5.7	7.2	3.6	5.5	3.8
Communication	18.9	1.1	14.5	1.7	25.6	2.7
Finance	9.3	8.7	6.2	8.4	6.8	7.9
Services	3.1	8.9	3.4	9.6	5.9	10.1
GDP	**7.9**	**100.0**	**4.5**	**100.0**	**5.6**	**100.0**

Source: CEIC Asia Database.

Note: Mfg: Manufacturing sector excluding oil and gas.

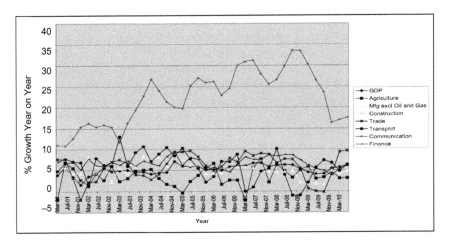

Figure 9.1 Sectoral GDP growth 2001–10

Source: CEIC Asia Database.

to around 4.5 per cent. Other sectors could not compensate since the slowdown took place uniformly across sectors.

The reason behind the slow growth of manufacturing can be explained by the same factors that make investment grow slowly, namely, deterioration of business climate, policy uncertainty and labor market rigidity.[1] Intense competition from cheap low-end manufacturing products from China may also be an

Table 9.2 Non-oil manufacturing average growth (p.a.)

ISIC	Average Growth p.a. Year on Year								
	2001	2002	2003	2004	2005	2006	2007	2008	2009
Food	1.1	0.2	2.7	1.4	2.7	7.2	5.1	2.3	11.3
Textile	3.4	3.2	6.2	4.1	1.3	1.2	–3.7	–3.6	0.5
Wood	0.5	0.6	1.2	–2.1	–0.9	–0.7	–1.7	3.5	–1.5
Paper	–4.8	5.3	8.4	7.6	2.4	2.1	5.8	–1.5	6.3
Chemicals	0.5	4.7	10.7	9.0	8.8	4.5	5.7	4.5	1.5
Non-metal	19.1	6.6	7.1	9.5	3.8	0.5	3.4	–1.5	–0.6
Basic-iron	–1.0	–1.3	–8.0	–2.6	–3.7	4.7	1.7	–2.1	–4.5
Machinery	17.2	18.1	8.9	17.7	12.4	7.5	9.7	9.8	–2.9
Others	12.6	–11.1	17.7	12.8	2.6	3.6	–2.8	–1.0	3.1
All	**4.9**	**5.7**	**6.0**	**7.5**	**5.9**	**5.3**	**5.2**	**4.0**	**2.5**
	Fraction of Share								
Food	0.33	0.31	0.30	0.28	0.27	0.28	0.28	0.27	0.30
Textile	0.14	0.13	0.13	0.13	0.12	0.12	0.11	0.10	0.10
Wood	0.06	0.06	0.05	0.05	0.05	0.04	0.04	0.04	0.04
Paper	0.05	0.05	0.06	0.06	0.05	0.05	0.05	0.05	0.05
Chemicals	0.12	0.12	0.13	0.13	0.13	0.13	0.13	0.13	0.13
Non-metal	0.03	0.03	0.04	0.04	0.04	0.03	0.03	0.03	0.03
Basic-iron	0.03	0.02	0.02	0.02	0.02	0.02	0.02	0.02	0.01
Machinery	0.23	0.26	0.27	0.29	0.31	0.32	0.33	0.35	0.33
Others	0.01	0.01	0.01	0.01	0.01	0.01	0.01	0.01	0.01

Source: CEIC Asia Database.

important factor. The appreciation of exchange rate due to capital inflows makes things more difficult for manufacturing.

Table 9.2 gives useful information regarding the manufacturing dynamic. In terms of value-added generation, machinery and food are almost always at the top. The dynamic is here too. Within a short time, in the post-crisis era, the position of food as value-added generator slowly is being edged by machinery. In 2009 the share of machinery within non-oil manufacturing was 33 per cent while food contributes to about 30 per cent of the total value added. These two branches along with chemicals and textiles comprise about 60 per cent or more of the non-oil manufacturing value added, so any poor performance of the manufacturing sector can be traced back to them. Other sectors are either too small or static or both to have significant impact on manufacturing growth.

After reaching its peak in 2004, manufacturing growth continued to decline which accelerated during the 2008 Global Financial Crisis or GFC (Table 9.2). The growth immediately fell to 4.0 and 2.5 per cent in 2008 and 2009, respectively, from 5.2 per cent in 2007. In 2008 the two mainstays of manufacturing, machinery and food, were resilient enough, with 9.8 and 2.3 per cent growth, respectively, while others with wood and chemicals as exceptions recorded negative growth. In the following year machinery eventually yielded with a negative growth of minus 2.9 per cent, while food did very well with exceptional growth of 11.3 per cent. Adding up all of these together resulted in a low, albeit positive, growth of 2.5 per cent for non-oil manufacturing because due to its sheer weight, it was difficult to fully compensate for the loss in machinery.

Despite a good development in machinery Indonesia is still locked in the specialization of low value-added products like shoes, low-end textiles and garments and so on. Other modern manufacturing branches like chemicals, non-metallic and basic metals are experiencing stagnation or a steady state situation with virtually constant shares from year to year. Some countries like South Korea and Taiwan have successfully graduated from low value-added producers to manufacturers of higher-value products with higher technology content. South Korea has even embarked on high technology products in electronics.

The story for Indonesia, however, is a little different. After having successfully undergone the first phase of export-oriented industrialization, the next phase of economic development would prove to be more difficult. Sooner or later the export-oriented development model based on cheap labor surplus with basic education would exhaust its potential as economic progress will drive wages and labor aspirations up. One plausible reason behind the slowdown of manufacturing is the nature of the products in that they are basically destined for low-end consumption and have relied on low-cost labor to be competitively priced. The erosion of competitiveness took place at a time when there was an increase in competition from other lower-cost producers such as China, Bangladesh, Sri Lanka, India and Vietnam (Pangestu, 1996). The natural solution is to move up the ladder, by moving to higher value-added products which could sustain higher wages.

One way to graduate from a low value-added producer into a higher position in the value chain is through innovations. One of the common misconceptions of innovations in developing countries is that any R&D activities are 'too advanced' or at least not yet relevant for the development process. R&D activities are considered as too luxurious for countries in the early stages of the development process where incomes are still low and the non-existence of modern sector beyond the primary sectors.

This however is no longer true. Between these two opposing views on innovations described above, some prefer to adopt a middle ground stance that globalization allows developing countries to jump up the learning curve without having to undergo the lengthy and expensive process of discovery so R&D does not necessarily have to be doing something sophisticated that is not immediately applicable to the real world. It could be a simple R&D – by accessing ideas and technologies developed elsewhere and putting them into practice after some modification (Bloom, 2002). In the next section we look into the nature of R&D activities in the large and medium sector of Indonesian manufacturing.

III.   R&D activities and globalization in Indonesian manufacturing

In this section we look the main data sets – the annual survey of large and medium manufacturing firms – to examine R&D activities and globalization. The biggest problem is that the data do not contain innovations per se, what is available R&D expenditure. Under this condition, one particular avenue to get around the problem is to model R&D expenditure as a conditional input-demand function representing innovation- generating activity.

The manufacturing data sets mentioned above are available from 1980 to 2007. So potentially one can construct a long panel data to study the dynamic of R&D activities. Unfortunately R&D expenditure is only recorded intermittently for the years 1995, 1996, 1997, 1999, 2000 and 2006 – nothing is before 1995.[2] A quick glimpse suggests that the R&D events are such a rarity that from the total of the combined sample from 1995 to 2006, the overall percentage of firms doing R&D rarely exceeds 8 per cent, which only happened in 1997 and 2006 (Table 9.3).

In observing the data sets, in particular we want to know the main motivation behind doing R&D. It is known that at the present stage of technology maturity, R&D has not been an important factor in affecting competitiveness (Kuncoro, 2002). Even if R&D activities do exist, mostly they are in the form of process innovation. Process innovation involves a substantially improved or new production process through the introduction of new process equipment or re-engineering of operational process. There are three situations where process innovation may take place: setting up a new production line, putting in a new production system and putting in new computer or information technology components to upgrade production facilities (Kraemer and Dedrick, 2000).

Table 9.3 R&D versus no R&D

Year	No R&D (%)	R&D (%)	Number of firms
1995	92.4	7.4	21,530
1996	92.8	7.2	22,969
1997	91.7	8.3	22,355
1999	94.7	5.3	20,445
2000	93.9	6.1	21,762
2006	91.2	8.8	29,421

Source: Calculated from the Annual Manufacturing Surveys.

Table 9.4 Firms investing in new machinery and R&D

Year	No New Machinery Investment		New Investment in Machinery	
	% Firms Doing R&D	Number of Firms	% Firms Doing R&D	Number of Firms
1995	5.4	18,246 (84.7%)	19.6	3,284 (15.3%)
1997	6.5	19,401 (86.6%)	20.3	2,954 (13.4%)
1999	3.5	17,347 (85.2%)	15.1	3,007 (14.8%)
2000	4.5	18,622 (85.8%)	15.3	3,100 (14.2%)
2006	5.6	25,342 (86.1%)	10.4	4,079 (13.9%)

Source: Calculated from the Annual Manufacturing Surveys.

The purchase of new capital equipment can be categorized as process innovation if it involves a new production process or at least it brings improvement in the production process. So a common occurrence is R&D activities taking place after new machinery is installed. To examine this, we tabulate new machinery investment and the incidence of R&D. The results are presented in Table 9.4.

For all years under observation firms making new investments in machinery are more likely to do R&D. In 1995 for example only 5.4 per cent of firms with no new machinery investment undergo R&D. The corresponding figure for firms with new machinery investment is almost four times higher at 19.6 per cent. For both investing and non-investing firms, the Asian economic crises obviously have significant impact on R&D activities. For investing firms the likelihood to do R&D declined ever since and it had not yet recovered in 2006 with a low figure of 10.4 per cent. The figures for non-investing firms are virtually flat. So if there is no new machinery investment – R&D must also be driven by something else like packaging, sales and so on. Investment in new machinery is only made after careful thought. Since the investment cost is sunk a careful consideration must be made taking into account business uncertainty and future profits; in effect it makes investment in machinery more volatile. Whatever the trend of the likelihood of doing R&D, Table 9.4 suggests that there is a relationship between new investment in machinery and doing R&D.

As mentioned above, it is hypothesized that a more intense competition as a result of globalization may force firms to do more R&D. For this we repeat the above simple analysis to two variables representing globalization, namely, being exporters and being FDI firms (Table 9.5 and Table 9.6).

Being an FDI is almost three times more likely to pursue R&D. In 1995 the percentage of FDI firms with R&D was 18.6 per cent in contrast to 7.1 per cent for non-FDI. The percentage of FDI firms doing R&D reaches its peak in 1997 just a year before the Asian crisis. Similar as the observed pattern before, the likelihood for FDI firms to do R&D fell after the Asian crisis almost by half (Table 9.5). Interestingly, the figures for non-FDI firms dropped only in 2000 – the number is practically the same for all other years. One logical explanation is that since R&D

Table 9.5 FDI firms and R&D

Year	Non-FDI Firms		FDI Firms	
	% Firms Doing R&D	Total Number of Non-FDI Firms	% Firms Doing R&D	Total Number of FDI Firms
1995	7.1	20,657 (95.9%)	18.6	873 (4.1%)
1996	6.7	21,988 (95.7%)	18.7	980 (4.3%)
1997	6.7	21,254 (95.1%)	20.9	1,101 (4.9%)
1999	7.7	18,926 (93.0%)	10.6	1,428 (7.0%)
2000	4.8	20,028 (92.0%)	13.1	1,734 (8.0%)
2006	8.7	27,252 (92.8%)	10.1	2,169 (7.2%)

Source: Calculated from the Annual Manufacturing Surveys

Table 9.6 Exporting firms and R&D

Year	Non-exporters		Exporters	
	% Firms Doing R&D	Total Number of Non-exporters	% Firms Doing R&D	Total Number of Exporters
1995	6.1	17,907 (83.2%)	15.1	3,623 (13.0%)
1996	5.5	18,614 (81.0%)	14.6	4,354 (19.0%)
1997	7.3	19,298 (86.3%)	14.8	3,057 (13.7%)
1999	3.9	17,553 (86.2%)	13.6	2,801 (13.8%)
2000	4.3	18,187 (83.6%)	13.0	3,575 (16.4%)
2006	8.5	24,422 (82.3%)	10.4	5,199 (17.7%)

Source: Calculated from the Annual Manufacturing Surveys.

is related to new machinery investment, the figure is less volatile for those that are less likely to make an investment, namely, non-FDI firms.

Table 9.6 shows how export is related to R&D activities. Manufacturing is dominated by non-exporters, which account for about 80 per cent of total firms. Definitely, exporting firms are more likely to do R&D. But like in the previous analysis, the likelihood to R&D diminishes after the crisis and by 2006 it has still yet to recover. To summarize there are three factors that may drive firms to do R&D: making a new machinery investment, being FDI and being exporters, all of which may be interrelated. To disentangle this we have to wait for a formal econometric analysis.

The above analysis yields the likelihood of firms to commit R&D but not the propensity or intensity to do R&D. To measure the intensity we use the ratio of R&D expenditures to the value of total inputs in percentage. The results are shown in Table 9.7. Of all figures, none of them is higher than 1.5 per cent. Interestingly for all variables supposedly to represent globalization namely, export orientation and FDI, the results do show that firms facing globalization

Table 9.7 Percentage of R&D expenditures to the value of total inputs

Category	Year		
	1995	*2000*	*2006*
Non-exporters	1.05	1.29	0.44
Exporters	0.88	0.87	0.70
No investment in new machinery	1.05	1.23	0.46
With investment in new machinery	0.90	0.92	0.65
No FDI firms	1.02	1.05	0.47
FDI firms	0.72	1.47	0.70
All firms	0.99	1.12	0.49

Source: Calculated from the Annual Manufacturing Surveys.

are not necessarily possessing higher intensity to do RD. Globalization may increase the likelihood or the incidence to do R&D but it does not necessarily mean at a high level.[3] Higher levels of R&D regardless of denominator used may indicate sophistication so these small values suggest that even if there are any, R&D activities may be directed only for simple activities. Another interesting observation is the observed turnaround in 2006 where in the categories of export orientation and FDI versus non-FDI, all respective firms have higher intensity to do R&D compared to their non-exporter and/or non-FDI counterparts, though all are at lower percentages. The Asian crises have lowered intensity of R&D in all categories. The same pattern can also be observed for firms with new machinery investment versus those without it.

R&D intensity across manufacturing branches

Intensity to do R&D certainly will differ from one industry to another. To provide more detailed pictures across manufacturing we redo the above exercise across two digits ISIC across manufacturing (Figure 9.2).

Overall, the intensity to do R&D declined after the Asian crisis. Taking out the outlier from paper (ISIC 34), both basic metal (ISIC 37) and machinery (ISIC 38) have the highest R&D intensity. Still, the figures are low, for example in 2006 none of them exceeds 1 per cent. One possible explanation is that since R&D is a risky adventure, the Asian crises have made firms more cautious. The other explanation links R&D decisions to that of new machinery investment since most R&D are done in the preparation of installing new machinery/ technology. With the same logic, since investing in new machinery in the face of a sluggish economy in the aftermath of the Asian crisis is a risky venture, R&D will also be affected.

Figure 9.3 divides the sample into exporter versus non-exporter category. The decrease of R&D intensity is also observed when comparing 1995 to 2006,

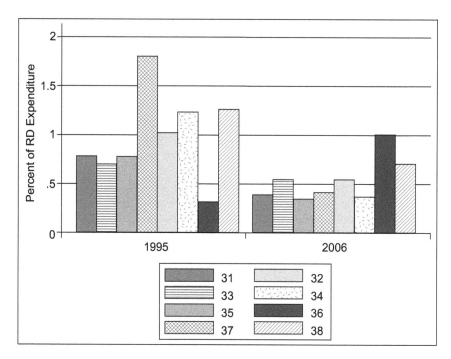

Figure 9.2 Per cent of R&D to input across industries

Source: Calculated from the Annual Manufacturing Surveys.

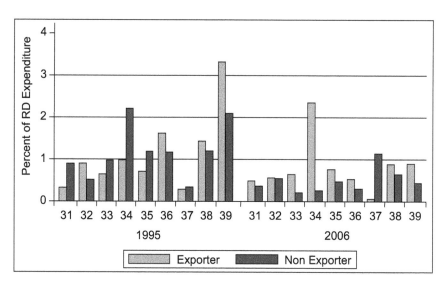

Figure 9.3 Per cent of R&D to input across industries

Source: Calculated from the Annual Manufacturing Surveys.

but the decrease for exporters is less pronounced than non-exporters. In 1995 non-exporters in food (ISIC 31), woods (ISIC 33), paper (ISIC 34), chemicals (ISIC 35) and basic metal (ISIC 39) recorded higher R&D propensity. But the situation is reversed after the crisis. It appears that in the face of increasing uncertainty, exporters facing competition abroad have to maintain minimum level or intensity of R&D expenditures which happen to be higher than non-exporting firms. One exception is heavily capital-intensive basic metal (ISIC 37) of which the steel industry is included. Even when the overall figures are declining between 1995 and 2006, non-exporters have always higher R&D propensity.

When comparing FDI versus non-FDI, there is no apparent clear pattern (Figure 9.4). The pattern is very noisy. For example in 1995 for food (ISIC 31), woods (ISIC 33), paper (ISIC 34), non-metallic (ISIC 36) and machinery (ISIC 38), the R&D intensity is higher for non-FDI. It is completely the opposite in 2006. For the rest the pattern is just as blurred. So unlike the case of being exporters being FDI may not be a strong driver behind R&D.

Next we turn to investment in machinery as a prime driver for R&D activities (Figure 9.5). In 1995 the pattern is less clear, but in 2006 with basic metal (ISIC 37) as a clear exception, in almost all other industries, machinery-investing firms tend to have higher R&D intensity. So in addition of a higher likelihood to do R&D (Table 9.4), the level of R&D expenditure is also relatively higher,

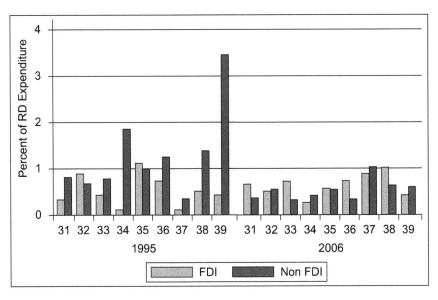

Figure 9.4 Per cent of R&D to input across industries: FDI vs. non-FDI
Source: Calculated from the Annual Manufacturing Surveys.

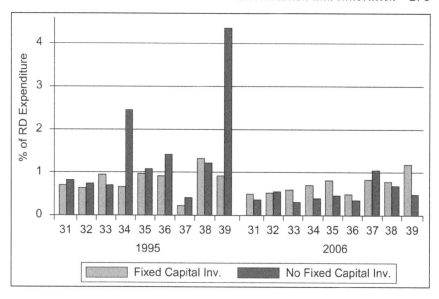

Figure 9.5 Per cent of R&D expenditures to input

Source: Calculated from the Annual Manufacturing Surveys.

which indicates a strong case for new machinery investment as a primary reason behind doing R&D.

Effective rate of protection

One way for a government to protect certain sectors from global competition is through tariff protection. This barrier will influence industry's relative profitability by creating an artificial price wedge. How the protection will affect R&D cannot be determined a priori. If the market is contestable enough then the extra profit can be recycled into R&D activities to boost firms' future profits once the protection is eventually lifted. On the other hand, high artificial profits could provide little incentive for firms to do R&D. Which forces are going to prevail is a matter of empirical analysis.

To measure this we mimic the concept of effective rate of protection (ERP) as in Amiti and Konings (2007).

$$erp_{it}^k = \frac{(tariff_t^k - \alpha_{it}^k inputtariff_t^k)}{(1 - \alpha_{it}^k)} \tag{1}$$

Where is the ratio of inputs to output for firm i in industry k at time t. A lower output tariff would decrease the protection received by industry k, while a lower input tariff would increase the protection received by industry k.

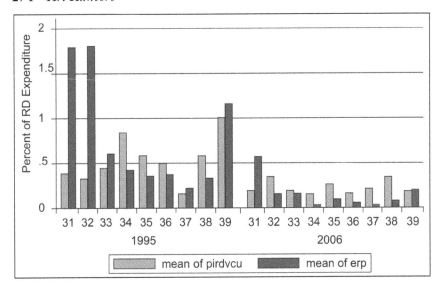

Figure 9.6 Per Cent of R&D versus ERP

Source: Calculated from the Annual Manufacturing Surveys.

To examine their possible relationship between the R&D intensity and ERP, we compare the per cent of R&D expenditures in total inputs to ERP in Figure 9.6.

The overall pattern suggests that the percentage of R&D expenditure declined after the Asian crisis. But one thing is clear that higher ERP is associated with higher intensity to do R&D. Lowering protection has encouraged firms to do R&D in order to stay competitive. If R&D is tied to new machinery investment then it is more likely directed to upgrade technology to boost competitiveness in the face of increasing competition from abroad.

Information spillover

Spatial centralization of resources and spatial concentration of manufacturing in a few of the largest metropolitan areas has been the hallmark of the modern economy. Centralization of industrial location at least in the early stages may bring benefits to firms (Hansen, 1990). One important benefit of agglomeration is cross-fertilization among firms conducting R&D creating a synergy that collectively improves their individual productivity. In this regard there are two types of 'positive' externalities. First is localization, in this respect knowledge is learned from their own industry, which in the dynamic form, is often called Marshall-Arrow-Romer (MAR) externalities. Alternatively, firms learn from all firms in a city, where the diversity of local industries enhance the local information environment. This type of externalities is called urbanization or in the dynamic context is termed Jacobs' externalities (Jacobs, 1969).

Which type of externalities is actually stronger for R&D in Indonesia is a matter of empirical investigation. If externalities are in the form of localization, smaller cities are more likely to be the places of R&D activities specializing in just one industry or closely connected industries. On the other hand if the externalities happen to be urbanization in nature, to advance R&D activities need to find a location in a diverse and large urban environment. R&D activities are therefore more likely to be found in large urban areas. Another related question is whether externalities are mainly static or dynamic. If it turns out that externalities are dynamic, then there is a systematic relationship between R&D past activities and the present productivity since a large body of knowledge will be accumulated over time in a particular location. The implication for R&D is that firms doing R&D would become more 'static' – tied to a particular industrial agglomeration – less willing to relocate to cities where historically R&D has never been present, and thus have no built-up stock of knowledge.

Localization/MAR externalities will be measured by total employment in the own industry in the respective districts. This measure is intended to capture interaction among firms within a district. Urbanization externalities are measured by a diversity index. For district i for example, the index of diversity is

$$g_i^s = \sum_{j=1}^{J} \left[\frac{E_{ij}(t)}{E_i(t)} - \frac{E_j(t)}{E(t)} \right]^2 \tag{2}$$

$E(t)$ is total national manufacturing employment and $E_j(t)$ is total national employment in industry j. Meanwhile, E_i and E_{ij} are the corresponding local magnitudes. The measure of urbanization economies $g_i^s(t)$ has a minimum value of zero, where in a district, each industry's share of local manufacturing employment is exactly the same as its national share, so the district is completely unspecialized because its industrial composition is just a replication of the nation. At the other end of spectrum, the maximum value of $g_i^s(t)$ will approach two for a district completely specialized in one industry, while at the same time national employment is concentrated in another industry. The higher is $g_i^s(t)$ the lower is the diversity, thus a district becomes more specialized.

To get better insight of the location pattern of R&D activities we compare the per cent of R&D expenditure to index of diversity given in (2) across industry. For easy exposition we choose the year 1995 and 2006. The result is shown in Figure 9.7.

Although the pattern is somewhat blurred in 1995, the overall relationship suggests that industry with higher R&D percentage tends to locate in a location with lower diversity index or less specialized location, usually in larger urban areas with a bigger, more diversified economy. Since previously it has been noted that most R&D are geared for preparing new investments in machinery and equipment (Figure 9.5), this type of R&D may need only general information

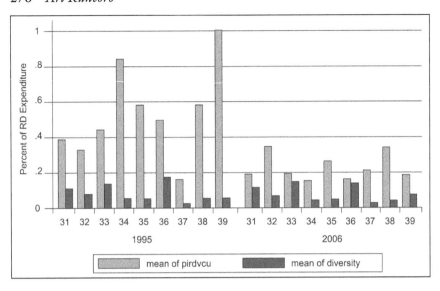

Figure 9.7 Per cent of R&D vs. diversity index
Source: Calculated from the Annual Manufacturing Surveys.

(market of capital goods, delivery time, general specification, after sales service and so on) from its industrial surrounding.

IV.   Direction of causality: from exports to R&D or from R&D to exports

Earlier we have argued for being exporters or going into export markets as a behavioral proxy for a globalization. As an issue here is whether exporting firms do learn from their activities in export markets or firms have to be innovative first i.e. doing R&D before they can go into foreign markets. Empirically, this is tantamount to investigate the direction of causality between export and R&D.

To examine this, after controlling for firm location and characteristics as well as industry and time fixed effects, we first regress firms' export on R&D and afterward reverse the regression. One after another exports and R&D along with output per labor are treated as endogenous – this necessitates the use of 2SLS method. The results are presented in Table 9.8.

We do not perform a formal causality test here, but from observing the Wald Chi-square value it is clear that the regressions where export is the dependent variable are stronger than when it is replaced by R&D expenditure. Furthermore, in the export regression R&D is positive and strongly significant at the 5 per cent level irrespective of whether time and industry dummies are included or not. In the reversed version where R&D expenditure becomes the dependent variable, export is not significant. So firms have to do R&D first to become

Table 9.8 Direction of causality between export and R&D (2SLS results)

Variable	Log (Export)		Log (R&D Expenditure)	
	Model 1	Model 2	Model 1	Model 2
Log(Output per labor)	2.50 **[7.11]	2.84 **[7.39]	0.04 **[2.37]	0.05 **[2.52]
Log(RD Expenditure)	3.39 **[4.26]	2.58 *[4.31]	– –	– –
Log(Export)	– –	– –	0.01 [0.83]	0.004 [0.66]
FDI Dummy	0.68 **[8.45]	0.65 **[8.01]	0.01 [0.81]	0.01 [0.70]
Effective Rate of Protection	0.00 [1.35]	0.00 [1.31]	–0.00 [–1.23]	–0.00 [–1.14]
New Investment in Machinery	0.43 **[11.85]	0.43 **[12.02]	0.01 **[2.90]	0.01 **[2.86]
Local Manufacturing Diversity (5 years lag)	0.31 **[2.16]	0.26 **[2.05]	–0.004 **[–1.97]	0.004 **[–2.25]
Log(Manufacturing Employment) (5 years lag)	0.01 **[2.25]	0.004 [0.99]	0.0004 **[3.81]	0.0003 *[1.95]
Industrial Dummies	No	Yes	No	Yes
Time Dummies	No	Yes	No	Yes
Wald Chi–Square	**443.27	**961.57	**71.40	**120.46
Number of Observation	109712	109712	109712	109712

competitive in the foreign market. The reverse, however, is not true. Since R&D is tied to new investment in machinery, presumably firms only need general information from the market as inputs to R&D process but not those of consumer and product specific.

Looking at other covariates, the dummy for new investment in machinery is positive and significant in all specifications with smaller coefficient in the R&D equation. The FDI dummy is only positive and significant in the export equation so FDI firms are more likely to have higher export. The R&D equation, however, suggests that FDI firms have done very little in R&D activities. The coefficient for the FDI dummy is very weak statistically. Effective rate of protection representing globalization at the 'macro' level has never been significant which is plausible given the fact that EPR is on its downward trend.

The coefficient of local manufacturing diversity is positive and significant for the export equation suggesting that export activities are more likely to happen in locations specialized in one or a few industries. This is in contrast with the R&D equation where the coefficient is negative and significant which points to more diversified, presumably urban areas, as the location of R&D activities. The coefficient of the log of employment is positive and significant except in the export equation where the control for industry and time fixed effects is included.

This suggests that localization forces which make industries concentrate in smaller cities are also at play. But judging from the magnitude of the coefficient and its statistical power, the forces of urbanization are still dominant. Since for export activity the direction of the diversity index and the localization is the same, in the future export-oriented firms will tend to concentrate more on smaller cities. One worry is that if R&D continues to locate in urban areas then there will be divergence between export and R&D activities. If R&D continues to be in house this means exporters are less and less relying on R&D for their competitiveness, which may imply they continue to specialize in low value-added products. In the modern concept of firm headquarters versus branch or production decentralization, there is the possibility, however, that R&D and production or export activities are not necessarily in the same location.

V. Conclusion

In this chapter we examine the impact of globalization on innovation in Indonesian manufacturing. The lack of innovation data in the manufacturing survey has necessitated the use of R&D expenditure as an input in the innovation production function. Globalization is represented by being exporters, FDI and effective rate of protection (EPR). The analysis is set up such that within the concept R&D as conditional input demand function.

The first important finding is that there is a relationship between new investment in machinery and doing R&D. The purchase of new capital equipment can be categorized as process innovation so R&D may be focused only on adapting new machinery to the prevailing condition in Indonesia. This suggests that some upgrading has indeed been taking place which brings improvement in the production process. One policy implication that emerges from this is that an improvement of business climate that make it easier for firms to improve their production processes would induce firms to do R&D that raises firm ability to compete globally.

In terms of globalization variables we find that there is a relationship between being exporters and committing resources to do R&D. Meanwhile the relationship between FDI firms and doing R&D is only on the incidence but not on the intensity of R&D. This phenomenon is also found for exporters. So for all variables supposedly to represent globalization, namely, export orientation and FDI, the results do show that firms facing globalization are not necessarily possessing higher propensity to do R&D. Globalization may increase the likelihood or the incidence to do R&D but it does not necessarily mean at a high level.

Also lower ERP would induce firms to spend more on R&D. So lowering protection or trade barriers will have a positive impact on R&D. But the main motivation to do R&D is in preparation for the installation of new machinery and equipment. Through this avenue the impact of globalization may come indirectly from the desire of firms to remain competitive by upgrading their machinery and equipment.

With regard to information spillover R&D activities are more likely to be found in less specialized industrial or economic agglomeration presumably in larger and diverse urban areas but not in smaller cities. This is consistent with the earlier finding that the primary motivation for R&D in Indonesia is for adaptation, accommodation and perhaps some modification of new machinery and equipment to meet operational conditions in Indonesia so the type of information needed is a general one and not a specific one associated with consumer needs. One policy implication from this is to maximize the gains from the current configuration of industrial agglomeration and minimize the negative externalities by improving the connectivity between agglomerations.

Notes

1 With the successive increases of national minimum wages, this competitiveness of Indonesian labor-intensive exports seemed to be eroded. From 1994–96, garment firms in particular had been hard hit by the sharp increase in minimum wages and changes in wage regulations pertaining to temporary and permanent workers (Kuncoro and Resosudarmo, 2006).
2 Although potentially one can construct a balanced panel data, the main hurdle is to link data sets before 2000 to that of 2006. We find that the firm identifiers are unreliable to link the same firms from different years. So at best one can use the data sets in a pooled fashion.
3 In our terminology the likelihood to do R&D irrespective of how much firms spend on it, while propensity is the percentage of R&D expenditure to the value of inputs which indicates 'level'.

10 Indonesia's democracy and decentralization in the post-1997 era

Maria Monica Wihardja

I. Introduction

Indonesia has historically been suffering from institutional issues since the Dutch colonial period in the 1830s: extractive and coercive institutions were introduced with the forced Cultivation System (1830–70); guided and socialist institutions during the Soekarno presidency characterized by a blend of nationalism, religion and communism; and predatory institutions during the New Order with a rise of rent-seeking behaviours, corruption, collusion and cronyism. The 'big bang' democratization and decentralization in 1999 (introduced only in 2001) posed new problems in the *Reformasi* period (the period after the fall of the 32-year dictatorship of Soeharto), including a fragmented and unstable presidential and multi-party parliamentary system, an increase of local inter-ethnic and inter-religious conflicts and violence, proliferation of autonomous district/municipalities, decentralized corruption and widespread local capture. The post-Soeharto government seems to be shadowed by a mix of the old and new oligarchic forces.

'Yet on balance, Indonesian democracy is more stable, more advanced and more deeply rooted in society than most observers would have expected in 1998' (Meitzer, 2013: 7). The next challenge is to ensure the consolidation of democracy, and not the persistency of or even the reversal to old institutional issues that have brought the Soeharto regime to a downfall. Decentralization must strive to bring local policies and local public goods closer and better to the people.

In this chapter, democratization and decentralization in the *Reformasi* period will be widely discussed. Relevant literatures on some of these issues will be reviewed. A question on why Indonesian democracy has not yet embraced the liberal democratic values but is still electoral and procedural is explored. Moreover, decentralization that seems to have failed to bring policies and public good provisions closer to people is also analyzed through a series of literatures on local political economy, economic performance with and without decentralization and endogenous institutions. Policy recommendations will be laid out in the concluding remarks.

II. Multiple meanings of institutions

The definition of institutions is broad and multiple. Here are some examples:

Preferences + institutions + physical possibilities = outcomes.

(Plott, 1979)

The alternative equilibrium standards of behaviour or conventions of behaviour that evolve from a given game described by its rules; properties of the equilibrium of games and not properties of the game's description; what the agents do with the rules of the game, not what the rules are.

(Schotter, 1981)

Reformulating Plott's equation:
Structure of an action situation + model of a decision maker = outcomes   (1)
Rules + physical laws + behavioural laws = structure of an action situation   (2)

(Ostrom, 1986)

Rules of the game as defined by three elements: formal rules, informal constraints, and enforcement.

(North, 1990)

A system that consists of rules, beliefs, norms, implied behaviours, players [or] organization that are in equilibrium.

(Greif, 2006)

In its simplest form, institutions can be compared to 'body organs', which need to function well in order for the whole body system to be in a healthy condition. All of the above authors' definitions fit the analogy of the body organs. The game-theoretical or equilibrium concept of institution as that of Schotter (1981) and Greif (2006) – it is a system in equilibrium – helps to explain why some institutions work and others do not work in order to improve a country's welfare. With the equilibrium definition of institution, we can use the behavioural argument of which institutions are functioning institutions, e.g. those with good rules, which are being obeyed and no one has an incentive to disobey, and which institutions are non-functioning institutions, e.g. those with good rules, but are continuously being violated or are simply being ignored, resulting in illegality. People react to incentives, and this allows us to study the strategic behaviour of individuals given the incentives and informational structures of their society. Ostrom's equation agrees in substance with Schotter's and Greif's definition of institution.

For the above reasons, we will generally define an institution as defined by Greif (2006): *a system in equilibrium*. It involves not only rules of the game (both formal and informal rules such as social norms) but also players who are essentially anyone and everyone who is in the system. It is worth noting that an individual is not narrow-mindedly defined as a selfish individual who maximizes her or his utility, as often assumed in many economic textbooks, but an individual is also an altruistic being with *other-regardingness* traits. A long-established institution is a state of equilibrium.

III.   Properties of institutions: endogeneity and multiplicity of equilibria

One interesting property of institutions is multiplicity of equilibria. Multiplicity of equilibria in the context of institutions means that there is no unique outcome that comes out from a certain incentive structure. This also means that two different institutions can arrive at the same outcome without necessarily having the same institutional trajectory. This is why studying institutions must involve both deductive and inductive methods done iteratively. A lot of times, it must also involve historical analysis.

Changing an equilibrium is not only about changing rules (such as revising regulations) or changing players (such as removing officials from office) alone. If the whole incentive structure is to change, it must also involve changing beliefs or expectations in order to arrive at a new equilibrium. Myrdal (1944: 77) wrote, 'a rational policy will never work by changing only one factor'. Basu (2010) talks about act versus rule sequentialism in which banning an act (such as not allowing an under-age child to work) is not the same as banning a class of actions (such as imposing a child labor policy). In the latter case, he argues, a society can move from one equilibrium (poor children working, increased labor supply, lower adult wages, poorer society) to another equilibrium (poor children attending school, reduced labor supply, higher adult wages, richer society). The question of how to move from the 'bad' equilibrium to the 'good' equilibrium is subtle.

Another interesting property of institutions is endogenity, which is reiterated by Myrdal (1944) and North (1990). In Myrdal's *An American Dilemma* (Myrdal, 1944), in what he called 'the theory of the vicious cycle', Myrdal argued that white prejudice and discrimination kept the Negro oppressed and more oppressions in turn exacerbated white prejudice. Moreover, he argued that the original change of either white prejudice or Negro oppression could set a different future trajectory that spirals either upward or downward. North (1990: 134–135) wrote:

> What makes for efficient markets? If poor countries are poor because they are the victims of an institutional structure that prevents growth, is that institutional structure imposed from without or is it endogenously determined or is it some combination of both? . . . Still to be undertaken is systematic empirical work that will identify the costs and underlying institutions that make economies unproductive.
>
> (North, 1990: 134–135)

The endogeneity of institutions may result in a 'middle-income trap' (Dixit, 2004) in which middle-income countries such as Indonesia, India and China may be trapped with a moderate degree of economic prosperity but with poor institutions and growing inequality. Or it may be trapped with an incomplete structural transformation to higher-productivity sectors before the population ages or the demographic dividend ends.

Because of the endogeneity of institutions, it is very easy to see that welfare and institutions may evolve to create either a virtuous cycle in which high welfare evolves with good quality institutions, or a vicious cycle in which low welfare evolves with low quality institutions. A persistent vicious cycle may lead to a revolution by citizens who suffer from high poverty and unemployment as well as corruption. Tunisia, Egypt and other Middle Eastern countries in early 2011 experienced such a revolution precisely because of some of these factors.

In the next sections, Indonesian political and economic institutions and how some of the above-mentioned theoretical conjectures about institutions, such as endogeneity of institutions and multiplicity of equilbria, apply will be discussed. Institutions are path-dependent and there is a need to conduct historical studies on past institutions. Institutions during the colonial, Soekarno, and Soeharto eras, mostly drawn from the work of Thee (2008a), Thee (2009), Thee (2010a), and Thee (2010b) will be reviewed to better understand the evolution of institutions that are path-dependent.

IV. Indonesian institutions: historical analysis

Interactive, deductive, inductive, context-specific and evidence-based model complemented by comparative, counterfactual and historical analysis is the method to study institutions proposed by Greif (2006). Since existing institutions are more often evolving rather than created, i.e. they are path-dependent, historical studies on institutions become important. A case in point is the deep-rooted extractive tendency: "Institutions and practices of extraction, leading to regressive distribution of assets, income and wealth, have been sustained during the post-colonial era. . . . The abuse of public resources by rent-seeking elites (including those during the Soeharto era), has been a constant factor in Indonesian history and the Dutch colonial rule set the example in its most extreme form" (Thee, 2013: 57). Indonesia continues to rely on its rich natural resources to support the economy. By 2013, two-thirds of Indonesia's gross exports rely on natural-resource-based products – mainly coal and palm oil export, and half of which are raw commodities. The current heavy reliance on natural resources is similar to that during the Dutch colonial period. Economic nationalism in which economic policies were designed to counterbalance the dominance of the Dutch and ethnic Chinese over the indigenous people also persisted (Thee, 2010b).

Extractive institutions in the colonial period of the Netherland East Indies (1830s–1945)

The Banda islands in Maluku hide a major historical importance of Indonesia today. As the only source of the world's supply of nutmeg (and nutmeg was more valuable than gold by weight then) and mace in the Middle Ages, the

Banda islands became the driving force behind the early history of colonialism in the East Indies from the 16th century onwards (Milne, 2011). After an island swap between England and the Dutch, in which the Dutch relinquished its control of Manhattan in exchange for the British-controlled islands of Banda, the Dutch gained sovereignty over all the Banda islands. So, Indonesian islands had been known and probably would always be known as treasure islands. Unfortunately, like many other resource-rich countries, this became more of a curse rather than a blessing for Indonesia to have such rich natural resources. Natural resources are exploited to serve the elites rather than to improve the welfare of the people as a whole and to build productive and efficient institutions.

Indonesian extractive institutions have gone back to the Dutch colonial period in the 1830s. The Cultivation System was in place to force Javanese peasants to allocate one-fifth of their lands or their labour time to cultivate profitable crops to obtain large profits to be remitted to the Dutch colonial government who was facing bankruptcy due to adverse impacts of wars in Java and elsewhere. Most important export crops were sugar, indigo and coffee. The coercive Cultivation System had adverse effects on the endogenous population, with famines spreading in Demak in 1848 and Grobogan in 1849–50 (Thee, 2010a). Under increasing pressures from Dutch private businesses keen on investing in Java, the Cultivation System was terminated in 1870.

Extractive institutions were less harsh on the poor peasants during the Liberal Era (1870–1900) but it did not lead to significant improvement in the welfare of the population (Thee, 2010a). In 1901, Queen Wilhelmina introduced Ethical Policy in the Netherland East Indies (NEI) – a name given to the Netherlands Indies government – due to a 'debt of honour' to the people of the colony for the Dutch having obtained large financial benefits from the Cultivation System. It focused on three issues: irrigation, education and emigration. However, the welfare ideology of Ethical Policy contradicted the colonial ideology. By the early 1920s, Ethical Policy was abandoned because of its failure to improve indigenous people's welfare. In the 1930s, depression hit the NEI very hard. A slight recovery after the mid-1930s came to a halt when the Japanese took over the NEI in early March 1942. New extractive institutions were introduced by the Japanese to support the war including by drafting forced labour – *romusha* – to work on infrastructure projects, such as railroads, including in other Japanese-occupied countries (e.g. Thailand).

Guided democracy and guided economy: putting politics above economics (1945–66)

In the late 1945, after Indonesia declared its independence, the Dutch army returned. Between 1945 and 1949 was the revolutionary period of sporadic and bloody armed conflicts and diplomatic struggles between Indonesia and the Dutch. On 27 December 1949, the delegations of the Indonesian revolutionary government and the Netherland government under the auspices of the

United Nations Commission on Indonesia agreed on the transfer of sovereignty, with the exception of Papua (Thee, 2011). The period between 1950 and 1955 was a period of economic recovery and nationalization of some of the Dutch institutions and enterprises as well as establishment of state-owned companies.

After the general election in 1955 failed to reach an agreement of the ideological base of the country – *Pancasila* or Islamic – the period between 1955 and 1959 was a period of political instability. Inspired by the People's Republic of China's Mao Zedong's strong leadership, President Soekarno, with the support from the military, put in place a political system known as Guided Democracy and Guided Economy in 1957. In 1959, he widened his political leadership by demolishing the legally elected Parliament and Constituent Assembly, and reinstated the Constitution of 1945 in which he became both the head of state and the head of government. Under this system, the Western-style parliamentary democracy was replaced by a form of government that was characterized by *Nas-A-Kom*, which was a blend of nationalism (*nationalisme*), religion (*agama*) and communism (*komunis*) to appease the three main factions, namely, the Army, Islamic group and the Communists. Since 1959, Indonesia did not see a state of liberal democracy until the *Reformasi* era started in 1998.

He also developed a 'Socialist Economy à la Indonesia', in which he held the view that politics came above economic policy and that political success would ultimately solve the country's economic problems (Thee, 2009). This concept – to put politics about economics – was wrong since worsening economic conditions drove people's sentiments on their government. Under his guidance, the economy fell deeply into a crisis that led to the 1965 revolution.

On Soekarno's leadership, 'Soekarno is like an ink blot test' said Kevin Fogg:

> Soekarno had a very broad and varied record when he took the reins of Indonesia in 1945, so everyone felt like they could identify with him. The left liked his talk of empowering farmers and laborers. Muslims liked his connections with Muhammadiyah (built during his time in Bengkulu and through his marriage to Fatmawati). Non-Javanese loved his Balinese roots. Urban elites liked his background as a Dutch-trained engineer. Thus, without a record of actual governance, all of the various interest groups in Indonesia were able to see Sukarno as a man who was 'probably on their side.' This mystique broke down for Soekarno when he started leading the independent government, at first in 1950 but more seriously after 1957.
>
> (Fogg, 22 November 2010)

From developmental to predatory states in the New Order period (1966–98): democracy Pancasila

The economic crisis in the early 1960s was followed by the *Gestapu* Coup on 30 September 1965, and in March 1966, Soekarno allegedly signed the *Supersemar*, which gave the then Army commander Lieutenant General Soeharto authority to restore order, but in effect gave a transfer of executive power.

Soeharto was officially sworn as the president in March 1968. With a change of power, there also came a change in the economic aspiration, policies and institutions. While Soekarno's economic institution was characterized by inward-looking, anti-Western sentiments, socialism and statist, Soeharto's economic institution was characterized by outward-looking strategies, open-door policies, capitalism and a development-focused agenda (Thee, 2008b). The economic agenda was focused on tidying up the economic mess from Soekarno's era, namely, hyperinflation, a huge budget deficit, dilapidating infrastructure and unproductive apparatus.

The economy under the New Order soon embarked on an episode of high growth and speedy socio-economic development, enabling Indonesia to 'graduate' from the 'low-income' economy to the 'lower middle-income' economy. Soekarno was often dubbed as the Father of Development. Despite the growth success, the high growth economy and miraculous development came at a cost. Because of the spread of rent-seeking behaviours and corruption that proliferated during the New Order era, Indonesian institutions had become a 'predatory state' from a 'developmental state' (Thee, 2008b). The economic fundamentals of developing Indonesia were greatly undermined by these structural and institutional issues. Economic crisis soon triggered a revolution by the oppressed and dissatisfied civil society to demand reforms in both the economic and political arena that finally toppled the 32-year authoritarian ruling of Soeharto. International pressures for reforms were also tremendous although some came at a high cost to Indonesia, such as the IMF's severe conditionality for a bail-out as stated in its Letter of Intent to the IMF.

V.   The *Reformasi* era: electoral democracy and captured decentralization

After the fall of Soeharto in 1998, Indonesia democratized and underwent a 'big-bang' political and economic decentralization in 2001. Indonesia is now the world's third-largest democracy. Democratization and decentralization came in a blink of an eye.[1] Although Indonesia had been successful in holding the first general elections and the first direct election since 1955 in 1999 and in 2004, respectively, Indonesian democracy has so far been electoral democracy.[2] Some experts call it 'collusive democracy' preferring co-option and consensus to competition ('SBY's Feet of Clay', 2002). Kristiadi, a senior political analyst at the Centre for Strategic and International Studies (CSIS), labeled Indonesian democracy as '*Demokrasi Tiwul*' (*tiwul* is an Indonesian traditional dish made of cassava, which is an inferior substitute of rice) (Kristiadi, 2011b). Another observer calls it 'democrazy' because of the proliferation of devolved authorities (districts and municipalities) and endemic money politics and political transactions ('Power to the People!', 2011). The Economist Intelligence Unit's Democracy Index 2010 ranked Indonesia at the 60th place (out of 167 countries) below Timor Leste, Papua New Guinea and Thailand, and categorized Indonesian democracy as a 'flawed democracy' ('Democracy Index 2010', 2010).

In 2005, regional governments (districts and municipalities) had their first direct local elections. Corruption by local leaders and provincial governors was rising after decentralization, which was often referred to as 'decentralized corruption' as opposed to 'centralized corruption' during the Soeharto era. As of February 2011, out of 524 local administration heads (including mayors/regents and provincial governors), 30 per cent of them were undergoing legal processes as graft suspects ('30% of Regional Heads Graft Suspects', 2011). Because of widespread local captures[3] that resulted in money politics and political transactions, the benefits of decentralization have not been optimal in improving people's welfare.

Many local-central divisions of official duties remain unclear as they are continuously being revised or created (or withdrawn), which often create legal uncertainty and ambiguous and overlapping regulations. By 2011, there were 3,080 local regulations that have been identified by the Minister of Finance as problematic and recommended to be withdrawn, but have nevertheless not yet been withdrawn (*Komite Pemantauan Pelaksanaan Otonomi Daerah*, n.d.). These problematic local regulations are likely to stay since National Law No. 28 of 2009, on local taxes and retributions, regulates that they can only be withdrawn by presidential decrees, which, due to the president's time constraint, would be unlikely to be issued promptly. This is certainly harmful to the local investment climate.

Despite the challenges, 'Indonesia has a functioning electoral democracy' (Meitzer, 2013: 6). By 2014, around 1,000 local direct elections were held since 2005 without any political strife nor conflict, with each of the 539 local administrations having carried out local direct elections twice. About 20 elections were held peacefully in the high conflict province of Aceh in 2006.

Moreover, Indonesia has avoided territorial disintegration. Despite all the struggles, we are safe from the revolutionary phase towards democratization, according to Kristiadi at CSIS.

> Our democracy is still a procedural democracy and not yet a civilized democracy. But, what we have is social capital, which has a long history. Despite the weak role of the government, our people are very much united without identifying themselves by ethics, religions, nor origins.
>
> (Structure: Kristiadi, March 2011)

In 2001, the controversial proposal by some political parties to turn Indonesia into an Islamic state, which might have caused a civil war, was resolved peacefully.

Indonesia's stability as a functional electoral democracy 15 years later is indeed a noteworthy achievement (Meitzer, 2013). Meitzer (2013) argues that democracy has been stable because, in combination, decentralization and democratization have given local people the opportunity to express their local identities and formulate their own policy priorities. He also argues that Indonesia has marginalized the military in political affairs. Other literature argue that Indonesia's transition has been relatively stable and consolidation has occurred because elite interests were never really challenged. All governments in the *Reformasi* era have been broad churches, being tolerant and accepting different opinions and ideas, including with and of most political parties.

In the following section, we will provide some analyses on Indonesian democracy and decentralization.

Electoral democracy

The thin definition of democracy, according to Diamond (2008: 21), follows Joseph Schumpeter's definition in the 1940s: a system for arriving at political decisions in which individuals acquire the power to decide by means of regular, free and fair elections. The thick definition requires other attributes on top of regular, free and fair elections. Unless these attributes are also ensured, it is not yet a democracy. The attributes include: freedom of speech; freedom of ethnic, religious, racial and other minority groups to practice their religion and culture; legal equality of all citizens under a clear and publicly known rule of law; an independent judiciary to neutrally and consistently apply the law and protect individual and group rights; freedom of individuals from torture, terror and unjustified detention or exile, or interference in their personal lives; institutional checks on the power of elected officials by an independent legislature, court system and other autonomous agencies; a vibrant civil society; control over the military and state security apparatus by civilians. All of the so-called democratic states should aspire to this thick definition, which is also called *liberal democracy* (Diamond 2008: 22).

We can use these definitions to characterize the democracy in Indonesia in the *Reformasi* era. We cannot deny that *de jure* Indonesia is a democratic country with regular direct elections both at the central and district levels (after 2004 and 2005, respectively), but *de facto* we cannot deny either that the elections, especially at the local level, have been marred by money politics and political transactions (Thee, 2007; Kristiadi, 2011a).

In 2005, President Yudhoyono decided to cut state subsidies to political parties by 90 per cent and this has made political parties fund-raise more aggressively. The cabinet reshuffle during the second administration of President Yudhoyono towards the end of 2011, which positioned his closest cronies in the most lucrative ministerial posts, including as the Minister of Energy and Natural Resources, invited many criticisms (Saragih, 2011; Kristiadi and Wihardja, 2011; Hill and Wihardja, 2011).

Many democratic values, as inspired by the above-mentioned liberal democratic attributes, are grossly violated or missing: doubling of the number of violent conflict incidents in the six 'high conflict' provinces (excluding Aceh) from 2004 to 2008 (World Bank, 2010b), 'vigilante justice' (World Bank, 2010b) with an absent or ineffective police and judiciary system to apply the law and protect individual and group rights, widespread and corrosive corruption at all levels of government (Thee, 2010c) and a weak rule of law with a lower score in 2009 than that in 1996 (World Governance Indicator, World Bank).

Conflict can be expected to increase in a young democracy.[4] In regard to the escalating conflict, Patrick Barron, co-author of 'Understanding Violent Conflict in Indonesia: A Mixed Methods Approach' (Barron, Jaffrey, Pallmer, and Varshney, 2009), asserted that the recent escalating religious attacks such as the attacks on the Ahmadiyah sect in Banten (February 2011) and attacks on Christians in Temanggung (February 2011), as well as other incidents in Jakarta, East Kalimantan, Lombok and West Java, are a result of failure to make progress on elements on democratic consolidation, especially the legal and security institutions as well as conflict management.

Meitzer also noted that,

> there is a noticeable deterioration in the protection of religious minority rights in post-Soeharto Indonesia. Attacks on Christian churches and Islamic non-mainstream group(s) such as the Ahmadis and the Shiites have increased dramatically under Yudhoyono's government, with the president unable or unwilling to confront the radical militias responsible of the violence.
>
> (Meitzer, 2013: 7)

Also, the fragmented and unstable presidential and multiparty parliamentary system erodes the efficiency and effectiveness of policy-making processes. The presidential and multiparty parliamentary system are often sources of ineffectiveness in the government, including in passing laws. Political authority of the House's right to investigate (*Hak Angket*) that should be used to protect people's rights, including by impeaching the incumbent president and vice president, has only been used as instruments to bargain political interests (Kristiadi, 2011c). A series of coalition battles, including the Bank Century scandal in 2010 and the House's right to investigate tax grafts in 2011, in which the supporting coalition parties, including Golkar and PKS, opted against the president and his party's stance, portrays the continuous struggle in the government to pass laws. In 2010, Parliament was only able to pass 7 out of 70 proposed bills ('House to Endorse', 2010). This certainly had an adverse effect on the economy.

There seems to be a misconception about democracy in Indonesia: a strong leadership and democracy cannot co-exist, as democracy does not leave any space for a strong leadership. 'Strong leadership is a trait. It can co-exist with any type of regime [democracy or autocracy]. Multi-party democracy with direct presidential elections definitely needs it to coordinate self-centered politicians from different parties', said Nico Harjanto, a public policy analyst at the Rajawali Foundation.

> For Indonesia, we need to create a moderate pluralistic party system [with only 3–5 seat parties] with a concurrent electoral cycle [legislative and presidential elections held at the same time]. We need one-time mid-term local elections to allow incumbents to be punished or rewarded.
>
> (Structure: Harjanto, N., March 2011)

A weak leadership and an increasing number of local conflicts and violence may endanger the unity of the people, which is one of Indonesia's strongest social capitals.

Although Indonesia's electoral democracy has been relatively stable for the past 15 years, this success cannot be taken for granted. There are serious challenges that threaten the consolidation of democracy, including political and economic corruption, transactional politics and escalating local conflicts. Indonesia may need to re-think where she wants to go – that is, whether this political system can continue to support the consolidation of democracy. By 2014, the youth unemployment reached that of Spain, at around 26 per cent. Although the number of people living below the poverty line was 12 per cent in 2012, an additional 27 per cent lived just above the poverty line and were highly vulnerable to slide into poverty. Inequality has also been rising since the start of the *Reformasi* era, from 0.30 in 2000 to 0.41 in 2012. Without any significant social safety net for this unemployed and highly vulnerable population, political and social cohesion are continuously under threat.

Captured decentralization

As she democratized in 1999, Indonesia also underwent a massive institutional change in 2001 following the administrative, political and fiscal decentralization enacted in 1999. Although decentralization is not the same as democratization, i.e. one can occur without the other, decentralization has some democratic values.

> Efforts to decentralize have taken many forms and have a variety of underlying motivations . . . The theoretical foundations of these efforts have been drawn from elements of democratic theory that stress the importance of participation by local people in the operation of their own public affairs.
>
> (Schroeder et al., 1993: 164)

However, in the Indonesian case, the decision to decentralize was also warily made under huge political pressures to appease the Indonesian people, who were disappointed with the New Order regime, when the economy plunged into a deep financial crisis in mid-1997.

> Lacking the past experience to calculate retrospectively the likely electoral payoff from supporting an effort to devolve political power to Indonesia's city [municipality] and regency [district] governments, New Order–era political elites in Jakarta gambled on the advice of a team of experts. The experts assured them that supporting the effort would give them strong and salient reformist credentials on the eve of free elections.
>
> (Smith, 2008)

VI. Is decentralization right for Indonesia?

The following pre-conditions are potentially problematic to begin with: (1) *de facto* judicial and legal systems were very weak and unreliable, (2) many poor and uneducated Indonesian citizens could not serve as an effective checks-and-balances mechanism (as of 2008, there are about 41 million 'very poor' and 'poor' people, and 61 million 'very poor', 'poor' and 'almost poor' people by PPLS 2008)[5], while the central government does not have power to discipline the autonomous local governments anymore, (3) there was no role model of 'quality' leadership nor governance prior to 2001, (4) the change in political structure created increased lobbying or local capture by the rich elites, namely, through local direct elections,[6] (5) local agencies with the autonomy to spend their budgets funded by the central government's money without a complete monitoring and information mechanism could easily create a moral hazard.

Essentially, fiscal and political decentralizations intertwine to give a different incentive mechanism than that of the New Order era for local leaders to deliver public goods and services. The central government essentially 'dumps' a lot of money to local governments – currently at about one third of the central government's budget in the forms of intergovernmental transfers – however, without any string attached. So, local governments spend a lot of local budget on administrations and paying personals. There is a principal-agent issue to incentivize local governments to deliver better public goods and services.

Because of this, quality of local spending is questionable. In 2012, 51 per cent of local budget was allocated to pay state apparatus, while 18 per cent was allocated to goods and services expenditure and 24 per cent was on capital goods (Temenggung, 2013). Sjahrir, Kis-Katos and Schulze (2014) argued that, on average, 30 per cent of district budgets are absorbed by expenses for district administration. Using data for 399 districts over 2001–09, they contended that local party composition, i.e. the intensity of political competition, influenced the extent of administrative overspending.

At the same time, the role of district governments (regencies and cities) becomes very crucial since the central government does not have direct state apparatus in the district level (except for some of public works and services). However, there is a lack of both upward and downward local political accountability for local governments to deliver public goods and services to their constituents.

Sometimes the implementation of public service delivery is impeded by a lack of institutional and technical capacity of the local governments (a rigid 'supply-side constraint'). So, even though, there is a political will, there is no capacity to implement. Moreover, because most of the local government fund is spent on operational costs, issuing policies that support public services and implementing them can be two different matters if funding to implement them is not sufficient. From the demand side, in general, Indonesia has a weak civic institutional life.

A growing decentralization problem in Indonesia is the proliferation of devolved authorities ('Power to the People!', 2011). In 1999, there were only 292 districts in 26 provinces, but by March 2011, there were around 491 districts in 33 provinces, and by 2014, there are 505 districts and 34 provinces. Given the money on offer for winning political candidates, this proliferation of new districts was hardly based on welfare consideration, causing huge cost, administrative and physical inefficiency.

In this section, we will review some quantitative as well as qualitative works on the above-mentioned issues, by looking at three issues: (1) local political economy in decentralized Indonesia, (2) economic performance with and without decentralization, and (3) how political and economic factors affect institutional quality.

Local political economy in decentralized Indonesia

Decentralization along with direct local elections give birth to a completely new politico-economic environment at the local level. Azis and Wihardja (2010) provide a game-theoretical approach to illustrate the strategic behaviors among local leaders, business elites and citizens under this new politico-economic environment. Using Azis's typology of leadership model (Azis, 2008), they theorize the evolution between low welfare level and poor-quality institutions, which creates a vicious cycle, through institutional mechanisms, such as local capture, poor local leadership and low participation level as well as a lack of local accountability.

In order to illustrate this local dynamic process, they took five Indonesian districts as case studies that varied in their initial conditions, namely, local leadership and socio-economic conditions based on prior knowledge about the districts – Balikpapan and Yogyakarta City for good leadership and high socio-economic conditions; Prabumulih for poor leadership and high socio-economic conditions; Sragen for good leadership and low socio-economic conditions; and Manggarai Barat for poor leadership and low socio-economic conditions. Based on a set of questionnaires, a series of in-depth interviews were conducted with high-ranking public officials (including district heads and/or mayors), political parties, opposition politicians, business associations, NGOs, local media, academics and poor families in each district.

The goal of these interviews was to assess the capacity and integrity of the local leaders; any practice of corruption/collusion/nepotism during the local budgeting process, public procurement and formulation of local regulations; the degree and quality of cooperation between local leaders and local business elites; and the quality and availability of social programs. The interviews were recorded and transcribed. Based on the transcription, each institutional indicator, namely, local leadership, local participation and local capture, as well as the socio-economic conditions, in each of the districts was given a score. The scoring system specified a set of requirements that have to be fulfilled in order to get a certain score. For example, for the public procurement indicator, a district

Table 10.1 Initial socio-economic conditions and local governance

Kabupaten	Province	Socio-economic Conditions	Participation	Local Leadership	Local Capture
Balikpapan	East Kalimantan	Good	High	Good	No
Yogyakarta City	Yogyakarta	Good	High	Good	No
Prabumulih	South Sumatra	Medium	Low	Bad	Yes
Sragen	Central Java	Medium	Low	Medium	Yes
Manggarai Barat	East Nusa Tenggara	Bad	Low	Bad	Yes

Source: Pepinsky and Wihardja (2011).

could receive a 'high' score only if there is no intervention from the local contractor association nor any special person or body. More detailed information about the data and methods for the field study are available from Azis and Wihardja (2008). The result of the field study is summarized in Table 10.1.

Azis and Wihardja observed a close link between initial socio-economic conditions and political participation, the quality of leadership and local capture. Regions with good socio-economic conditions, namely, Balikpapan and Yogyakarta City also received high scores for local participation and local leadership supported by welfare-enhancing cooperation between local leaders and business elites. Regions with moderate socio-economic conditions but with some institutional deficiencies, such as low public participation and/or poor leadership, namely, Sragen and Prabumulih, were found to be prone to local capture. A region with poor socio-economic conditions, namely, Manggarai Barat, received low scores for local participation and local leadership supported by a high degree of local capture.

The result suggests two reinforcing factors to create the evolution between welfare and institutional qualities. The first one is through local participation. In regions with poor socio-economic conditions where citizens were uneducated or poorly educated and not politically well-informed, citizens could not elect a good leader. The second is through local accountability. In regions with poor socio-economic conditions, citizens could not hold local leaders accountable and hence, cooperation between local leaders and local business elites are more prone to money politics and political transactions, creating intense local capture. These in turn create poorer socio-economic conditions. However, these results are only suggestive. A repeated study over time is needed to study the co-evolution of welfare and institutions, especially since sufficiently long time-series data on institutional quality and local governance at the district level in Indonesia do not yet exist. This can be an agenda for future research.

'The welfare-enhancing local capture in Azis and Wihardja (2010), in which cooperative relationships between local leaders and business elites generate pro-investment and pro-development outcomes, is consistent with what Luebke et al. (2009) calls "heterodox reform symbiosis"' (Pepinsky and Wihardja, 2011). Von Luebke et al. (2009) found that relation-based institutions as opposed to rule-based institutions, such as those found in Solo and Manado, contribute to a high level of investment and growth, although in the medium run, they may not be stable as legal issues may start to arise.

The policy implications that we can draw from these literature are (1) the attempt to solve how to break the vicious cycle between low welfare and poor institutions must be made exogenous to the system, multidimensional and context-specific, which takes into account social norms and culture in each district (Azis and Wihardja, 2010), (2) local capture is always present but in different scales (Azis and Wihardja, 2010), and the symbiosis between local leaders and business elites can be welfare-enhancing (Luebke et al., 2009), especially under better local participation and local accountability that are supported by politically informed and well-educated citizens, (3) 'institutional innovations are neither necessary nor sufficient to create developmentalist policy-making, but a strong civil society, which has a space in a democratic Indonesia may be the key to making decentralization work'[7] (Pepinsky and Wihardja, 2011).

Although there are no two regions observed in the study that have the same initial conditions, such as geography, the fact that there are regions in Indonesia with similar initial conditions such as neighbouring districts having completely different development outcomes would be an example of the multiplicity of equilibria discussed earlier. There are many remaining unobserved factors that affect the evolution between institutional trajectory and welfare of a district. Historical analysis is indeed needed. Although it is true that institutional trajectory is not always smooth (i.e. they neither follow the vicious nor virtuous cycle) and many internal and external shocks (including natural disasters) could abruptly change institutional trajectory (like Aceh), the persistent inequality between East and West Indonesia may be an evidence of the existence of this virtuous and vicious cycle model. Other evidence include the lower health and education social program expenditures in poorer districts in Indonesia than in richer districts, according to the Partnership Governance Index 2008 (Kemitraan, n.d.).

Economic performance with and without decentralization

Using a *synthetic case control methodology* formalized by Abadie et al. (2010), in which a 'synthetic Indonesia who did not decentralize' is created, Pepinsky and Wihardja (2011) show that Indonesian decentralization has had no discernable effect on the country's overall economic performance. A synthetic Indonesia is created by first choosing the weight that minimizes the metric distance between Indonesian determinants of economic development, say $X1$, and a weighted mixture of sample countries' determinants of economic development, say $X0.W$, prior to the decentralization. The weighted mixture of sample countries becomes the synthetic Indonesia whose growth trajectory after decentralization simulates the counterfactual of Indonesia's growth trajectory who did not decentralize. A placebo test was then performed to test robustness, which if, on average, the estimated effect of decentralization for Indonesia is large (small) relative to the estimated effect from a placebo case chosen at random, then this provides a robustness check that the decentralization truly had (did not have) an effect.

Using four different sets of sample countries, namely, a restricted set of countries, an expanded set of countries, Asian countries only and countries who did not decentralize only, Pepinsky and Wihardja (2011) found that in all cases, the development trajectory for Indonesia since decentralization is nearly identical to what is expected from a country with similar economic, demographic and political fundamentals but which did not decentralize. In other words, the growth trajectories of real and synthetic Indonesia trace each other very well in all cases. The placebo results also support the finding that decentralization has not had any significant effect on Indonesia's economic performance.

Pepinsky and Wihardja then probed two political economy mechanisms – interjurisdictional competition[8] and democratic accountability – that underlie all theories linking decentralization to better economic outcomes. Their findings suggest three issues contributing to the above-mentioned decentralization outcome. First is the extreme heterogeneity in endowments that may actually make the disadvantaged governments more likely to adopt predatory local regulations instead of trying to compete with the advantaged regions by adopting good policies (Cai and Treisman, 2005). Second is the endogeneity of institutions in which unfavourable initial conditions in a district such as uneducated and politically uninformed citizens can create a perpetuating self-reinforcing vicious cycle between low welfare and low institutional qualities (Azis and Wihardja, 2010). Third is factor immobility, including natural resources and labour, that undermines the interjurisdictional competition.

How political and economic factors affect institutions' institutional quality

Both literatures above propose endogeneity of institutions as one of the main threats to welfare improvement in poor districts. One of the issues to study institutions is precisely the endogeneity issue that makes it difficult to disentangle between cause and causality (see 'properties of institutions' above). While most studies on institutions look at how various institutional indicators affect economic development (e.g. IMF, 2005), which suggest a positive effect of institutions on economic performance, hardly any study discusses the reverse relation. Baryshnikova and Wihardja (2013) look at cross-country evidence of how inequality, democracy and GDP per capita may affect institutional qualities, controlling for natural resource endowments and population using an empirical model suggested by Savoia, Easaw and McKay (2010).[9]

Baryshnikova and Wihardja (2013) construct a dynamic model of institutions where the current institutional quality depends on the institutional quality in the previous years and the political and economic factors in the country. The model accounts for the sluggish process of institutional adjustment, the heterogeneity of countries, the non-linear effects of the independent variables and endogeneity in inequality, democracy, GDP per capita, endowment and mineral depletion. The authors take the data on 76 countries from 1984 to 2006 with institutional quality indicators – government stability, corruption, investment profile and bureaucracy quality – and merge the dataset with the political and economic factors in these countries. They use both lagged and collapsed instruments sets and estimate a panel AR model using the difference GMM.

Their result shows significant effects of political and economic factors on government stability. While the effect of log of GDP per capita is always positive for all countries, ceteris paribus, the effect of inequality and democracy can range from positive to negative depending on the country's current conditions with regard to the rest of the indicators. Intertwining these effects shows that the relationship between institutions and political and economic factors is much more complex than ever thought in the literature before. Population size is shown to positively affect government stability, while evidence of resource curse is not found. The authors find no effects of these factors on any other indicators of institutional quality considered in this chapter. It is still unclear why the results on government stability do not apply to other institutional variables, namely, bureaucratic quality, corruption and investment profile. Perhaps a different model would provide this explanation in the future.

VII. Concluding remarks

Democratization and decentralization happened without any paradigm nor consensus among the policy makers. It is therefore not surprising that more than a decade later, democratization and decentralization are still yet to consolidate with laws being continuously revised. This chapter attempts to give insightful analyses on institutional constraints and review progresses of Indonesian democracy and decentralization since 1997.

Democracy in Indonesia has not yet fully embraced the liberal democratic values. It is still an electoral democracy that is procedural. One of the main issues of Indonesian democracy is the dual presidential and multiparty parliamentary system. Although a president may win a landslide victory at the presidential direct election, he or she must still form a coalition in Parliament in order to be able to pass a law. The forming of a coalition results in public policies being transacted as political commodities, in which the president and his or her political party must sacrifice his or her political stance to appease the coalition parties. Combined with a weak leadership, democracy that must face dissenting voices from different political parties with different political interests is not only noisy, but also messy and no longer represents people's interests. Indonesia needs to think whether the aspiration of democracy can ever be achieved under this unstable and fragmented political system. Otherwise, it must be amended. As this chapter is being written, Indonesia just completed its third direct presidential election on July 9, 2014, which marked a positive development to Indonesia's democracy with a tight competition between the two presidential-vice presidential candidates and enormous public participation through electronic uploading of voting results, social media and online organizations guiding the election processes. The future of democratic consolidation in Indonesia is promising.

The important essence of decentralization is to bring policy making and public services closer to the localities. The principal-agent issue in the incentive mechanism of the decentralization system combined with a lack of institutional and technical capacity of the local governments (a rigid 'supply-side constraint') has impeded further improvement in the delivery of public goods and services as expected from decentralization. This chapter has suggested not only a supply-side but also a demand-side approach to better public goods and services delivery.

There has been some evidence on the endogeneity of institutions and welfare. Policies to break the vicious cycle are subtle and they remain an agenda for future research.

Notes

1 'We are not ready and there is no time to think' (Structure: Kristiadi, March 2011).
2 Diamond (2008) describes electoral democracy as the minimal level when a people can choose and replace their leaders in regular, free and fair elections.
3 Local capture is defined as a condition under which local business elites capture or influence local economic and/or political institutions. This rise of local capture is not surprising since many local political candidates needed financial supports from local businesses, which, due to meager salaries once elected as local leaders, they pay the business elites in the form of contracts, projects and even local policies.
4 'Conflict is actually very healthy for democracy because it shows that democracy is functioning and that people are allowed to express their disagreements with the government and also horizontally with other groups. . . . But the problem begins when conflicts start to be resolved by using violent means', said Sara Jaffrey, the team leader of ViCIS, World Bank. Moreover, Ashutosh Varshney, Professor of Political Science at Brown University, asserted, 'conflict development, and conflict and rule of law, . . . are vitally important components of the way we think about consolidating democracy itself in Indonesia' (PSFconflict, 2010).
5 Author's own calculation using PPLS 2008 (CBS 2008). PPLS (*Program Pendataan Perlindungan Sosial*) is a survey on 40% bottom of low income households population conducted by Central Bureau of Statistics.
6 'Given the rewards on offer for a successful local politician – free money from the centre and the power to raise local taxes – perhaps it is not surprising that local electoral politics has become mired in corruption. Prospective candidates rack up big debts to bribe voters and political parties. Then, they resort to embezzlement in office to pay the debts' ('Power to the People!', 2011)
7 These are drawn from the 2010 *Human Development Report,* pp. 61 and 63.

8 Tiebout (1956) famously argued that decentralization enables asset holders to compare expenditure and revenue policies across jurisdictions and allows them to 'vote with their feet' for preferable service-tax packages. Besley and Case (1995) confirm the importance of neighbours' taxes both on the probability of incumbent re-election and on tax-setting behaviour.
9 Due to the data limitation, it is impossible to do the same analysis on Indonesia alone (in which a long time-series of district-level institutional qualities does not exist).

References

Abadie, A., Diamond, A. and Hainmueller, J. (2010) 'Synthetic Control Methods for Comparative Case Studies: Estimating the Effect of California's Tobacco Control Program', *Journal of the American Statistical Association* 105(490), 493–505.

Aghevli, B.B. and Khan, M.S. (1977) 'Inflationary Finance and Dynamics of Inflation: Indonesia 1951–72', *American Economic Review* 63(3), June.

Aizenman, J. and Lee, J. (2006) 'Financial Versus Monetary Mercantilism: Long-Run View of the Large International Reserves Hoarding', *IMF Working Paper* No. 06/280, Washington: Internationanl Monetary Fund.

Amiti, M. and Konings, J. (2007) 'Trade Liberalization, Intermediate Inputs and Productivity: Evidence from Indonesia', *American Economic Review* 97(5), 1611–1638.

Andersen, E. (1970) 'Asymptotic Properties of Conditional Maximum Likelihood Estimators', *Journal of the Royal Statistical Society* 32, 283–301.

Ando, A. and Modigliani, F. (1963) 'The 'Life-Cycle' Hypothesis of Saving: Aggregate Implications and Tests', *American Economic Review* 53(1), 55–84.

Ando, M. and Kimura, F. (2003) 'The Formation of International Production and Distribution Network in East Asia', *NBER Working Paper*, 10167.

Andrle, M., Freedman, C., Garcia-Saltos, R., Hermawan, D., Laxton, D. and Munandar, H. (2009) *Adding Indonesia to the Global Projection Model*, IMF Working Paper No.WP/09/253, November.

Arellano, M. and Bond, S. (1991) 'Some Tests of Specification for Panel Data: Monte Carlo Evidence and an Application to Employment Equations', *Review of Economic Studies* 58, 277–297.

Ariyoshi, A., Habermeier, K., Laurens, B. Otker-Robe, I., Canales-Kriljenko, J.I., and Kirilenko, A. (2000) *Capital Controls: Country Experiences with Their Use and Liberalization*, Occasional Paper 190. Washington, D.C. IMF.

ASEAN Secretariat (2011) *Economic Integration*. Online. Available HTTP: http://www.aseansec.org

Asian Development Bank (2008) *Emerging Asian Regionalism: A Partnership for Shared Prosperity*, Manila: Asian Development Bank.

Asian Development Bank and World Bank (2005) Improving the Investment Climate in Indonesia, Joint ADB-WB Report, May.

Asian Development Bank Institute (2010) *Free Trade Agreement Trend*, Asia Regional Integration Center: Asian Development Bank Institute. Online. Available HTTP: http://www.aric.adb.org/ftatrends.php

Association of Indonesian Mutual Fund Managers (2011), 'Tantangan dan Peluang Industri Pengelolaan Investasi 2011', Powerpoint presentation by the Vice Head of the Association, Jakarta.

Aswicahyono, H., Bird, K. and Hill, H. (2009) 'Making Economic Policy in Weak, Democratic, Post-Crisis States: An Indonesian Case Study', *World Development* 37(2), 354–370.

Aswicahyono, H., Hill, H. and Narjoko, D. (2010) 'Industrialisation after A Deep Economic Crisis: Indonesia', *Journal of Development Studies* 46(6), 1084–1108.

Aswicahyono, H., Hill, H. and Narjoko, D. (2011) 'Indonesian Industrialization: Patterns, Issues and Constraints', *Critical Development Constraints*, ADB.

Aswicahyono, H.H., Basri, M.C. and Hill, H. (2000) 'How Not to Industrialise?: Indonesia's Automotive Industry', *Bulletin of Indonesian Economic Studies* 36(1), 209–241.

Azis, I.J. (2008) 'Institutional Constraints and Multiple Equilibria in Decentralization', RURDS 20(1), 22–33.

Azis, I.J. and Wihardja, M.M. (2008) *Field Survey in Five Districts in Indonesia on Local Capture and Social Welfare,* Cornell University and KPPOD: Internal Report.

Azis, I.J. and Wihardja, M.M. (2010) 'Endogenous Institutions in Indonesia', *Economics and Finance in Indonesia* 58(3), 309–334.

Bagus, I. (2010) 'Jual KPD Natpac, Bank Bumiputera Terancam Sanksi BI, *detik-finance* 11 November.

Bahl, R. and Wallace, S. (2007) 'Intergovernmental Transfers: The Vertical Sharing Dimension', in J. Martinez-Vazquez and B. Searle (eds.) *Fiscal Equalization: Challenges in the Design of Intergovernmental Transfers.* New York: Springer.

Balassa, B. (1964) "The Purchasing Power Parity Doctrine: A Reappraisal", *Journal of Political Economy,* 72(6), 584–596.

Bank for International Settlements (2010) *Annual Report.* Chapter 2.

Bank Indonesia (2013) *Indonesian Banking Booklet.* April.

Bapepam-LK (2003a) Annual Report for 2007, Jakarta.

Bapepam-LK (2003b) *Annual Report*, Bapepam LK.

Bapepam-LK (2008) Annual Report for 2007, Jakarta.

Bapepam-LK (2009) Annual Report for 2008, Jakarta.

Bapepam-LK (2010) Annual Report for 2009, Jakarta.

Barron, P., Jaffrey, S., Pallmer, B. and Varshney, A. (2009) 'Understanding Violent Conflict in Indonesia: A Mixed Methods Approach', Social Development Working Papers, No. 117/June, World Bank.

Baryshnikova, N. and Wihardja, M.M. (2013) 'Do Political and Economic Factors Affect Institutional Quality?' Working paper, University of Adelaide and University of Indonesia.

Basri, M.C. and Hill, H. (2004) 'Ideas, Interests and Oil Prices: The Political Economy of Trade Reform During Soeharto's Indonesia', *World Economy* 27(5), 633–655.

Basri, M.C. and Patunru, A. A. (2008), 'Indonesia's Supply Constraints', *Background paper prepared for OECD.*

Basri, M.C. and Rahardja, S. (2010) 'Indonesia Beyond the Recovery: Growth Strategy in an Archipelago Country', chapter in *Growth and Sustainability in Brazil, China, India, Indonesia and South Africa*, Paris: OECD.

Basri, M.C. and Rahardja, S. (2011) 'Should Indonesia Say Goodbye to Strategy Facilitating Export?' in Mona Haddad and Ben Sheppard eds., *Managing Openness: and Outward-Oriented Growth after the Crisis*, Washington DC: World Bank.

BCBS (2010) Basel Committee on Banking Supervision.

Beim, D. and C. Calomiris (2001) *Emerging Financial Markets.* Boston: McGrawhill/ Irwin.

Bernhardsen, T. and KarstenGedrup (2007) 'The Neutral Real Interest Rate', *Economic Bulletin* 2/07, Oslo: Norges Bank.

Bertscheck, I. (1995) 'Product and Process Innovation as a Response to Increasing Imports and Direct Investment', *Journal of Industrial Economics* 43(4), 341–357.

Besley, T. and Case, A. (1995) 'Incumbent Behaviour: Vote Seeking, Tax-Setting, and Yardstick Competition', *The American Economic Review* 85(1), 25–45, available HTTP://www.jstor.org/stable/2117994.

Blinder, A.S. (1998) 'Central Banking in Theory and Practice', Cambridge, MA: MIT Press.

Bloom, D. (2002) 'Mastering Globalization: From Ideas to Action Higher Education Reform', unpublished paper.

Boivin, J., Kiley, M.T. and Miskin, F.S. (2010) 'How Was the Monetary Transmission Mechanism Evolved Over Time?' *Finance and Economics Discussion Series,* No. 2010-26. Divisions of Research & Statistics and Monetary Affairs, Federal Reserve Board, Washington D.C.

Braga, H. and Willmore, L. (1991) 'Technological Imports and Technological Effort: An Analysis of Their Determinants in Brazilian Firms', *Journal of Industrial Economics,* 39(4), 421–431.

Brodjonegoro, Bambang P.S. (2004) 'Three Years of Fiscal Decentralization in Indonesia: Its Impacts on Regional Economic Development and Fiscal Sustainability', Paper delivered in 2004 APPP Symposium, Hitotsubashi University.

Bryan, M.F. and Cecchetti, S.G. (1993) 'Measuring Core Inflation', in N.G. Mankiw (ed.) *Monetary Policy.* Chicago: University of Chicago Press.

Bussière, M. and Mulder, C. (1999) 'External Vulnerability in Emerging Market Economies: How High Liquidity Can Offset Weak Fundamentals and the Effects of Contagion', IMF Working Paper No. 99/88. Washington: International Monetary Fund.

Cai, H. and Treisman, D. (2005) 'Does Competition for Capital Discipline Governments? Decentralization, Globalization, and Public Policy', *American Economic Review* 95(3), 817–830.

Calvo, G.A. and C.M. Reinhart (2002) 'Fear of Floating' *Quarterly Journal of Economics* 107(2), 379–408.

Calvo, G.A., Leiderman, L. and Reinhart, C.M. (1992) 'Capital Inflow and Real Exchange Rate Appreciation in Latin America: The Role of External Factors', IMF Working Paper 92/62. Washington: IMF.

Calvo, G.A., Leiderman, L. and Reinhart, C.M. (1993a) 'The Capital Inflows Problem: Concepts and Issues', IMF Paper on Policy Analysis and Assessment 93/10. Washington, D.C.: IMF.

Calvo, G.A., Leiderman, L. and Reinhart, C.M. (1993b) 'Capital Inflows to Latin America: The Role of External Factors', *IMF Staff Papers* 40, 108–151.

Caprio, G. and Klingebiel, G. (2003) 'Episodes of Systemic and Borderline Financial Crises', Washington, D.C.: World Bank.

Carbo-Valverde, S. and Fernandez, F.R. (2007) 'The Determinants of Bank Margins in European Banking', *Journal of Banking and Finance* 31(7), 2043–2063.

Carbo-Valverde, S., Humphrey, D.B. and R.L. del Paso (2005) 'Explaining Bank Cost Efficiency in Europe: Environmental and Productivity Influences' Fundacion de las Cajas de Ahorros Working Paper No. 208/2005.

Caruana, J. (2012) *The Need for Effective International Collaboration in Time of Financial Stress*, Speech at the Seminar on 'Long-Term Growth Organizing the Stability and Attractiveness of European Financial Markets', Berlin, 20 January.

Casario, M. (1996) 'North American Free Trade Agreement Bilateral Trade Effects', *Contemporary Economic Policy* 14(1), 36–47.

CBS (2008) PPLS: *Program Pendataan Perlindungan Sosial* Survey, Central Bureau of Statistics.

CEIC Database (2010).

Cerra, V. and Saxena, S. (2005) 'Did Output Recover from the Asian Crisis?', *IMF Staff Papers*, Vol. 52. No. 1. Washington: International Monetary Fund.

Chamberlain, G. (19920 'Comment: Sequential Moment Restrictions in Panel Data', *Journal of Business and Economic Statistics* 10, 20–26.

Chia, S. Y. (2010) 'Accelerating ASEAN Trade and Investment Cooperation and Integration: Progress and Challenges', *Competitiveness of ASEAN Countries: Corporate and Regulatory Drivers, New Horizons in International Business* (in Philippe Gugler and Julien Chaisse Edition), London: Edward Elgar.

Cihak, M. and Richard, P. (2006) 'Is One Watchdog Better Than Three? International Experience with Integrated Financial Sector Supervision', *IMF Working Paper* No. WP/06/57. March.

Clarida, R., Gali, J. and Getler, M. (1999) 'The Science of Monetary Policy: A New Keynesian Perspective', *Journal of Economic Literature* 37, 1661–1707.

Cole, D.C. and B. F. Slade (1996) *Building a Modern Financial System*, Melbourne: Cambridge University Press.

Crepon, B. and Duguet, E. (1997) 'Estimating the Innovation Function from Patent Numbers: GMM on Count Panel Data', *Journal of Applied Economics* 12(3), 241–263.

Critical Review of Recent Research (2010) *World Development* 38(2), 142–154.

Dahlby, B. (2009) 'The Marginal Cost of Public Funds and the Flypaper Effect', *Working Paper No. 2009-17*, Department of Economics, University of Alberta.

Daniel, J., Davis, J., Fouad, M. and Van Rijkeghem, C. (2006) 'Fiscal Adjustment for Stability and Growth', Pamphlet Series No. 55, Washington: International Monetary Fund.

Darby, J., Hallet, A.H., Ireland, J. and Piscitelli, L. (1999) 'The Impact of Exchange Rate Uncertainty on the Level of Investment', *The Economic Journal* 109(March), 55–67.

Deloitte (2008) *The Structure of Financial Supervision: Approaches and Challenges in a Global Marketplace*, Washington: Center for Banking Solutions.

Deloitte Center for Banking Solutions (2008), "The Structure of Financial Supervision; Approaches and Challenges in a Global Marketplace", Report for the G-30, Washington, DC.

Demirguc-Kunt, A. and Huizinga, H. (1999) 'Determinant of Commercial Bank Interest Margins and Profitability: Some International Evidence', *The World Bank Economic Review* 13(2), 379–408.

Democracy Index 2010: Democracy in Retreat (2010) *The Economist Intelligence Unit*. Available HTTP: *//www.eiu.com/public/topical_report.aspx?campaignid=demo2010*

Diamond, L. (2008) *The Spirit of Democracy. The Struggle to Build Free Societies Throughout the World*. New York: Henry Hold and Company.

Dixit, A.K. (2004) *Lawlessness and Economics*. New Jersey: Princeton University Press.

Dubin, J. (2004) 'Criminal Investigation Enforcement Activities and Taxpayer Non-compliance,' paper written for Internal Revenue Service Research Conference, June.

Dubin, J., Graetz, M.J. and Wilde, L.L. (1990) 'The Effect of Audit Rates on the Federal Income Tax, 1977–86', *National Tax Journal* 43, 395–405.

Durdu, C.B., Mendoza, E. and Terrones, M. (2007) 'Precautionary Demand for Foreign Assets in Sudden Stop Economies: An Assessment of the New Mercantilism,' *IMF Working Paper* No. 07/146. Washington: International Monetary Fund.

Ebrill, L., Keen, M., Bodin, J. and Summers, V. (2001) The Modern VAT, Washington: International Monetary Fund.

Edison, H. (2003) 'Are Foreign Reserves Too High?' Staff Studies for the World Economic Outlook, September, Washington: International Monetary Fund.

Eichengreen, B. and Hausmann, R. (1999) 'Exchange Rates and Financial Fragility', NBER Working Paper No. 7418, November.

Enoch, C., Frecaut, O. and Kovanen, A. (2004) 'Indonesia's Banking Crisis: What Happened and What Did We Learn?', *Bulletin of Indonesian Economic Studies* 39(1), 75–92.

Eurasia Group (2010) *Global Political Risk Index.* New York: Eurasia Group.

Fane, G. and Condon, T. F. (1996) 'Trade Reform in Indonesia, 1987–95', *Bulletin of Indonesian Economic Studies* 32(3), 33–54.

Fauziah (2008) 'Fiscal Decentralization and Economic Growth: Evidence from Indonesia', *Journal of Economics and Finance in Indonesia*, February.

Filardo, A. and Genberg, H. 2009. 'Targeting Inflation in Asia and the Pacific: Lessons from the Recent Past'. BIS Representative Officer Asia and the Pacific. August.

Fisher, Ronald C. (1996) *State and Local Government Finance.* Chicago: Irwin.

Fogg, K. (2010) 'Islamic Organizations and the Borders of Politics in the 1950s', Presentation at CSIS, Jakarta, 22 November.

Frankel, J.A. (1994) 'Sterilization of Money Inflows: Difficult (Calvo) or Easy (Reisen)?' *IMF Working Paper* 94/159. Washington, D.C.: IMF.

Frecaut, O. (n.d.) 'Indonesia's Banking Crisis: A New Perspective on $50 Billion of Losses', *Bulletin of Indonesian Economic Studies* 40(1), 37–57.

French, K.R.M., et. al. (2010) *The Squam Lake Report: Fixing the Financial System*, Princeton: Princeton University Press.

Friedman, M. (1957) Introduction to "A Theory of the Consumption Function", NBER Chapters, in *A Theory of the Consumption Function*, Princeton: Princeton University Press.

Friedman, M. (1960) *A Program for Monetary Stability.* Fordham, NY: Fordham University Press.

Friedman, M. (1968) 'The Role of Monetary Policy' *American Economic Review* 58(1), 1–17.

Friedman, M. (1969) 'The Optimum Quantity of Money', in *The Optimum Quantity of Money and Other Essays.* Chicago: Aldine Publishing Company.

Ghosh, A., Zalduendo, J., Thomas, A.H., Kim, J.I, Ramakrishnan, U. and Joshi, B. (2008) 'IMF Support and Crisis Prevention' *IMF Occasional Papers* 262, International Monetary Fund.

Giap, T.K., Abeysinghe, T., and Yam, T.K. (2011) *Chapter 6: Opportunities and Strategies for ASEAN 2030: Forging a Competitive and Innovative Region.* A paper prepared for presentation at the conference on 'ASEAN 2030: Growing Together to Shared Prosperity' organized by ADBI, 11–12 July 2011, Sheraton Hotel, Yogyakarta.

Goeltom, M.S. (2008) *Transmission Mechanisms of Monetary Policy in Indonesia*. BIS Papers 5(January), 309–332.

Gonçalves, F. (2007) 'The Optimal Level of Foreign Reserves in Financially Dollarized Economies: The Case of Uruguay,' *IMF Working Paper* No. 07/265, Washington: International Monetary Fund.

Goodhart, C.A.E. (2011) 'The Squam Lake Report: Commentary', *Journal of Economic Literature*. 49(1), 114–119.

Gray, S., Felman, J., Carvajal, A. and Jobst, A. (2011) 'Developing ASEAN5 Bond Markets: What Still Needs to be Done?', *IMF Working Paper*, No. WP/11/135. June.

Green, R., and Torgerson, T. (2007) 'Are High Foreign Exchange Reserves in Emerging Markets a Blessing or a Burden?', Department of the Treasury, Office of International Affairs, Occasional Paper No. 6.

Greif, A. (2006) *Institutions and the Path to the Modern Economy*, New York: Cambridge University Press.

Guided Democracy in Indonesia. (n.d.) In *Wikipedia*. Available HTTP: //en.wikipedia. org/wiki/Guided_Democracy_in_Indonesia.

Hadisoesastro (1989) 'The Political Economy of Deregulation in Indonesia', *Asian Survey* 29(9), 853–869.

Hansen, B.E. (2000) 'Sample Splitting and Threshold Estimation', *Econometrica* 68(3), 575–603.

Hansen, N. (1990) 'Impacts of Small and Medium-Sized Cities on Population Distribution: Issues and Responses', *Regional Development Dialogue* 11, 60–76.

Harmanta, M., Bathaluddin, B. and Waluyo, J. (2011) 'Inflation Targeting Under Imperfect Credibility: Lessons from Indonesian Experience', *Bulletin of Monetary, Economics and Banking* 13(3), 271–306.

Hauner, D. (2005) 'A Fiscal Tag for International Reserves,' IMF Working Paper No. 05/81, Washington: International Monetary Fund.

Hausman, J., Hall, B.H. and Griliches, Z. (1984) 'Econometric Models for Count Data with An Application to the Patents-R&D Relationship', *Econometrica* 52(4), 909–938.

Hill, H. (1996) *Southeast Asia's Emerging Giant: Indonesian Economic Policy and Development since 1966*. Cambridge: Cambridge University Press.

Hill, H. (1999) *The Indonesian Economy in Crisis: Causes, Consequences and Lessons*. Singapore: ISEAS.

Hill, H., and Wihardja, M.M. (2011) 'Indonesia's Reform Reversal,' *The Wall Street Journal*, November 30.

Horaguchi, H. H. (2007) 'Economic Analysis of Free Trade Agreements: Spaghetti Bowl Effect and a Paradox of Hub and Spoke Network', *Journal of Economic Integration* 22(3), 664–683.

Hoshi, T. (2011) 'Financial Regulation: Lesson from the Recent Financial Crises', *Journal of Economic Literature* 49(1), 120–137.

House to Endorse Only Seven Out of 70 Priority Bills for 2010 (2010) *The Jakarta Post*, 26 October.

IMF (2003) 'Public Debt in Emerging Markets,' *World Economic Outlook*, September.

IMF (2005) 'Indonesia, Selected Issues,' *IMF Country Report* No. 05/327.

IMF (2007) *Regional Economic Outlook: Asia and Pacific*, World Economic and Financial Surveys, Washington, D.C.: International Monetary Fund.

IMF (2009) 'Annual Report on Exchange Arrangements and Exchange Restrictions 2008'. Washington, D.C.: International Monetary Fund.

IMF (2010) *Financial Access Survey*, Washington D.C.: International Monetary Fund.

IMF (2011a) *Indonesia: Selected Issues*. IMF Country Report No. 11/310, October.

IMF (2011b) *Indonesia: 2011 Article IV Consultation-Staff Report; Staff Statement; Public Information Notice on the Executive Board Discussion; and Statement by the Executive Director for Indonesia*. Country Report No. 11/309, October.

IMF (2012) *Indonesia: Financial Sector Assessment Program-Basel Core Principles Assessment-Detailed Assessment Compliance*, IMF Country Report No. 12/335. December.

Indonesia-Japan Economic Working Team (2004) 'Strengthening Tax Policy Through Tax Reform', pp. 15–16.

Ing, L. Y. (2009) 'Lower Tariff Rising Skill Premium in Developing Countries: Is It A Coincidence?' *The World Economy* 32(7), 1115–1133.

Ito, T. and T. Hayashi (2004) 'Inflation Targeting in Asia'. Hong Kong: Hong Kong Institute for Monetary Research. HKIMR. March.

Jacobs, J., 1969, *The Economics of Cities*, New York: Random House.

Jeanne, O. (2007) 'International Reserves in Emerging Market Countries: Too Much of a Good Thing?' Brooking Papers on Economic Activity.

Jeanne, O. and Rancière, R., (2006) 'The Optimal Level of International Reserves for Emerging Market Countries: Formulas and Applications', *IMF Working Paper* No. 06/229, Washington: International Monetary Fund.

Jin, H. J., Koo, W. and Sul, B. (2006) 'The Effects of the Free Trade Agreement among China, Japan and South Korea', *Journal of Economic Development* 31(2), 55–71.

Kauffman, D. and Kraay, A. (2002) 'Growth without Governance', *World Bank Policy Research Paper* No. 2928.

Kawai, M. and Pomerleano, M. (2011) 'Who Should Regulate Systemic Stability Risk? The Relevance for Asia', in Masariro Kawai and Edwar S. Prasad (ed.) *Financial Market Regulation and Reforms in Emerging Markets*, Washington, D.C.: Brookings Institution Press.

Kawai, M. and Wignaraja, G. (2010) 'Free Trade Agreements in East Asia: A Way toward Trade Liberalization?', *Asian Development Bank Brief*, 1 (June).

Kemitraan (n.d.). Available HTTP://www.kemitraan.or.id/govindex/metodology.php.

Kenward, L.R. (2011) 'Developing Indonesia's Mutual Fund Industry: Booms, Busts, Frauds and Scandals'. 3 April.

Komite Pemantauan Pelaksanaan Otonomi Daerah. Available HTTP: www.kppod.org.

Kraemer, K.L. and Dedrick, J.L. (2000) 'The Information Technology Sector and International Competitiveness: A Background Paper', paper presented at the ADB Consultation Meeting, Asian Institute of Technology, Bangkok.

Kristiadi, J. (2011a) 'Political Projection and Dynamics in 2011' A handout for CSIS Seminar on January 11.

Kristiadi, J. (2011b) 'Demokrasi Tiwul', *KOMPAS*, 11 January.

Kristiadi, J. (2011c) 'Investigations without Luck, *Pansus* Resembles Political Acrobats (*Angket Tanpa Tuah, Pansus Mirip Akrobat Politik*)'. *KOMPAS*, 1 March.

Kristiadi, J. and Wihardja, M.M. (2011) 'Indonesia's Cabinet Reshuffle: How Low Can It Go?' *East Asia Forum*, 1 November.

Kuncoro, A. (2002) 'International Trade, Productivity and Competitiveness', in J.S. Fanelli and R. Medhora (eds), *Finance and Competitiveness in Developing Countries*. New York: Routledge.

Kuncoro, A. (2007) 'Manufacturing Growth in a Country Undergoing Political Transaction: How Firms Cope with Changing Business Environment in Indonesia', paper presented at GDN Medal Competition, Beijing.

Kuncoro, A. and Resosudarmo, B. (2006) 'Understanding Economic Reform in Indonesia, 1983–2000', in J.M. Fanelli and G. McMahon (eds) *Understanding Market Reforms; volume 2: Motivation, Implementation and Sustainability*. New York: Palgrave Macmillan.

Laeven, L. and Valencia, F. (2012) *Systemic Banking Crises Database: An Update*, IMF Working Paper No. WP/12/163, June.

Lall, S. (2000) *The Technological Structure and Performance of Developing Country Manufactured Exports, 1985–1998*, Working Paper, Q. E. House, University of Oxford.

Lane, P. and Milesi-Ferretti, G.M. (2007) 'The External Wealth of Nations Mark II: Revised and Extended Estimates of Foreign Assets and Liabilities', *Journal of International Economics*, 73, 223–250.

Lane, T., Gosh, A., Hamann, J., Phillips, S., Schulze-Ghattas, M. and Tsikata, T. (1999) IMF-Supported Programs in Indonesia, Korea, and Thailand, A preliminary Assessment, IMF Occasional Paper 178, Washington D.C.: IMF.

Lebow, D.E. and Rudd, J.B. (2006) *Inflation Measurement*, Finance and Economics Discussion Series. Divisions of Research & Statistics and Monetary Affairs, Federal Reserve Board, Washington, D.C. 2006–43.

Levy Yeyati, E. (2008) 'The Cost of Reserves', *Economics Letters*, 100(1), 39–42.

Lewis, B. D. and Smoke, P (n.d.) 'Incorporating Subnational Performance Incentives in the Indonesian Intergovernmental Fiscal Framework', 101st Annual Conference on Taxation, National Tax Association Proceedings.

LPEM (2005) 'Inefficiency in the Logistics of Export Industries: The Case of Indonesia', Report in collaboration with Japan Bank for International Cooperation (JBIC), Jakarta.

Magud, N.E. and Tsounta, E. (2012) 'To Cut or Not to Cut? Thai is (Central Bank's) Question', *IMF Working Paper*. No, WP/12/243, October.

Mahi, R. (2002) 'Three Years of Fiscal Decentralization In Indonesia: Its Impacts on Regional Economic Development and Fiscal Sustainability', *ISP Working Paper 02-28*, Georgia State University.

Mahi, R. and B. Brodjonegoro (2004) 'The Indonesian Political Economy of Decentralization', Paper presented in International Sympossium on Indonesian Decentralization: Problems and Policy Direction, Hitotsubashi University.

Manning, C. and Roesad, K. (2006) 'Survey of Recent Developments', *Bulletin of Indonesian Economic Studies* 42(2), 143–70.

Marks, S.V. (2005) 'Proposed Changes to the Value Added Tax: Implications for Tax Revenue and Price Distortions', *Bulletin of Indonesian Economic Studies* 41(1), 81–95.

Marks, S.V. and Rahardja, S. (2011) 'Effective Rates of Protection Revisited for Indonesia', mimeo.

McCallum, B.T. (1988) 'Robustness Properties of a Rule for Monetary Policy', *Carnegie-Rochester Conference Series on Public Policy* 29(Autumn), 173–203.

McCallum, B.T. (2000) 'Alternative Monetary Policy Rules: A Comparison with Historical Settings for the United States, the United Kingdom, and Japan', Working Paper 7725, National Bureau of Economic Research.

McCulley, P. and Toloui, R. (2007) 'Perils of Plenty: Can Foreign Reserves Growth Forever?', Global Central Bank Focus, PIMCO.

Meitzer, M. (2013) 'A Strong Base for Democratic Development', *East Asia Forum Quarterly* 5(4), October–December.

Milne, P. (2011), 'Banda, the Nutmeg Treasure Islands', *The Jakarta Post*, 22 March.

Ministry of Finance (2011) 'Provinces and Local Governments APBD Realization (various years)', SIKD.

Ministry of Trade (2011) *Data on Exports and Imports of Indonesia and Its FTA Trading Partners*, Research Division, Directorate of Foreign Trade Affairs, Ministry of Trade of Republic of Indonesia, Unpublished.

Mishkin, F. and Schmidt-Hebbel, K. (2001) 'One Decade of Inflation Targeting in the World: What Do We Know and What Do We Need to Know?' *NBER Working Paper No. 8397*, Cambridge, MA.

Myrdal, G. (1944) *An American Dilemma. The Negro Problem and Modern Democracy.* London: Harper Brothers.

Narjoko, D. and Hill, H. (2007) 'Winners and Losers during a Deep Economic Crisis: Firm-level Evidence from Indonesian Manufacturing', *Asian Economic Journal* 21(4), 343–68.

Narjoko, D. and Jotzo, F. (2007) 'Survey of Recent Developments', *Bulletin of Indonesian Economic Studies* 43(2), 143–69.

Nasution, A. (1983) *Financial Institutions and Policies in Indonesia.* Singapore: Institute of Southeast Asian Studies.

Nasution, A. (1995) 'Financial Sector Policies in Indonesia, 1980–1993', in S.N. Zahid (ed.) *Financial Sector Development in Asia*, New York: Oxford University Press.

Nasution, A. (1998a) '"Big Bang" versus "Go Slow": Indonesia and Malaysia', in J.M. Fanelli and R. Medhora (eds.) *Financial Reform in Developing Countries*, London: MacMillan.

Nasution, A. (1998b) 'Trade and Industrial Policies in Indonesia in the 1980s', ECLAC – Economic Commission for Latin America and the Caribbean.

Nasution, A. (2001) 'Financial Policy and Financial Sector Development in Indonesia since the 1980s,' in Masayoshi Tsurumi (ed.) *Financial Bing Bang in Asia*, Aldershot, UK: Ashgate.

Nasution, A. (2002) *Bank Restructuring: Strategy, Progress and Outlook*, Mimeo.

Nasution, A. (2010a) 'Berbagai kelemahan penanganan PT Bank Century tahun 2004–2008' (Various Weaknesses in Handling PT Bank Century during 2004–2008), Hearing before PT Bank Century Committee, DPR-RI (The Parliament of the Republic of Indonesia), Jakarta, 15 January.

Nasution, A. (2010b) 'Building Strong Banks and Bond Markets in ASEAN+3 Countries', International Conference on A Perspective of Asian Financial Sector on the Global Financial Crisis, January 21, 2010.

Nasution, A. (2011) 'Banking Supervision in Indonesia,' in Masahiro Kawai and Eswar S. Prasad (eds.), *Financial Market Regulation and Reforms in Emerging Markets.* Washington, D.C.: Brookings Institution Press.

Nasution, A., Griffith-Jones, S. and Montes, M.F. (2001) *Short-Term Capital Flows and Economic Crises.* UNU/Wider Studies in Development Economics. London: Oxford University Press.

North, D. (1990) *Institutions, Institutional Change, and Economic Performance.* New York: Cambridge University Press.

Oates, Wallace E. (1972) *Fiscal Federalism.* New York: Hartcourt Brace Jovanovich, Academic Press.

Obstfeld, M., Shambaugh, J.C. and Taylor, A.M. (2010) 'Financial Stability, the Trilemma, and International Reserves', *American Economic Journal: Macroeconomics, American Economics Association* 2(2), 57–94.

Okun, A. (1981) *Prices and Quantities: A Macroeconomic Analysis*, Washington, D.C.: Brookings Institution.

Organization for Economic Co-Operation and Development, various years, OECD Outlook.

Organization for Economic Co-Operation and Development, various years, OECD Revenue Statistics.

Orphanides, A. (2007) *Taylor Rules.* Finance and Economic Discussion Series, Division of Research&Statistics and Monetary Affairs, Federal Reserve Board, Washington, D.C.Staff Working Paper No. 2007-18. January.

Ostrom, E. (1986) 'An Agenda for the Study of Institutions', *Public Choice* 48, 3–25.

Pangestu, M. (1996), *Economic Reform, Deregulation, and Privatization: the Indonesian Experience.* Jakarta: CSIS.

Pangestu, M. and Habir, M. (2002) 'The Boom, Bust, and Restructuring of Indonesian Banks,' *IMF Working Paper,* WP/02/66. April.

Park, C. (2011) 'Asian Financial System: Development and Challenges' *ADB Working Paper Series* No. 285. November.

Patunru, A.A. and von Luebke, C. (2010) 'Survey of Recent Developments', *Bulletin of Indonesian Economic Studies* 46(1), 7–31.

Pepinsky, T. and Wihardja, M.M. (2011) 'Decentralization and Economic Performance in Indonesia', *Journal of East Asian Studies* 11(2), 337–371.

Plott, C.R. (1979) 'The Application of Laboratory Experimental Methods to Public Choice'. In C.S. Russell (ed., *Collective Decisions Making: Applications from Public Choice Theory.* Baltimore, MD: Johns Hopkins University Press.

Plumley, A.H. (1996) 'The Determinants of Individual Income Tax Compliance: Estimating the Impacts of Tax Policy, Enforcement, and IRS Responsiveness', Internal Revenue Service Publication 1961 (rev. 11-96) pp. 35–36.

Power to The People! No, Wait . . . (2011) *The Economist,* 18 March.

PSFconflict (2010) Counting Conflicts. In English and Indonesian with subtitles [Video File]. April 6. Available HTTP: //www.youtube.com/watch?v=UCngGGjxhE4 accessed 1 March 2011.

Putnam Investments, Two Ex-Officers Accused of Fraud (2003) *Times Online,* October 29.

Qibthiyyah, R.M. (2008) 'The Impact of Local Government Formation on Health and Education Outcomes'. Chapter in Essays on Political Decentralization. PhD Dissertation. Georgia State University.

Qibthiyyah, R.M. (2011) 'Review of Incentives and Sanctions Linked Intergovernmental Transfers', *Local Government Finance and Governance Reform ADB-INO. TA 7184,* Asian Development Bank.

Reisen, H. (1993) 'Macroeconomic Policies toward Capital Account Convertibility', in H. Reisen and B. Fisher (eds.) *Financial Opening: Policy Issues and Experiences in Developing Countries.* Paris: OECD.

Resosudarmo, B.P. (ed) (2005) *The Politics and Economics of Indonesia's Natural Resources,* Singapore: Institute of Southeast Asian Studies.

Rich, R. and Steindel, C. (2007) 'A Comparison of Measures of Core Inflation', *Economic Policy Review,* 13(3), 19–38.

Rodrik, D. (2006) 'The Social Cost of Foreign Exchange Reserves', *NBER Working Paper* No. 11952.

Roger, S. (2009) 'Inflation Targeting at 20: Achievements and Challenges'. IMF Working Paper No. WP/09/236. Washington, DC: IMF. October.

Romer, D. (1996) *Advance Macroeconomics*, New York: McGraw-Hill.

Rosengard, J.K. and Prasentyantoko, A. (2011) 'If the Banks are Doing So Well, Why Can't I Get a Loan? Regulatory Constraints to Financial Inclusion in Indonesia', *Asia Economic Policy Review* 6, 273–96.

Rosul, M. (2002) "The Capital Market in Indonesia's Economy: Development and Prospects", Center for Policy and Implementation Studies, Jakarta.

Rouwenhorst, K. Geert (n.d.) 'The Origins of Mutual Funds' Yale International Center for Finance *Working Papers* No. 04-48.

Rouwenhorst, K. Geert (2004) "The Origins of Mutual Funds", Yale International Center for Finance Working Paper No. 04-48. Available at http://ssm.com/abstract=636146.

Ruiz-Arranz, M. and M. Zavadjil (2008) 'Are Emerging Asia's Reserves Really Too High?' IMF Working Paper. WP/08/192.

Saad, I. (2001) 'Indonesia's Decentralization Policy: The Budget Allocation and Its Implications for the Business Environment', *SMERU Working Paper*, London.

Samuelson, P. 1964. "Theoretical Notes on Trade Problems", *Review of Economics and Statistics* 46(2), 145–154.

Saragih, B. BT. (2011) 'SBY Controls 'Lucrative' Posts', *The Jakarta Post*, 19 October.

Saunders, A. and Schumacher, L. (2000) 'The Determinant of Bank Interest Rate Margins: An International Study'. *Journal of International Money and Finance* 19(6), 813–832.

Savoia, A., Easaw, J. and McKay, A. (2001) 'Inequality, Democracy, and Institutions: A Critical Review of Recent Research. *World Development* 38(2), 142–154.

SBY's Feet of Clay (2002) *The Economist*, 21 October.

Schaechter, A. (2001). *Implementation of Monetary Policy and the Central Bank's Balance Sheet*, IMF Working Paper No. WP/01/149. October.

Schotter, A. (1981) *The Economic Theory of Social Institutions*. Cambridge: Cambridge University Press.

Schroeder, L., Ostrom, E. and Wynne, S. (1993) *Institutional Incentives and Sustainable Development: Infrastructure Policies in Perspective*. Boulder: Westview Press.

Scott, H. (2011) 'Little to Celebrate on Dodd-Frank's Birthday', *Financial Times*, Wednesday, July 20, p. 8.

Simatupang, Renata (2009) 'Evaluation of Decentralization Outcomes In Indonesia: Analysis of Health and Education Sectors', PhD Dissertation, Georgia State University.

Sjahrir, B.S., Kis-Katos, K. and G.G. Schulze (2014) 'Administrative Overspending in Indonesian Districts: The Role of Local Politics,' *World Development* 59(C), 166–183.

Smith, B. (2008) 'Origins of Regional Autonomy in Indonesia: Experts and the Marketing of Political Interests', *Journal of East Asian Studies* 8(2), 211–234.

Soesastro, H. and Basri, M.C. (2005), 'The Political Economy of Trade Policy in Indonesia', *ASEAN Economic Bulletin*, 22(1), 3–18.

Statistics of Industry, 2006, Statistics of Industry, 1993–2004. Jakarta: Central Bureau of Statistics.

Structure: Harjanto, N. (March 2011). Personal Interview.

Structure: Kristiadi (March 2011). Personal Interview.

Summers, L.H. (2006) 'Reflections on Global Account Imbalances and Emerging Markets Reserve Accumulation', L. K. Jha Memorial Lecture. Reserve Bank of India, Mumbai, March 24.

Suta, P.G.A. and Musa, S. (2004) *Indonesian Banking Crisis. The Anatomy of Crisis and Bank Restructuring.* Jakarta: Yayasan Sad Satria Bhakti.

TADF (2008) 'Evaluation of Deconcentration Fund and Tugas Pembantuan (TP)', Assitance Team to Ministry of Finance on Decentralization (TADF), Ministry of Finance.

Tanuwidjaja, S. (2011) 'Indonesia's Electoral System: Finetuning the Reforms', *East Asia Forum*, 6 January.

Tatum, B.P.T. (2012) 'Determinants of Credit Growth and Interest Margins in the Philippines and Asia', *IMF Working Paper* WP/12/123.May.

Taylor, J.B. (1993) 'Discretion versus Policy Rules in Practice'. *Carnegie-Rochester Conference Series on Public Policy* 39(December), 195–214.

Taylor, J.B. (ed.) (1999) *Monetary Policy Rules.* Chicago: University of Chicago Press.

Taylor, J.B. and Williams, J.C. (2010) *Simple and Robust Rules for Monetary Policy.* NBER Working Paper Series No. 15908, http://www.nber.org/papers/w15908.

Temenggung, Y. (2013), 'Kebijakan Pengelolaan Keuangan Daerah', Orientasi Kepemimpinan dan Penyelenggaraan Pemerintah Daerah Bagi Bupati/Walikota dna Wakil Bupati/Wakil Walikota Tahun 2013, Jakarta, 13 March.

Thee, K.W. (2007) 'Indonesia', in A. Chowdhury and I. Islam (eds.) *A Handbook on the Northeast Asian and Southeast Economies.* Northampton, MA: Edward Elgar.

Thee, K.W. (2008a) 'The Impact of the Two Oil Booms of the 19790s and the Post-Oil Boom Shock of the Early 1980s on the Indonesian Economy', A paper presented at the Third AFC International Symposium 'Resources under Stress—Sustainability of the Local Community in Asia and Africa', Ryukoku University, Kyoto, February 23–24.

Thee, K.W. (2008b) 'Indonesia's Economic Development During and After the Soeharto Era—Achievements and Failings', A paper presented at the International Workshop for the Stocktaking Work on 'Asian Experiences of Economic Development and Their Policy Implications for Africa', organized by JICA and JBIC, Tokyo, February 5–6.

Thee, K.W. (2009) 'Indonesia's Two Deep Economic Crises: The Mid-1960s ad the Late 1990s', *The Journal of the Asia-Pacific Economy* 14(12), 49–60.

Thee, K.W. (2010a). 'The Introduction, Evolution, and End of Colonial Extractive Institutions in the Netherlands Indies, 1830–1942', A paper presented at the Workshop on 'Colonial Extraction in the Netherlands Indies and Belgian Congo: Institutions, Institutional Change and Long Term Consequences', Utrecht University, December 3–4.

Thee, K.W. (2010b) 'Understanding Indonesia—The Role of Economic Nationalism', Indonesian Journal of the Social Sciences and Humanities, LIPI and KITLV, 1.

Thee, K.W. (2010c) 'Does Indonesia Have the Potential to Join the BRIC Group'. A paper presented at the Seminar on 'the Prospect for Indonesia–China Relations', Jakarta, 23 November.

Thee, K.W. (2011) *Indonesia's Economy Since Independence*, ISEAS Publication.

Tiebout, C. (1956) 'A Pure Theory of Local Expenditures', *The Journal of Political Economy* 64(5), 416–424.

Tobin, J. (1960) 'Towards Improving the Efficiency of the Monetary Mechanism', *Review of Economics and Statistics* 42(3), 276–279.

Tobin, J. (1969) 'A General Equilibrium Approach to Monetary Theory', *Journal of Money, Credit and Banking* 1(1), 15–29.

Toder, E. (2007) 'What Is the Tax Gap?' prepared for the American Bar Association Conference on the Tax Gap, June 21.

Truman, E.M. (2003) *Inflation Targeting in the World Economy*. Washington, D.C.: Institute for International Economics.

Truman, E.M. (2011) *Sovereign Wealth Funds: Is Asia Different?* Working Paper Series. WP 11-12. Washington, D.C.: Peterson Institute for International Economics, June.

UNCTAD (2010) *UNCTAD Train Database.*

von Luebke, C. (2009) 'The Political Economy of Local Governance: Findings from an Indonesian Field Study', *Bulletin of Indonesia Economic Studies* 45(2), 201–230.

von Luebke, C., McCulloch, N. and Patunru, A.A. (2009) 'Heterodox Reform Symbioses: The Political Economy of Investment Climate Reforms in Solo, Indonesia', *Asian Economic Journal* 23(3), 269–296.

Walsh, J.P. (2011) 'Reconsidering the Role of Food Prices in Inflation', *Working Paper No 11/71*, International Monetary Funds, Washington, D.C. April.

Walter, S. (2011) *Basel III: Stronger Banks and a More Resilient Financial System*, a paper delivered at Conference on Basel III, Financial Stability Institute, Basel, 6 April.

Weingast, B.R. (2007) 'Second Generation Fiscal Federalism: Implications for Decentralized Democratic Governance and Economic Development', USAID.

Wicksell, K. 1936. *Lectures on Political Economy*, Vol. 1: *General Theory* (trans. E. Classen). London: G. Routledge and Sons.

Wie, T.K. (2009) 'The Development of Labour intensive Garment Manufacturing in Indonesia', *Journal of Contemporary Asia* 39(4), 562–578.

Wijnholds, J.O. and Kapteyn, A. (2001) 'Reserve Adequacy in Emerging Market Economies', IMF Working Paper No. 01/143, Washington: International Monetary Fund.

Windmeijer, F. (2002) 'Expend: A Gauss Programme for Non-Linear GMM Estimation of Exponential Models with Endogenous Regressors for Cross Section and Panel (Dynamic) Count Data Models', UCL, IFS Working Paper CWP 14/02.

Woo, W. T., Glassburner, B. and Nasution, A. (1994) *Macroeconomic Policies, Crises, and Long-Term Growth in Indonesia, 1965–90*. The World Bank Comparative Macroeconomic Studies. Washington D.C: The World Bank.

Wooldridge, J.M. (1997) 'Multiplicative Panel Data Models Without the Strict Exogeneity Assumption', *Economic Theory* vol 13, 667–678.

World Bank (2006) *Unlocking Indonesia's Domestic Financial Resources: The Role of Non–bank Financial Institutions*, Washington D.C: The World Bank.

World Bank (2007) *Investing in Indonesia's Education: Allocation, Equity, and Efficiency of Public Expenditures*, Washington D.C: The World Bank.

World Bank (2010a) *World Development Indicators*. Online. Available HTTP: http://devdata.worldbank.org/dataonline

World Bank (2010b) 'New Patterns of Violence in Indonesia: Preliminary Evidence from Six 'High Conflict' Provinces', Policy Brief. Understanding Conflict Dynamics and Impacts in Indonesia, Edition III.

World Bank (2010c) Report on The Observance of Standards and Codes (ROSC) Indonesia. Accounting and Auditing, April, Jakarta: World Bank.

World Bank and International Finance Corporation (2009) *Doing Business 2010: Reforming through Difficult Times*, Washington, D.C.: World Bank, IFC, and Palgrave Mcmillan.

World Trade Organization (2010). Online. Available HTTP: http://www.wto.org/english/tratop_e/tariffs_e/tariffs_e.htm

Wyplosz, C. (2007) 'The Foreign Exchange Reserve Buildup: Business as Usual?', Paper presented at the Workshop on Debt, Finance and Emerging Issues in Financial Integration, at the Commonwealth Secretariat in London, March.

Xu, B. (2003) 'Trade Liberalisation, Wage Inequality and Endogenously Determined Nontraded Goods', *Journal of International Economics* 60, 417–431.

Zee, H.H. (1995) 'Value Added Tax', in P. Shome (ed.) *Tax Policy Handbook*. Washington, D.C.: International Monetary Fund.

Author Index

Subject Index

For Product Safety Concerns and Information please contact our EU
representative GPSR@taylorandfrancis.com
Taylor & Francis Verlag GmbH, Kaufingerstraße 24, 80331 München, Germany